WORLD WAR II GENERATION SPEAKS IV

THE THINGS OUR FATHERS SAW SERIES:

VOL. IX: HOMEFRONT/WOMEN AT WAR
VOL. X: OVER THE HUMP: CHINA, BURMA, INDIA

MATTHEW A. ROZELL

WOODCHUCK HOLLOW PRESS

Hartford · New York

World War II Generation Speaks IV

Copyright © 2025 by Matthew A. Rozell. WW2 GEN 4 VOLS 9-10. 6.15.2025. All rights reserved. No part of this publication may be reproduced, distributed, or transmitted in any form or by any means without the prior written permission of the publisher. Grateful acknowledgment is made for previously published material used with permission and short quotations credited to other previously published sources. Please see author notes throughout the following works.

Front Cover, "Pilots running towards Warhawks." 1940s. US Signal Corps. National Archives, public domain.

Back Cover: "Women workers groom lines of transparent noses for deadly A-20 attack bombers." Alfred T. Palmer, Office for Emergency Management. Office of War Information. Public Domain Photographs, National Archives.

Any additional photographs and descriptions sourced at Wikimedia Commons within terms of use, unless otherwise noted.

Publisher's Cataloging-in-Publication Data

Names: Rozell, Matthew A., 1961-
Title: World War II generation speaks 4 /Matthew A. Rozell.
Description: Hartford, NY: Woodchuck Hollow Press, 2025. | Series: The things our fathers saw: the untold stories of the World War II generation, vol. 9-10. | Includes bibliographical references.
Identifiers: | ISBN 978-1-948155-54-0 (pbk.) | ISBN 978-1-948155-55-7 (hbk) |
Subjects: LCSH: World War, 1939-1945--Personal narratives, American. | World War, 1939-1945 --Biography. | Military history, Modern--20th century. | BISAC: HISTORY / Military / Veterans. | HISTORY / Military / World War II.

MatthewRozellBooks.com

MATTHEW A. ROZELL

THE THINGS OUR FATHERS SAW

HOMEFRONT/WOMEN AT WAR

THE UNTOLD STORIES OF THE WORLD WAR II GENERATION

VOLUME IX

THE THINGS OUR FATHERS SAW

THE UNTOLD STORIES OF THE
WORLD WAR II GENERATION
FROM HOMETOWN, USA

VOLUME IX:
HOMEFRONT/WOMEN AT WAR

*GOLD MEDAL WINNER OF THE 2025 AUDIOBOOK FOR NON-FICTION PERSONAL-INDEPENDENT PUBLISHER BOOK AWARDS

Matthew A. Rozell

WOODCHUCK HOLLOW PRESS
Hartford · New York

Copyright © 2023 by Matthew A. Rozell. V.12.29.2023. All rights reserved. No part of this publication may be reproduced, distributed, or transmitted in any form or by any means without the prior written permission of the publisher. Grateful acknowledgement is made for the credited use of various short quotations also appearing in other previously published sources. Please see author notes.

Front Cover: "Stars over Berlin and Tokyo will soon replace these factory lights reflected in the noses of planes at Douglas Aircraft's Long Beach, Calif., plant. Women workers groom lines of transparent noses for deadly A-20 attack bombers." Alfred T. Palmer, Office for Emergency Management. Office of War Information. Public Domain Photographs, National Archives Number 535577, Unrestricted.

Back Cover: "Women workers install fixtures and assemblies to a tail fuselage section of a B-17 bomber at the Douglas Aircraft Company plant, Long Beach, Calif.". U.S. Office of War Information, 1944, public domain.

Any additional photographs and descriptions sourced at Wikimedia Commons within terms of use, unless otherwise noted.

Publisher's Cataloging-in-Publication Data

Names: Rozell, Matthew A., 1961- author.
Title: Homefront/women at war : the things our fathers saw : the untold stories of the World War II generation, volume IX / Matthew A. Rozell.
Description: Hartford, NY : Matthew A. Rozell, 2023. | Series: The things our fathers saw, vol. 9. | Also available in audiobook format.
Identifiers: LCCN pending | ISBN 978-1-948155-89-2 (hardcover) | ISBN 978-1-948155-40-3 (paperback) | ISBN 978-1-948155-76-2 (ebook)
Subjects: LCSH: World War, 1939-1945--Personal narratives, American. | Civilians--United States--Biography. |
www.matthewrozellbooks.com
www.teachinghistorymatters.com
Information at matthewrozellbooks.com.

*~To the Memory of the Women
Of the World War II Generation~*

"There was one good thing came out of it. I remember going to [a] Sunday dinner one of the older women invited me to. She and her sister at the dinner table were talking about the best way to keep their drill sharp in the factory. I had never heard anything like this in my life. It was just marvelous! I was tickled."[1]

— Young Woman, Recalling Women Workers
During World War II

THE THINGS OUR FATHERS SAW IX: HOMEFRONT/WOMEN AT WAR

The Storytellers (in order of appearance):

Helen Quirini
Mabel Colyer
Frances Cooke
Ethel Severinghaus
Ruth A. Bull
Leonard Amborski
Jane Washburn
Elaine Curren Sommo
Spencer Kulani
Kathryn Goodman Frentzos
Katherine G. Denegar
Lillian Lorraine Yonally
Rose Landsman Miller
Margaret Doris Alund-Lear
Helen Marcil Brennan
Kathleen Mary Davie
Joyce Griffin
Joan Hoffman
Halina Roman
Eva Koenig
Lily Muller

THE THINGS OUR FATHERS SAW IX: HOMEFRONT/WOMEN AT WAR

TABLE OF CONTENTS

AUTHOR'S NOTE	17
THE WATERSHED	19
PART ONE	23
THE LABOR ACTIVIST	25
Pay Discrimination	27
Wartime in the Factory	28
Recruiting Women Workers	30
The Union	32
'We Felt the Danger to Our Country'	35
'I'm Doing a Good Job Where I Am'	36
SHIFT WORK SISTERS	41
'You're More Talented Than That'	43
Thirty Cents An Hour	44
THE LOS ALAMOS SECRETARY	47

DR. FERMI AND DR. TELLER	49
'AS IF IT WAS NOONTIME'	50
HOME	51
'NEVER QUESTIONED ME ABOUT THE BOMB'	52

THE RESEARCH PHYSICIST — 55

'NOT ALLOWED TO DISCUSS THE NATURE OF OUR WORK'	56
'I LOST TWO BROTHERS'	59

PART TWO — 63

THE SCHOOL TEACHER — 65

DEPRESSION DAYS	66
'NOBODY REALLY KNEW'	69
RATIONING	70
ENTERTAINMENT	74
TEACHING	75
MARRIAGE DURING WARTIME	79
THE BOYS IN THE WAR	81
D-DAY	83
'THEY JUST WOULDN'T TELL ANYONE'	85

THE SCHOOLGIRL — 87

THE VICTORY BIKE	89
SCHOOL	90
CULTURE AND MUSIC	92

THE NEIGHBORHOOD	93
'WE FELT SO BAD FOR THEM'	95

THE PEARL HARBOR KID — 99

FAMILY IN PEARL HARBOR	100
GOING ACROSS THE PACIFIC	101
PEARL CITY	101
MARTIAL LAW	103
'THEIR HAIR HAD TURNED WHITE'	104
'THIS WAS THEIR LAST CHANCE'	105
'JUST ONE OF THOSE THINGS'	106
THE END OF THE WAR	107
BACK IN NEW YORK	107

PART THREE — 111

US ARMY NURSE, EUROPE — 113

THE DEPRESSION ERA	113
'ONCE YOU DO THIS, YOU'RE THEIRS'	114
PEARL HARBOR	115
OVERSEAS	116
NORTH AFRICA AND CORSICA	117
MT. VESUVIUS	120
THE END OF THE WAR	120
'WHAT ARE YOU GOING TO DO FOR ME?'	121
'THEY ARE MOSTLY GONE'	122

US ARMY NURSE, PACIFIC — 125

'I Would Kill You' — 126
Overseas — 127
Home — 129

THE WASP — 131

The Women Airforce Service Pilots — 133
Training at Sweetwater, Texas — 133
B-25 Training — 140
Target Towing — 141
Disbanded — 145
Keeping In Touch — 146

THE FLIGHT NURSE — 149

'I Didn't Want to Tell My Father' — 150
'We Didn't Know Where We Were Going' — 152
'This One Needs Me' — 154
'A Planeload of Psychos' — 155
'We Flew the Entire Pacific' — 157
Olivia De Havilland and Betty Grable — 161
The Philippines — 162
Tarawa — 163
Food — 164
Marriage — 165
The World War II Flight Nurses Association — 167
'Leave Me Alone' — 167

THE WAVE — 169

THE WAVES	170
WAVE QUARTERS ONE	171
MAPWORK	173
CELEBRITY BOND DRIVE	174
THE FLAG	176
A COSMOPOLITAN WEDDING	177
INTERESTING PEOPLE	178
DISCHARGED	178

THE RECRUITER — 181

AWAY FROM HOME	182
'I FEEL RESPONSIBLE HE'S DEAD'	183
SMALL TOWNS	184
THE BAND CIRCUIT	185
FAMILY	186
BROTHER JACK	187
THE END OF THE WAR	188

THE WREN — 191

DOODLE BUGS	192
LIFE IN ENGLAND	194
THE GIRL GUIDES	195
THE WRENS	196
WAR'S END	199
'LIFE HAS CHANGED'	200

ANTI-WAR	201
PART FOUR	**203**
THE WAR BRIDES	**205**
THE ATS	206
BOMBINGS	208
'A LIFE'S SOUVENIR'	209
VE DAY	211
THE RIDING SCHOOL	213
LEADING THE HORSES	214
AIR RAIDS	216
THE GIS IN ENGLAND	217
WAR BRIDE	218
LONDON	220
'SHE'LL NEVER LEAVE ME'	222
SINGING WITH THE WOUNDED GIS	223
THE NEW YORK SKYLINE	225
'LIFE IN AMERICA WAS VERY DIFFERENT'	226
PART FIVE	**229**
THE REFUGEE	**231**
ARREST	233
SIBERIA	234
'I DO NOT THINK I COULD FIND THEIR GRAVES'	235
EAST AFRICA	241

TANZANIA	242
TO THE UNITED STATES	243
'WHAT WAR DOES TO WOMEN AND CHILDREN'	244

THE GERMAN SCHOOLGIRL — 247

'OUR WAR STARTED'	250
'A VERY HARD TIME'	252
'THE RUSSIANS WERE REACHING THE BORDER'	253
DIFFICULT JOURNEY	254
'WE LEFT EVERYTHING'	254
'THERE WAS NO ONE ELSE TO BLAME'	256
REBUILDING AFTER THE WAR	259

THE HOLOCAUST SURVIVOR — 261

THE ARRIVAL OF THE GERMANS	263
THE WARSAW GHETTO	264
THE GHETTO UPRISING	265
BERLIN	267
'NO ONE SURVIVED FROM MY FAMILY'	268
'I WANTED TO LIVE'	268
TO THE UNITED STATES	270
'I KNOW WHAT WAR IS'	270

TO KEEP THEM WITH US — 273

'General Electric's Fort Edward plant is the only completely government-financed factory in the Glens Falls area. A half of its workers live in Glens Falls. Above, Jean Fitzgerald, Eleanor Penders, Phoebe Francato and Ruth Lopen test synchronous motors for automatic gun turrets on our largest bombers.'
LOOK Magazine, 1944.[1]

---

[1] Fort Edward High School's sports teams are still known as the "Flying Forts," after the Boeing B-17 Flying Fortress heavy bomber and the motors for the gun turrets built here.

Author's Note

The photograph on the facing page, a 1944 staged shot for a patriotic piece in a national news tabloid magazine showing young women employees of the General Electric plant—less than a five-minute walk from my childhood home—opens my first book in *The Things Our Fathers Saw®* series. Now returning nearly full circle, it is appropriate that I present it again here in the ninth volume, *Homefront/Women at War*.

This is one of the last, and one of the most difficult books in the series that I have undertaken, which was a bit unexpected when I began to lay it out. It turns out that many of the storytellers were relaying different versions of a similar story—that of being tasked with stepping up to answer their nation's call to fill the shoes of the boys and men called overseas, only to, when those veterans returned home, be expected to return to a form of second-class citizenship, in many cases giving up their newfound freedoms outside of the home, relegated to then wait decades for formal recognition from their country for their efforts.

My wife was reading a widely popular book series, which she enjoyed, but she noted that it seemed that every title carried the same plotline, but told it from a different perspective. So maybe something similar is going on with this book. Here is the perspective from the home front, featuring mostly women, from the eyewitness accounts of persons relatively ignored—over half the population.

I remember a quote from years past, which went something like, 'If it had not been for the women going out the door, there would have been no spring in 1944.' How very true.

Matthew Rozell
Labor Day, 2023
Washington County, NY

CHAPTER ONE

The Watershed

'The war changed my life completely; I found a freedom and an independence I had never known,' said one woman defense factory worker. Another recalled, *'[It] was the beginning of my emancipation as a woman. For the first time in my life, I found that I could do something with my hands besides bake a pie.'*[2]

World War II was a watershed moment for the United States of America, and for the world. The America that emerged from the Great Depression and 'the War' would be in many ways almost unrecognizable. Yet when we think of the war today, how many of our countrymen stop to wonder how in the world we came together to fight the existential threat? And what about the seismic domestic change on the home front, in the absence of fathers, brothers, and sons? How did the lives of women change as they left the home, while still having to run the household?

Congressionally authorized conscription on a limited basis began in 1940 as war clouds darkened over Europe. After Pearl Harbor, the Selective Service had more than twelve million men in active service at its peak strength in 1945, with around sixteen million Americans serving in the military during World War II.[3] The economic and social effects and ramifications would be felt for generations as big government and big business worked hand in hand,

and side by side with labor; even with postwar cuts, "the federal government in 1950 still had nearly twice as many civilian employees as it had in 1940, spent four times as much money, and had greater power."[4]

In July 1943, President Roosevelt said that, 'Every combat division, every naval task force, every squadron of fighting planes is dependent for its equipment and ammunition and fuel and food on the American people in civilian clothes in the offices and in the factories and on the farms at home.'[2] By 1944, a Liberty ship was made ready every two weeks. A B-24 Liberator heavy bomber rolled off the line every sixty-three minutes.[5] People moved from rural to urban areas in service to wartime industry or auxiliary assignment. Entire cities were created from nearly scratch, the Manhattan Project, which produced the atomic bomb, being the prime example. Oak Ridge, Tennessee, and Hanford, Washington, grew seemingly overnight where uranium and plutonium were extracted and processed by well over a hundred thousand workers; at Los Alamos, New Mexico, the bomb was developed and tested by legions of engineers and scientists with thousands of support staff. Dozens more related facilities rounded out the atomic effort.[6]

These massive production gains came at a high cost. Huge fractures in the tractional seams of American society were compounded on families already stressed by the absence of male members' military service. And what of the children? Many were left to grow up at a young age, unattended. Others were blessed with older sisters, who, though barely out of their own childhood years, assumed the duties of the frequently absent parents. Is it any wonder that some women never spoke of their wartime jobs?

School-aged children endured practicing drills, listening to frightening news reports dramatically broadcast over and over,

---

[2] Franklin D. Roosevelt, "Fireside Chat," July 28, 1943.

hearing no word from brothers and fathers in uniform. It must have boosted anxiety levels sky high, although, comparatively speaking, American children were much better off than their counterparts in the overseas war zones. Imagine being a child refugee, watching as your younger siblings died, one after the other, *being on the run for an entire decade...*

*

Americans didn't physically suffer at home. They didn't starve, they were not subject to bombardment or invasion. The only continental US war dead directly due to enemy action on American soil came in May 1945 when a church youth group fell victim to a fluke small Japanese high-altitude balloon incendiary bomb in Oregon.[3] Americans flocked to the movies every week, listened to the radio, read their newspapers and comic books, enjoyed outings and other diversions. Still, nearly 185,000 American families didn't get to welcome a father, brother, or son back home, to say nothing of the psychological distress caused by the war. One girl remembered, 'Beginning on the first night Dad left, my mother had awakened me with her crying. I can remember going into her room and stroking her forehead while telling her everything would be all right, that Daddy would be home as soon as he could. I became what I was to remain for the rest of my mother's life—her daughter, her best friend and, in a sense, her mother.'[7]

Like the 'hard times' of the Great Depression in the preceding decade, this war affected every family. Few American communities would remain unscathed by the emotional detritus of World War II.

---

[3] *The only continental U.S. war dead*-For further information, the reader may wish to visit www.history.com/news/japans-killer-wwii-balloons.

PART ONE

WORKING

"We developed relationships with our co-workers, because if you have ever worked in any place for a long time, the people you work with are mostly people that you see every day. In fact, in a lot of cases, they're closer to you than your family. Of course, we all realized that when the guys came back, we would have to give up our jobs."

—Woman worker, General Electric Plant, Schenectady, New York

United States Office of War Information. Credit: George Roepp. Public Domain.

CHAPTER TWO

The Labor Activist

In the late 1800s, inventor Thomas Edison's business interests merged, with a main part forming the basis of the General Electric Works complex in Schenectady, New York, which would become one of the major industrial contributors to victory over the Axis powers on land, sea, and air.

For the Navy and the Merchant Marine, GE researchers, engineers, and workers created new types of propulsion systems that sped up ships and reduced fuel consumption; in fact, three-fourths of the World War II fleet's auxiliary turbine horsepower emanated from GE.

GE researchers had also developed early versions of radar, which would help Britain triumph in the Battle of Britain, and later, brought forth the radar jamming systems essential to Allied landing invasions. They also developed the autopilot systems and remote turret controls that increased the efficiency of air crews in the heavy bombers; by the end of the war, GE was producing the most essential components of the new B-29 Superfortress bomber, including power systems and heated flight suits necessary in the higher altitudes.

For land-based forces, this Schenectady plant also specialized in the construction of large motors for heavy vehicles and tanks. Smoke generators, lamps, lighting systems, and aerial searchlights were also a specialty. Because the rubber supply was strained by Japanese Pacific occupation, GE Schenectady developed high-performance polymers, molded plastics, and invented silicone.

X-ray technology was improved specifically to examine ordnance issues and determine if unexploded bombs were live. GE Schenectady also developed the appliances we take for granted today; advanced refrigerators, freezers, cooking ranges, and fire suppression systems aboard ships and in the field all improved the quality of life and hastened the end of the war in Allied victory. GE Schenectady was awarded the Navy 'E Ribbon' in 1942 and the Army-Navy 'E Ribbon' three times between 1942 and 1945.[8]

*

It may not have been glamorous work, but the men and women who labored here, epitomized by natural leaders like Helen Quirini, likely cut years off the war. Helen Quirini worked at the General Electric plant in Schenectady, New York, for thirty-nine years, beginning in April 1941, before Pearl Harbor, and retiring on her work anniversary in 1980. She followed her siblings into the war effort there but instead of an office job, she chose to work on the factory floor, due to its higher pay and her interest in saving for college. Instead, she became a pioneer of workers' and women's rights in the factory, the nascent union movement, and later, the national labor scene.

Helen Quirini

I was born on March 9, 1920, in Schenectady, New York. I had graduated high school and I started working at General Electric on April 1, 1941. I think Pearl Harbor happened after that. I worked in a factory. I did all kinds of jobs, assembling and wiring panels and little equipment needed for the war effort. I worked at General Electric for thirty-nine years. I started on April 1, 1941, and I ended on April 1, 1980. It was a great experience. I got active in my union because I fought this discrimination.

I [originally] didn't want to work at GE, for various reasons. My whole aim was to get enough money to go to college, [but for me], by the time the war was over, my father had died, so forget about college. But I was appalled about the bombings of England and knew that eventually, our country had to go to war. [At the time], my brother and I, we had started a grocery store [near the factory]. He went into the plant before I did because we were a little store, and we worked twelve hours a day, seven days a week. He went in, and then I went in. Of course, we developed relationships with our co-workers, because if you have ever worked in any place for a long time, the people you work with are mostly people that you see every day. In fact, in a lot of cases, they're closer to you than your family. When somebody died or something, we were there. When somebody had a child, we were there. When somebody was sick, we were there. It's something that today, they're not going to know, because what they say now, a person is going to work seven years or something, three or four jobs during their lives.

Pay Discrimination

When you first go into GE, you go on a training program, and they try to figure out where they can place you after the training program. I worked on some miscellaneous assembly and wiring, and then they moved you someplace else, which required a little bit more knowledge in reading blueprints and wiring diagrams, and handling a soldering iron and screwdrivers, and things like that.

I think [the pay] was two cents an hour, if I'm not mistaken. I think that was the minimum, and I am going to point out that women were paid less than men, which was shocking to me.[4] Also, males under the age of twenty-one were considered at the boys' rates. I used to go to [workers' lectures] during the Depression, and I'd meet young men, and I'd say, 'How come you're not working in GE?'

This was before the war, and they would say, 'We're too old.'

I said, 'What are you talking about?'

'We're over twenty-one and they're only hiring males under the age of twenty-one, so they can pay us boys' wages.'

We had three shifts, and we worked eight hours, but when the war started, we worked straight through for two weeks. They had to get special permission to let us work that long, but there were three different shifts, so we had to leave so the second shift could come in, and then the second shift had to leave for the third shift to come in. But there were times when we worked overtime, when the second-shift person didn't show up. But the regular hours, if I remember right, was the eight-hour shift plus overtime, and every Saturday and Sunday.

Wartime in the Factory

I was the chairperson to hold bond drives and blood donor drives and we had [bond] rallies. Three other women and I did that in our spare time. The company gave us that great big board, which is something like eight-by-sixteen. We had a crepe paper behind it, red, white, and blue. We had a cafeteria there and it was between the two doors in the cafeteria, and so it has a whole lot of things on

---

[4] In 1940, the median pay for an American male worker was $956 annually. On average, an American woman earned 62% less than her male co-worker. Source: NPR, *The 1940 Census: 72-Year-Old Secrets Revealed*, April 2, 2012.

it. There were also blood donor drives competitions throughout the whole plant. You can see on there if you read what the different areas were. And then, we also had little blood containers that were made into cardboard that we wore around our necks. So much for one pint, and so much for two, and so much for a gallon.

I used to write for the *General Electric Work News*, a history about what was happening there. We would put in who got married, who had a baby, who went to war, who came back to visit. And we had a fund, I think it was ten cents for each person a week; we gave to this fund, and if a service person ever came back [to work], we gave him ten dollars. But we had these rallies, especially to sell war bonds. During the rallies, we also talked about our co-workers [now overseas]. We were constantly reminded that we were at war, and we felt very deeply that we were important because without the materials that were created by the factories during this war, the war couldn't have been won.

We all had little badges in order to get into the factory, and there's that kind of security, and in order to get into certain rooms, you have to have had another badge, you know, so there was no doubt that we felt strongly about the war and cared about it very deeply because some of our people started losing their lives. In one of my articles I wrote for the news, I'm pleading for people to give blood and to buy bonds. Then I say something that, if you think you're making any sacrifice, look in front of the city hall, you will see sixteen thousand flags of the servicepeople from Schenectady, and if you look another place, you will see X number of flags for those who have already given their lives. So, it was a constant reminder of what had been happening. These friends of mine and I spent our time after work writing the names on those [displayed] nameplates and crosses. Those crosses have the names of the soldiers, the people who lost their lives. I think the big stars on nameplates are the names of the people who gave a gallon of blood, and the rest are the names of people in the services. And on top, it says, 'Lest we forget.' So, it was a constant reminder, if anybody had any doubts that we were at war or that we cared, this is a living proof of what has happened.

Recruiting Women Workers

Of course, everything was the way GE advertised it, [in recruiting women into their workforce]. We got wonderful restrooms and all this kind of junk, but anyway, that encouraged people to go in.

One of the articles [I worked on] said that some women [workers] were giving up their children because they could not find a place for them. So, I was now active with the union, and we got involved. During the war, there were special committees set up to talk about daycare. I mean, professional daycare, it is almost something that you don't even think about [today]. But, you know, when you read the article, [you learned that] women were giving up their children because they couldn't find a place and they had to work. And so, afterwards, I became president of a daycare center.

GE had classifications of men's and women's jobs. We, as women, could never even think about getting on a so-called man's job, and the differential in their rates was about three quarters. What GE used to do is, they'd set up a job description of what a job consists of, including safety and common knowledge and all that kind of stuff. And then when it went to a woman, they automatically cut it to three-quarters rate. So, most of us, not having the opportunity to work on so-called men's jobs, in most cases, we assumed they were very difficult. When the guys went to the service, and we went to work on those jobs, they weren't any more difficult than our jobs! Of course, the company always said, 'Well, it requires a lot of lifting,' but that was a lot of bull, because a lot of jobs don't require a lot of lifting! And so, we were kind of shocked. So, we worked on so-called men's jobs, and took the same skills that we had to do the little panels. In fact, the company, we used to have these, I think they were transmitters, and they used to be about that square [*gestures with hands*] and about six feet high, and so, you would wire everything in between. So then, the company got a great idea. They broke it down into little panels. They gave the women the little panels, and then they put connections between the panels so that they downgraded the man's job. I'm just trying to point out to you how much skill it took, but as a matter of fact, the skill was probably harder to do with the little panel [for women] because you didn't have that much room.

Of course, we all realized that when the guys came back, we would have to give up our jobs. One of the things that we had during some of this time, is the company had a double seniority list too. In other words, when the war was over, a man could bump a woman if he had less service. The whole country was in sort of a letdown in a sense because there were going to be a lot of layoffs when the men came back, and there were. And so, we had to fight all this kind of discrimination against women. Now, [don't forget], women were very tired because women in a lot of cases, they had to take care of the children and the houses, because you men did not do housework! It was beneath you! So, they had to do all this stuff. [A woman worker wrote in and] told about how she did her housework [and worked in the factory]. She was on second shift, she did her housework first, made do for the grandchildren, and she was very tired. She worked in a [position in] a place that was dirty, and GE—I don't know about today, but GE never had air conditioning in the plant. So, when it was hot, it was hot!

It didn't bother me that much, but I thought about the guys who worked in the foundry. I mean, they used to take their shirts off and work with no shirts on, because it was so hot. So, she's coming home, tired, and a couple of guys were talking about why the hell don't women stay at home and take care of their kids. She was so disgusted because, number one, she is trying to help out the war effort, and also to try to keep the family together. So, we had that fight! Of course, you get the idea, women's place is in the home and [they] used to say that we should be pregnant and barefoot, you know. That was the feeling in those days in a lot of things. How would you guys like it if you went on a job and you were told, 'Well, you can't go on that at all, because of your sex?'

The Union

[In the beginning], I was against unions, because in the schools and in the newspapers, like a lot of the right-wing things are today, they're not very complimentary, especially in a place like Schenectady, where GE controlled everything. And so, my [first] ideas about unions were 'a bunch of Reds' and all this kind of stuff, and 'they take money away from you.' I had to do a lot of searching. My father hated unions, and my father worked three days for GE and quit. And so, I said to him one day, I said, 'How come you quit?'

He said, 'Don't be impertinent.'

In those days, you didn't talk back to your father, and so, he was mad because I got involved. He was mad because I went in the factory. My sister said to me when I came home, 'Let me see your hands.' She worked in the office. I've always worked around my house. I've always worked on my car. So, my hands were not any more calloused or swollen because I was working on jobs that required small tools. The thing is that I was on piecework, and when you're on piecework, you got to learn how to move, and you don't waste any time because you're getting paid by the piece.

Anyway, then I saw that discrimination; even when the first group came in, they had women leaders. I met with a very nice shop steward, and I said, 'How come you don't do anything?'

She said, 'Because nobody wants to put in a complaint.' And you have to have grievances.

So then, I got involved with a couple of other things; I went to a meeting. The woman there said, 'Any organization'—she wasn't just talking union—she said, 'Any organization, if you belong, take part in it. Make sure things are run right.' And if you look around at some of the things that are being done, in some of the organizations today, where the board of directors are not even doing what they're supposed to...

Then, I decided to go to another union meeting and sat and listened. The union was fighting some good cases about discrimination. They won a case with the War Labor Board, and the company stalled long enough, so when the war was over, they didn't put it into effect. So, having this kind of situation, I really got involved more with the 1946 strike, because I realized how important it was, and that I was going to be staying in GE, whether I liked it or not, because there were no jobs on the outside, you know, and where do you go without an education?

Now, during the war, our union was honored by the federal government and everything because of the great job that they did. While the war went on, the company got what you call 'cost plus.' Whatever they put in for a cost, they got a certain percentage above, so they were making money, not just them—I think the auto industry is the first one who started it. Through all of the country, the auto industry and everybody else was just reaping in money like mad. So, when we went in '46, we asked for some share of it, and they refused.

A labor historian interviewed Helen Quirini in 1993 where she recalled the 1946 strike, which was national in scope, as a turning point in her life, prolonged when the union refused to accept an inferior raise for woman members. "We stayed out for a couple of extra weeks, and I thought, 'Boy, isn't that great!' That... people were willing to sacrifice those weeks—and this is a lot of men, of course, mostly men!" [9]

I was active in the strike, with a lot of people, a lot of activities. Two of the same women who helped me with that were working in the factory, and we got tired of working the picket line. And so, we commandeered a beat-up truck that had a loudspeaker on top of it. Of course, if you know the General Electric plant, you have quite a few gates, and it was nine weeks in the winter. It was cold.

Anyway, we ran around with this truck, playing music, dancing with the guys. Lo and behold, when the thing was settled, there was an election for a secretary. I wasn't even running, and I was elected! I told the guys, 'I'm not qualified.' But when they took the job over, they weren't qualified either! I [filed] all the grievances for a couple of years. I worked that for two hours a day, I went in from seven to nine, and every grievance that was put in against the company, I recorded. Well, the guys before, they just put a couple notes on it, they had such scribbling! If a grievance went up to the next level, they would depend upon this paperwork for the business agent, to see what the arguments were. So, I brought in carbon paper, and I wrote in detail. I learned how to write nothing but the important things. And then, I put a copy of that in every grievance so that the business agent would have a copy. It wasn't just something [scribbled]. So, when I said I wasn't qualified, they said, 'Why do you demean yourself?' But that's how life is, you know? You can never understand how a woman feels being discriminated against the way we were, that you're not good enough to go on this job, you're not good enough to go on this job, and all that kind of stuff.

'We Felt the Danger to Our Country'

We had all kinds of rationing, you know, gas and butter and meat, and all that kind of stuff but, you know, this is a sacrifice. That's what's wrong with the [Iraq] war today, who the heck is sacrificing anything except the soldiers? We felt the danger to our country. As a matter of fact, and I'm speaking from memory, I think we were one of ten places in the country that if we're going to be bombed, we would be the place because of GE, the locomotive company, the Watervliet Arsenal, and the closest to the [state capital] at Albany. We had men and women standing on top of hilltops, watching for airplanes. All of the factory windows were blocked. We never saw the sunshine when we worked. There was a feeling of responsibility and even joy in being part of the sacrifice for something as important as that war. And as I say, that's what's wrong with this [current] war, who is sacrificing anything?

I remember, we laughed like mad because somebody said, 'Hey, I got some gas coupons, but you got to go to the certain garage.'

And so, if somebody went out a couple of miles to go there, spend all of his time with these [illicit] gas coupons, when he got there, he [would find] a gas lock on his tank.

I said, 'See, you're cheating, and that's what happens.' *[Laughs]*

But you got to remember that there was such a tremendous drive that people were bringing in their old furnaces, anything with steel. And if you went down some of the streets, you would see, there would be a big drive because the Japanese bought our steel from us, and then they made it into bullets and sent it back to us in that manner, for Pearl Harbor. So, we collected tin foil, grease, all that.

I'll talk a little bit about something that most people don't know about. There was an outfit called the block plan that was set up during the war. The block plan took every city. I'll just talk about Schenectady. It took Schenectady and it divided it down to blocks, but first, they divided down with, like, divisions. I headed a whole area, Mount Pleasant area, and each one, I had a block person in every block in that area. We used to have meetings once a month or even frequently, if there was news that had to be talked about the war. And if there was a push for blood, if there was a push for bonds, if there was a push for scraps, it was there. So, anything that could help, like the scraps that were so badly needed, we're constantly talking about it and talking about saving grease, and all this kind of stuff.

'I'm Doing a Good Job Where I Am'

I remember, one of the things I had done as chairperson, I brought in a recruiter. A very nice woman, looked very sharp. As she's talking about the need for people to sign up, somebody said, 'Helen, why don't you sign up [for the military]?'

And I said, 'Sure.'

She said, 'You know, you'd be a good candidate to go to officer school because of your experience. You're a shop steward, you know how to handle people, blah, blah, blah.'

She put her coat on me, and I must say, I looked pretty sharp. Then, I asked the sixty-four-dollar question.

I said, 'Let me ask you something. You're promising me that you're going to send me to the Paul Smith College or someplace, where my experience and my leadership and everything will be taken into consideration?'

She said, 'I can't do that,' and I said, 'Forget it.' Because you know what happened? Some of our women joined up. They were doing a good job in the factory, and they ended up in the kitchen someplace. They wrote back and said, 'Helen, we're all sorry we signed up, because our skills were more needed where we were!'

As I say, they almost hooked me, but I figured, hey, I'm doing a good job where I am, because of the leadership that I showed about blood and bonds, and the *GE Work News*, which kept everybody connected. I was on a war production console during the war that was set up by the union and the company. We met regularly to talk about what can we do better in the shop to increase production. And so, I felt like I was doing my bit for the war effort.

You've got to remember that there were 40,000 people working at GE and women were thirty or thirty-five percent of them. We had a General Electric Athletic Association, and they had a tennis court, they had a ballpark, they had bowling alleys, they had places where you can play pool, they have places where you could meet and it was a great place for people to socialize. And so, and I was the only woman on that board, and so I worked hard too. I was a basketball player, I was a baseball player, I bowled, and so I worked very hard to let the women know that there was a place that was safe because some of the women came in from the [mountains and farms], and, I hate to say this, but boy, they had a ball taking these women out, you know, who were very inexperienced.

We stopped having some section nights for the union because it seemed like the guys—I don't want to be too derogatory, but you know what I'm saying—well, they had a ball with these young women. So, I finally got to the point where I told them, 'Look, you got all these women in the plant, you need a woman staff person' and they refuse to do it. I said, 'Look, I'm doing it already.' I'm working and trying to arrange all this stuff and put out publicity, but then they were too cheap to do that, so I resigned.

[When the men came back], we even had people come in from the federal government, the services, and we sponsored them. This one woman talked about syphilis, you know, I wrote an article for the *Work News* and they wouldn't put the word 'syphilis' in! 'Mrs. Kidman, you're going to talk about social diseases?' But one of the things that she said is very shocking because young men used to come home or come back from the service and have syphilis or something and they would say, 'Who were you with?' and the guy would say, 'We don't remember.'

'Oh, come on now. Who were you with? This person, if she gave that to you, is a danger.'

And so finally, they'd say, 'Well, you know, her name was Mary and she had blue eyes and I think it was in a section of Mount Pleasant.'

So, pretty soon, Mary got a knock on the door, 'We want to see you.' So this is some of the stuff that I did, you know. And that's why I felt like I was, in my estimation, more important here on the home front than if I had gone into the service. I know some of my friends joined the service and they were shocked. I mean, 'Geez, Helen, you were smart not to go in!'

*

You asked the question about the men's attitudes. Hey, the men have always resented women coming into the shop. Let's be honest. The attitude has changed lately, because of circumstances, but they have always resented the fact, I mean, you know, we used to stand in line at the clock and somebody would say something about, you know, 'Why don't you stay home and have a baby,' and I said, 'You know, guys,' I always had an answer for them.

I said, 'You know, get off of it,' and they'd laugh like mad because they knew that I always had an answer for them, you know, but they resented the fact that we were there. Let's be honest, though, regarding the amount of work that was after the Depression, if there had not been a war, there would have been a lot more people unemployed. But the fact is that one of the strengths that we had in Schenectady in the 1880s was led by women workers, but nobody knows about it because we have always been involved and the company used to say, 'Women work for pin money. Women can't lift, that's why they can't do jobs in the shop.' And the fact is that history has shown that 80% of the women who work support themselves and/or families, you know, so that knocked it off. We had to fight this whole thing about women.

Helen Quirini died on October 4, 2010, at the age of 90 after years of service to GE workers and retirees, a pioneering voice for women.

The Long Sisters. NYS Military Museum.

CHAPTER THREE

Shift Work Sisters

The Long sisters of central New York, like many young women, played a critical role in supporting the nation's war effort by working a major defense plant in Sidney, New York, during World War II. Frances was born December 30, 1916, in Syracuse; her sister Ethel followed on December 10, 1918, and Mabel came along on April 3, 1921. They sat for this interview with the New York State Military Museum in 2003.

Mabel Colyer
Frances Cooke
Ethel Severinghaus

Ethel: We worked in the same defense plant, the Bendix Scintilla Airplane Magneto Plant in Sidney, New York, [supplying the starting engines for the US Navy planes].[5] It went from that, to Bendix, to another name before Amphenol, which it is now.

---

[5] During World War II, the company was a major manufacturer of magnetos used on American aircraft engines.

Mabel: They still make connectors and stuff for planes, although they make more domestic products now. In fact, back then, it was the only decent employer in the whole area. People would come in from Pennsylvania and everywhere to work there. It still is, really.

Ethel: The railroad brought people from Middletown, to Edmiston, to Sidney for work. The train had three shifts, it would bring a group and then go right back and get another group. I was there briefly, just several months, between one thing and another. I was in the inspection, inspecting cams and a few other things they dragged me into. We had no experience, except my sister had been in inspection for a long time. I knew a little bit about it from her. I was there from September to December, 1941.

Frances: I was there from the fall of 1936 to the fall of '44. I worked on Rockwell machines, which had a diamond point and an indicator you pressed down to metals to find out if they were the correct hardness that was needed. I also worked on the springs, which were very important, used in cam followers; they were little pieces of felt fastened to a spring and the spring had to be tested 100% for each piece, because it was very important. They were used in the airplanes. I also worked with other things, like cable screws and stuff they used in the molding room. I am trying to think of what else.

Mabel: I worked there from 1940 until 1945 when the war was over. I worked on the magneto spark plug assemblies, and it was mostly just general assembly work. They all went into the ignition system for airplanes. It was mostly all airplanes, magnetos, and assemblies. We really don't know whether they made as many during the war as before, but they were building all these extra planes and everything. It was Scintilla Magneto, originally started by German immigrants, and they, by the way I was told, made just about all the magnetos that were used on the planes at that time. There was no country or place that made them more than they did, Scintilla, in

Sidney. But we really don't know who did it, if it was men, before we went there, because there were just more women and they had to split mica, and make the center core of the spark plugs, and assemble them. At that time, you did one or two jobs and that was it. That's the way they made production.

Frances: [Being there well before the war], I'd say [the sex ratio of the workers was] half and half.

'You're More Talented Than That'

Interviewer: Why did the three of you end up there?

Frances: I started out to be a nurse, and my father kept complaining that he wanted me home helping him. I got so tired of his complaining that I told him I guess I would stop my nursing for a while. I went there and my Aunt Louise said to me, 'Well, Frances, you shouldn't just work in my store. You're more talented than that. Why don't you go down and apply to the plant?'

They told me they wouldn't hire me for quite a long time, but the next morning, I got a call to come in.

I said, 'Well, why would you hire me?'

They said, 'Because you had physics and chemistry in high school.' They figured that would go along with their metals.

Interviewer: What kind of shifts did you work, did you work a swing shift?

Frances: I worked the day shift, but during the war, I worked from 11-7, nights, and sometimes the next day shift. Sometimes I was working sixteen hours a day.

Mabel: The war was on by then, we worked ten hours a day, seven days a week. The only time you saw daylight was if you went outdoors at your lunchtime, because the windows were all blacked over. I lived in Oneonta at the time, and they used everything that moved on the road to get people back and forth to work. I remember the old bus which had school seats like they had in old schools, bolted to the floor. That's what we rode. A lot of people from other towns took the train, any way they could get to Sidney, because Sidney was the only defense place in the area.

Mabel: The plant was secured by the military with a fence all around. There were guards, they had Army and Navy personnel in the plant to make sure that quality control was kept the way it had to be, and things like that.

Ethel: Well, [for me] it was a day shift because I had to go down with the riders from Sidney Center. I was a schoolteacher, and I was really working during the four months between my summer work and marriage. I was married in December, and of course, the war was declared three weeks before I was married. I had to move to Saranac Lake where my husband was a regional game supervisor.

Thirty Cents An Hour

Frances: We were paid thirty cents to start out with and I ended up with a dollar and a quarter when I quit.

Mabel: I don't really remember what my early wage was.

Frances: At Christmastime they gave us a little piece of ham.

Mabel: The only thing we got was extra stamps for gas, but then everybody carpooled. And of course, as I said, we rode on the bus. At the time, my husband was in the National Guard, and he was down in Alabama, Fort McClellan. Everybody from Oneonta got to the plant any way they could. It was mostly carpooling and these old buses. They would put anything on the road that traveled and could take people to work. Anybody driving in carpools got some extra stamps for gas if they took passengers.

Frances: They pushed a lot of war bonds, they had to ask us to buy them. We were supposed to buy a $25 one every month. We got a $25 bond for $18.75. With our small pay, you can see how much we gave up.

Mabel: When the war ended, we had a celebration, everyone went crazy. We were laid off, they closed the plant right down, and everybody went home. About a week later, if they wanted you to come back, you got a letter. I received a letter, but I didn't go back until five years later, and then I put in another twenty-one years there.

Ethel: We were very conscious on the job because we knew those planes were dependent on our doing our job properly. At one time, a fellow who had been an upperclassman when I was in college crashed in a plane in the Pacific and died while I was working there.

Mabel: Everybody was working long hours, but we took it in stride because we had a good purpose for doing it. It wasn't like we were working long hours for somebody else's profit. We were doing it because of the war effort. That's all you did, went to work and came home. We felt quite proud of the work we were doing; it was worth it.

The Long sisters lived rich, full lives into the 2010s, with the oldest, Frances, passing at age 102.

CHAPTER FOUR

The Los Alamos Secretary

Ruth Bull graduated from Schenectady High School in 1938 and soon after, she was employed as a secretary at General Electric in Schenectady and worked on the Manhattan Project in Los Alamos, New Mexico, during World War II, with an eyewitness view to the goings-on surrounding one of the most important projects in history.

Ruth A. Bull

I was born in Rotterdam, New York, on February 7, 1920. I finished high school, in a commercial course [with secretarial training].

I remember about Pearl Harbor that it was on Sunday, and I was working down at General Electric at that time. That day, I was home and getting ready to go out for the day, but instead we stayed home and listened to the radio. Well, it felt so sad, so bad. Didn't know what was going to happen next. That's what was so bad. And the next day, of course, going to work on Monday, and it was talk about what was going to happen.

Interviewer: How long did you stay at GE?

I was there from 1940 to 1945, doing secretarial work. I ended up with the Los Alamos Project when my sister and my brother-in-law were called. He was a glassblower at GE, and he was personally asked to go to Los Alamos. And so, he went, and my sister went with him. I said to her, 'Well, I'd like to come out. Maybe I could be your maid. I'd like to see what New Mexico looks like.'

And so she turned my name into personnel, and then they sent me an application and information about going, so I applied; my fare was paid by the government. And that's how I got out there, to be a secretary; we didn't have to have any specific training, but you couldn't leave the Hill. They called it the Hill. It was 2,000 feet above sea level and then it was like a mesa up there. [There was a lot of security around it]; you couldn't get in or out without identification. And you had to sign in the time you left and the time you came back.

I enjoyed my work there. I lived in a dormitory, with about twenty people in each dorm. They were all men and women. My sister lived in a house, apartment, or duplex house. We were well supplied with food. We didn't have to worry about any food. They had a commissary, and you were able to buy your own. They also had a mess hall facility.

Were there any special precautions you had to take with the kind of work you did at all?

No, not at that time. We handled some things that were contaminated; you had to be careful what you handled and to know how you had to handle it, get it out of the office fast and do not handle it too much. I had a Geiger counter on my desk. And if it flipped, well, then you had something in there that was contaminated, and you had to get it out of there. Get it moving.

We worked a full eight hours and sometimes more, depending on what job had to be done. You couldn't say anything about where you worked, how you worked, or what you did. It wasn't much for me, but I worked in an office. The military took care of the civilians. There were three or four people that worked in our office who were civilians. After I got there, there were more people that were hired civilians in our office, but we had a couple. I know that one of my best friends was in the Army. She was in charge of radiation reports. She had to be locked in when she was doing those reports. We were all combined all the while. At the door, we had about four MPs because you couldn't go in and out of the building unless you identified yourself with a pass, in every building.

Dr. Fermi and Dr. Teller

I met [the scientists], Dr. Fermi and Dr. Teller, they all worked in the technical area. We all worked in the same area. They were nice, especially Dr. Fermi. He was my favorite. Everybody looked the same. The only one you could tell was different was Teller. Do you know Dr. Teller? I didn't [really] like him, he was so boisterous. There were dances. We had dances on weekends; not every weekend, but once in a while. Dr. Fermi liked to do square dancing with me. His wife did not dance, she didn't want to square dance. So he picked me. It was fun. Everybody was very friendly. I only saw Robert Oppenheimer a few times. Half the time he was incognito; he was working all the time or somewhere else, he was always on the move.

The [scientists] lived in private homes. Originally, it was a private school. That's where Oppenheimer went to school as a child.

They had a few homes that were very well-built—stone and brick. He lived in one of those, not too far away, all the dorms and everything were built around it. It was a very small area.

We had quite a few movies in one building. We had church there, too. Just entertaining. I met a lot of my sister's friends that were married people. I spent a lot of time with them. I had dinners with them, and we played cards a lot. But then, after the drop of the bomb, they were more liberal. Some of the GIs were able to bring their wives up on the Hill.

'As If It Was Noontime'

Do you have any memorable events that you think stood out more than others while you were there?

The night before the first test of the bomb. I mean, they had several different tests down in the southern part of New Mexico. We would hear about them being duds or not or about them being successful. But the night that the big one was going to be dropped, it was a sort of funny feeling because you got the feeling that you didn't know whether it was going to be successful or not. And they were worried. They were worried, because they didn't know whether it was going to start a chain reaction and start the world on fire. They were pretty sure of what was going to happen, but they weren't positive, so we stayed up all night waiting for that first test. And it happened at 5:30 a.m. We were 250 miles away from it, but it was as if it was noontime. But everybody that went down to see the test, to be there, all had to have permission to go. My boss went. And they couldn't watch it anyway because they had to turn away from it and they had to wear special glasses. They couldn't look toward it at all. And so we saw more of the fire and the color and it was just like fire. And it just kept rolling and rolling. It was so bright. It wasn't close, but you could hear the rumble at 250 miles. And see, that was the southern part of New Mexico, and we were in the north, so the sound rose higher and came up high.

This is what the bomb did, it turned the sand to glass. This is kind of crude, but some of it was beautiful. The colors in it were really nice. I had a pail of it. My boss brought up a pail. And so, then we had this GI, anyway, he worked in the department where he could put it in plastic. He made bookends and different things like this for everybody to have a piece to take home.

Why didn't you let the family look at this for a long time?

Because it was contaminated. It isn't too big a piece, but it was radioactive.

Home

From there, I went to Columbia University. The professor I had in our department was Dr. Mitchell from Columbia. He was a physicist. He was the head of our department. And so, I followed him to New York, and I worked at Columbia University in the government contracts office at the time. And then I didn't stay there very long, and then I worked in... I ended up working in the alumni house, and then after that I had to come home because my twin sister was supporting my mother. Well, I was too, but indirectly. Finally, I did come back home.

I came home in 1946. My sister and her husband went directly to Oak Ridge, Tennessee, and continued to work with atomic energy, for twenty years or more, until he retired.

'Never Questioned Me About the Bomb'

I was still in contact with one engineer friend that I had that was in the Army, and we still write Christmas cards. And another girl that moved up to Seattle, I kept in contact with her for many years. I have a certificate for working on the Manhattan Project, and the pin was also issued to each one of us, signed by the Secretary of War, Mr. Stimson, a kind of [token] that at least we did something for the war effort.

What was your reaction when you heard about the atomic bombs being dropped on Japan?

Terrible. Also, we had to go to a couple of lectures because of it being dropped on so many women and children. It was so bad, so that we didn't... At first, I didn't know what they meant, what they were [having us be briefed for]; why? But afterward, I thought about it. Because after you start thinking about it, you think how terrible it was. It was so that we didn't feel so guilty. But, we did. We had those lectures afterward. Since then, though, we went to a talk about Los Alamos, just a few years ago, and one man came up to me after we talked about how I got there. He said, 'I want to thank you for working on that atomic bomb.'

I said, 'Oh, gee, thanks.' And he noticed my pin.

I said, 'That's the first time that anybody's ever said anything to me.' That's when I quit feeling guilty. You can't help thinking of it all these years.

He said, 'You saved many, many more people than were killed by that bomb.' And it's true. And we were good friends with a Japanese girl, after the war. But she never questioned me either, did she? Never questioned me about the atomic bomb.

Ruth Ann Bull passed on February 10, 2008, at the age of 88.

CHAPTER FIVE

The Research Physicist

Leonard Amborski was a civilian teaching physics when he was called upon to go to Washington, DC, working on new secret magnetic compasses for the military, to gear up for the anticipated invasion of Japan. He gave this interview in 2008 at the age of 86.

Leonard Amborski

I was born on August 23, 1921, Buffalo, New York.

I was at my date's house on a Sunday afternoon, we had the radio on and we got the message about Pearl Harbor then. I never heard about Pearl Harbor until then, didn't know where it was. Most people didn't. It didn't take long to find out what happened and so on, further comments on the radio filled us in on the details.

I was still a student at Canisius College. I graduated March 1943 and started teaching Army Air Corps cadets who were stationed at the college. They had just started the program, the college training detachment, at that time so I taught them physics and I also taught the civilian classes in physics at Canisius starting in May 1943. The Air Corps students had just arrived that month, there were two hundred of them in the original group. They were taking a five-month course, four months were classwork and one month they spent learning how to fly. We taught them pertinent physics subjects that might be important for them to know as flyers in combat.

We designed the course. We selected the parts that we thought were important for them to know. We tried to teach them some of the mechanics of airplanes, why they fly, the Bernoulli Principle, what kept the plane up in the air.[6] We taught them things on computers, computing distances and time so they would have some idea of instrumentation. We taught them things like electricity, a little bit of meteorology, too.

'Not Allowed to Discuss the Nature of Our Work'

In May 1944 they were ending the college training detachment program for the Army Air Corps. At that time, they had a need for scientists at the Department of Terrestrial Magnetism, which is the Carnegie Institute in Washington. There were eight of us on the faculty who went to Washington, D.C. to work at the Carnegie Institute. We were assigned to various activities; I was doing work on magnetism, studying the magnetic effects of the earth. I also worked on magnetic compasses and compasses for the Air Force, the Navy, and Coast Guard. Of those eight people, many of them were sent overseas because we were compiling data on the ionosphere, which is related to radio transmission. People were sent as far as Baffin Bay, Alaska, Christmas Island, Trinidad, and they were at these

---

[6] *Bernoulli Principle*- 1738 theory of flight that states "an increase in the speed of a fluid occurs simultaneously with a decrease in pressure or a decrease in the fluid's potential energy" and is to calculate the lift force on an airfoil. Source: www.skybrary.aero/articles/bernoullis-principle.

stations where we were compiling magnetic data as well as ionospheric data. Fortunately, I happened to be staying in Washington where I worked on the compass work and also on detecting and deactivating mines. We were anticipating an invasion of Japan at that time so they brought in a lot of Japanese mines and we were doing research on how to deactivate these particular mines to protect our troops if they were going to invade Japan.

We designed compasses specifically, one of the most detailed ones was for the Air Corps. These compasses were designed to make sure pilots would get to their destination and get back. We also were designing compasses for the Coast Guard and were actually on a Coast Guard ship in Glen Burnie near Baltimore where we were testing these compasses. They were automated and they would be recording the data as you went along. Rather than just looking at a compass, they would have recording devices, the early stages of computerization.

We worked five and a half days, Monday through Friday and then half a day on Saturday. It was a beautiful setting in Rock Creek Park. The buildings I worked in primarily were non-magnetic buildings because we didn't want the outside influence of the building having any steel or magnetic material. The building that I worked in was a rather unique building in that it was all wood and they used copper nails to put it together. We studied compass deviations and how they might be affected by the outside influences.

We were essentially qualified [with a high security clearance] by the War Manpower Commission. They looked at our credentials in terms of training and knowledge and experience, so they gave us an exemption from being military people. At one time they considered putting us into the military, but they said what's the point, we're doing the same work anyhow, so the War Manpower

Commission kept us as civilians. We were not allowed to discuss the nature of our work.

I worked in Rock Creek Park, which was northwest Washington, but I lived right across the street from the US Capitol building. I got married when I was there and we lived in an apartment directly across the street. If you were in our bathroom, you could look out the window and see the dome of the Capitol. *[Laughs]* We didn't have a car, we used public transportation. For $1.25 we had a pass, you could go anywhere in the city on a trolley or a bus. I also taught night school there; I taught chemistry in one of the public high schools, Theodore Roosevelt High School, but I lived at the other end of town. We had a lot of exciting days because we lived right across from the Capitol and any dignitaries coming in, we'd get a chance to see them. One of the most notable things I remember is seeing President Roosevelt the day he left the White House to go to Warm Springs, Georgia, before he died. He was in an open car with his fedora and I took a picture of him. That was the last time I saw President Roosevelt. To me he was a hero. I felt very badly about that.

On the way to work one day, I met, coming out of the apartment building, on Connecticut Avenue, President Truman, the day he took over the office. He lived in an apartment; I saw him come out of his building that morning after Roosevelt died. I also remember seeing General Charles de Gaulle, he was on the street one day. Those are the two dignitaries other than Eisenhower and Wainwright whom I saw in parades. But I got pretty close to President Truman at the time and de Gaulle.

We also enjoyed the parades they had when Eisenhower came to Washington and General Wainwright, there was great celebration. We also had a daughter born that year, and when the Japanese war ended in August 1945 my wife and I were pushing the baby carriage down Pennsylvania Avenue rejoicing with everybody else.

My two-month-old daughter was sound asleep in the carriage, she didn't hear anything.

We knew nothing about [the dropping of the atomic bombs]. When it happened, having been alerted to the possibility that we might have to invade Japan, knowing the consequences of our people being killed, I was very happy to see that we saved a lot of our own lives. Probably tens of thousands of American lives were saved as a result.

[Rationing was a part of our lives], definitely. My wife used to go to the local store, and he'd give her a package. You didn't know what it was you came home with, probably hamburger so you never knew what you got. Butter and meat were very scarce, hard to come by. We had a lot of Spam. *[Laughs]* My wife was pregnant, so we did a lot of walking, a lot of sightseeing. We got to see many things in Washington, Glen Echo Park, we went to the Franciscan Monastery, so we got around the town to see what was there. Of course the Lincoln Memorial, we walked around the Tidal Basin, we always enjoyed the cherry blossoms there. So we did a lot of sightseeing around the town, that was our major effort. I don't think we even went to movies in those days, we just did sightseeing.

'I Lost Two Brothers'

My brother and I started school together at Cleveland and went through every class together through freshman year at Canisius College. He was eleven months older than I was, so we were almost like twins. He spent one year at Canisius and then went in the Coast Guard and ultimately went to the Merchant Marine Academy on Long Island. Part of their training was to be on a merchant vessel. He was assigned to a merchant vessel which went to England. On the way back they were torpedoed and that's where he lost his life. I spent four years researching this in recent years and published a book.[7] That was the most tragic event in my life. I still recall my mother when she screamed when she got the message. All we learned at that time was that he was missing in action. It wasn't until about three months later that my mother got a letter from the mother of one of the survivors of the ship, giving us the details of how it happened. My mother was in a bad state of mind for a long time after that. It did affect the family very strongly. My father kept writing letters trying to find out more information. I still have copies. It was a real tragic event for the whole family.

I also lost a cousin, Arthur Amborski, whose mother and my mother were sisters and our fathers were brothers. They were married in a double wedding. He was like a brother to me. He went to Bergen High School, he was a four-star athlete, he was in football and basketball, he was class president, he was an honor student. He had an offer to play professional baseball with the Cleveland Indians but when he graduated in 1943, he joined the Air Force and ultimately wound up in Italy and he was a gunner on a plane.

They were shot down over Vienna, Austria, and he was killed. He was buried in a cemetery in Austria and four or five years later they exhumed his body and he's now buried in Ardennes, Belgium. So I basically lost two brothers in the war.

After the war I joined DuPont where I worked forty-four years. During the course of my career at DuPont I went to night school at the University of Buffalo and got my Master's and PhD at night school. I was the first student to do that. I got my PhD in chemistry and worked for DuPont in research and I got to do environmental work. I got to do fitness work and got to be an industrial hygienist. I had to take a training program and pass a certification exam and I was the first certified hygienist in western New York. That entailed my efforts to look after the health of our workers. We tested the

---

[7] *The Last Voyage: Maritime Heroes of WWII.*

area for toxic material, noise, radiation, stress, mechanical stress. I got to be an industrial hygienist as well as a research chemist. It's just an inherent interest I had in research, I still have that same interest. Now I do my research in genealogy. I'm still researching all the time, I guess that's my nature. I started out that way and I maintained that same interest in looking into new things. *[Laughs]*

Leonard Amborski passed away on January 8, 2014 at the age of 92.

PART TWO

HOME & SCHOOL

"The servicemen, most of it was just party time, really. Servicemen came in and all they wanted to do is eat, sleep, and drink, they figured this was their last chance. They would have a big party and they figured if they left Hawaii, they would be dead, so all they wanted to do was party. A lot of them did not even come back."

—School kid remarking about his family's restaurant, Pearl City, Hawaii

CHAPTER SIX

The School Teacher

Jane W. Washburn was born a week before the Armistice ceasing the hostilities of the 'Great War' was signed in 1917. She grew up on a farm during the Depression in Gansevoort, New York, and graduated from Glens Falls High school in 1935. Unlike many in her generation, she went on to graduate from a private college in 1939, earning a degree in home economics, remembered by her students for holding high standards in her classroom. She gave this interview to a pair of my high school seniors in 2003, having enjoyed many days of travel in her retirement. On one of her many travels, she visited Japan; she was very impressed with their lifestyles and friendliness, but, as she stated, her 'old feelings towards them still remained.' Here, she offers her insights into growing up in 'Hometown, USA' as the Great Depression and World War II and its aftermath unfolded.

Jane Washburn

I was born on this property and my grandfather was four years old when he came here to live back in 1854. He came, so the Washburns have lived here all this time. How I feel about the wars and the Depression are somewhat colored by my family's background for generations, if you know what I mean.

I was born before the Armistice. Therefore WWI, WWII, Korean War, Vietnam War, Palestine, and Israel, Wars in Africa, Gulf War, and the present two wars have all been a part of my life. I have had very few years in my life when there's been total peace in the world. Too bad, isn't it? *[Pauses]* Now you want to know about the Depression?

Depression Days

The big crash came in 1929. I was a teenager, of course, during the Depression. Nobody had any money, anyway. At first, I went to a little private school, then I went to school in South Glens Falls. I took the trolley! I had to walk up the road here and took the trolley from there, from South Glens Falls. At the end of seventh grade, I was sent to the Glens Falls High School because it had a better curriculum. My parents, neither one of them had education beyond high school; they wanted it for their three daughters. So, my sisters and I, all of us graduated from the Glens Falls High School. My family paid tuition for that. So we didn't have any money, but living on a farm made a difference.

We always had plenty of food. Plenty of milk, plenty of eggs, plenty of butter, plenty of meat, lots of vegetables. If you wonder what might have contributed to the fact that today I'm 86 and still navigating, it might be because I had a long walk every day to catch the bus. We got plenty of exercise; we didn't have time for a lot of foolishness. *[Laughs]* We took piano lessons, you know, and all of those things.

My older sister graduated two years ahead of me and went to Russell Sage [College]. So when it was time for me to go to college and I was interested in home economics, Russell Sage was the place. They had a very good economics department there then. My sister graduated two years ahead of me. It was Depression days, but we each got an allowance of four dollars a month. A dollar a week! How would you like that? *[Laughs]*

Miss Jane Washburn, 1939. Source: Jane Washburn.

In fact, I was a sophomore in college before we got electricity. One of the biggest things that Franklin D. Roosevelt did as President was to bring about rural electrification. It was a wonderful, wonderful thing to be able to flip a switch and have a light. This is digressing, but my mother and father heard about this, you know. So-and-so out in such-and-such a place is getting electricity. My mother said, 'Why don't we have electricity?' So, she called Niagara

Mohawk [Power Company] and they said, 'If you want electricity, you get all the people in the community together that want it and I will come and tell you about it.' So everybody called everybody, and they all met down there at the farmhouse and had a big meeting. One month later, they had electricity, it was just wonderful!

We didn't have a lot of clothes. We didn't have cars, but we did have a very good education. I graduated in 1939 and it was right around the time when schools were beginning to centralize. With centralization, they put in a lot of new departments. Home Economics was one, agricultural courses was another, industrial arts courses, all things that were going to be helpful to train people in the Depression days.

So I went out to western New York to teach for 1,200 dollars a year. Worked ina school that had no economics department, nothing, but I got it going. I was there for six or seven years, and I was there during Pearl Harbor.

I didn't know anything about it until that night. [*Pauses*] When I heard, somebody had the radio on. This was in [Ripley], New York. That's the last town left of New York State, it's right on the Pennsylvania border. My sister was teaching at Newfield, which was just south of Ithaca. She taught French! Somebody always had a radio on. When they heard a piece of news, they immediately got onto the telephone and then that person got the radio on. This is how news got around, and that's how I got the news. Somebody had the radio on and heard about Pearl Harbor. As I told you before, I was indignant because I had been to the movies previous to this and knew that two ambassadors from Japan had come to visit Franklin

Roosevelt at the White House, the day before the seventh.[8] They never let on that all of this was being planned, you see. We all knew that something was going on; we didn't know what it was.

'Nobody Really Knew'

As I told you I think previously too, my roommate's boyfriend joined the [Army] Air Force in the summer of 1940, and he was a pilot on the B-17s. He flew to Manila, the plane had all the armaments it needed, but it had no ammunition. He was there when Clark Field was bombed. The only thing he saved was his camera. Then he had a hard time getting out. It took months to get out of the Philippines, you see, all this time the war with Europe was going on too. Here again, if you wanted to know something, you had to go to the movies. To see the Pathé newsreels they used, to see about the battles and things and whatnot. There was lots of talk about what Hitler was doing, but nobody really knew. The terrible things, we had rumors of it, but nobody really saw it. No one ever knew! Then when Pearl Harbor came, all the Japanese [-American] people were rounded up. You've probably seen pictures of that, haven't you? They had prisoner of war places for them. Many innocent people were [rounded up]. People of foreign descent! [A friend] who was up here on Mount McGregor, she'd been there for 20 years, a Japanese girl, but after that she was temporarily relieved of

---

[8] *two ambassadors from Japan-* Secretary of State Cordell Hull met with the diplomats at 2:20 pm, Washington time, on December 7, where they were to deliver the message that the Japanese government was formally breaking off relations with the United States. Unbeknownst to the officials, the Japanese had commenced their attacks. Hull, now aware of the perfidy, lectured them and dismissed them after ten minutes.

her job as caretaker up there.⁹ We had German people, we had Austrian people and we were very suspicious, we couldn't help it.

Rationing

It was really after Pearl Harbor that things began to tighten up. You couldn't buy an automobile, you couldn't buy tires, and gasoline was rationed. Here on the farm, of course, we were able to get more gasoline, because we didn't live in town.

Now to get back to after Pearl Harbor, we began to have rationing; sugar was one of the first things to go, butter was another. We had olio, which was just the color of Crisco, you know. You had to put colored things in it to perk it up. Meat was terrible, Spam, I can't eat it even today. Hot dogs you could get, they were the mixtures of things. We had lots of vegetables; we had our own pork. Now and then we would have a piece of beef. We had a dairy farm, so that's why we had beef. In the town where I was teaching, they got the rationing. The teachers were one group of people that could always get together to get a job done, so the teachers were responsible for signing all the people in that town up for rationing. You got stamps for gasoline and for butter, and for various foods. Canned foods and

---

⁹ *Mt. McGregor*-Mt. McGregor, located in Wilton, New York, about 10 miles south of Glens Falls, has an interesting history. Originally settled by Native American survivors escaping King Philip's War, it boasts spectacular views. Duncan McGregor built a hotel called the Mountain House in 1876; in 1885, the new owner, Joseph Drexel, loaned the use of his personal cottage on the mountain to his friend, then seriously ill former president Ulysses S. Grant, where Grant finished writing his war memoirs in just six weeks before he died there that July. Today, the Grant Cottage State Historic Site is preserved exactly as it was at the time of his death. In 1945, New York State used it for convalescing WWII veterans, and from 1976-2014 it was used as a minimum-security state prison.

meat and meat products, you see. This is beside the point, but we had one famous person in this little town. He was a Civil War veteran, and he was one of the last ones to die. He was over a hundred years old when he died, but he was a vegetarian. So anyway he was very, very patriotic. So when rationing came along in that little town, everybody who had any extra stamps or canned vegetables or canned fruits, they gave to the grocer for Grandpa Rounds when he did his shopping. But Grandpa Rounds would never ever give anybody one of his meat stamps, because he thought it unpatriotic. Yet, he never knew that everybody in that town was keeping him well fed with their extra stamps. We all knew! *[Laughs]* He was rather interesting!

Paper Salvage scrap drive: "A young woman, Jean F. Casey, staffs a booth on Glen Street, Glens Falls. Sign reads, 'WANTED 250 MEN to help win the war.' Banner below her reads in yellow, 'It is a weapon of war,' and in white, 'SAVE WASTE PAPER.'" Source: LOOK Magazine for 'Hometown USA' series, 1943-44. The Folklife Center at Crandall Public Library, Glens Falls, NY.

We all got along somehow or another with what we had. We had lines that would form! If you were walking along Glen Street in Glens Falls, and you saw a line, you would know someone had cigarettes or they had candy or some little thing. You would get into line, whether you would want it or not. Buy the product, maybe for somebody else who did want it and couldn't get there, you know.

Stockings, we got so we couldn't get nylon stockings. We had to wear rayon stockings, which would run. It was weak when it was wet, so you would get runs in them all over. We had to wear cotton stockings but somehow, we managed to do that, too.

Travel was very hard! I sat on my suitcase from west of Buffalo to Albany on the train one day. Now that's a long time, it's about six hours. I had to sit in the aisle on my suitcase because there were no seats on the train, you see. The train, well there would always be men on the train, servicemen on the train. That was the first time I think when gentlemen did not have to give up their seats to a lady! If you saw a serviceman on, he got to sit. I took a trip on an airplane and if you were changing planes in like Chicago and there was a serviceman waiting to get on that plane, he got on, you were bumped. They had priority, which was probably right because many of them were tired and many of them didn't know where they were going or what their futures were going to be. In 1945, I went to Galveston, Texas, to see this college roommate of mine who had a new baby. Her husband had come home and was flying out of the airbase there, he was a weather expert. I got bumped every stop from Buffalo, then Detroit, then I think it was Chicago and Kansas City and Dallas, Texas. It took me 24 hours to get there, which now you would do in about 4-6 hours. Then the planes were not big planes like they are today, of course.

There were a lot of recipes by the way, too, for egg-less cakes and butter-less cakes and sponge cakes and things like that. It was amazing what women did to give variety to their foods. [With the rationing], all rubber things… You couldn't buy a pair of rubber overshoes, you know, that were made of rubber. You know your underpants have elastic around the waist, they did away with that. They were stitched around and buttoned on the side. *[Laughs]* I had a college friend, and she was very proper, you know, she was walking down the street one day, and the button fell off her pants. She was in the middle of the street. She said, 'I just stood there a minute and let them drop down and reached down and picked them up and went on.' *[Laughter]* But the babies, you see, babies [before rationing] would always have rubber bands. No rubber bands, they were not to be had. But…this was very hard on the mothers, there were no Pampers and things of that sort, you know. It was bad, the problem was very, very bad. The rubber was needed for jeeps and trucks that were part of the war effort, airplane tires and things, you see. So we knitted soakers, they were three corner pieces of wool yarn because wool holds the moisture and wool keeps you warm. Our bathing suits were all wool then because you get out of the water, and you wouldn't feel cold. But then they stopped all that, you know, when you got swimming pools. This was because wool has lint, and it would clog up the swimming pools. So now you don't have wool, very rarely would you find wool bathing suits. This sounds unbelievable but when you went to buy a tube of toothpaste it was in aluminum tubes you had to take back to get a new tube. That was because the aluminum then would be converted for the war effort. You gave in your old pots and pans that had holes in them. If they were aluminum, they would be reprocessed for that. Everything was converted to the war effort that was possible to do. We were very careful about coffee. You didn't waste coffee… but we always had some, but we drank a lot more tea probably, which wasn't so scarce.

Our clothes, the skirts were very short. Actually, the government regulated the width of the waistbands and belts and the pulls on the skirts, saving money on materials, the quality on material, you see. *[Pauses]* The quality of the materials was rather shabby too.

We all wore hats; hats were very fashionable. A good hat would be made out of a fur product with a …sheep hats were made just of wool and then they began to put other products in, you know. Another thing, our underwear was silk. We wore slips which were silk satin and they had to be ironed too, but they were nice. Our stockings were silk, nylon stockings didn't come in until about 1940. That was one of the big graduation gifts girls got when they graduated from high school, a pair of nylon stockings. They had seams in the back; you know you had to be very careful that your seams were straight, never twisted stockings. We rolled our stockings because with silk you could roll them. Of course girls got this habit of always pulling up their stockings, then when rayon came through you couldn't, you couldn't roll stockings because they would stay up. So that's where the two-way stretch came in and that had its problems too. I think back now and think probably the happiest moment of my day when I was teaching school was when I could get home and get the girdle off. Now girls don't wear things like that, you see.

Entertainment

Everything was kind of closed down, you know. You couldn't go any place because you didn't have a car [Laughs]. Quite different from today. We did not hear a lot. What was in the paper, what was on the radio. Lowell Thomas was on every night like, you know, like Dan Rather is now. They would tell us stories and then if you really wanted to see it, you went to the movies. We went to the movies a lot. It was cheap and you really got a good… You got the feature movie, and you got the previews, and you got the Pathé News.

The [Pathé] News would come on; it would show the ships that were being burned and the soldiers that were marching and the tanks that were down in the mud and all those things. That's the only way you got any pictures of anything, except *Life* magazine would come out with pictures. They would show a picture, that's why it was so popular. Oh, and at Christmas time, I think this must have been about Christmas of 1939, probably. The radio had a program where the children, the British children who had been sent to the United States for safekeeping could talk to their parents on the radio. It was just, it was just the most heart- wrenching experience. To hear these children seven and eight years old, you know, talking to their parents out there. But they had been sent here to be safe, you see, to be safe from the bombing. There were a lot of care packages too, at Christmas time. Even though you didn't know the boys, you know, you would collect them. The Red Cross did a lot of getting people involved in things. We also had airplane watch, you know, right on top of the school. Where every plane that went over, you reported it. They kept track of things. Of course, along the coast there were submarines and all kinds of things that people had to watch for.

Teaching

[The teacher shortage], well, that was very difficult. We had a lot of people in and out, in and out. Usually, they were people that were not successful from just the beginning. I think we had a lot of bad education. I remember at that time the state of New York enacted a law that all students had to take a health course. Who was going to teach it? Turned out that the home economics teachers were going to, because we all had a science background. We were very health conscious, we all had to do first aid. Home nursing courses, all the women did. Men and women took first aid courses. *[Laughs]* You had to learn how to do artificial respiration. They would get you down on the floor and push your chest and you'd be aching for about two weeks after that, but everybody did that. We rolled bandages, we knitted a lot, hats and scarves, and some did sweaters. We made bob cats, which were little toilet bags, and then filled it with things, you know. If you knew someone was in the service, you made a lot of cookies. Some goodies, you know, and tried to write letters. You keep writing to them to let them know what is going on here. The air raid drills, they were a big pain in the neck. In your high school today was one of the places that they had the air raid drills, you would hear things [*raises voice*] 'clang,' you know, and everybody would get up. Each homeroom had its assigned place, as I remember it. It wasn't your class you were in; it was your homeroom. You had an assigned place to be, it was all along the corridors, and it was inside the stage. All up against the wall, and you stood face to the wall and waited. Until…you were protected by the walls, you see, rather than being in the corridors. I don't remember if we had to get down on our hands and knees or not, but I don't think we did. But we did have to stand there until it was all over. It was like a fire drill in a way, but the rules were a little different. Some people had air raid shelters too, you know. They stockpiled canned food, sugar and milk, dry milk and so that when we had a bombing they would be protected. It was a very big fear, a very, very big fear later that Russia would bomb us. We lived with that!

[For first aid], well, we had to learn how to bandage. We had to learn about what we should use for certain problems. Bleeding was the main thing, and how to put a splint on if you had a broken limb and artificial respiration for drowning, you see. Also, how to protect against smoke inhalation and fires. [*Pauses*] I guess that was about it. Now, England, of course, had terrible air drills and lots of their families were lost. I know one young man who ended up in Bermuda and he lost his whole family. His mother and sisters and all of them, you see, the whole town would be wiped out. The bombings were so terrible, you see. The whole town would be wiped out, the bombings were so terrible in parts of England.

Then of course, you watch the newspaper because it would give a list of all the local people that had been injured or killed. All the towns had these big signs out, you know, of all the people in the town who were in it.

Roll of Honor, 1946, Hudson Falls High School yearbook photo, which stood before the town library.

Now, I don't know where Hudson Falls had theirs, but they must've had one that had a list of all the people who were joining the service. It also changed your social life for women particularly, because there wasn't anybody to go out with. Unless he was '4-F' and *[Laughs]* there was something 'with him,' you know. That was the first that women felt free to go to a restaurant or a movie unescorted. It was really rather an uncomfortable time, we weren't used to that, you know.

There were a lot of women that had always just stayed home and looked after the children. Now, they got out and got jobs and earned money. Of course it was Depression time too, so that extra money was wonderful to come by. One person would have a car, and everybody would pay him or her so much to ride to, say, Glens Falls. One of the places we had for women was McMullen's [three-story brick factory] that made men's shirts originally. Then it went into making women's dresses, very fine quality, very attractive dresses. The women learned very good sewing techniques by working in the shirt factories and the dress factory. Then a lot of women went to the [local] General Electric, located in Fort Edward, which wasn't too far, as they couldn't drive back and forth from [the main plant infrastructure] in Schenectady; GE took on a lot of people from this area.

We knew we were going to have sugar rationing, so my mother stored sugar! Now my mother canned a lot, she canned peaches and pears and she made jellies, and we needed sugar for those things, you know. So she…we had these great big tin cans, that I guess originally potato chips came in. They were probably ten gallons or so, they were like lunch pails, but were only metal. She would get sugar and put it up in the attic, so when necessity rose, we would have sugar. We never really did run out of sugar, but we were very careful. Soap was another thing, very hard to come by and you would be very careful with the soap. Of course, we didn't have laundromats and we didn't have automatic washing machines either. So you would have to wash with the old-fashioned washers with a spin dryer on it. If you had a modern one, it had a spin dryer and you would put it in this one to wash them, then you would take them out and put them in this, and it would spin them out. Then you could put them in a tub of water to rinse them, you know, then place them in the spinner to get the water out again so they would dry faster. No dryers either…even after the war.

My father [was a dairy farmer, and], yes, there were milk strikes. The price of milk was just terrible, just terrible, and farmers wanted more pay for their milk, so they went on strike. They called people who continued to sell their milk 'scabs.' Farmers normally would take their milk to the milk man, who was over there in Gansevoort, [near the railroad], right near where the post office would later be.

A lot of men dumped their milk. But, of course, they were small dairy farms. Early on in my father's life they made butter. My grandmother made butter; I can remember it very well. She had butter customers in Glens Falls. So, my father just got out the old churn and made butter, we had plenty of butter! When the war was finally over, they raised the price.

Marriage During Wartime

There were a lot of quickie marriages. The boys would come home for a furlough and knew they were going back and felt if 'I don't get married... [*pauses*] and get this woman pregnant, I will have no offspring to carry on my name.' There were a lot of marriages of that sort. Then, of course, when the war was over, the marriage was no good. They just didn't get along. Then it started this terrible time with lots and lots of divorces and separations. There were a lot of girls who settled for anybody who came along because it was a time when every girl was supposed to get married, settle down and keep house. That was the main objective in many families. That all the daughters should get married, keep house, and have children. Then, when the war came and so many thousands of men were lost, there were not many available men of the quality that a girl would like—good education or talented—so they married whoever came along and that did not make for a happy marriage either when the war was over, because they didn't have anything in common. I will say, too, that there was a lot of drinking going on, terrible, not only during the war, but after the war. These men that came home, they were going to party and live it up. There was a lot of drinking going on. I think about that, and I think, how did anyone survive, because we didn't have laws about not drinking and driving. Cars were not as safe as they are now. Roads were not as well kept as they are now. But there were a lot of people who were killed too, but almost not as bad as they are now. Well of course they didn't have the speed that we have today. But there was a lot of drinking going on, which is very regrettable for both men and women. I was going with a fellow who was a metal artist, I didn't think much of it at the time. But he didn't go to war, and I know now that it was because he was a metal artist and the Americans didn't want him in the war effort, which he didn't talk about. Well, I didn't see anybody I thought I wanted to spend the rest of my life with. There wasn't too much to choose from. I had my chances but I'm glad I didn't take them. [*Laughter*] I don't regret it, no.

[After the war], we had the materials then to make clothes and make shoes and automobiles. My father kept saying… I didn't have a car, you see, of course, and he said, 'Well, as soon as the war is over, then they will make cars again.' They were not making any, so of course when the war was over, I was ready to buy a car. The price moved up considerably. My father said, 'If you only wait a year or two, the price will go down.' Of course, it didn't happen, so it was 1950 before I got my first car, and it was a brand-new Pontiac. I paid $1,700 cash for it, because I saved my money for it. That was my first car, some of the first cars that came out were very poorly made and very unsatisfactory. So probably waiting a little while didn't hurt, but there was a big boom. There was also a building boom, because there were no apartments, there were no houses being built. There were these young couples, that was the time when girls and young men were getting married, and then there was the baby boom. There was no place for them. My sister lived down there at the farmhouse for I think about two years while her husband was in the service. Then when he came home and they began looking for houses, it really was very, very hard. If you knew somebody who had died, then you would get a hold of the relatives to find out what was going to happen to the house. *[Laughs]* Then they started making and building a lot of houses too. Have you ever heard of Levittown? It's a very large town, city now, down on Long Island because that was near New York City, you see, and they needed houses. They built hundreds of houses in this area. They were all alike and they were all small houses. Beginners houses, you see, for these young couples that were getting married and having children. They had to have places and so the whole town was built. Schools were built, the whole thing. I wonder sometimes what happened to it.

The Boys in the War

[Several local families had their sons in the war], two brothers I knew, they both were Marines. One was in Guadalcanal and the other was in Iwo Jima. They both came home safely but they don't talk about it. This little project that you've got has probably started a lot of people talking. I have a magazine here, which I don't know where it is now, a little article in it about three men who have been in the war, and they were just beginning to talk about it now. So you're going to find out maybe a lot of things that people kept kind of in the background. My sister was in the Navy, my younger sister. During the WAVES, she was down in Virginia. Some of the folks that came in were a lot of burn patients. She doesn't ever talk about it. Of course, she wouldn't sail out of the country, either. *[Pauses]* She saw the men when they came home, and the condition they were in.

82 | THE SCHOOL TEACHER

"'Four *star mother*,' probably *Mary Marcantonio, the mother of four children, one adopted, who were all serving in World War II. Source: LOOK Magazine for 'Hometown USA' series, 1943-44. probably photographed by Harold Rhodenbaugh. The Folklife Center at Crandall Public Library, Glens Falls, NY.*

I think at the time of World War II, [the draft] was very essential. There are a lot of people that wouldn't have gone into it if they hadn't been drafted. It was getting down to the point where they were going to draft men as old as 38, you know, which seems pretty old, but that's how hard up we were. All the young ones as soon as they got out of high school, they joined up. I remember one boy in particular we were very fond of, and he wasn't over there very long, and he was killed. He was probably nineteen, a lot of them very, very young. Mothers, little things they hung in the window, you know a little red, white, and blue sign and it had stars on it. When you had one son in you had one star, two sons, two stars, and so on. Then if you had lost a son, you had a gold star. You could go by the houses and see these gold stars and you would know where there were men in the service and who had lost sons.

I don't think [draftees] were eager, but I think the draft was very efficient. It was the Vietnam War where the men went to Canada and there was a draft then too, but somehow it wasn't as strict as it was in WWII. The feeling was totally different because of the Japanese. We were mad, and my sister, the younger sister, lives down in Georgia, is still mad. To some degree I am still indignant. I went to Japan on one of my trips. Beautiful country, friendly people, clean, very clean, but I didn't trust them. I'm not sure if I do today, I don't know. Marines were a tough bunch and you had to be ready to do all kinds of things to join the Marines. They were tough and a lot of them were sent to the Japanese war.

D-Day

I remember D-Day with the most jubilation, and we got the day off. We got the rest of the week off, as I remember it. We were very happy. We knew it was coming. We didn't know about Normandy until it happened, you see. That was a very, very great secret. We did not know…We figured something big was going to happen, but we didn't know when exactly. It was a terrible thing for a lot of those fellows. In fact, to do all this embroidery I do, I took classes in Massachusetts, for several years I went after I retired. One time there was a man there and his wife had been interested in embroidery and he went with her, and he became interested. He had only one arm and he had been in the battle for three hours and lost his arm. He did very, very nice work with one hand. But he was maimed for life, you see, because the way it hurt his shoulder. No, he never did talk about that, he just said three hours and his arm was gone. It was a very violent thing, very violent.

These men keep going back, you know. Like the Marines they have meetings every year and then they go back to some of these places and see what has happened, you know. It was a terrible thing, so many of them so young, not much older than you are, you see. We had a family in Hudson Falls who lived over on the road to Hartford, a German family. I won't say the name because I might have the wrong name. But I remember the father's brother came over from Germany and they had been in the war over there. They had been deprived, of course. I seemed to remember another young man who had been taken prisoner. He was in the Air Force, that had come down and gotten into some German area, you know. He had been taken prisoner there, he got out of it eventually. [*Pauses*] We were all glad when it was finally over.

*

[When President Roosevelt died], we all knew he wasn't well, you could look at him and know he wasn't well. I was a Republican and I knew I made a mistake in feeling he had been in too long. He had been in for sixteen years, and previous to that he was Governor of New York State. So he was in the limelight for a long, long while. There was a slogan, 'You can't change horses in the middle of the [race],' which meant you can't change presidents while a war is on. That was one of the reasons he was put in year after year. It was to maintain his position to knowledgeably be able to help us with the war. He was probably the best equipped that we had. He wasn't afraid of Stalin, and he and Churchill were great friends, you know. But as he got older, he was less and less able to get out and around. They only showed us what they wanted us to see, they didn't want us to know he was in such poor health. That was probably smart.

Harry Truman was an entirely different kind of man. Roosevelt was a very highly educated man and spoke very beautiful English, you know. Harry Truman was just an ordinary man who had worked in a men's clothing store and sold suits and hats and things. I don't know how he ever got into politics the way he did. But he had a sign on his desk that said, 'The buck stops here,' and by golly, nobody could talk him into spending money that he didn't feel was right. He was actually a very good president.

'They Just Wouldn't Tell Anyone'

I think [the atomic bombing of Japan] probably was the only way to get things done. It was just going on and on and on. It ended things in a hurry. We spent a lot of time getting it ready. I knew of a young woman who worked at Oak Ridge. She didn't know what she was working on. So even the people who were making the parts for the atomic bomb didn't know about it, you see. The *Enola Gay* was the airplane that carried the crew that dropped the atomic bomb. It was named for the mother of one of the men on that plane. It was very, very, very secret. There was a lot of secret stuff that went on very, very quietly, part of it probably because we didn't have television because you know we've got people over in Iraq right now. Well, you probably watched it, sat right there in the truck with them while they're going down there towards Baghdad.

Now, [when servicemen returned from World War II], it wasn't that they were secretive about their experiences. No, they just wouldn't tell anyone. Well, if you were polite you wouldn't ask, you didn't try to dig it out of them. I think even their parents didn't know.

High school interviewer: So what do you think about the war today? The Iraq War?

I feel we had to do it for the safety of the world. I feel indignant that France and Germany won't help. After all, who were the troops that went marching into Paris when the war was over? Who was it that helped to get that Berlin Wall down? How much money did we put into all of this? Now this terrorism is a worldwide thing that has to be stopped. It's been an unexpected situation where we have been...we've lost many men and we've been badly hurt by it because their way of life is entirely different from ours and I don't think we've understood it. Also we're not always right, Americans are not always right. People don't always like us because we may appear to be cocky and superior and we're not always right.

I want to say this, too. When I was young, my grandfather would tell me stories, I didn't listen very well, now I wish I did, my grandma too, I didn't listen. How are we going to keep these things, don't you agree? They're very precious, really! Little things that I think about my grandparents, the little sayings that they've had.

Miss Washburn died on April 8, 2007, at the age of 89, three and a half years after this interview with my students.

CHAPTER SEVEN

The Schoolgirl

Elaine Sommo, born Elaine Curren, was the second of five children—all girls—who grew up in Vermont during the Great Depression. Her father was a steam shovel operator, and her mother worked as a waitress when times were tough. Like her older sister, she trained as a registered nurse. Elaine entered high school as the war began. Though too young to serve in World War II, she gave her teenage interviewer insight into her own teenage years during the war, her fears and dreams shared by a generation of young people across the United States. She sat for this interview in 2003 at the age of 75.

Elaine Curren Sommo

I was born in Fair Haven, Vermont, on March 26, 1928. I am now 75 years old.

During the Great Depression, goods and materials were short, however, we learned to get along without these things. A really vivid memory is that my father had a job at the Stasel Milling Company in Castleton, Vermont—they made roofing material. They would dig this material from the earth; my father ran a steam shovel. There was not enough work for civilians at the time, so he was transferred to Willimantic, Connecticut. My mother had five girls; I have an older sister ten years older than I, and the other four, starting with myself, have two-year differences in age, so we were all little girls. We took a train to Willimantic—we were there only three months—and then we returned to New Haven. The school we went to in Willimantic was called the Nantauk School, a wonderful school; we loved it. Two of my sisters were too young to go to school, but my sister, who is two years younger than I am, was in first grade and I was in third grade. To this day I still remember both the teachers' names, they were wonderful.

My father got a job with the WPA, the Works Progress Association. My father adored President Franklin Roosevelt, he thought that he helped a lot. I know that many people did not like Franklin Roosevelt, but I, to this day, like him. He also developed a program called the Civilian Conservation Corps. That was mostly for young men that needed jobs.

We received the daily paper. It was called *The Rutland Herald*, published in Rutland, Vermont. It was delivered to our door. I was frightened when I heard the news about Pearl Harbor. Our radio was on; it was on a lot, just like a lot of people have their televisions on. I was in the living room of our house in Fair Haven, and I could not believe it. I said to myself, 'We are going to be bombed!' I will tell you why I felt that way at thirteen. Germany had pummeled London, England, night after night after night—I do not know how London survived. This was all I could think of because we used to hear about it on the radio and the newsreels. I think we tried to act normally; I think everyone pretty much acted the same. We did the best we could with what we had, we got through it. At the time the war started, I remember being really afraid. As time went on, we had blackouts at night. We had dark green shades, and we had to pull them at night. One could not even light a cigarette on the street, or a flashlight, or anything, in case there were planes. Thank goodness. It was a terrible thing, there were so many hundreds of planes that bombed Pearl Harbor, the big carriers that came over. It was amazing, when I think of it, that we were not aware of it before it happened—that there was a possibility that it could happen. The Nazis especially impressed us a lot, they were the 'bad guys.' I think we heard more about them than the Japanese. [In school], I remember a quote, 'The only good thing about war is a geography lesson.'

The Victory Bike

We had a lot of rationing, of course. We had rationing stamps, which we got monthly. They were for basic things: eggs, sugar, and butter, actually I should probably say 'oleo.' It is what we had back then; oleo is substitute butter. It would come in a big brick, it looked like pure lard. We had a little yellow coloring thing that came with it. We had to let the oleo soften up, then mix in the coloring so we could use it. It was not the best tasting thing in the world, but we did get along, most people had it. We had a bicycle. In order to get a bicycle during [those times], someone, either your mother or your father, had to have it to go back and forth to work. That was the only way you could get one. We were a little underhanded in getting ours; my father said he would ride it back and forth to the Stasel Company, it was only three miles from Fair Haven. He rode it a couple of times and that was it; the bicycle was handed over to us girls. It was called a 'Victory Bike.' It had two wheels, handlebars, and that was about all; it was stripped of everything else. The tires were very, very thin due to the shortage of rubber. But four little girls had a very good time on that victory bicycle! We had it for quite a long time—sometimes there were arguments as to whose turn it was to ride it, but we managed. I guess that when you are faced with obstacles, like the Depression, it is like anything you are faced with that is not pleasant; you try to do the best you can with it.

I think how brave our parents were to have fed all those little mouths, maybe not knowing where all the food was coming from. They did have stations where you could pick up things like flour and sugar. We young girls were very proud and did not like to do that. We would go to this gentleman's house at night—we did not want anyone to see us, because we thought people would call us poor. We did not want to be known as poor. *[Laughs]* We did get through it, but, as I said, I do admire the parents; it was hard for them.

School

When I went into high school in 1942, we could not take typing because typewriters were short; you could not buy them. Soon after I graduated, things changed and typing started up. As the war went on, of course, young men went to war; help was short in every little town and city. It was apple-picking season, and Allen Orchards in Fair Haven had a huge orchard. They needed pickers. In the morning, they brought a big truck to school, we had lunch, and down we went to the orchard to pick apples. They paid us ten cents a bushel. I was never a very fast picker, but some of the kids were, and everyone tried to see if they could outdo the others. We did that for quite a few days; we thought we were helping the war effort; the young men were not around to do it.

In our park we had a big pile where you could put anything you had. Rubber was another thing as well. They needed all the rubber and metal they could get at that time for guns and equipment like tanks.

We lived in a home that did not have much yard, but my father worked for a gentleman who was in charge of a slate quarry in Fair

Haven—a lovely man, he lived across the street from us, he had a huge garden. My father went over there and helped tend the garden for him; the gentleman was very generous. A lot of people had victory gardens; we just did not have the room. I know they did not have to be very big, but we did not have one. *[Laughs]* When we went to the pictures on Saturdays, they would always have a newsreel, quite involved. They would always show the planes bombing and this and that, all pertaining to the war. It was very informative.

There was V-mail, we did that; I think I wrote to a cousin. We wrote them and they were somehow reproduced on very thin, small paper, very fine print.

A teenage culture began to grow in America, as a result of the war. With labor shortages, teenagers were more able to get jobs early, earn money, and pursue a modicum of independence.

At thirteen, I started babysitting—my sister and I did a lot; I even babysat the child of my eighth-grade teacher. When I was older, I worked in a jewelry store in Fair Haven, and a bakery—I loved that, not just because it was a bakery, but because the people I worked for were lovely. I made fifteen dollars a week in the summertime, which was pretty good for only being fifteen years old. I did a lot of that until I was eighteen and went into training.

Now, I never really had a lot of extra money. I probably gave my parents some of the money. If we had extra money, then we had ten cents to go to the movie. The thing to do after school was to go down to the local drugstore and get a Coke float. *[Laughs]* We gathered there, and the gentleman who ran the pharmacy, the pharmacist, was wonderful to us kids. We behaved; we knew better than to act up. That was our thing to do. I loved sports, of course. I cheered for our team; I helped sell tickets to the basketball game. I was pretty active in high school; I joined in a couple of one-act plays, was president of my freshman class, treasurer of the senior class, belonged to the glee club—which a lot of people also did. In my senior year, I was an honors student and received the DAR award, which is quite a prestigious award. I never realized that until I was older—you were chosen by the faculty and your peers, quite an honor. I enjoyed school. One day I came here to the local high school and sat in on one of the classes. I thought, 'I wish I were back in school again!' [Laughs]

Culture and Music

[Frank Sinatra became popular during this period], but I did not like him. It took me years and years to like him. The thing I remember about him was that he had the microphone in front of him, and he was always shimmying up and down the pole. And he was skinny! I just did not like him, but in later years I learned to love him. We were all bobbysoxers. The girls wore skirts and peasant blouses, saddle shoes and ankle socks. That was the look back then, and it was fun. [Laughs] There was a sandlot near my home, and we played softball there. The boys and the girls played together and got along; there was not anything structured, anyone who was there played.

The Andrews sisters had a lot of songs, 'The White Cliffs of Dover,' 'When Johnny Comes Marching Home'; I am not sure if that is a World War II song, it might have been a Civil War.

[Laughs] There was a lot of Big Band music and sounds. Abbott and Costello were our favorites. When I look at them now, I wonder why we thought they were so funny. [Laughs] Judy Garland, Mickey Rooney, wonderful. MGM had a lot of beautiful musicals as well. We liked Tom Mix, cowboys, Gene Autrey. Those were the main ones when I was young. The girls especially liked Shirley Temple; Jane Withers was her friend. As we got older, we got to know some of the actors, Barbara Stanwyck, Ginger Rogers, and Fred Astaire. Some actress donated the bumpers off her car to a scrap metal drive. I think it was Barbara Stanwyck. *[I remember the posters around during the war]*; 'Uncle Sam Wants You!' 'Loose Lips Sink Ships' was another one. *[Laughs]* I remember when I was a sophomore in school, we had to write an essay on citizenship; I think it was, 'Duty, God and Country.' A boy and I won that essay contest. I wish I had it today, but you throw things away.

Elaine Curren during the war. Credit: Sommo Family.

The Neighborhood

[I did not know of any women who went to work in factories]; of course, there were no big factories in our area, not even Rutland. I do not know any young women in my area who did [factory work, but my mother was forced to become] a waitress. Back then, the men worked 12-hour days. We saw very little of the father, except on weekends. They all worked very hard. My older sister became like a mother to us, helped us get off to school, even though she had to get to school herself. We were very fortunate to have her.

In 1942, I was a freshman in school, and I developed a severe strep infection. I got to the point where I could not even move in bed; I had developed acetonemia, or, as the layperson would say, blood poisoning. My sister, Mary, had just graduated from the hospital in Rutland. Aqueous penicillin had not been on the market for very long—Sir Alexander Fleming discovered it way before 1939, when it was put on the market. My sister was available to give me injections every three hours; it saved my life. Mary was an RN—that influenced me more than anything. I have never regretted [becoming a nurse], although I have often thought about what it would have been like to be an English teacher.

[The neighborhood had an air raid warden]; they wore a patch on their sleeve and a hard hat. There was a group of men who did that. I knew there had been bombing—it was all we ever heard on the radio or at the movies—all this bombing, the V-2 rockets. I thought, 'They are going to come and that is all there is to it.' I was afraid; I was a child.

*

My [future] husband was nineteen when he was recruited. He went into the Army and became an MP, military policeman. He had not been there too long, when his contingent—most of them from Long Island, most of them nineteen years old—went right over to Europe. He did not talk much about it; a lot of servicemen do not. He would tell me, 'I was only just an MP, I did not do that much.' But they did have a lot of responsibility. They had to guard prisoners, direct traffic; I am sure there were other duties they had to perform. He was also in the African campaign. From the day he went into the service, it was three years until he came home again. He had a baby brother when he left, and when he came back, he was already three years old. Think how much a lot of men missed by going away.

We were sad when Roosevelt died. Very, very sad; anyone who liked him felt the same way. But when he met with Churchill and Stalin on that ship at Yalta, he was not well. He probably never should have been there; you could tell by his look. I never realized that until I was older, and if you see pictures of that you can tell he was not well. But he probably felt it was his duty and he had to go.

[When the atomic bomb was dropped], I had mixed emotions. I was thinking, 'What a terrible thing this is.' Another thought: 'If it is going to stop all this fighting, maybe it is okay.' But as I got older, I realized all the innocent people that it killed. Really mixed emotions.

'We Felt So Bad for Them'

[When the war ended], it was unbelievable; the country went wild, we were so thrilled. Everyone was happy and full of talk. For a small town we had quite a few fellows come back. I had two cousins that were over in Europe, they came back, and, of course, they had no jobs. They were not first cousins; they were my mother's cousins and we felt so bad for them. These two young men had mental and emotional problems until the day they died; they could not get over it. It was very hard for them, one in particular. There were a lot of young men who hung around on the street corner; they had no place to go. They could go to the American Legion rooms, but as far as jobs, there was nothing for them. It was very difficult for a lot of them. It was also sad; a lot of men were killed. Some men from my town never came back, people you knew. In a small town, everybody knows everybody else. I felt very thankful, glad and sad.

There were problems, but we coped the best we could. We did not get all bent out of shape; we went along with what had to be done. I'm not sure I am in total agreement with the phrase, 'The Greatest Generation'; perhaps not the greatest, but a great generation. I think there were other generations that had to go through terrible times of war and famine. I would not want to brag and say we are the greatest, but I think we were great. Later on after the war, things picked up, jobs came along. People went about doing what they had to do. Goods were more available, but it took a little time. Of course, we were happier. We were glad to see the war over and hoped it would never happen again. I think General Douglas MacArthur did a grand job over there; it certainly was not easy for him. I think he was a wonderful commander. Patton and Eisenhower, General Mark Clark, they are the other ones I remember the most. I think that they were very intelligent men, knew their job, and carried it out to the best of their ability. Maybe a lot of people would not agree with me, but that is my thought.

High school interviewer: Do you think, in the midst of all the destruction the war brought, the world became a better place?

Hopefully it did. I would hate to say, 'No, it did not.' It is too bad that we have to have war in order to make things better, but it has been that way since time began. I have mixed feelings about [the idea of parents having to] send their children off to war. I probably did not even think of it then; I was so young. If there is a conflict, it would be terrible for a parent to send a child off to war. But in another vein, somebody has to do it. It is not very pleasant, that is for sure.

I think the war made everyone stop and think, to maybe make you a better person, in trying to make sure it does not happen again. [As for women's rights], if women can do that economically, [it follows that social change [would come], toward equality to men. I never believed we had to be subservient to a man. But I think the women's rights groups carried it a bit too far, they have to have this and that, and they have to join men's groups. What harm is there in a man having his own group? Why do we always have to be intermingled? We can still get along.

We lived through the war and got along, and we are here to talk about it. But like any parent with children, you want the best for them, and the safest for them, and the kindest for them. It would be kind of hard to watch your children's generation go through it again. Let us hope we, especially you, growing up, do not have to go through anything like that.

We survived; you either survive, or you sink. You can get up and do something about it, or you can sit in a chair and wither away.

CHAPTER EIGHT

The Pearl Harbor Kid

Mr. Spencer Kulani was born in Brooklyn, New York, in 1935. As a child after the attack on Pearl Harbor, his family moved to Oahu, Hawaii, where he spent most of his childhood. Much later, he enlisted in the Marine Corps and was stationed at Camp Pendleton, but his formative memories were as a child living near Pearl Harbor at his family's restaurant. He sat for this interview in January 2006 with one of my students at the age of 70.

Spencer Kulani

On December 7, 1941, I was in Brooklyn, New York, on 53rd Street and 3rd Avenue. We had just come out of the movies, and we were going to a candy store. We were on our way to Chinatown, and we went to the candy store to buy some gum because the young lady that was with us had motion sickness, and she had to chew gum while she was on the subway. And when we went into the store, we had heard on the radio that Pearl Harbor had been attacked; that was in the afternoon when we got the news.

Family in Pearl Harbor

I was really too young to really realize. All I knew was that my brother was over there. Most of my emotions were taken off of [being near] my father; whatever emotions my father had, I had them too. As far as my own emotions are concerned, if he would have smiled and laughed, I probably would have smiled and laughed. I was really too young to really realize what was going on.

My parents were hurt and worried about my brother because he was in Pearl Harbor at the time; [we had family there.] Al was probably twelve years old at the time, and they were more worried about him and the rest of the family. But as far as other people around me and how they reacted, I really do not remember. The big thing was we really had food [rationing] stamps and such, buying meat, but it never really affected us as kids, but it did affect the family. We had victory gardens going and drives for tin cans, rubber drives and all kinds of waste material that they would put in a pile where scraps would actually be. They had scrap drives and then they would have victory gardens for people to have enough land to plant their food and stuff. That is about all I saw as far as support; I mean you always have the flags out, of course, and such.

Around December 1942, we got on the bus from New York to go to Hawaii, we left for San Francisco by bus. My dad was a musician, and we got a flat tire in some state, I do not remember which state. We spent about six hours on the side of the road waiting for someone to come fix the flat tire on the bus. My dad played music and the guys played cards and everyone just had a good old time traveling by bus. We got to San Francisco and stayed in a hotel most of the time while we waited for transportation to go to Hawaii; you had to wait your turn until you got a ship that left San Francisco that left for Hawaii.

Going Across the Pacific

There were a lot of civilians on the ship that we were on, an awful lot. And a lot of them, mostly, I imagined were defense workers going to work in the shipyards, welders and the like, people that did not actually qualify for the actual service or were too old for the service.

Going across we all ate at the big chow table; we were just like servicemen. The ship was made and built for servicemen, and we ate just like them. The seas got rough, and they had blackouts, the lights went out on the ship, they shut all the doors. You could not open any of the doors on the ship at night, everybody had to stay inside, except of course for the crew, and they had big canvases. They would open the door and first they would step in the hallway, close the canvas, then open the door so no light could get outside. They were worried about submarines attacking the boats and stuff like that. But it was a good cruise, I had a lot of fun. There was no big fanfare when we got to Hawaii; there was no Hawaiian aloha band or anything like that. We just docked and everyone just got off the ship and that was it. There was no fanfare. It was the first time I had ever been there.

Pearl City

The land we lived on in Hawaii was called Pearl City Peninsula. Before the war my grandmother was leasing the land off a big and rich family, and when the military came, they said, 'You cannot have this land, it is going to be turned over to the military.' They just took it away from her. Financially they gave her the money for what she leased it for, but it was not hers no more. We had what they called Queen's Pond right there in Pearl Harbor. When we were kids we used to play in it; the Navy filled it all in and made docks and piers for the ships to pull up and load and unload. They made a big storage area out of Pearl City down in the peninsula, which is for cargo ships. That is how it changed.

Pearl City's peninsula is in Pearl Harbor. We stayed there from 1943 until we left in 1946, and that was after the war. And it was one of those things that happened and as the war progressed things got easier. We did not have food stamps, not there, not in Hawaii. But they had an old car, and gas was hard to get; they had some aviation gas off the airport over there and they stuck it in the old car and burned up the valves because the aviation gas was too much of a high octane. It burned up all the valves in the car, had to get a valve job on it. But they needed gas to move the car. That is one of those things you know you do.

[Coming from Brooklyn], well, Hawaii was just a lot of fun. I mean, you were living in New York, you needed a lot of clothes, but in Hawaii you went barefoot, things like that. You hardly ever wore a shirt, especially when you are kids. Nobody wore shoes over there, you had to get used to that. It took about six months before you could walk the way everybody else could walk, until it did not hurt your feet as much, but there were kids over there that could put cigarettes out on the bottom of their feet, that is how tough it got out there. All in all, as a kid, it was just one big party. You go to school just like any school. You had air raid drills where they would run everybody, once a week, under the bomb shelter, which is a hole dug in the ground about six feet down. Then they would just put a big mound over it with wood and you would crawl down inside. They would have big benches, and everybody would just sit down and look at each other, sit there for about five or ten minutes, then they would blow the alarm, and everybody would come out. That is the way they [practiced for] war in school. Of course, we had victory gardens and stuff like that. Most of it was playing, they had a big dump, and they would dump everything they had, new ball bearings, parts of airplanes; of course, we kids would go through it to see if we could find anything. Things like that, you would just ride your bike. There was no restriction on us, we just went wherever we wanted to go. Of course, the only place you could not go was the Navy base, and you cannot do that today.

Martial Law

When Pearl Harbor was attacked it then became a martial law, which means the military has more say than anyone else on the island. It was their law, there were guys that got shot because they did not stop, and the military shot them. But they were scared of spies because there was an awful lot of Japanese at the time. I do not think, in all the people in Hawaii that were Japanese, I do not think they found one Japanese that was ever a spy or ever proved that there was a Japanese in Hawaii that was a spy.

Most of the Japanese in Hawaii were hurt, just like the rest of the people. That was their home and to have their own country bomb their own home hurt them. The people in Hawaii, the Hawaiian people, the Japanese, the Filipinos, the Orientals, and the whites, they all got along pretty good, the people that knew Hawaii. The servicemen that came there had a lot of what you would call 'hate' because with some of the Japanese Americans, all they would see is Japanese, but they did not care. It is just like today a lot of people see Arabs, and they get all excited, and blame the Arabs for everything; they get all shook up about Muslims, but every Muslim is not the same, they all do not believe in killing everybody. The same thing happened in Hawaii, and as most people know a lot of Japanese in this country, they were put in a concentration camp; now, they did not say it was a concentration camp, but more or less that's what it was. But in Hawaii they did not do that to them; half the people over there were probably [of Japanese descent], they could not stick half the island in a concentration camp. But they proclaimed martial law, and the military took care of their own. Of course, the Hawaiian police took care of their own too. We had curfews and stuff like that, but for most of the people it was good, as far as us kids go it was really good, but you know older people are different.

'Their Hair Had Turned White'

I had about four cousins who were all in the service; most of them were in the Navy. They were all in the European theater. Most of the rest of the family worked in Pearl Harbor, there was a restaurant and a bar, but that is all. That is all we ever did, work. You know there are different things that happened to them over there; when we got there, most of them had been through the attack at Pearl Harbor. There was the old fellow, grandfather, step-grandfather actually, he just passed away two years ago, he was 103 years old. He was born in 1901 and he had talked about different things that happened to him on the day of the attack on Pearl Harbor. He was saying that when Pearl Harbor was attacked, all the civilian workers ran for the gate, they wanted to get out of there, but the military stopped them from leaving Pearl Harbor because they needed people to repair and fix the area. He said when they all attacked, they were working on the different ships in the area, and he had got behind a telephone pole and he had got strafed by a Japanese airplane, they were just strafing the whole area. And he said that he had thought that he had been shot, but what had happened was the bullets hit the gravel around his legs, and he thought they had hit his legs with the bullets, but it was just the gravel that hit him in the leg, and he got all excited about that. Then they kept him there all night and he said that in the middle of the night, he would go over there to all the secretaries. He went over to the side of the building and picked up a bunch of gravel and he threw it on the roof. It sounded like bullets hitting the roof, and they all got underneath the desks and he stuck his head in and started laughing at them. Of course, they did not appreciate that one.

About twenty years later he had worked for the bank and one of the women that made out the bills was one of the women that was inside that building when he threw the gravel up. She had called him up and said, 'Are you that stinker that threw that gravel on the roof, I was in Pearl Harbor.' And of course, they got together, and they had a good time, they had dinner and all that, but it was just remembrance.

Those were different things that people remember about Pearl Harbor. He said that a lot of the boys got stuck in the ships. Phil was in supplies and what they would do was, they would supply the different ships with the different everything, food and stuff. And a lot of the young sailors would come by and get the supplies from the ship, and he says a lot of them are storekeepers on the ship. And a lot of those kids got stuck in the bottom of the ship. They got them out, but a lot of their hair had turned white, that's how scared they were. Which was a hell of an experience, stuck in a hole underneath water, figuring you would never get out of it. A lot of kids came out with white hair, and they were only 19 and 20 years old. Those were the different things that happened there.

'This Was Their Last Chance'

My dad worked in the family restaurant as a bouncer when he got over there, because my grandmother had a restaurant and he worked for the shipyard for a little while as well. The servicemen, most of it was just party time, really. Servicemen came in and all they wanted to do is eat, sleep, and drink, they figured this was their last chance. They would have a big party and they figured if they left Hawaii, they would be dead, so all they wanted to do was party. A lot of them did not even come back. The family had quite a few friends in the restaurant that did not make it back. Owning a restaurant like that, you see a lot of servicemen, but me myself, we were all kids then, it was no big deal for us. We would just go down to the beach, and we would watch them load ammo, doing whatever they were doing.

I saw two planes crash up in the air when I was a kid. We were out there swimming in a swimming pool and two guys up there in the air, we could see they were chasing each other, and all of a sudden, they turned around, and both of them came together and boom, they just collided in the air. I saw one of the men's parachute come out and down he went. I do not know what ever happened to the other guy; of course, I did not read the paper back then.

'Just One of Those Things'

As far as war stories go, these guys would come back; in a bar one time, a jarhead he was, and Indian, he came back and he had a Japanese ear inside of a bottle of alcohol, it was his souvenir. People talk about how rotten the different countries are and how nasty they did things. If you talk to some of these guys that had really been over there, they did some bad stuff over there. They were actually giving bounty for the ears. From what I understand they wanted to go out and get the snipers, they were giving money for the ears. So these guys would go out and hunt these Japanese down and kill them and cut their ears off so they could get some money. And that is how they got the Japanese snipers, because nobody wanted to go out there. This is a story, I have no written proof of all this, but I did see that ear come in in a jar, and I understand what was going on, that is how they got the Japanese snipers out of there. They had to stop it because these guys were going and cutting ears off of dead guys and tried to come back and tried to claim the money for them. In reality, we may not have started it, but we did some awful things, things that a lot of the guys are not proud of, but that is all a part of war, it is just one of those things.

The End of the War

After the war ended, they had a USO club. Well, actually before the war ended, they had gotten together with Love's Bakery and made what they called already-made sandwiches. That was one of the first civilian outfits on base that delivered lunches. I do not know what you call them; you see them in convenience stores, pre-packaged sandwiches. They were the first ones to make them, and my dad used to deliver them to all the different Navy facilities; he would go out there, making deliveries of sandwiches. At the end of the war, my father was offered a machine gun, a rifle, and the guys were just giving them away because the guys were so happy that the war was over. They did not have to be accounted for, so they were going to give them to all of them. He did not want any of it, they were all automatic weapons, and he knew it was against the law to have them, so he did not touch any of it. But those were the things that happened, but when the actual war ended, I was in Pearl Harbor and they were firing live ammo in the air, shooting all over the place, shooting live ammunition all over the sky when the war ended.

Back In New York

After the war was over, we ended up back in New York. And then, of course, we stayed there a little while and things did not go well so we ended up back in Hawaii again. We stayed there until the Korean War started. So, I probably came back here to New York from about 1946 until about 1948, then we went back to Hawaii in 1951. That is about the time I spent in Hawaii. I went back there in 1985 and we tried to get down in there and they would not let us in there anymore. I just wanted to see what it looked like, but you had to be in the military to get down there and of course I was not so they would not let me down there. A lot of USOs turned into different night clubs. The military still had a good hold in Pearl Harbor. Now the sugar cane companies are all folding up, I think they are getting outsold from Mexico, I think that is what's happening there. A lot of the farms and all that, now they are going to coffee. Their land is very fertile; they can get three crops of corn in Hawaii in one year. Now they cannot get sugar, they cannot get any money for their sugar, and the mangos, and the pineapples, and the papayas. They are all coming out of South America and Mexico. Actually Hawaii, before World War II, was the third largest beef producer in the world for export. Parker Ranch had a million-acre ranch on the island of Hawaii. And they were the third largest export producer of beef in the world. Of course, Argentina and the US were fighting for first place. Hawaii was really considered a territory during World War II, it was not part of the United States as a territory, like Puerto Rico is today. In fact, we had American money in Hawaii that was all stamped 'Hawaii' on it and that is what they used for currency, and it was illegal to bring it to this country. It was the same money that you have today, of course there was that silver certificate, but it was the same money you have today only it had 'Hawaii' stamped across the front of it. If you have got any of them now, they are worth a little bit of money.

*

What else can you say? I think World War II was a necessity and there is no getting away from that. You have to talk to some of the guys over there, who have been there and done it. Especially some of these guys that were ground troops, they are the ones that know what it is really all about. Of course, I was a kid and I had fun; they did not, but I did. We used to go along the beaches, and you would find washed-up C-rations on the beach. We found life rafts made out of balsa wood; we would cut up the balsa wood and make little boats out of them. In fact, there was a lieutenant in the Navy who would carve boats for us. He made some beautiful models for us, and it was all out of these balsa wood rafts. You would go along the shore and cans of C-rations, you would open it up and there would be candy and of course we would eat them. They all floated in from a sunken ship, who knows where it came from? You would find them on the beaches all the time, in Pearl Harbor, all along, all along the beaches in Hawaii. That was some of the different things I remember; [in the big picture], when you are a kid you do not realize what is going on.

Spencer Kulani passed away in November 2022 at the age of 87.

PART THREE

SERVICE

"There was one psycho case who saw ducks, he was in New Guinea, wherever he went he saw ducks. Well, the psychiatrist tried to rid him of the ducks. Finally, they sent him back but he still saw his ducks. They decided, he's no good, we'll send him back to the States as a Section 8. Well, it's four hours from New Guinea to Guadalcanal, another twenty hours to Hickam Field, another fourteen hours to San Francisco. All of this time he saw his ducks. Finally, about an hour out from San Francisco he calls the flight nurse over and said, 'Lieutenant, you can have the ducks now, I don't need them anymore.' [Laughs]"

—Flight Nurse, Pacific

CHAPTER NINE

US Army Nurse, Europe

Kathryn Goodman Frentzos was interviewed several times by my students for this project. Raised in a very rural Adirondack Mountain setting, she rose to the rank of major during the war.

Kathryn Goodman Frentzos

I was born on September 20, 1912, in Athol, Warren County, New York. I have two sisters and four brothers. Three of my brothers went into the service, one in the Pacific and two in the European theater. I was the second oldest. Both of my sisters were also nurses.

The Depression Era

My first few years I grew up in Johnsburg, New York; it's a small, little village, really a hamlet, in the Adirondack Mountains. It was just like a wide place in the road, a few houses and a grocery store, a post office, and they also had a cobbler, that sort of thing.

I had a rather routine childhood. We didn't have electricity in our house, until like sometime in the 1930s when Roosevelt became president and the Rural Electrification Act was passed, then we had electricity, and we got a bathroom in our house and things like that. Growing up during the Depression didn't bother us at all. Some people were better off. But I lived on a farm when I was growing up and we always had food because we had a garden. And we had chickens, and we had a cow, so we always had milk and we really didn't suffer. We just thought everybody was poor, like us, but of course that wasn't true, but we did very well during the Depression.

I really had only seven years of grammar school, because at the end of the seventh year, the teacher asked me if I wanted to take the eighth-grade Regents [examination]. So, I took the eighth-grade Regents, and I passed them, and I went into high school right out of seventh grade! I had four years of high school and four and a half years of college, so I had, you know, a pretty good education.

'Once You Do This, You're Theirs'

I graduated from North Creek High in 1929. From September 1931 to January of 1932, I attended Albany State Teacher's College intending to become a teacher. The courses I liked best in college were anatomy and physiology, and I decided I'd rather be a nurse; accordingly I applied to and was accepted as a student at St. John's Long Island City Hospital School of Nursing. I graduated in September 1935, took and passed my state board examination and became a registered nurse. My nursing career took me from general duty nursing at Polyclinic Hospital in New York City in 1935 to the Albany visiting nurse service from 1937 to 1940. While attending teacher's college at Columbia University, fall session 1940, on a New York State scholarship, I saw a recruiting poster urging nurses to join the Army Nurse Corps. I was interested, so I immediately joined the Red Cross Nursing Service, which was a prerequisite to joining the ANC. Soon I was requested to make an appointment at 90 Church Street in New York City to take a physical exam. I was a little less than five feet tall, but the examining physician, who wasn't that tall himself, told me to stand as tall as I could. I just barely made the height to pass.

When I joined up, my father was a little bit concerned because he said, 'Kathryn, once you do this, you're theirs, you know, you belong to them. You don't have any say in what's going to happen to you,' which was true. You went where they sent you. They owned you.

Pearl Harbor

I took my oath of office on February 21, 1941, and then took a standard train to Tennessee. When we got to Camp Peay, the name had been changed to Camp Forrest. I stayed there for twenty-two months, during which I was promoted to first lieutenant and eventually to captain.

On December 7, 1941, I was still in this country, and I remember that day very well, it was a Sunday, and I was going off duty at three-thirty in the afternoon and the nurses coming on duty were crying and I said, 'What's the matter, what happened?'

They told me that Pearl Harbor had been attacked by the Japanese. Well at that time I had no idea what Pearl Harbor was, I didn't know that it was an Army base in the Pacific, actually. [Later], the nurses in the [Philippines] were not so well taken care of. They were in [the service of] of General MacArthur, and MacArthur [later] got on a submarine and went to Australia and left his soldiers and his nurses there at the mercy of the Japanese.

Several months after my promotion to captain, I received orders in early December to proceed to Camp Kilmer, New Jersey, to join the 500 bed 40th Station Hospital in the unit as chief nurse.

Overseas

Camp Kilmer was the pits. It was the least accommodating, the most uncomfortable billet I have ever experienced in my five years in the service. I joined my unit on December 6, and on December 12, we boarded a troop ship for an unknown destination. Throughout the voyage we were required to wear helmets and life preservers and to carry canteens full of water at all times. We had many lifeboat drills also; we sailed under strict blackout conditions. We were constantly in danger because we were on the ocean between America and North Africa, which was constantly being patrolled by German submarines, and we never knew when we might meet German ships and then be conquered by them. The ship ride over was an experience in itself. Because we sailed from New Jersey, about three days' out we got a storm at sea, it was really a very bad storm. And on the tables that we ate at, they put rims around the edges to keep the dishes and the food on the table and everybody got sick, but I think I was the only one of the nursing and doctor's staff that didn't get sick, and our chief surgeon always said after that I kept him alive; I saved his life. Well, I didn't do anything to save his life except to tell him, 'Don't eat anything except crackers!' And he always swore that I saved his life.

We had to have helmets on all the time while we were on the ship, and we had to have a canteen always filled with water in case you had to get off the ship and get onto the lifeboats, where there would be no drinking water. Of course we didn't have any lights on at night because we were traveling in a convoy with other ships, and there were German ships all over the waters, but we never had any problems, we got there safely.

North Africa and Corsica

When we reached Oran, in Algeria, on December 25 of 1942, we couldn't depart until the next day because French Admiral Jean Darlan had been assassinated in Algiers on Christmas Eve and it wasn't clear what kind of reception we would get.[10] We did have a traditional Christmas dinner on board the ship on Christmas Day.

We were in Algeria, then French North Africa, for thirteen months where we lived in old French foreign barracks. Finally, we went by plane to the island of Corsica where we stayed in several locations.

As a chief nurse, I was in charge of 55 women. We went from 250 patients to 500. So, as the war went on, we got more and more patients, our hospital got bigger. And sometimes our hospital was in tents. And other times it was in buildings. For example, in Corsica, we were in tents all the time. And that was interesting. One time we had a big wind blow through it, and it blew down all of our tents. Nobody got hurt, but we had to put the tents up again and put everything back in order. There were three types of hospitals. There were field hospitals, which were sort of like *M.A.S.H.* units; you know, you must've watched *M.A.S.H.* on television? Well, there was that, and then there were station hospitals, and then beyond us were the general hospitals, they were closer to home, not physically closer, but the soldiers were closer to [getting] home. While we weren't exactly like *M.A.S.H.*, which was a Mobile Army Surgical Hospital unit in the war area, we did have the mail call [you see in the television series], and mail call was the most important time of the day because you might be getting letters from home. I got letters from my brother John, who was the oldest of my three brothers who were in the service, in the Pacific theater, in the Navy. We

---

[10] *French Admiral Jean Darlan-* Pro-German Vichy French naval commander-in-chief in North Africa.

wrote letters back and forth but that was all. We had no personal contact. We were too far apart.

World War II was an unusual experience, because the ordinary person doesn't get to go overseas and work in tents and such. At one time our hospital was set up in a small hotel and an apartment house and in a school, a children's school. You did your work every day; we had things to do and you did them and I had to see that the nurses did what they were supposed to do because as a chief nurse, that was my job. For our overseas duty the nurses were all adequately clothed in government-issued duty uniforms and outerwear. We always had sheltered living quarters whether in tents or buildings, and toilet facilities with latrines if we lived in tents or regular bathrooms if we lived in buildings. Food was adequate and well prepared and good; we used our mess kits only occasionally when we were breaking camp in our location and preparing to move. The hospital, wherever the setting was, provided all the necessary equipment. The welfare of all the personnel was a priority, from the commanding officer down through the ranks. We didn't get homesick because we were so busy all the time. You know, when you're nursing you have wards full of injured people; you don't really have much time to do anything except work.

When the soldiers came to us, they had already had first aid and they were bandaged, you know, whatever immediate care they needed they had and they came to us and it was just like any other hospital that you would work in. You give them whatever care they need and you try to get them healed so they can go back to duty, but sometimes they went on to another hospital, which was called a general hospital, and if they couldn't get the soldier to go back to duty, they sent them home. We had an adequate staff for the daytime shift, the afternoon shift, and the nighttime shift. The nurses wanted to work around the clock, but in the effort to keep them from getting sick or too tired out, we kept them to their regular schedule.

When we had days off, we usually had two days off, I think, so we went on trips to other places in the area and we saw whatever scenery there was to see wherever we were. We had recreation, we had dances, and of course there were so many more men than there were women, that we were never without a date if we wanted to go.

One memory that sticks out [in Corsica] is that in June of 1944 [just before D-Day], when they had the battle in southern France, we got a shipload of soldiers who had been wounded in that. They came to us, and they were mostly burn cases because they had jumped into the ocean and the ocean was literally on fire, so they got burned. When they came to us they were wrapped in medic's [bandages] and probably only a little bit of their faces was showing and they looked like the Michelin Man, you've seen pictures of the Michelin Man?[11] That's what they looked like, and they were youngsters, German soldiers, they were fifteen, sixteen years old or so, they were like our little brothers, you know? And their shoes were so thin, there were holes in them, you know, and Germany was running out of everything then, so that battle was really the end of the war for them. At our triage point they were sorted, and the ones that were the worst off were taken care of first, and that was when my nurses wanted to work all night, no matter what their normal tour of duty was, they just wanted to work all night because there was so much to do, but I had to let them work just their shift and let another shift come on, so they wouldn't get exhausted.

---

[11] *Michelin Man*- mascot of the Michelin tire company, a bloated human-like figure consisting of stacked white tires, introduced in France in 1894.

After the Battle of the Bulge, which began on December 16 of 1944, we were again on the move, this time to Italy outside of Rome. We lived and set up our hospital in what had been Mussolini's glass factory, where all personnel of the hospital were housed in buildings.

Mt. Vesuvius

I have one very fond memory; people are always surprised when I tell them this. We had a colonel who was the head of our unit and there were other men who were assistants of his, and one day a general came to visit our colonel and he had lunch with us. He said to the colonel, 'I would like to take you on a trip down over Mt. Vesuvius this afternoon,' and of course being the chief nurse, I was asked to go, too. So, he had a B-17 with a plexiglass nose, and when we go into the plane, it was the control room, we got into the plexiglass nose and I had to lie on my stomach so I could see everything, and so he took us down over Mt. Vesuvius, which of course is a volcano, you know churning and burning and all, whatever burns in there. Well that was really interesting, and being in the nose of a B-17 was like being on a magic carpet and that was really the highlight of all the things I did. After that we flew back up over the north of Rome, over the Pope's summer palace, Castle Gandolfo.

The End of the War

While we were in other countries, if you were an officer, enlisted men had to salute you and it was very funny when they would see me with the captain's bar on my hat and so forth, and they'd say, 'Ma'am/Sir?' They were surprised and they would do a double take and then they would salute, because they weren't used to saluting women.

We were all very sad when Franklin Roosevelt died. A lot of us had never had any other president other than Franklin D. Roosevelt and we were very sad that he had died. It was like losing a close relative. Germany surrendered unconditionally in May of 1945, so the war in the European theater was over. In July 1945, after nine months of living in Rome, we moved to Naples. We did not set up a hospital in Naples; most of the time was spent watching training films and wondering what was next for us. The plan was that those with the longest length of service would eventually go home, and others would be sent to the Pacific theater. However, that never happened, because on August 14, the Pacific war was over and eventually everyone was sent home.

'What Are You Going to Do For Me?'

[When the war finally ended], I was very, very happy. I didn't like the idea of so many people being killed [by the atomic bombs], but the other thing about that was we were really told that it shortened the war, so it saved a lot of lives also. But things had changed when we got back home. You know before I went in the service, if I went somewhere to get a job my question was, 'What can I do for you, what do you expect from me?' you know. After the war when I came back and I worked again in the hospital, when they had people coming looking for jobs, their questions were, 'What are you going to do for me?' instead of 'What can I do for you?' to get a job, you know, 'What do I get out of this?' It was a very different attitude.

'They Are Mostly Gone'

In November of 1946, I was promoted to the rank of major. My post-war nursing experience was all in teaching and administration. The most rewarding thing [to come out of my experience, for me], was that I had a profession in which I could help people, sick people and wounded people. It's pretty hard to just tell somebody, in a couple of hours, about the war. One thing is that we were always treated very well; the nurses were treated extremely well, which wasn't true in the Pacific theater. It's pretty hard to describe the war, but I wouldn't have missed serving in it. I was very happy to be able to serve in the war. I kept in contact with some of the nurses [after the war]; I did that for a long time. But they're mostly gone; I think the ones I kept in contact with are all gone. You know, World War II nurses and soldiers are dying off at a very fast rate. You won't find very many 99-year-olds like me. I'll probably live a couple more years anyway. [Laughs]

Nobody ever asked me anything about my service except when I first came home, I went to church one Sunday with my father, and some little girl came up to me and said, 'Did you ever ride in a jeep?' [Laughs] That's the only question anybody ever asked me. But you know, when I was in the service, times were not so good here either, because everyone was on rationing, shoes were rationed, certain foods were rationed, sugar was rationed, but we had everything we needed overseas. People in America were rationed, and they had blackouts—as we did, of course. Another thing that I found out after I came home—I didn't know it when I was in the service—there was a big tent on our front lawn, and I said, 'What in the world is that?' They said it was for plane spotting, and there were people in the community who would come to our house to spot planes going over, and the tent where they stayed was still on our front lawn!

And I didn't know anything about it while I was overseas, nobody thought to tell me or write me or anything about it. So, people here didn't have it too easy either, they suffered probably more than we suffered, because we really didn't suffer, we were extremely well taken care of. And I've always been so happy that I had it so good, believe me.

Kathryn Goodman Frentzos passed away on June 2, 2015, at the age of 102.

CHAPTER TEN

US Army Nurse, Pacific

Katherine Denegar joined the Army Nurse Corps after Pearl Harbor, serving in the Pacific theater in the Philippines. Like most of our women veterans, she was motivated to serve her country, but even after the war she had to deal with pushback from a veterans organization that denied her a membership, solely because she was female. She set the record straight, refusing to join with auxiliary status. She sat for this interview in 2003, just before her 87th birthday.

Katherine G. Denegar

I was born in Youngstown, Ohio, in 1916. [By the time of the war], I was a registered nurse, and I also had a bachelor's degree in psychology. [I remember that when I heard about Pearl Harbor], I was working nights and I just couldn't believe it, it's like yesterday; you don't forget these things. We were all, of course, terribly excited when we got into the war and realized the damage that was done to our Navy.

I enlisted in Youngstown, Ohio. I knew the Army nurses went overseas and at that time I didn't think the Navy nurses did and I just liked the Army. I had further training when we went to Fort Knox, Kentucky, and then of course I had the usual training that they give you; in other words, crawling on the ground, the whole thing, even marching. I did a terrible job because I'm left-handed and left-footed and everything else, but the second lieutenant passed me. I guess they were desperate.

'I Would Kill You'

We had basic training at the hospital, them telling us, 'You know how to do your work, but now you do it the Army way,' and we understood it from that. The first thing after I left Fort Knox, Kentucky, I went to Newton D. Baker Hospital in Maryland, and that I think is mostly psychology. And unfortunately, the major there wanted to keep me as a psychiatric nurse, and I had never done it and she said, 'Well, you have a bachelor's in psychology; you could do quite well.' But I was put in the most mentally disturbed ward. Which was quite an unhappy situation. You realize what war is like when you see these men coming back like that, as a result of the European theater mostly. I had never had psychology, all I had was the study of the different diseases in psychology, and to go into this most mentally disturbed ward, I remember feeding a young, very strong-looking man and he said, 'You're pretty, but if I could get you, I would kill you.' I mean, we had that sort of problem, and we had these catatonic patients that would stand for hours at a time and then rush and try to destroy their beds, that sort of thing.

I read a lot of their histories, which I found very interesting. This one particular man that was catatonic had been made to bury the dead in Europe and he just couldn't handle it. I also realized by reading all their histories, that some of them should have never been in the Army, but with the excitement of World War II, if you could walk in, you were taken.

Overseas

I complained that most of my friends had gone already overseas, and I just didn't want to stay there, and the major said, 'Well, we're going to give you first lieutenant, and you can help us.'

I said, 'I'm really not comfortable with this kind of thing.'

I think I must have been there three months and I finally headed overseas. Of course, we never knew where we were going, but we ended up in Manila and the sad thing about that is, there were about 375 of us, and we weren't welcomed. The major, who was female, came out and said that on the way over there had been nurses that had been stealing the narcotics, and there was venereal disease, and conduct certainly unbecoming an officer. That was our beginning in Manila, then we were sent to Mindoro, Philippines, and I understand Lingayen Gulf had been captured before they got to Manila, and they set up in Mindoro, it was a jungle really. I never saw anything, just the jungle and the monkeys, but they did set up an airfield, and they did that by [putting down] metal tracks, and they were able to fly the planes in and they had attacked the Japanese in Manila, but that was before I got there.

[We were at what] was called a station hospital, but it was really kind of like a lab. We had beds with mosquito netting and just canvas overhead; everything was open. We did not have any [casualties at that time] coming in from the war. We had yellow fever, we had jungle rot, we had venereal disease, we had everything like that, and malaria and dysentery. Later, much later, we were sent on to Batangas, Philippines, and right then they were beginning to get ready for the invasion of Japan. We were going to be the first ones going, but fortunately there were the two atomic bombs, and you have probably heard so many times the criticism of the atomic bombs, that the Japanese would have fought to the death and there would have been hundreds of [thousands] of Americans killed, and we knew that. So we were delighted, delighted. So many of the men had been there for about three years, and the fact that they weren't going to encounter [an invasion], that now there was a good chance they'd get back to the States, and no, I heard nothing but elation over [the bombs] and I felt the same way, but many times I heard people criticize [the decision to use them], but they were not in the war.

We still had 50,000 Japanese up in Baguio, [and their commander, General Yamashita], I guess he thought he was going to fight until the end, and the Japanese always did it that way. But they finally conquered them, and I can remember he was brought down to Manila.[12] We were still around, because we were told we could go down and visit if we wanted. I had no feeling of going down to see a man I knew would be executed, even though we had a very poor opinion of the Japanese, we now had them around the area cleaning up and they never looked at us. But [later in the United States], we also had the German prisoners, they were used in the wards, and they were having a grand time. They were trying desperately to learn English, they were wonderful.

[I returned to the States] not too long after the war. From the time we got to Fort Knox, Kentucky, there were already a lot of prisoners there. Very few Japanese, but quite a lot of the Germans

---

[12] General Yamashita-Tomoyuki Yamashita (1885-1946) was the Japanese defender of the Philippines later in the war, and he was able to hold on to part of Luzon until after the formal surrender of Japan, and afterward, he was tried for war crimes committed by his troops. It became a landmark case that affirmed the legal doctrine of command responsibility, in which a commanding officer could be held accountable for war crimes committed under his authority if he did nothing to mitigate or stop the atrocities from occurring. It is now known in international legal circles as the Yamashita standard.

that had come from the European theater. They were used in the wards, and also in the kitchens, and cleaning the area, and of course it was immaculate.

Home

There was something about the war, you didn't have to be beautiful, all you had to be was be a woman and be there. There were some romances. I myself didn't approve of them because I was afraid that in the excitement of the war, they weren't going to last, but I always did a lot of sewing and crafts, so making use of old parachutes, I rigged up a couple good [wedding dresses].

When I came back, like I said, I had my bachelor's degree, but I intended to work with a doctor and handle his clinic and I did not know the [new] medical technology part. [I used the GI Bill to] graduate with a degree in medical technology, which took me a year. I was very pleased.

[You want to know if I ever joined a veterans group?] Oh, don't start me. When I came here, I was married to a veteran who has long since died, 1973. He had been a captain and was almost called back to the Korean War again, but fortunately, he had high blood pressure and didn't get in. He had five years of [membership in a veterans group]. I said, 'Well, I want to join,' so I went over to the local [chapter].

They said, 'You cannot join as a veteran, you have to be an auxiliary.'

I said, 'Forget it!' And that was the end of that. I felt I had earned a place there, but of course, it's changed since then.

*

[How did my time in the service affect my life?] I think when I came back home, I can still remember being on that ship [coming home], I felt we had so much, so much over here and so much poverty everywhere else; of course, I had never been overseas before. And I think I'm more compassionate, I believe that in being a nurse, you have to have a lot of that. [The war did change my life], and it also made me change my thinking on a lot of things.

One soldier dead is one too many.

Katherine Denegar passed away on May 9, 2011 at the age of 94.

CHAPTER ELEVEN

The WASP

Lillian Lorraine Yonally began learning to fly at age fifteen, and at age twenty-one, became an aviation pioneer upon being accepted into another new military program for women, the Women Airforce Service Pilots. These women had to undergo the same rigorous training as their male counterparts; thirty-eight were killed in service to their country, but because at the time they were considered civilians with no military status, their fellow women classmates would often pool their money to ship the body home, with no military honors.[10] She gave this interview in 2009 at the age of 87.

Lillian Lorraine Yonally

I was born in Lynn, Massachusetts, in 1922. I moved to New Bedford, Massachusetts, and grew up there and attended school there through high school. I graduated from high school, Lincoln School in Providence, Rhode Island, a Quaker boarding school. At that point, my father remarried, because he was divorced before, and he started a second family, and I flew the coop.

Then I went to Katherine Gibbs Secretarial School in New York City. At the same time, occasionally on weekends, I took flying instructions. I finally got my private pilot license.

I [began flying] in Rochester, Massachusetts, which was actually a little field with two airplanes. I soloed there in the summer before I went to Katherine Gibbs. I think my father thought it would be a good idea for me to tackle something else, rather than see how I could drive his car. *[Laughs]*

I trained on mostly the Piper MJ-3 Cub and some Aeroncas. Both my aunt and uncle started flying at the same small airport as I did in Massachusetts. They both ended up with commercial licenses and airplanes.

So, I had a private license and was looking for a job. I got the secretarial job, which I had to stay in for six months, because that was the requirement. After that I tried Pan Am, but I did not fit in there very well. I got a job at Grumman Aircraft Engineering Corporation in Bethpage, Long Island. I was the secretary to the vice president for a while. They were building a new hangar and it was going to have a new control tower, so they needed more personnel than the two men who were doing it at that point. So they asked my boss if he would let me go, because I had a license and understood a lot about flying. I think he probably was very glad; anyway, I was! *[Laughs]* I got to go to the old control tower until the new one was built.

I was not flying on the weekends then because they closed flying on Long Island because of submarines and so forth. Everything was blacked out at night; I believe it was still before the Pearl Harbor attack. I finally bought a car—it was a Model A Ford—for thirty-five bucks and felt really special. I could now drive to Grumman instead of taking the Long Island Railroad.

I think the Pearl Harbor attack was the final blow for getting the WASPs [Women Airforce Service Pilots] going. It was so obvious that there was going to be a shortage of men flying, and they did not need them to be delivering airplanes back and forth or doing any of the other jobs they finally let us into. They started us out fairly small, but there was one group, Nancy Love's, that had pilots, some who had logged a thousand hours. They were mostly wealthy and had their own airplanes and so forth. They formed a group and worked for the ferry service.

The Women Airforce Service Pilots

The Women Airforce Service Pilots was established in August 1943. Eventually just over a thousand women were selected from over 25,000 who applied. During the war, they flew a total of 60 million miles in a host of missions.[11]

I had to be twenty-one to join. I turned twenty-one on May 5 and I had already applied for the WASP. I had a physical at Mitchell Field in Long Island by a male doctor who had never done a female, which was interesting. *[Laughs]* I passed all the way through so I was ready to go whenever they called, which was about mid-May when I got the telegram saying, 'Please show up in Sweetwater, Texas, for the seventh class.'

Training at Sweetwater, Texas

My previous boss gave me some money to work with, loaned me some money. I got a flight to Chicago, Illinois, and a flight down to Dallas, Texas, and then took the train. There were a lot of gals on the train that were coming in for that class. At Sweetwater, it was hot and dirty. It wasn't dressy, it was very casual. And it was fun with a lot of nice people.

Once we got out to the airbase, which was a couple of days later after we stayed at the hotel there for two nights, they gave us GI coveralls, the kind the mechanics wear, size forty or up! And we weren't that big. *[Laughs]* So we went back into Sweetwater and bought heavy shoes to wear, tan pants and white shirts and an overseas cap for our uniform. We found out a good system for washing them was with a scrub brush and a cake of soap. You stand in the shower, get wet, and scrub them. Then you rinse off and hang them on a hanger and in Texas they dried fairly fast; it was the only way to do it! *[Laughs]*

We had both alternating flight line and ground school. We would have flying in the morning and ground schooling in the afternoon. And then the following week we would reverse it. We started off with primary training and a PT19-A was the airplane that was low-wing with an open cockpit. It was entirely different from a Piper Cub, believe me, but great fun.

The Fairchild PT-19 was used by the USAAF during Primary Flying Training. Credit: Unknown. Licensed under CC BY-ND.

We did a lot of things I had not done before but they were explained to you and there was no problem with doing them.

[We did minimal aerobatic training]; I think the pilots liked to do that too, so we cut loops and, of course, spins. We did snap rolls and slow rolls, that kind of thing, but not anything major. The Air Force pilots, the guys, were going to do combat so they were flying in all positions. Our main thought at that time was just delivery of airplanes, to relieve them so they could do other things. At the end of primary training we had a check ride by Army personnel.

A lieutenant gave the physical training, and he yelled a lot of 'hip-hip-hop,' you know. He wasn't taking anything slowly, it had to be right, and he would call you out if you did not do it right. You were pooped when you were finished, but he wanted healthy gals. Some girls did drop out, some were excused and left. You would come back to your bay. We had six people in our long barracks, which we called bays. There were six in one room at the end, a bathroom with two stalls, and then six in the next room—that is twelve girls to a bathroom with two stalls, it kind of got busy. But you got to be very quick at things and you had to fall out into position in a marching group, squadrons with a flag. Wherever we went, we sang.

Jackie Cochran, center, with WASP trainees. Public Domain.

Jacqueline Cochran was a famous flier and a wonderful person. She was the one who started the WASPS. She was very secretive about what we did in the beginning. She did not want pictures taken. I have met her once and I'm very proud of her. She believed that girls could do this! I don't think anyone in the Army thought so. General Arnold did not think that was the place for ladies.[13] But Eleanor Roosevelt said, 'Put the girls in,' and President Franklin Roosevelt sanctioned it. It was needed, it really was. I mean there were girls flying combat in Russia, and before we were started Cochran took a group of girls over to England to fly! There were people from eight other countries who were helping fly in England, both men and women. So it was proven it could be done.

---

[13] *General Arnold-* Henry Harley "Hap" Arnold (1886-1950), then commander of the Army Air Forces.

After primary training, basic was BTs aircraft and they had a large radial engine whereas the PT19 was inlaid and they fired and made a great racket and it was entirely different.[14] They also had the blackout front section so that you could practice instruments, and that was the beginning at that point of our training, we had a great deal of learning in ground school. The worst deal of flying at that point was the radio and signals with the Morse code. I did a lot of that. Then we were checked out on instrument training—that is, flying in the front, not seeing anything, just doing it all by the needle, ball, airspeed, and a gal sat in the back, so you trusted one of the girls and she trusted you to watch, making sure you did not run into an airplane or do something silly up there. There were quite a few airplanes up there while you practiced. So you learn to trust whoever was with you and you made good friends that way.

We finished that, and the check ride by the Army, which was a sweat job, you were scared because they threw everything at you; they wanted to be sure you could do this, and I think that was wise probably. The AT-6 came next, they are used all over, they are wonderful airplanes. They will do anything. We had BTs at night, so we did night flying also.

A major part of our training was the cross-country [run]. We had to know map navigation, et cetera, because that is what they thought we would be doing, flying airplanes from the factory to the base, and returning flying deficient airplanes to the factory to be fixed and so forth. They did not know what size we would be capable of handling, but as time went on, we got more and more convinced that we could fly the bigger ones.

After the check ride with the AT-6s, which was much tougher because our instructor wanted that spin to come out right where he

---

[14] *BTs* -The Vultee BT-13 was the basic trainer aircraft for American pilots during the war.

wanted it. The first one I tried did not happen that way, and I was scared.

North American AT-6C-NT Texan trainer, 1943. Credit: USAF, public domain.

He said, 'Try it again, I think you can do it,' and I did. But you were to come out on a certain heading when you do a spin. They don't teach spins, incidentally, anymore. That guy who was in Buffalo who pulled up when he should have pushed down and stalled the airplane and killed the people should have had our training or better training. You don't pull up when you are shaking, you get some air speed first.

After the AT-6 airplanes, we went to the UC-78s. We called them the 'underpowered coffins,' [the 'UC' stood for that]. It is a Cessna twin-engine, and we learned to manipulate two throttles and fly with one engine and do all of those things.

Cessna UC-78 Bobcat in flight. Used in training to bridge the gap between single and multi-engine aircraft. Source: Unknown, public domain.

The last thing we did was the night cross-country training in one of those. That was interesting. We would leave, check in, and come back. So as I said, ground school was extremely tough and a lot to face. We had Link Trainers to give us more help with night flying and blind flying.[15] When I found out you could spin in them, they went 'whoosh-whoosh!' I thought they were fun, 139ut they were very confining, and when it was hot, they were hot and sticky, though it was a good way to learn.

I got my wings in November of 1943, I had been there since May of '43. They changed as time went on, they took girls who were younger and people with less flying background training, etc. They were trying to figure out just where we fit in and how much you could ask, I think. It made a lot of sense because this was something that was new at that time.

---

[15] *Link Trainers*- flight simulators produced during the early days of aviation for U.S. military between the 1930s and 1950s by Link Aviation Devices of New York.

B-25 Training

When I graduated, twenty of us were chosen to go to Mather Field in Sacramento, California, for B-25 training. And except for one girl who found a guy she wanted to marry and quit—I can't imagine picking a guy over an airplane! — [we all went]. I mean, those B-25s were beautiful, I loved them! *[Laughs]* I stayed until I graduated with the class.

North American B-25 Mitchell. Twin engine American medium bomber, used in every theater of World War II. Source: USAF, public domain.

The B-25 makes a heck of a lot of noise. We did all kinds of special things. Colonel Wimberly was in charge of us, and he was great for that type of job. He would try new things with us and so forth. He didn't figure we had any problems at all, which was a good way to approach it, so we didn't. Of course we had ground school, engines, weather, and cross-country information training there. All kinds of stuff. We were young with open minds, a lot of room to set new things in. We did a day/night cross-country trip with two gals. This was in the winter by the way, which meant sheepskin-lined pants, jacket, helmet, boots, and heavy gloves. We always carried a flashlight with our parachute on our backs and books, so we were well loaded and strong. On this day/night cross-country trip, we went down in the daytime in Texas, just north of Mexico, then we flew back at night over the mountains so it was proof that you could do it. Two girls, no men, no one else, it was fun. It felt good.

Target Towing

Douglas SBD Dauntless; American naval scout plane and dive bomber, generally carrier based. Source: Tomás Del Coro, CC BY-SA 2.5.

When we graduated, we had a break, but I did not go anywhere. Then about half of us went to Biggs Field in Texas and the other half to March Field in Riverside, California, for the 7th Tow Target Squadron. Now I did not know what tow target was going to be. In the Mojave Desert at Camp Irwin, it was very deserty and had a lot of people working as non-coms along with our regular guys and the flight line.

Our job was to tow targets in SBDs. When you get a sleeve [a target flag trailing behind the aircraft] out back, you would fly with a tow-reel operator in the stern of the airplane. They would let the sleeve out from there when you were on course, and it would take all of the power for that SBD, having the throttle almost full forward, [because] there was a lot of drag. That was fine, we would tow the target for four hours, two two-hour shifts for the guys down below, who would be firing live ammunition at the sleeve. Each group, or battery, would dip their bullets in a different primary color. When they hit the sleeve, which was made of clear nylon material, you could read who had made hits and who did not. After the two-hour flight you would drop the sleeves as close as you could to the battery and go off and put on another sleeve for the next two hours.

This went on most of the time until the end, about December 1944. I went to Orlando, Florida, to learn how to become part of the Army Air personnel, but I did not like the idea of sitting behind a desk. When I came back from Orlando, I was shipped to Hamilton Army Airfield in San Francisco, California, where the people were returning from the island battles. [Pacific theater battles]. I did not do many things there; I could fly anything they had, and I did. I was used as a co-pilot on one flight to Mitchell Field in Long Island. Then I returned in a Grumman TBF [Avenger Torpedo Bomber] and I flew in the back of them, in the gunner's section.

Grumman TBF Avenger. Credit: U.S. Navy, 1942. Public Domain.

[The male pilots and ground personnel], they kind of avoided us, I think. Though in the officers' mess we did not have any confrontations or anything. It was generally accepted that we had qualified, and we were doing our thing. So that was good, but I did have one dispatching officer who did not like us. He gave us some bum jobs, but that was all right as long as we could do them. For example, flying a BT [Vultee-BT 13] as high as you can get it at night for searchlight training, especially on my birthday, but that is what he chose, so that is what I did. *[Laughs]* He designated what we did. Anyway, we were available for anything with any of the airplanes that we had qualified to fly.

We also did radar-tracking out of the Pacific with A-24s [Douglas A-24 Banshee Dive Bomber aircrafts], which are rather big and clumsy.[16] When you get in one of those, you don't know what you are going to be doing, but you find out before you land how to make

---

[16] *A-24s*-Douglas A-24 Banshee Dive Bomber.

it work. Three of us would go out in formation and someone in the back would drop out cut-up aluminum foil and see if they could track it from one place, and then another place. It was the beginning of radar work; that was interesting.

Then we would be sent to other fields for a week or less. We did whatever they wanted us to do with the airplane we had or what they had. It was getting more interesting for the girls because tow-target work was one thing they decided to see if we could do. We proved that we could. I think it was done with twin engines in other places, but we were given SBDs so that is what we did with them. We did have one really interesting trip with them. Three of us were asked by the head of the camp if we would come out early in the morning, before everything started, and do some diving on the troops who were in hollows between the hills; they wanted to give the troops a feeling of airplanes and so forth. We were very willing and had a great deal of fun. We stayed out for about a half hour. When I landed, the fellow who took care of my airplane said, 'Did you know that your propeller is green on the ends and your wings have green along the leading edge? And your air scoop underneath is quite green?'

I said, 'No, and I did not hurt anybody, nor hit anyone.'

He said, 'No, and you came back in good shape, but you were kind of low. Your plane has sagebrush in it!' So they did not ask us to do it again; that was too bad.

We also did what they call equiangular firing at nighttime in twin-engine aircraft, usually Beechcraft or such with two of us. This was without a horizon; it was total blackness up there, you had to use instruments. They would aim at you, but the guns would fire to the side of you. It was done with mirrors or something. So you would be flying, and these great bursts would come along side of you, so you had better focus on what you were doing.

We went into Palm Springs after that, and they had a young male cadet group, and that was kind of fun too. You could not get into March Field until about ten in the morning because of the fog, always. Flying out of there was okay going up over the mountains and into the desert, but not flying into it until after ten.

During time off, we had dates, we had a lot of things to do between us. Sharing, laundry, and all of that stuff, too. They kept us pretty busy.

Disbanded

When the WASPS were disbanded, they said, 'Thank you.' I think they said thank you, at the time I wasn't listening very closely. It was December 20 and they said to get home however you can. *[Laughs]* I wondered when they started this officer training at Air Force Strategic Air Command in Orlando if there wasn't something in the wind. I mean rumors go around all the time in the service. So when I was sent to Hamilton Field I thought, well, this is sort of a goodbye place probably. I caught a B-24 part of the way and then I don't remember what I got into, whatever I could find. I also took ground transportation and showed up on the east coast on Christmas Eve. I chose to become married with six children rather than continue, and that's okay, we all have our priorities.

I don't remember [any sort of discharge pay] or rank. I met my [future] husband when he was down on the firing line. I did not marry Jim until he came back from Korea. He had been in England, France, and Germany, through all the worst of that. After I got married, my husband did not want much to do with the WASPs and said to give my uniforms to the Salvation Army and I was a fool, I did. So I don't have a uniform, I don't think I could wear it even if I had it. *[Laughs]* I do have my wings, I had them made into a bracelet.

We were the last class that was a Woman's Air Force Flying Training Detachment.

I got a job on Long Island finally. I worked for Sperry Gyroscope Company in the lab for a while testing Venturi tubes. Then I got a job as the secretary to one of the head guys and stayed there for a while. I left to get married and got a job in the Department of Aeronautical Engineering, an interesting job really and it worked out very well. They had a part of the Sperry company in Mineola, and I lived in Garden City at that point near Roosevelt Field. I bought an airplane with three guys; it had a radio in it, I'll say that for it. *[Laughs]* Because my family was near Cape Cod, I could fly it home on the fourth weekend, I could just go off Montauk Point. I did not have to take the Long Island Railroad; it was so much more convenient. I flew it to many other places too.

Keeping In Touch

When you go through something like that, you are really quite close. I met a lot of people that I would not have met because there would not have been this connection. We've had reunions and the last reunion was this past year. At the reunions, you see everybody and have a wonderful time. It makes you feel like you are young again!

The WASPs were not recognized for their military service until the US military began to admit the first women military pilots in the mid-1970s; it took two years of lobbying for retroactive military status to be enacted.

[We finally got our veterans status through President Carter], in 1977. It was also through Barry Goldwater and some other people who worked for us to get us that. It was a blessing because it made it possible to be a veteran and go to the Veterans Affairs for physical needs. It was something we really needed.

[My time in the WASPS definitely affected my life] a great deal. I have a very high respect for the government in flying connections; I don't think I would have been as fussy about flights going up and coming down at the right time. Yes, I am very proud of my country.

The women WASPs of World War II were finally formally honored in 2010 with the Congressional Gold Medal, sixty-six years after the Women Airforce Service Pilots was disbanded, with over 200 traveling to the US Capitol to receive the honor.

Lillian Lorraine Yonally passed away on December 31, 2021, at the age of 99.[17]

---

[17] Interested readers can view an NPR interview and slideshow of Lillian's color photographs from her service at this link: https://www.npr.org/sections/pictureshow/2010/03/a_contraband_camera_photos_of.html

CHAPTER TWELVE

The Flight Nurse

During World War II, the ranks of US military nurses expanded exponentially, from just under two thousand to nearly six thousand in the combined Army/Navy ranks. Nurses served with skill and determination in field and evacuation hospitals, and on hospital transports, including medical transport planes in the Pacific. Rose Landsman Miller served with the 809th Air Evacuation Medical Squadron in the Pacific theater. Like many, she answered the call of her country; she wanted to fly, but she became just as important as a pilot, a flight nurse ferrying wounded boys her age across the Pacific. She was a recipient of the Army Air Corps Air Medal in 1945. She sat for this interview at the end of 2009.

Rose Landsman Miller

I was born July 24, 1916, in Massena, New York. I [started] grade school in Massena and finished grade school in Syracuse. I went to Wilmington High School in Delaware for two years and finished up my high school in Massena, New York. I graduated in 1933, and I went to nurse's training in 1934 in Brooklyn, New York, in a Jewish hospital and graduated as a registered nurse in 1937. I did staffing for about a year, then I did private duty in the hospital for about three or four years before going into the service.

[When] the attack on Pearl Harbor took place, I remember I was ready to go off duty; it was about four o'clock in the afternoon and we heard this horrible news that we were at war. Now, I had had visions of flying; I had been taking flying lessons for several months. I was even taught how to land on the water, and I had to learn how to land on the land. I got as far as soloing. Everybody who flies remembers the first time they took a plane up alone. You come down, you think you were in paradise. That's the feeling that you get. I will never forget it. I learned on the Piper Cubs. Today, you get into a machine and learn everything there. Then, a number of my classmates from training were going into the service.

'I Didn't Want to Tell My Father'

I had already enlisted, in July; I didn't want to tell my father I was going into the service. You have to stop and consider, way before the draft, if someone had joined the Army at that time, [some people got the idea that there was] something wrong with them. It was almost like they [must have been] the dregs of society. So my father always had an idea that the service was something else, and I was very reluctant to tell him. But my oath had already been in, and when my orders came home that's when I told him. I think by that time he kind of accepted that this was war. I guess he was very proud of the fact that I was the only one in the whole family that was able to put my time and energy into helping people. My brother could not go for physical reasons and the rest of us were all women. I had gone down, and I applied, but we had to go through the Red Cross; at that time, nurses had to go through the Red Cross. We were not considered part of the service. It was all complicated. But once we were in the service, we were given the rank of first lieutenant.

We were sent to Atlantic City; Atlantic City at that time was an air base. There, we encountered everything that was thrown at us. I'll use that word. We weren't receiving any wounded at that time, it was just an enlisted base. We were issued white uniforms, white caps, and shoes. We encountered meningitis there. In fact, [in one instance when I was there], the base was almost closed to anybody coming in or going out, even by train. I would say because we were alerted and knew about a lot of these things, we saved an awful lot of these boys. I know that there were over five of them we could not save. That was unfortunate. We just couldn't, and that was it.

One time, at lunchtime, all the officers would go to lunch and leave [one of us] on. When I was there, they were ready to admit a patient with a temperature, and I loosened his coat. I took a look and said, 'You have a stiff neck.'

I saw these marks on his neck and called down to the admitting office and said, 'I'm not admitting him to a pneumonia ward. I am sending him upstairs to the meningitis ward.' That's how quickly we saved all the rest of them—that we knew.

Well, things changed, and spring came, everything was fine again. Then in April or May, there were two of us who had applied for flight training. I was a little bit annoyed [when she was tapped for the program before me, having had earlier flight training], because I said, 'Why did they call her before me?'

Anyway, I knew a number of the officers, and they said, 'Well don't worry about it because you're gonna be in the next class.' Turns out they had to take her because of her age; if they didn't call her, she was going to be over the age of going [next time].

So I was in the next class, and they sent me to Bowman Field for flight training. We had to adapt how to conduct ourselves in the plane. They were all mockups like the C-40, we'd go in with equipment and come out with patients. In the interim, once the equipment was unloaded, they had to set up what is called a litter strap.

The litters were just slipped into the litter straps. We had to learn all these things in order to do our jobs.

'We Didn't Know Where We Were Going'

In the meantime, they sent us to different hospitals to do this and that. Around November, they had already broken up our class and put us into our squadrons. The squadrons consisted of twenty-five nurses. There were four flights of six nurses, plus the chief nurse. Around the end of October, our squadron was called to attention, and [the commander] said, 'The first group of you will be leaving in four hours to San Francisco.' So that meant packing up quickly and getting everything ready to leave in four hours! We got down to the plane; they bumped everybody else off. They broke us up so that each group went onto a different plane, and we all met in San Francisco. We didn't know where we were going.

When we got to San Francisco, they equipped us with arctic gear boots, parkas, you name it! Around the first week of November, we were alerted for our next flight. We were leaving on four C-54s, they weren't passenger planes. They were these big C-54s and they were able to fly long distances. Three of us left on time, and one was a little delayed because of engine problems. We got there on a Friday. The plane that got left behind, one of the nurse's husbands was based at Wheeler Field with the fighter planes.

She said to the chief nurse, 'Would you please call when you get there and tell Ray I'm coming down.'

So she called the commanding officer when we landed and he said, 'When she comes in, have her call me.'

Well, Sunday morning their plane landed, and she called the commanding officer and he said, "You stay right there, I'm sending him down to get you!'

The husband was probably a first lieutenant at that time and he's fussing and fuming, 'Why should I go down and pick up a lousy second lieutenant?' He doesn't know who this is, you know. The crew was alerted when they landed, and the crew disappeared as he was about to pick her up. When she got out of the car, her husband said to her, 'Annie, what are you doing here? Go on home!' *[Laughs]*

Anyway, like I said, it took us close to four or five months before Admiral Nimitz decided that flight nurses were okay in the Pacific, because he had said there's no place for them here. Well, I would like to say we proved him wrong.

The first group was sent down to Port Moresby to evacuate anybody coming up. They were to bring all the injured all the way up to Hickam Field, which would have been over thirty hours. There would be two nurses coming up alone only with their crew and their patients. When they finally got up, they decided it was too much. I mean you can't put someone on a plane and ask them to take care of their patients for thirty-six hours all alone. So they decided no, they broke that up, so then they were going from Port Moresby, New Guinea, into Guadalcanal. From Guadalcanal they would go into Kanton Island, then back to Hickam Field [Army Air Base, Oahu, Hawaii].[18] Then another flight would be taking the States runs, which would have been anywhere from twelve to fourteen hours, depending on the winds. Finally, they sent the second group down to Guadalcanal and that was going to be almost twenty hours in the air. The third group would be taking them to the States and the fourth group was going on to Tarawa.

---

[18] *Kanton Island*- Coral atoll in Kiribati in the Central Pacific. Tarawa is the capital of Kiribati.

I remember the first flight, we hadn't really begun our runs [but] then suddenly they said, 'The two of you will be going to Kanton Island to pick up five burn cases.'

You see, a plane had hit a bunker and blew up, and five of them were burned, so they sent us down to bring them back. When we got down there—that's almost nine to ten hours down and nine to ten hours back—the patients were just swathed completely. The treatment that they got down in Kanton Island must have been so good that when we met one of them, all he had was just a little scar on his nose. The treatment that we were getting in the Pacific was unbelievable.

'This One Needs Me'

From that time on [we were assigned to] the four spots. I was down on the Guadalcanal run and I picked up a flight there, that one had just come out of New Guinea.

[An officer] said, 'I think you had better prepare a blood transfusion when you get to Kanton Island.'

'Why?' You see, this was sixty-five years ago, and everything was different then.

'He has aplastic anemia.' Now that could have been anything, he probably could have had leukemia, or whatever. The poor boy was oozing blood from his mouth, all he was doing was spitting. So before we took off, I wired ahead for whole blood transfusion. So for nine hours from when we took off I strapped on the oxygen, all we had was a little tank. No sooner did I have it on, he said, 'I have to spit.' Off comes the mask, put it back on, 'I have to spit.' You fly with one nurse and one corpsman for about thirty-five patients. So I said to my corpsman, 'You look after all these others, this one needs me.'

So for the rest of the flight I took the mask on, off. On, off, you know what I mean? We landed on Kanton Island, they took him off and they gave him a transfusion.

As soon as the transfusion was over, he was loaded back up. We took off and it was fine, I could strap the mask on and attend to the other ones. When we landed at Hickam Field, I told my commanding officer I would suggest that this boy remain on the ground and have him transfused before going out on the next leg of the flight. He said, 'I'm sorry but he's going out in about four hours.' Well, he was the commanding officer, there was nothing else I could do, but let me put it this way, if it had been one of the other girls, the southern girls, he would have listened. This commanding officer was a southerner from maybe Mobile, Alabama. *[Laughs]* I had two strikes against me, he didn't like me—firstly, I was a damn Yankee, and secondly, I was Jewish, so he didn't like me, period. Anyway, the boy went out four hours later and they almost lost him. My roommate was on that plane and she said they almost lost him—the only thing they had [onboard] was plasma. To this day I only hope he was able to get home before he went.

'A Planeload of Psychos'

He wasn't a war wounds patient, but we evacuated everything from war wounds to psychos, to medical problems and whatever. We also evacuated more psychos and more jungle rot. If it wasn't our turn to go out, we would have had a little clinic and we would bring our patients in there for a few hours. While I was there, they brought some of these jungle rots in, and the stench was overpowering. Now how the girls sat there for eight hours and smelled that, I really don't know. We never knew what we were picking up. Over the years, you remember the bad ones. You remember the psychos. For every planeload of patients we were bringing out of the South

Pacific, we had to have five psychos on the plane. They tried bringing out a planeload of psychos one time and it didn't work.

Anyway, on one of my planes we had a latrine, and one of these patients decided to get up and streak up and down the plane. *[Laughs]* Like I said, you look at it and see a bit of humor in spite of the war. There was one psycho case who saw ducks, he was in New Guinea, wherever he went he saw ducks. Well, the psychiatrist tried to rid him of the ducks. Finally, they sent him back but he still saw his ducks. They decided, he's no good, we'll send him back to the States as a Section 8. Well, it's four hours from New Guinea to Guadalcanal, another twenty hours to Hickam Field, another fourteen hours to San Francisco. All of this time he saw his ducks. Finally, about an hour out from San Francisco he calls the flight nurse over and said, 'Lieutenant, you can have the ducks now, I don't need them anymore.' *[Laughs]*

Later I was on the Kwajalein run. From Kwajalein we went off to Saipan and Guam. When hospital ships picked up the wounded in Saipan, they unloaded 1,500 sick and wounded at Kwajalein. We had all of those sick and wounded back in Hawaii in the general hospitals in less than a week. Where if the hospital ship had gone, it would have taken them three weeks out and then three weeks back. I guess we proved Nimitz wrong.

My last flight, we went from Kwajalein into Guam and Saipan. I think it was in Saipan that they gave us the quarters just beyond the hospital so that we wouldn't interfere with the nurses and all; [I was at Saipan right after the bonzai attack.] The Japanese that were still there did not want to be taken by the Americans. Whether they were afraid or whatever, I don't know. All the families committed suicide. There was a section there called Suicide Cliff.[19] They would

---

[19] *Suicide Cliff*-She most likely refers to Marpi Point. One veteran in Volume 8 remembered: 'At the end of the battle, [I witnessed] the most eerie, bizarre thing that I ever saw in my life. Up at the end there was a place called

line up their children and push them off the cliff! Then the second one would push the other until the father was left and then he would jump. These were high cliffs, so you can just imagine. They also had a lot of sugar cane factories there and it was a very peculiar smell, very unpleasant. Most of us were pretty close to the air base so it didn't bother us that much.

'We Flew the Entire Pacific'

People used to say, weren't you afraid of flying that whole distance with nothing in between? We said no, it never occurred to us. There was a plane going from Hickam Field to Saipan and the plane went down. What happened, no one will ever know. They never found [them]. And yet, we flew the entire Pacific.

Marpi Point. We were there for two or three days, just watching people commit suicide, civilians basically jumping into the water, blowing themselves up with grenades, having their own soldiers shoot them.
What had happened was the end of the island was covered with a shrubbery very tight, like a hedge. It was also coral, and it was pockmarked with these holes, so people could get in these holes all along there. Then there was a cliff just about a thousand feet from the edge, which had caves in the underside. There was a path going down into the flatland before you got into the water.
There were some Japanese soldiers apparently up in the cave underneath where we were standing. A lot of other people were hidden in these caves all along. But they had gotten the people afraid of us, probably terrified of [us] coming. So, we went down there, we sent scouts down there [first]. A couple of them got killed by the snipers, so we pulled back to the cliff line and then had the Japanese speakers try to convince the people that we weren't going to harm them. But I would imagine [they were] like, 'Who are they kidding?' There was nothing much we could do at that point. The killing just started. I saw whole families standing on a rock, right along the ocean, and explode a grenade, and then maybe a survivor would crawl off into that water. [But as an eighteen or nineteen-year-old in combat], I think by that time, I was a little deadened about anything shocking me. I thought much more about it in years after.'

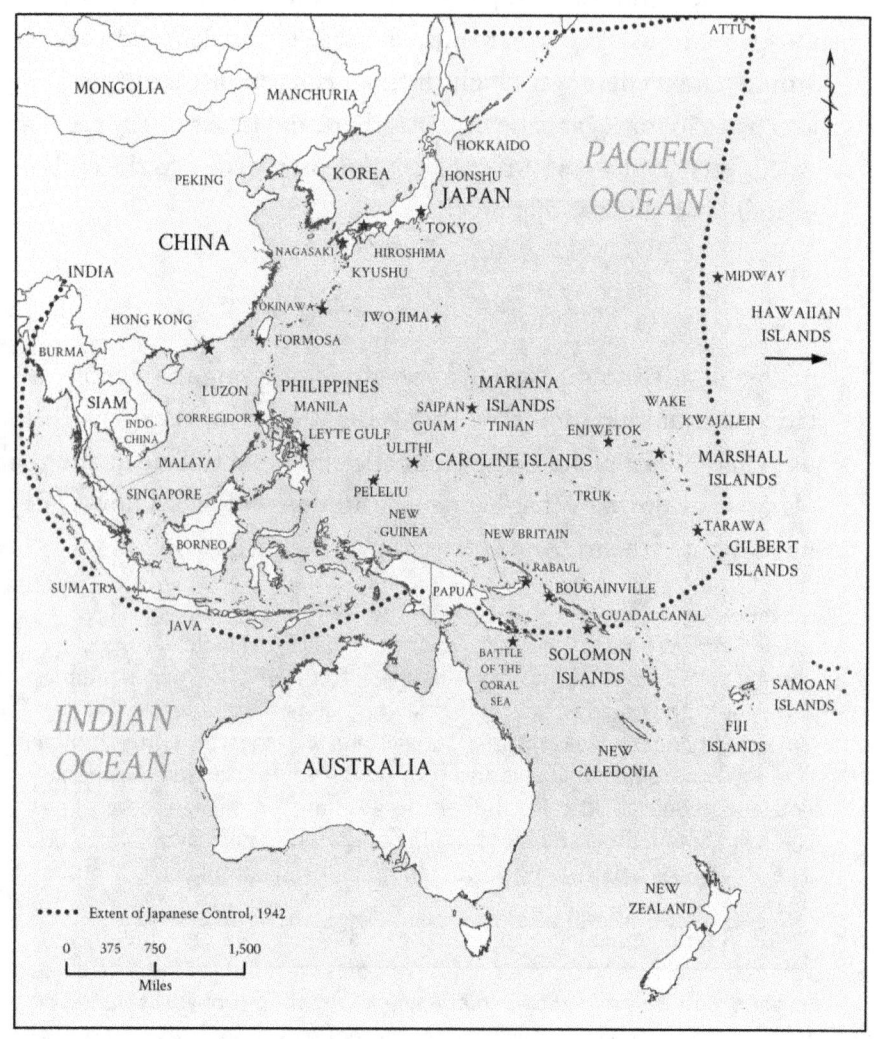

The vastness of the Pacific Theater. Extent of Japanese control, 1942. Drafted by Susan Winchell, after Donald L. Miller.

Yes, many times we came in on three engines and hoped to God we didn't feather another one. Now, coming into San Francisco in the middle of winter, the fog hangs over there like pea soup. You can't see in front of you. We had no radar then. There were four airfields that we could use; you never knew where you were going to land. One plane came in and it was all fogged out; [the pilot radioed that] he's going over the mountains. I guess they tried to reach Reno, but they had to land on a fighter training strip because they were running out of fuel. We came in once, again practically closed in with fog and cloud cover, and our pilot said, 'I'm going to try Oakland!', and so help me God, he found a hole in the clouds and came down in Oakland. We just would never know. We could be losing fuel or hitting a mountain, because all along the coast are mountains. And yet, I guess our faith in our pilots was such that we didn't really think about it; it's a job to be done, and that's it.

People would say to me, 'What did you see when you were over there?' I said, "See? Sky, water, and telephone poles!' They would say, 'Telephone poles?' 'Yes, when you bomb an island, what do you think is left standing? Telephone poles!' *[Laughs]*

On Guadalcanal, New Guinea, Saipan, Guam, and Tinian, nurses were quartered behind fences and guarded and escorted to their hospitals and activities by MPs. They were subject to evening curfews and armed escorts after 1800 hours. Women's Army Corps (WAC) members here received the same treatment. Women were restricted ostensibly to protect them from the Japanese, but in reality, it was to cut down on incidents of sexual intimidation or harassment, and fraternization.[12] MacArthur's orders fooled no one.

Nurses relaxing, Guam. Donald P. Quarters collection. Courtesy Jackie Quarters.

In between our flights, it might have seemed we had a lot of time off because for every twelve hours in the air you had to be on the ground a full two days. They had one flight down in the South Pacific doing the New Guinea to Guadalcanal run, which was four hours in and four hours back with your patients, which was eight hours in the air. Then another twenty-eight hours to Hickam Field. If they didn't have enough of their nurses, they would pull ours. That meant these girls were in the air twenty-eight hours. We would come off like this *[shakes both her hands in a nervous gesture]*. We couldn't eat, we couldn't sleep. At one time we were all taking Seconal to help us sleep. Even that didn't work, so they issued a command that we had to be on the ground for at least forty-eight hours. There was one ground nurse who had to be flown out somewhere and when she got off, she said, 'I would not want your job!' We were considered the elite. We were different, you know. Now, it doesn't make any difference. When you take a look at the equipment on the plane that we had, you would not believe how primitive it was. We had no penicillin at that time.[20] We had sulfur, sedatives, and pain killers. But there were a lot of things we just did not have. Sometimes you wonder how in the world we ever won the war *[Laughs]*. We had used up a year's supply of aspirin in six months. At one time in the hospital, we had about 1,500 patients of various conditions, they had no urinals. So what do you do? You need the urinals. They went to the Red Cross, who brought back all types of shapes and sizes of vases to use as urinals. *[Laughs]*. That's why I said, how we won the war, I don't know. It was just persistence, I guess.

Olivia De Havilland and Betty Grable

We saw an awful lot of USO shows. But most of the time when we were there, we didn't have very much time to sit in on them, because we were either coming or going. I was coming up from Guadalcanal, we were on Kanton Island, and we heard a VIP was coming down. Everybody was saying who's this VIP? It could have been a general. The plane landed and what came off the plane was a lady. Have you ever heard of Olivia De Havilland? She was beautiful. But more than beautiful, she was a lady. She came off the plane

---

[20] *We had no penicillin at that time-* While penicillin production was being ramped up, especially in the buildup to the June 1944 Normandy campaign, it was also in short supply. It was not until June 1945 that large-scale mass production enabled by the War Production Board was reaching its peak. Source: Parascandola, J. *The History of antibiotics: a symposium.* American Institute of the History of Pharmacy No. 5. 1980.

in a simple dress, normal high heels, but gracious. I'm a woman and I look at her and just say, 'Oh!' The aura that she expelled was like the essence of womanhood. She wasn't Betty Grable, excuse me, *[laughs]* but like I said, she was a lady. She could have been your sweetheart, your wife, your mother, your sister, everything. I mean, that is the way I looked at her and I think the men looked at her the same way.

Betty Grable was, I'll use the word, a bore. There was an occasion in the South Pacific with the USO troupe, and Betty Grable was there. She happened to ask one of the flight nurses if they could iron her costume for her. I hate to tell you what they told her to do. *[Laughs]*. The idea is that we're working our necks off and she's enjoying herself, I'll use that word. Oh well.

The Philippines

We never experienced a bombing, but once when we went into Okinawa, we went in on red alert. Anything could have happened, a bomb or an airplane could have come over and hit the airfield. We were down there for only two hours, enough to load up our patients, refuel, and get the hell out of there. When we went into the Philippines [in 1945], my husband and I were on our honeymoon; we had a week to ten days of R&R. That's the time that they went and evacuated all of the internees [of the Japanese, from the conquest in 1942]. They said these girls, these nurses, were coming out almost like skeletons. For three years they were interned.

One of the stories that came out of the Philippines was about a Japanese soldier who had appendicitis and had to get his appendix out. So they made sure the American doctors and nurses took care of that. They were standing over them with guns. Fortunately, he recovered, and because of that they got an extra ration of rice or something. So there were all kinds of stories that came out.[21] One of these days I will get that book about these nurses that got caught in the Philippines. Now as far as MacArthur is concerned, we did not like him, period. He was a very selfish man. Instead of trying to get some of the other Americans out, he loaded up his plane with his household goods, things like that.[22] The people who were down in the Philippines, who got captured and even after we went in, they did not like him, period. You read the history books and you think, well that didn't happen like that. History actually distorts reality. I suppose that's the way it is.

Tarawa

When we were on Tarawa, the Navy had no idea how to set up a ground facility. Two of our girls came down with dysentery and they were isolated for about six weeks. Like I said, the facility wasn't the cleanest and that was the Navy. Maybe it's different today, but it wasn't then.

Sometimes we were housed in a Quonset hut, but sometimes it was just a wooden shack to keep the rain off. That was just about it. When you were down in Tarawa, it was just a small wooden building. The water was brackish. If we wanted to go out and bathe in the ocean, we wanted to be sure the squids weren't there. There was

---

[21] "In February 1945 U.S. troops liberated the sixty-seven Army nurses who had been imprisoned in Santo Tomas Internment Camp since 1942 and evacuated them to a convalescent hospital on Leyte. Although suffering from malnutrition and beriberi, they recovered from their ordeal fairly quickly. The duty they performed in combat and the hardships they endured as prisoners of war are testaments to the professionalism of the entire Army Nurse Corps throughout the war." Source: *The Army Nurse Corps in World War II.* U.S. Army Center of Military History, p. 30.

[22] *he loaded up his plane with his household goods* -General Douglas MacArthur and his family, ordered by the President to leave, were evacuated from Corregidor in a risky PT boat operation in March 1942.

a little ledge, and very often they would be hiding under there. Not too bad, but you had to be careful. On Kanton Island, there were two coconut trees and some desert bushes and that's it. A number of our girls were fair-skinned; fortunately my skin is not fair. But if they went from our quarters, which is about from here to that chair [*gestures across room*], they would be burned. A lot of the girls came down with bad sunburns. Me, I just turned so dark; my daughter has a picture somewhere in which I look like one of the natives. Yet when I got back, all I did was this [*rubbing her forearm*]; I didn't burn, fortunately; I just flaked off a little bit.

Food

[In the mess hall, we had] Vienna sausages, pancakes, and anything that was canned, powdered eggs. When we went to the States and back, we would pick up the things we didn't have before. I remember once we had strawberries or something and we would come back, and we would share it. For some reason or other we couldn't get very much chicken, so we would bring that back from the States, the makings for dinner. In Hawaii, we would get fresh fruit, but wherever else we were, we didn't get it. If we were on Kwajalein, there was nothing there but coconuts, Guam and Saipan [also]. Everything was being brought in by ship. Everything was canned, the fruit, vegetables, everything like that. I think 'oleo' got started there too. We had heard something about a substitute for butter, we didn't know what it was, but it was used. Today, it was probably a form of oleo. When you get home, you want all the things you didn't have before. You want to go out for dinner and get a good steak. Or you want something fancy that you hadn't had in years. So in a way, you begin to enjoy yourself.

Marriage

I met my [future] husband at Hickam Field. I was in the [Army] Air Force and he was in the Signal Corps, in the ground force. One time he was telling me they had to set up communications in Kauai. Now Kauai is a peculiar island, I'll say it that way, because you can't go all the way around the island because the mountains go right through to the end all the way down. You have to use a boat to go all the way around. They had to set up communications right through the mountains, through the forest, all the way through. They had to set up communications in Hawaii on top of the mountains. That was his job.

Of course, like everything else, you're on Hickam Field base and you get to know all the officers there.

I had gotten quite friendly with the general next door; he would send his orderly in and invite me to dinner. I complained to him that my husband could not get off the island at all. He said, 'Don't worry about it. You set up the time you want to get married and I'm sure he'll be there.' Anyway, we didn't know when the war was going to be over. I had already been overseas eighteen months and he had been overseas longer than that. The next thing I knew, I got a letter from my husband setting up the time that he would be there! I guess it's important that you get to know different people.

We were married in February 1945, by the chaplain from Pearl Harbor. The chaplain was from the Navy, a little Chinese boy played the organ, a Marine sang the hymns. So, it was kind of an international wedding. At that time, you couldn't be married and be on the same base. We were talking about it [beforehand] and decided that if we got married and went back to the States, I'd be on one end, and he'd be on the other. So, we decided I'll get out of the service. I'll get pregnant.

*

My last flight was to Okinawa. I was getting morning sickness, and it was a little bit too much. I just turned myself in to the Medical Department and was discharged in San Francisco in June, but it didn't take effect until August. I should have waited a little bit longer because in August they dropped the bomb and that was it.

After that, I went to my husband's folks. They were waiting for me; they had only met me once in San Francisco. My father-in-law was a theatrical lawyer, and he had some business out there. My mother-in-law came out first. I met them both in Los Angeles. They were very anxious for me to come back; they had heard I became pregnant. I stayed with them. I went back to Massena for a while to see my folks. We couldn't even find housing; at that time, even after the war was over, there was no housing available. If you had a room in a house, you were lucky. Nothing was available until the new housing developments went up.

In September, my husband was discharged, right after the war ended. There was something very funny. We went to a party, by this time I was about eight months pregnant. There was a fella there who asked, 'When did your husband get back?'

I said September, and here I am like this. [*Holds hands out in front, showing pregnancy*]. He looks at me, and his face dropped!

I said, 'Oh, I forgot to tell you, we were married overseas!' [*Laughs*]

[When my husband was discharged, he made use of the G.I. Bill], he went back to law school. He was supposed to have joined his father in the law business, but like everything else, a lot of things fell apart. His father died, and like I told you, things fell apart. By that time, I had the one child and then fifteen months later my daughter was born. So with him going to school it was impossible for me to go back to school. I just went back to nursing. At one point someone had asked me, when you went back to work, how did the other nurses treat you? I couldn't understand what she meant. Then I began to understand what she meant, because I didn't go back to work until seven or eight years later. By that time, the war was over and I said, 'They treat you like any other nurse.' They didn't ask you where you were or anything else.

The World War II Flight Nurses Association

About four or five years after the war, the flight nurses decided they were going to have their own group. There were 1,500 flight nurses worldwide. We covered everything from North Africa, all of Europe, England, the CBI (China, Burma, India) route; the girls flying that route, they were flying the Hump, [the eastern end of the Himalayan Mountains]. And of course, we flew the entire South Pacific. Because there weren't that many of us, when you compare the 1,500 of us to those [thousands] of nurses on the ground, we weren't very many. So we decided to form the World War II Flight Nurses Association. We more or less once a year have a reunion, but since we are losing more every year, it has dwindled down. If we have one hundred fifty nurses in a year, that's an awful lot. In January we hope to have the last reunion, I hope it isn't. There's a lot that I know we have lost contact with completely, and we know those that have gone, but outside of that, we don't know where a lot of them are. And that was it.

*

'Leave Me Alone'

It's difficult to say [how the war affected my life] because once you come back and you pick up ordinary life again, it's almost like a bad dream—or a good dream you had, depending how you look at it. I really don't know, [but I had no trouble adjusting to civilian life].

When I first got back, my mother-in-law asked me if I wanted to go to the Congregational church meeting? I said, 'No, I am very happy just sitting here.'

Nobody's going to tell me when to get up, nobody is going to tell me when to go to bed. Nobody's going to tell me when to go out. Just let me sit for a while. That's the way I felt. Leave me alone.

Less than four percent of American soldiers who received medical care in World War II were lost. Just forty-six of the nearly 1.2 million patients flight-evacuated during the war did not survive. This is a testament to the professionalism and standards that our nurses created, and lived by.[13]

Rose L. Miller was honored as the grand marshal of her hometown's Memorial Day parade in 2012. She passed at the age of 96 the following November.

CHAPTER THIRTEEN

The WAVE

Margaret Doris Alund-Lear was a 1942 graduate of Catholic Central High School in Troy, New York. In 1943, she joined the US Navy WAVES training program at Hunter College in the Bronx and then was posted to Washington, D.C. at the Naval Air Station in Anacostia, preparing flight maps for pilots. Later, she was chosen to participate at the famous Sixth War Loan Drive in Chicago, which brought 600,000 people a day to the Navy Pier to meet the famous movie personalities and view the latest equipment the Navy was using. Later, she was assigned back to Washington at the largest WAVES station, with 5,000 women serving there. She was a chaplain's assistant, visiting the hospitals for the sick and wounded in the war.

Margaret Doris Alund-Lear

I was born in Watervliet, New York, on September 21, 1923. I went to Catholic Central High School. I majored in business, but I studied drama and art. I did a lot of public speaking and was in various plays and things in school.

[The attack on Pearl Harbor] was such a shock at the time to all the seniors. Everyone seemed to want to do something. What can we do? I remember talking about it and then my brothers went into the service, one in the Army and one in the Navy. I was very close to my brothers, and it was quite a loss without them at home. That was when I saw pictures of women and I thought, this is for me. I'm going! I really felt that I wanted to do something. I was working in the telephone company, and I said no—I want to leave and go into the service. And my girl chum was going to go with me. We were to meet the next day; I showed up, and she didn't. I enlisted in Troy, New York, the third week in March 1944.

The WAVES

I went into the WAVES when they were new to the country.[23] That was for me, I was really excited about it. My parents, of course, said, 'Well now, a third one going, but we can't stop you.' I said, 'No, you can't.' I had never been to a big city, but I had my orders and went down. I was amazed at New York City and had to go to a center where they did all the health checkups and everything. I came back home, and they told me I was leaving for the boot camp training at Hunter College in the bronx. So here was a little girl from a small town going down by various means on subways and so forth to get around New York City. But it was exciting, and I really felt I was getting somewhere at that point.

My active duty began April 6. I had six weeks of boot camp at Hunter College. The day we arrived, we received all of our clothing and the next morning at six we had to march to breakfast. The marching was new, the clothing was new. We had cotton stockings because of the war. And to a woman who loved nylons, that was something different to wear! The cotton stockings were heavy, believe me. The short, flat oxford shoes were different also, but we

---

[23] *WAVES*- Women Accepted for Volunteer Emergency Service/US Navy Women's Reserve, established on July 30, 1942 to free up men for sea duty.

found out we needed the oxfords because of all the marching. They gave us a song sheet and we had to sing on the way to breakfast. Then they informed us there was such a thing as 'captain's inspection.' So we girls had to learn how to have everything in the drawers a certain way, and everything had to hang a certain way. And in between times we were so busy marching, and there was so much to learn. For example, we never knew about certain ships and Link Trainers and all these different things. So we had to learn as the men learned about the Navy and the chain of command.

Another thing we learned was we could no longer decide what we were going to do, we were told what we were going to do for six weeks. It was wonderful training and we shaped up. I enjoyed that. Waiting for our billet [postings], we had a graduation ceremony in one of the huge armories down there. The experience was very exciting, [leaving me] to swell with pride, believe me. When you were marching and doing it right, that took six weeks to be perfect, but we were perfect! The other thing was the people in the Bronx would watch us marching. They would be so excited, to see these women learning how to conform. Then we had our shipping orders, we were all going to various places. We had our picture taken all together, we had a lot of camaraderie. It was very, very good. We did a lot of studying and took tests. I would like to say that I ran a switchboard in the telephone company, but I never had to do one in the Navy.

WAVE Quarters One

My first billet was Washington, D.C.; when we got there, that was a shock. It was so beautiful! We were sent to WAVE Quarters I, which was on the Potomac River. We could see the Jefferson Memorial and the Washington Monument; it was just breathtaking.

We had three airports that formed a 'V', and all the military planes were coming and going all the time.

Believe me, for a sailor woman, it was inspiring at the time. At WAVE Quarters I, they said, 'Well, we don't know yet what we are going to do with you. Everyone serves a mess detail in the Navy, so until we get you a billet, we are going to have you in ship's company and you will have to do a mess detail.'

We would feed two thousand a meal, and they kept coming from all over, officers and enlisted men as well. After each meal, we would have to clean the floor. I had never scrubbed floors and we had large, large mops. You had to squeeze the mops out, and the floors in our mess hall were wooden. We would also have to perfectly line up the salt and pepper shakers with a string on all these long tables. I had to take care of the coffee urn, which meant I had to climb up onto a bar and get down into it with steel wool. You had to keep going over it with your hands so that there was no residual coffee marks on it. I was down into it practically to my head to clean it. All the [large pans that the food was in] also had to be cleaned. Then the officer would come and check everything afterward; we made sure they were cleaned. You wondered, is that what I'm going to do? But you took it, you didn't complain.

We had to wear jeans; I had never worn dungarees. But that was the Navy, you wore the shirts and the dungarees. I [also] had to pluck chickens, I was so sick plucking chickens that I thought I was going to faint one time! *[Laughs]* They said, 'Well, we will take you off the chickens. You are doing good on the cleaning!' We used to go back to the barracks and laugh and say, 'Look what we are doing!' But it was interesting.

Mapwork

After the ship's company, they said, 'You are going to be down at the Naval Air Station. You are going to paint maps. We understand you took art.'

'Yes, I used an airbrush.'

They added, 'But understand, it is going to be secret. You cannot tell anyone what you are doing. You cannot tell your parents; you are not to talk about the work. You will be there, but you won't talk to anyone, and you will be inspected every day.'

So we would carry our purses, we wouldn't take any junk in them. They inspected us as we went in and when we came out. We sat at long tables, you could see the maps in the room, whatever they were made with, big white things that they would spray green. Then we would see all these designs that we had to put the roads, the pillboxes and the hills in. We had everything to do on these maps. We were painting them all the time, some of them with an airbrush, others with the tiniest of brushes, to paint everything perfectly. A steady hand was needed; I was able to do it, and I enjoyed it. But you would see the other women working but you did not talk to them. You kept your mind on your work. There were large and small maps. Some of the large ones I had never seen until I watched a history program. I got so excited one day, I said, 'There is my map!' and my husband said, 'You finally saw one.' I said, 'Yes, that is what we were doing!' It was only after the war when they told us we could discuss the maps that we had painted. It was kind of hard not being able to tell your parents what you did.

Oh, we worked all day. We would get there at eight in the morning and then at four o'clock the bus would come. We would go outside, get inspected again, and then be taken back to the barracks. It was very interesting; I did that for roughly four months.

Celebrity Bond Drive

Then the commander said, 'You have been chosen to go to Chicago. They are having the biggest bond drive of the war, and you will be a representative of New York State.' I said what do I do, sell bonds? She said, 'You will do everything. The commander there will be your boss. You will follow him around and do whatever he wants you to do. You will greet the people coming in, hand out programs, familiarize yourself with the area so you can talk about it. They are going to sell bonds and will have all the radio and movie people there. The Admiral is coming, everyone is coming to see the new equipment we are going to use in this war!' When they said you are going to see a lot of people, well, I didn't realize I was going to see 500,000 people all in a group! [The *Chicago Sun* newspaper with the headline '*Navy Bond Show Attracts 500,000*' is displayed. It was all day long, but it was an honor. It was wonderful, they put us up in The Drake Hotel, which is a gorgeous hotel. They had given it over to the war effort, so it was all military people, and it was beautiful. We met so many people there, I can remember a baseball team [owner] and he was quite famous. I met Gloria Vanderbilt's husband at the time, his name was Pat DiCicco. He was a very interesting man. I also saw Judy Garland and Eddie Cantor, Dorothy Lamour and Red Skelton, he was wonderful. So many movie stars, we would escort them to the stage, and they would do their bits; it was very, very nice.

After us girls did our duty, we would walk down to Chicago. I remember seeing the Christmas tree at Marshall Fields. One of the girls told me to meet her and we would have lunch. I did not know they had seven cafeterias in the place so you can imagine my feelings about trying to find her! I was a lost country girl, but it was a wonderful experience to meet all of these people. I was right at home with them, everybody was so nice to me, it was very exciting. I have pictures of the girls from the tour; when I came back from the tour, I was so exhilarated. I thought the experience was so grand, I thought, 'I don't know what I'm going to do now!'

They said, 'Well, we have a new job for you. You are going to WAVE Quarters D in Washington, D.C., [the largest, state-of-the-art training facility]. Well I loved WAVE Quarters I, which was new, Quarters D was an older one.

'You are going to be a chaplain's assistant. You can be a yeoman striker,' [administrative position], which takes a year to do it. Commander Tom Fallon was going to be my boss. He was a very nice Irish priest and very direct to the point when he wanted something. He would say, 'Get this off!', and then I would have to get a letter off to this or that person. He had been on a battleship, and he was very interesting. He told me about all the people on the ship when it was hit. He had brought a lot of rosaries with him, but he said even those who were not Catholic wanted rosaries. The fellows were really scared; that battleship was being bombed, and many sailors were badly hurt. He was a very dedicated man who would do everything for the men.

He started retreats and brought Monsignor Fulton Sheen to speak.[24] I would like to say, Fulton Sheen was remarkable. We arranged for a retreat and had the lights off. Monsignor Sheen came down the aisle then onto the stage looking down on the audience; he scared the daylights out of us. He said loudly, 'Where are you going?'

We all said, 'What did we do?', but he was such a wonderful speaker with penetrating eyes. He came several times just to see us! What a remarkable man; if you did not have some kind of faith, he

---

[24] Fulton J. Sheen (1895 -1979) was a Catholic bishop of the Catholic Church highly regarded for his work in television and radio.

would give it to you. He would make you feel that you better get to church once in a while or something.

The Flag

Every day in our place, we had to have the flag ceremony. I was part of the ship's company, so we would have to go out and march; all of the WAVES would march out and raise the flag. I think today, since 9/11 when people see the flag, they are getting the feeling that I, and many of us in the service, had. We all stopped. If you were on the street, all the cars around the Communication Annex where I worked all stopped until that flag got up. It was something, to look around and see this happening. The cars, kids going to work, and we ourselves being in it, it was very exciting. Then, at eight o'clock at night, it would come down. To this day when I see a parade, people look at me because I am saluting. I feel so deeply about the country and the flag means something.

I was only twenty years old, and it was just grand to grow up like that and know what life was about. I also did a lot of writing. I had to answer letters regarding girls that were going to be married or the young men from Communications across the street. We had to get all their records so they could get married. The chaplain would take me to Bethesda Hospital, it was one of the biggest hospitals I had ever seen. It would make Albany Medical look small. If people want to see what war is, they should go in the hospital. Some men had no faces, no legs, no arms. I saw so much, to this day, I still think about it. I did see them all doing little things to keep busy. What the chaplain said was, 'You'll notice some of the men are walking around with toilet paper. Everybody in the Navy that can walk does a job. It restores their dignity and lets them think they can do something.'

I can remember the chaplain saying, 'You girls go out with all the young, good-looking fellas, but how about taking some of these guys out?' So we started saying, 'Would you like to go to lunch with us?' Cabs were cheap then, thirty-five cents for a whole zone in Washington. The boys would say, 'I would love to go out!' I have a picture of a young man that I took out, he had only one leg. My girlfriend was going with her boyfriend who had come home, and we took this young man with us, it was my last night in Washington. I had been married the month before and I called my husband. I said, 'I'm going to take a young man out.'

He said, 'Do it!' I just felt that I should let my new husband know that I was going out with someone. *[Laughs]* It was quite an experience to work for the chaplain and see all these things.

To me, to this day, I feel I would have gone now if my country needed me. I believe America is a wonderful country. I've been to Europe, and I have seen people are not as fortunate to work, like we could work and have the things we have here. I'm very dedicated to this country.

A Cosmopolitan Wedding

Oh, I have to tell you about my wedding! I had a plumber that used to come in and out fixing things. Even if our typewriter broke, he would fix that, he could do anything. When I was going to be married, he said, 'I would like to see you get married.' I said yes. I also had two African American women that were maids. In Washington, in the days of segregation, when you went down to Thirteenth Street, they had barricades. You could not go over there. The two girls that cleaned the office were so lovely to me, I got along with everybody. They said, 'We are coming to your wedding.' They had saved their money and bought me the most beautiful negligee I ever had in my married life. I had some of the Marine boys there, the Protestant chaplain stood by me, and the Catholic chaplain married me. So I had a very beautiful military wedding. When we went down to my wedding dinner, a gentleman came over and said how wonderful you and your husband are, you are so happy. He said, 'I am the head of the Library of Congress, and it is my pleasure to buy you all a drink.' He was so nice to us.

Interesting People

I have met many interesting people. I also used to babysit to make money. I made sixty-two dollars and fifty cents a month, which wasn't much. And when you had to buy stockings, lipstick, and various things I babysat for extra money. One of the gentlemen I babysat for was Colonel Beirne Lay, Jr. He wrote *Twelve O'clock High*. He said 'I have a manuscript here all typed, call me if you want to read it. When you get through it, tell me what you think. I hope someday, I can get something for it. Maybe publish it or have a movie made.' He did have a movie made of it! I took care of his baby, and he was a wonderful man. I also took care of a little child for the Biddle family. They were very, very well-known and he was in the Embassy. I met so many people, it was wonderful. I had the pleasure of being in the parade for Admiral Nimitz. Of course, I was one of hundreds of women, but I was in the parade.

Discharged

[I was in the service] from April 6, 1944, through October of 1945. My husband was discharged before me. He was in the Army, in the Signal Corps and discharged in September. I was going to go to Hawaii, but I was married. It was embarrassing for him to be home while his wife was still serving. So I came home. It was the most wonderful time of my life, I thought. I really enjoyed all of it.

The WAVES have their national group. I brought my cap to show you, we wear caps. I thought you should also see the current WAVES paper we have. We keep up with things. The girl that stood up for me at my wedding has come every year to see us. She liked [Saratoga Race Course] horse racing, laugh if you will. I liked it, but I would be working so I would let her go with my husband. Then we got together when I retired. She called about two weeks ago, we keep up. I write to other girls, and we meet up at these conventions that the WAVES nationally have. I am a very fortunate woman.

After the war I was very busy, and I'm still busy being involved with things. I was always happy with people, and through the years I have done a lot of lecturing for women's places in unions. I decided to go back to the telephone company and worked there until my children came along. Then I did not work for sixteen years. Afterward, I went back to the telephone company again, but everything was different. They were going into computers. Then I was asked to be a union representative. I said, 'Well I don't know,' and they said, 'Oh, you are going to do it.' I only lasted a few months being a representative and then went on the executive board of the union. I then felt I might as well go back to school and went to Russell Sage College and Cornell University, for a two-year program for labor management. I came out with all A's and B's, and A's in economics, which was good at the time. I was one of two women in a class of twenty-six down in Albany in the Russell Sage/Cornell group. The men at that time in the 1970s were very insulting. They felt a woman's place was in the home. I remember a couple of them saying, 'Why don't you stay home with your children?'

I said, 'No, I am going to work, and I am going to learn!'

Before I was through, all of the men all stood behind me and said, 'You did fine,' and were really nice to me. I felt that once they knew me, it was great. I loved the union work. After that I did a lot of lobbying in Washington, D.C.

When Hugh Carey ran for Governor of New York, I was non-political as far as saying who I would vote for. But Mary Anne Krupsak, his lieutenant governor, asked me if I would help them. I said I would speak on women's rights and getting out to vote. My children used to say, 'Mom's going to be on TV again.' And I was many times... but I had a strong belief in my country. I believe if people have a mouth, they should open it and speak their opinion. They should not say what anyone should do and then expect to have things done for you, when you don't take an interest in it. So I would go to town meetings and various things, but that is the way I am.

It came easy for me to be in the service. I would write letters and correspond, so I just loved every day of my military career. There were so many things that I was fortunate enough to be involved in and enjoyed meeting people.

Margaret Doris Alund Lear passed away on November 19, 2005, at the age of 82.

CHAPTER FOURTEEN

The Recruiter

Helen Marcil went into the service from a working-class family, following her brothers when the Coast Guard opened up their Women's Reserve, the SPARS. She served as a recruiter, traveling the country. She gave this interview in 2012, at the age of 82.

Helen Marcil Brennan

I was born in Cohoes, New York, on August 21, 1920. I went to Saint Bernard's Grammar School. For high school I went to Catholic High in Troy.

[I remember where I was when I heard about the attack on Pearl Harbor], very vividly I remember. It was on a Sunday, December 7, and we were getting ready for dinner, and we heard it on the radio. My mother started to cry very softly, and I thought, 'Why is she crying?' But she was thinking that she had two sons and she figured they'll be going into the service. My brother and my boyfriend immediately went down the next day and volunteered to enter the service.

My boyfriend, who later became my husband, joined the Navy, and my brother joined the Coast Guard. Years later, I visited the *Arizona* in Pearl Harbor, Hawaii, and what a feeling to know that all those bodies were down there. It was a wonderful experience to go there.

One day I was on my lunch hour from the FBI and there was a recruiting trailer on North Pearl Street [in Albany] and I went over. It was for the SPARS, and so I got all the information. I decided to go into the Coast Guard, the SPARS, because my brother was in the Coast Guard. When I went home, I was all enthused about going into the service. Now, at that point, I was in the FBI, I can just say that I was in correspondence. I ran the switchboard, and I did teletype and all sorts of communications, but we couldn't talk about it. I had a hard time getting a release to go into the service because they said I was doing my duty there, in the FBI. I said I really wanted to go, and I still have a letter from J. Edgar Hoover giving me permission to resign and saying he hoped I'd have a good time in the service.

Well, my father was very old-fashioned, and he had an idea that all servicewomen were 'fast,' as he used to say. He didn't want me to go in, but he didn't stop me. After I was in, he was very proud of me and my sister and my two brothers. He was in World War I, in the Army.

Away From Home

I was sworn in in Albany in August of 1942; I had to meet a group of people in New York City, and I had two suitcases and I thought, 'I'll never make it.' I went all by myself, and I was just about dying, holding my two suitcases. It was my first time away from home and it was my first time going to New York City alone. I was very sheltered, so to speak.

I missed the people at Grand Central Station, and we had to wait and we had a military train, and it took us forever to get to Palm Beach. It was two days for us to get down there, and when we got there to the SPAR station, they billeted us in the Biltmore Hotel, a very swanky hotel that had been taken over by the government. We got in line to get in there and we were starving, and we went right to the mess hall, and when we got to go into the mess hall, the girls that were dishing out the tomatoes and stuff, they all started to say, [*sings in singsong fashion*] 'You'll be sorry!' [*Laughs*]

But it was wonderful, really. The Biltmore Hotel in Palm Beach, we went to classes from nine o'clock in the morning until ten o'clock at night, but it wasn't all classes. During that time we would have drills, we would march, we would have swim and surf, so it was broken up with the classroom studies. It was really wonderful training, and I graduated first in my class from yeoman school.

My sister went in a year after I did; she had to wait to be old enough to go in. I was way ahead of her in yeoman school. Later, it was a good advertisement for the SPARS that two sisters were there. They took advantage of that and let us both be at the same station, to be stationed together, but I was in travel status, and I went all over and did the speeches and all that. My sister was in yeoman work, she did clerical work in the office, she didn't do the traveling I did.

I could have gone to New Orleans or St. Louis, the headquarters. I picked St. Louis, and from St. Louis, because I was a recruiter and I was a good speaker, I used to speak at all of the Rotary Clubs at the towns I went to.

'I Feel Responsible He's Dead'

I had two speeches. I'd look at the crowd and if it looked low key and I thought it should be higher, I would talk more about the casualties of war. But not always. I had a problem that bothered me for years after I got out of the service. When I was up in North Dakota, I was recruiting 18-year-old boys and a young man came in and I interviewed him. He was so thrilled to go into the service! He did the exam and all that, and then he went down to Omaha to be sworn in; it was all through me that he came in. He asked me to come to Sunday dinner with his family, and after always eating in restaurants and hotels, I was thrilled. So on Sunday afternoon, I met his mother and his father, and they told me how thrilled he was that he was going into the service, that he was on cloud nine.

About six months later, he was shipped out and he was on a ship that was torpedoed, and he was killed. I felt responsible for that, I really did. I thought that if I hadn't recruited him, maybe he wouldn't have gone in the Coast Guard. It troubled me a lot. So the next time that I had to go up there to recruit in North Dakota, I thought, 'I can't visit his parents, they'd probably kick me right off their porch.' But I thought, 'I have to do it,' so I called them up and told them I was in town to recruit again, and they invited me to dinner. I went over and I told them how sorry I was.

They gave me a big picture of him.

I said, 'I can't get him out of my mind, I feel responsible that he's dead.'

They said, 'Don't feel like that. It was the most wonderful thing that happened to him. He was so happy.'

So instead of them saying to me, 'You recruited our son and he's dead,' they had open arms for me. I had such a feeling of gratitude that they did that. But that's the only bad memory I have of the service.

Small Towns

A lot of times, I had to go by myself. When it was very small towns in North and South Dakota, I would go by myself and on the train. I remember one small town that I went to, and I wondered why they had sent me there. When I got off the train, I had my suitcase and all sorts of pamphlets and posters, and I asked where I could get a taxi. The man said to me, 'We don't have any taxis, where are you going?'

I told him the hotel and he told me it was about three blocks down, he told me how to get there. So I walked there, and it was like something out of Norman Rockwell. There were four men sitting around a pot-belly stove and when I came in the door, they all turned around and looked at me.

One man stood up and said, 'You must be the recruiter that's coming,' because the Coast Guard had sent my reservations in. They didn't have to because I was the only one in the hotel. *[Laughs]* He brought me up to the second floor, there was no elevator, and I asked him for my key. He said they didn't normally use keys. I said I had to have a key and he gave me a skeleton key, that's the type of place [it was]. I spent a whole week there by myself. I recruited out of the post office but then when I'd get out of there and go look for a place, there were no restaurants. I went to a bakery and bought food there and went and bought milk. I called up my recruiting office in Omaha and asked if I had to stay a whole week. I didn't interview anyone, and I didn't have any speeches because there was no Rotary or anything like that. *[Laughs]*

The Band Circuit

Another thing, out of St. Louis, they had all the men that were in all the bands, Glenn Miller and all that, they had a group that went all around the country, like they do now. When they came into Omaha, they came into our office and said they were going to be in the area and going to North and South Dakota and they wanted to take a recruiter with them. They figured the band was there, they'd put on this wonderful concert in the town and the recruiter would be there, maybe getting some people into the service.

So they picked me and said that I would go, so I went. I rode in the bus with all of the musicians, and I remember, I was never so cold in my life. We were in Fargo, ND, and it was so cold, unbelievably cold. We put on a concert and as we were coming out of the stage door, there were a lot of grammar school kids there with their autograph books and one little girl came over to me and said, 'Are you anybody?' *[Laughs]*

I told her, 'No, I'm really not.'

I enjoyed that. I traveled with them through Iowa and North and South Dakota while they did their concerts and I sat on the stage. I do not have any musical talent but the man that was in charge of them said they had one number and they were going to use maracas.

He said, 'Helen, when I do this *[motions with hand]*, I want you to [shake] the maracas.'

I said, 'Really, I don't have any rhythm, I'm not going to be able to do it.'

'You'll do it.' So I said okay.

When it came time, he went like that *[makes hand motion]* and I threw the whole band off. I did it all wrong and I was so embarrassed.

I said to him, 'I told you I couldn't do it,' and he never asked me to do it again.

He said, 'Stick to your speeches!'

I said, 'I told you I'm not musically inclined!'

Family

When we closed our recruiting station in Omaha, we had our choice of three places to go: Alaska, Hawaii, or Washington. I picked Washington because in the meantime, my husband had come home, and we were married in Omaha. He was a radioman in the Navy. He was on a sub chaser, the same sub chaser for four years. He was in the South Pacific the whole war, but he was going to be discharged from Guam. I wanted to go to Hawaii but I thought I'd better go to Washington, he'll come home in the meantime. He was out on Guam when I was discharged so I really could have gone to Hawaii, but I wouldn't do that, thinking maybe I'd miss him.

Brother Jack

One other very nice thing happened to my sister and me. I was in Omaha at the recruiting office and a military policeman came in.

He said, 'Where are the Marcil sisters?'

We both looked up and said, 'Here we are.'

He said, 'Your brother, Jack, is on a troop train here in Omaha and we have a delay. He said that his sisters were here, and we want to bring you down to see your brother.'

So they brought us down and there was this troop train, all military, and they walked us down and they let my brother get off the train, but we had to stay right there. But we hadn't seen my brother in almost three years so when he said how that happened, he had been in Germany, and he was just ready to come home, and they needed an electrician first class, and they sent him out to the west coast so that he would go to the South Pacific. He was on an LST (Landing Ship, Tank). He mentioned that his sisters were stationed in Omaha so the officer in charge told him that they were going to be in Omaha for a couple of hours and that he would go and get his sisters. I thought that was so nice that they brought us down and that we got to see Jack. We hadn't seen him in three years. We had to stay right there down by the tracks.

My brother, Jack, the one that I'm talking about, he and I are the only two that are still living. My sister's dead and my brother that was in the Navy, the youngest one, he was a pharmacist mate attached to the Marine Corps, he's dead.

One morning I was called, it was the middle of the night, they said, 'Your husband's calling from Seattle, WA.' I spoke to him and I cried through most of the phone call and he said, 'Helen please, let me talk to you. Stop crying!' *[Laughs]*

He came to Washington. He was discharged from Seattle, Washington, and if your husband was discharged, you automatically could be discharged. All I had to do was produce his discharge and I was discharged, too.

The End of the War

I was in Omaha when [I heard about the death of President Roosevelt], and I was going up the stairs into the USO and two women who were Army recruiters—you knew most of the recruiters of the other services because we would attend different meetings together—were coming down and they told me. That's where I was, in the middle of the flight of stairs on the way to the USO, when I heard he was dead. Another thing that was very emotional for me was seeing General Wainwright; he was in [the Bataan Death March].[25] He came to Washington, and they had a special parade in his honor.

---

[25] *General Wainwright*-Jonathan Wainwright IV (1883-1953) was the Commander of Allied forces in the Philippines at the time Japan surrendered to the United States. In May 1942, with food and firepower running out, he made the difficult decision to surrender the remaining Allied forces on the Philippines. He became the highest-ranking American prisoner of war, and with his men, suffered the rest of the war maltreated in Japanese prison camps.

General of the Army Douglas MacArthur and Lt. Gen. Jonathan Wainwright greet each other in Yokohama, Japan on August 31, 1945. U.S. Department of Defense, public domain

He was in an open car, and we had to line the streets, all of the different military, and as his car passed where you were standing, you would salute him. He looked like he was coming back from the grave, he was so thin, but I always remember that. That was a highlight in my life, too, that I was there when he was in Washington.

I never regretted my service. I was very patriotic; my whole family was patriotic. My mother and father were so proud of the four stars in the window. The people next door to us had three children in the service and they had three stars. When my youngest brother, Ned, the one that was in the Navy, went in and we got the fourth star, my father and mother were thrilled.

*

How did the war change my life? It broadened me, meeting so many different types of people from different parts of the country. I never had any negative other than when that young man was killed. It just enriched my life, going into the service. If I hadn't gone into the service, I would have been living in Troy, working at the FBI in Albany, and that would have been it. But I got to go all over the Middle West, and I enjoyed all the people I met. I treasure the years that I was in the service.

CHAPTER FIFTEEN

The WREN

Born near London, England, Kathleen Davie joined the Women's Royal Naval Service at age 17 during the war.[26] Afterwards, she felt a calling to serve God and started training to become a nurse at St. Bartholomew's Hospital in London. Later, she met a Congregational minister who asked her to go to Michigan with his family to care for his three-year-old twins while he did an exchange pastorate for three months. She quit her job and moved to the United States. She married Ralph, a Baptist minister, in February 1966 and moved to New Rochelle, New York, in 1967. She sat for this interview with

---

[26] *Women's Royal Naval Service* – "The WRNS was reformed as an auxiliary service for women in April of 1939. It started with 3,400 volunteers working as storekeepers, engineers, draftswomen, radar operators, and weather forecasters. Some also worked as paymasters, secretaries, coders, decoders, writers, depth charge fitters, boiler cleaners, life-belt washers, torpedo net repairers, and hostesses of hostels. WRNS plotters helped with the secret planning for the D-Day invasion. Many Wrens served abroad during the war, in the Middle East and the Far East. By the end of the war, there were 72,000 Wrens." Source: Shuler, Megan, Hudson Falls High School World War II Living History Project, 2006, as researched from Guddant, Soujanya, *In Air and Sea (WAAF and WRNS)*, The Living Archive; *The Women's Royal Naval Service (W.R.N.S.) - A Celebration of Their Lives Then and Now*; Simkin, John, *Auxiliary Territorial Service*. Spartacus Educational; Harris, Carol, *Women Under Fire in World War Two*. BBC.

one of my World War II Oral History Project students in 2006 at the age of 79.

Kathleen Mary Davie

I was born on January 28, 1927, in Chiswick, London, England. We were living in a place called Wembley, which is where the soccer cup finals are held, and one of the things that we did when the war broke out was to stand on the landing, halfway up our stairs, and look out over London. At the time that they were announcing the war had started, on September 3, 1939, there was an air raid siren that immediately went off, and of course we were a little scared, and we looked out over London to see if we could see any action, but we couldn't, and it finished shortly after that.[27]

Doodle Bugs

Later, there were bombs around us and we used to hear them. The thing that was the most frightening really was not so much the bombs, because you usually would hear a plane come before you'd hear the bombs, but when they started these unmanned planes called 'doodle bugs.' You'd just hear the engine suddenly start, shut off, and then you'd wait for the crash because there'd be a bomb at the end of that. So, that was a bit unnerving.

---

[27] "The news that Britain was at war was broken by Prime Minister Neville Chamberlain at 11.15am on Sunday 3 September 1939. In a 5-minute broadcast on the Home Service, he announced that as Hitler had failed to respond to British demands to leave Poland, "This country is at war with Germany". Source: 'Chamberlain announces Britain is at war with Germany,3 September 1939.' British Broadcasting Company, www.bbc.com/historyofthebbc/anniversaries/september/war-announced

My father's cousin went into the Women's Naval Service, and I think she went in after I did. I was in the Women's Naval Service. The war broke out when I had just finished the first year of high school, it was county school, and my father decided we had to have an air raid shelter. So, my doll carriage, which was quite a sizeable one—you could have put a small baby in it—became a wheelbarrow for carting rocks and so on for making the air raid shelter, which we did at the bottom of the garden. Most of my high school was during the war. So, we used to sleep in the air raid shelter on a plank about 10 inches wide—amazing, we slept pretty well. And most of our schooling was done either between the classroom or the air raid shelter. We used to take sandwiches to school with us so that if the air raid warnings stayed on too long, we would still have things to eat.

We always had all kinds of snacks. And we had most of our classes in the air raid shelter, a good deal of the time; it just went off at different times, and we would all go to the shelters. We were so used to the routine by the time I got to leaving school, it was just one of the things we did. It was most of my high school.

I left school in '43, so my service was in the fall of '44, after I had spent a year doing secretarial training. My mother thought I would be exempt from military service if I did that, so I volunteered for the WRENs. I don't know that we really thought anything about it until we went to a cousin of my mother's in East Anglia, where part of his farm was annexed to make the aerodrome which was taken over by the American soldiers and fliers. So, I think my mother was a little anti-American, but I married an American, so she had to get over that.

Life in England

I was only in my teens, and I wasn't very politically astute. I don't think that many of my school friends were particularly up on what was happening in politics and national life—we were more concerned with what Germany was doing. Of course, we didn't have television, we had radio, and I remember different things being told to us, that the Germans had bombed this town or that town, and what we had done in retaliation, but of course there were no pictures or anything, like now we have instant pictures of everything. I don't remember being told how many lives were being lost or anything like that. There was also a program that described how the British were putting misleading notices out by radio to Germany, so that they didn't know what damage they had done where. We had code names; I don't remember what they were, but there were code names for different places. I remember we learned a lot more about what had happened, what had been bombed, months afterward.

We had ration books, and a number of coupons had to last for each month and so on, but we didn't have our tea, for instance, we didn't have our tea very strong. We were rationed for meat and eggs, and milk, and sugar and tea, and coffee, mostly the basics. Flour was rationed. My father gave up sugar, and we were always having some things left over that we could hand on to other people who found it more difficult. To this day I only use about one bag of sugar a year, simply because we got used to doing that. And we had coupons for everything, and it lasted for quite a while. We used to eat and sleep, and we used to play games, like board games. 'Old Draughts' we used to play, which is the same as your checkers. We'd do that, but we read a lot, my sister and I were both readers, and we'd sit and read, talk.

We had an incendiary bomb land on our house, but the air raid warden saw it very quickly and put the fire out. We never even lost the house; we lost the front gate; the incendiary bomb destroyed the gate in the front yard. We were very blessed. The Jerries were really smart; they used to have a high-explosive bomb that started things off, and then they put an incendiary bomb just as everybody was trying to rescue people. Our shelter was in the backyard, way at the farthest end of the backyard. My father had built a rockery, a rock garden, with a channel down the middle of it, and the shelter was right behind it, so it sort of looked like it was part of the rock garden.

The Girl Guides

My father was in the Signal Engineer Office for London Transport, and was seventy feet below ground in an office for London Transport. If there was a bomb on the land destroying some tunnels or train tracks or anything like that, he would be the one that would have to stop and repair and make sure that the trains didn't go into the danger area. So, he had an interesting time, but it was mostly nighttime work for him. He used to write to me when I was in Ireland, and the letters used to come like a paper doily with chunks taken out of it, because of the way they used to censor everything. It was just from Britain over to Ireland, and I used to think it was crazy that they censored so much, but they did it so that the enemy would not find out what was happening. Nowadays, I don't know how they do the censoring at all because of the e-mails and everything else. It's just a mind-boggling task.

One of the things that I volunteered to do was to go and do dishwashing at the hospital. We didn't have dishwashers in those days, we didn't even have refrigerators. I was in the… well, you call it Girl Scouts, Girl Guides they call it.

We used to go and work at the hospital and do all sorts of volunteer work during the war. Bicycles were very much used. You either walked or we rode places. I mean we lived in London, but we used to bike ride a lot when we were kids. Nowadays it seems strange that kids can't go out. We went miles, we were gone for a whole day and our parents never even thought anything of it. Now, you're sort of checking in with your parents all the time if you go out. Kids—we were very free and the war changed a lot of that. I'm sure it did here too. Our private lives are more restricted nowadays.

There were times when we felt threatened, and there were times when we were pleased. Everybody was rejoicing at the news of the D-Day landings. Of course, the thing that had been badly fought at was the Dunkirk debacle. A lot of my friends were evacuated to country places, so that was another difficult thing for a lot of people, to have their kids go away. Some even sent them to the States. Every so often I meet someone who came over as an evacuee. They married an American and stayed.

I think the morale was exceptionally good. I really do. I can't remember any specific ways in which people did it, but of course Winston Churchill was the prime minister that really boosted people's morale, I think. We were so busy, involved in the war effort in different ways. People were air raid wardens, and people were volunteering—everybody volunteered in some way to do something that would help the war effort. The threat of Germany invading Britain, I think, increased the amount of activity that people were involved with. We were at war now, but we're not at war on our own land, whereas the bombs were falling all the time.

The WRENs

In the WRENs, I did mostly the typing of signals. Many of them had been decoded by the coding group, and then we would type them and send them to the admiral and various other people. It was quite an interesting job. We did shift work—working all night and then having the day off, and then working the following evening, and then the next morning and so on, and then it would be the same over again. So, we never knew, we had to get used to sleeping at all odd hours.

I enjoyed being in the WRENs, in Northern Ireland; the Irish Sea separated England from Northern Ireland, and when I was first sent there, it was very, very rough. We were hanging on for dear life in order to stay on the boat, and it was a small boat; people talk about the Irish Sea being rough all the time. We weren't allowed to go over the border into southern Ireland because they were not involved in the war, and if we did, we were told we had to take off our uniforms and wear [civilian dress]. In Belfast, the problems that the Catholics and the Protestants had, even then, was quite strong. I remember I was very friendly with a Catholic girl who was my bunkmate, and I took her to the Baptist church with me, and the preacher inveighed against the Catholics in such a way that I said I would never go back to that church. So, although I'm now a Baptist minister, I would never have gone back to that church. And I went to her church with her most of the rest of the time I was in Belfast.

Religious wars were still going on during the war; it's never really been settled, even though there's peace there now. That was very strange in Belfast because the Catholic population in Belfast were against the war and were against the British—they have always been against the British, I guess. So, we were told never to go down certain streets, which was largely a Catholic area in Belfast, in our uniform. But I loved Ireland; it was a beautiful place. If we were in the Castle, which was up on a hill, we used to be able, early in the morning if we'd been there all night, we'd look out toward the sun rising over the hills of Scotland across the Irish Sea, and we were able to see from there. Princess Elizabeth came over when she was, I think, eighteen, which was evidently a year after I had been in Belfast for that time. She came over and launched an aircraft carrier, and I don't remember the name of it, but I was down at the docks and watched her throw the bottle at the hull.

[The Castle] was where we did a lot of decoding of messages. Things were sent from ships in the Irish Sea, and around Britain and Northern Europe. Messages were sent and decoded, so that we knew what the Germans were doing. It was all very hush-hush, but when the things were decoded, they had to go to the various people who could take any action, if there was action needed. It was very interesting. Of course, now it's all done with computers. We had teleprinters, which were ways of sending messages that would be like the forerunner of the computer, I think. Sending messages from England to Northern Ireland, or from ships at sea, would come by teleprinter and telephone messages, too.

I didn't hear about [the atomic bombs and the fallout] until quite a long while afterwards. I was horrified that we would use a nuclear bomb. I think that was something that we never should have done, but we did it. There's a lot of things we regret about the war. There's a lot of things that are still only now coming to light about that war. I saw a program on television just recently that showed some places that nobody knew anything about at the time. I think there were ways in which the lack of communication, such as we know communication nowadays, was probably useful to the war effort, because the enemy couldn't find out an awful lot. Whereas now, I cringe sometimes when I see things on television that I think could help Al Qaeda or the insurgents in Iraq. I just wonder sometimes whether a lot of the things that we talk about, our security things and everything, whether we're being wise in publicizing as much as we do. But that's probably because I was so lacking in information during the war.

War's End

I was in Belfast at the time the war ended, on duty in the Castle of Belfast, which had been taken over by the Navy, and we decided we had to celebrate somehow, so a group of us walked down the hill to the bottom where there was an ice cream shack, and we brought back ice creams to everybody to celebrate. And then there was a big celebration in London. I think it wasn't until the next year, if I remember rightly, and there was a big celebration in London and we went. Some friends of mine that now live in Canada and I went into the city. We were young enough to not mind the crowds then, but it was a fun time. Everybody was just waving flags and just having a good time. It was a bit like Times Square at New Year's. It was very busy. I don't know how we got there—probably by subway.

*

I think, in general, most of us felt bad that civilians were being killed. Factories that were turning out good things for people were also being bombed because we had ideas that they were producing munitions. I think a lot of things happened where we think something is true, and then after we bombed it, we discover—like we did with weapons of mass destruction in Iraq—that it wasn't true. I don't really know anything about covert operations during the war, but I'm sure there were. We had a young man come from France who was British—he'd grown up in France—and his father was killed and he went underground with the French Maquis to fight against the Germans in a sort of underground way. He came and lived in Britain, lived next door to us for quite a while. He and his friends were all sort of underground. The Germans didn't even know about what was going on, and what they were doing, sabotaging a lot of German things.

I went into nursing after the war. The war was over in '45, in May, and then in August, and in '46, in September, I started nursing training, because I felt called to do missionary work. I applied to the hospital and was accepted and did four years at St. Bartholomew's Hospital in London. Part of that time we were still evacuated. Some of the wards had been evacuated during the war and they hadn't moved back to London because there wasn't really any room.

It seemed to me that even after I was doing nursing training, after the war, in some ways things were not greatly changed even though the war was over. We were still rationed for a while.

'Life Has Changed'

I didn't move to the United States until 1960. That was partly because I had gone to India as a missionary, and was there for two years, and I went to India expecting the culture to be very different and the language to be different. When I came to the States in 1960, which was seven years after I had gone to India, I expected the language to be the same, and it isn't by a long way. It's even worse now, I don't understand half the language that you guys talk about. *[Laughs]* And I really suffered a great deal more culture shock coming here than I did going to India, because I was prepared for it there. I had to learn to talk American, and now it's gotten to the point where I can't tell the difference—I don't know whether an expression is a British expression or whether it's an American expression.

So, life has changed a great deal in fifty years; I think the world has changed a great deal. We didn't have television until 1952. My father built his own television set. I watched Wimbledon. That was the first thing I saw. I had just had an appendectomy, and I lay on the couch and watched tennis and Wimbledon on this new TV that my father had built. That made a big difference to our lives. I still prefer the radio. I like to use my imagination when I hear stories and so on, instead of having it all presented to me in picture form.

Anti-War

Student interviewer: How do you feel about bombing against civilians in Germany by the British and Americans?

I just thought it was terrible that we were bombing, and they were bombing us. But what can you do? I've never felt that we should ever retaliate against somebody, because usually what happens in war is you bomb each other to death, and then negotiate afterwards. Well, we could negotiate beforehand. I think we very often want to show our power or something and we are not so willing to go the whole mile with negotiation. I'm very anti-war. Mostly I think because I was in it. I don't know whether if I were seventeen and a half now, whether I would volunteer to go to Iraq. I rather think I would not because I just don't feel that war is the answer. Maybe if I was younger, I'd be... I'm more politically astute now than I was when I was seventeen. There's a lot of difficult questions that we all have to think about.

Kathleen M. Davie passed away on January 1, 2020 at the age of 92.

PART FOUR

WAR BRIDES

"My sister had a falling out with the local vicar because he was against our marriage and saying [bad] things about the American soldiers. My sister was in the church youth group and stood up for me, saying, 'That is my sister, and she is married to an American. I wish you would not talk that way.' And she never went back to the youth center. There were reservations about it. Some had horror stories, other brides. I was lucky. Yes, we were warned about how there were mixed feelings about it."

—War bride, Great Britain

CHAPTER SIXTEEN

The War Brides

Joyce Griffin was raised in England on the family farm with her sister. During the war years she served in the British Women's Army as a physical education instructor and then as a secretary and married US Army Sgt. John J. Griffin, who was serving there at the time. John was injured and returned to the United States for medical treatment; Joyce followed aboard a Red Cross ship with many other war brides several months later. This interview was given at our high school in 2004, when she was eighty-two years old.

Joyce Griffin

I was born October 6, 1922, in Helsby, in the county of Cheshire, England. My father was a British naval officer in World War I. It was very strict during the war. For example, you would have only two ounces of butter, two ounces of margarine, and four ounces of cheese. Everything was rationed like that. It was very difficult. I was lucky because I was raised on a poultry farm. We had all those supplies—even though I did not like any of those products and still don't! At least we could exchange them on the black market.

I eventually came to join the British Army Auxiliary Territorial Service. My parents did not object to it. I had wanted to go into what was called the Women's Land Army where you were assigned to farms and so forth. I had an interest in nature. But my father did not think that was appropriate for a young lady. You had to be checked out by your own doctor rather than a military doctor. So my father beat me to my doctor, they had a discussion, and I was turned down. *[Laughs]* So then I was conscripted into the women's services; at that time it was just the Army that had opened. At age nineteen you were conscripted.[28]

The ATS

In the ATS, we took shorthand and did typing.[29] Originally, I was the secretary to a naval commander. He was getting rather old

---

[28] *Women's Land Army*-"Though not strictly a military auxiliary force, the Women's Land Army greatly aided the war effort. About 80,000 women joined this group, which had also been in existence during the First World War, in order to grow enough food to support their country. The volunteers learned basic skills that they needed at places such as Agricultural Colleges and then went to live in hostels with other WLAs. They worked several farms, traveling between them during the day and returning to their lodgings at night, sometimes as late as 9:30 PM. They had to take over any work that had been left by men who went to war. Sometimes, they worked alongside Italian and German prisoners of war. They were paid very low wages by the government but were sometimes hired by a specific farmer." Source: Shuler, Megan, Hudson Falls High School World War II Living History Project, 2006, as researched from Kemp, Pat. *First-Hand Account of life in the WLA.* The Wartime Memories Project.

[29] *ATS*-"During the 1930s, when it seemed obvious that a war would start, Britain decided to resurrect her World War I era auxiliary services. In September 1938, the Auxiliary Territorial Service was formed; women aged 17 to 43 worked as clerks, cooks, and storekeepers. They received two-thirds the pay of male soldiers and were volunteers. In 1939, 300 ATS women were

and being phased out. His replacement was chosen, and I had to replace a civilian testing the rockets, so I wound up being with a battery of men who were a unit who were experimenting with rockets. It was a highly secret place because rockets were unknown in those days. We would freeze some of the rockets to see how they would fire at low temperatures. And then heat some to see how they would fire in hot countries. We would fire them over the Cardigan Bay, part of the Irish Channel. I was also the physical education instructor. There were different phases. I don't know, there was a unit of ATS girls, but everyone was secret from the others. Soldiers were in each place. It was in South Wales and quite fun. I used to be able to go up onto the lookout area on the roof of the building with the captain of the unit. We would have stopwatches and time the explosion of the rockets in the air and as they splashed into the sea. Then I would have to compile the two results. Sometimes we had visiting officers from other countries. I was there for three years; we could not talk about it. But some of my most memorable experiences were, number one, I met my husband. He was with an American company stationed not too many miles from where we were. They were sort of experimenting with the same ideas about rockets and tanks.

---

with the British Expeditionary Force in France working on anti-aircraft crews. They were not officially allowed to fire the guns but worked on searchlight crews instead. Some of these women who had been serving as telephone operators were with the last people to be evacuated from Dunkirk on May 26, 1940. In July 1941, the ATS finally earned military status; by September of the same year, it boasted 65,000 women serving as orderlies, postal workers, drivers, and ammunition inspectors in addition to their previous employment. By 1945, 190,000 women worked in increasingly demanding jobs, such as radar operators, military police, and gun crews." Source: Shuler, Megan, Hudson Falls High School World War II Living History Project, 2006, as researched from Simkin, John, *Auxiliary Territorial Service*. Spartacus Educational, and Harris, Carol, *Women Under Fire in World War Two*. BBC.

Bombings

When the bombing of London occurred, I was mostly in South Wales. The bombing had started before I was in the Army; my mother, my sister, and I used to sleep under the stairs every night. We could hear the hum of the German planes coming. They had a very distinctive sound. I don't know how my poor mother ever slept since there was not very much room with the three of us there. My father worked nights then. But we survived. We did not have too many bombs around us, [but the ones that fell] did kill some cows and made a few craters in the ground. It was scary, though, because you would get the impression your name could be on that bomb coming down. I was in Liverpool during a bad bombing raid. We were two stories underground. We were fine, but when we came out in the morning the stores had been bombed, the goods were all over the street, and you heard people calling out that had been buried under the rubble. It was a horrible experience.

[The bombing of Pearl Harbor in Hawaii was not a big deal to the British people], I don't really think so. Just like the bombing of London did not mean much to the American people because it was so far away. Pearl Harbor was the same story. We were still going through the war ourselves in England. We talked of invasions and so forth while we were battling over there; we had landed on the beaches. That is what we were more interested in at the time, I guess.

It was alarming because we did not know if we were going to be overrun at any time. The bombs kept falling. We had the ack-ack [anti-aircraft] guns going off all the time, shooting at the German planes. We witnessed a few [Royal Air Force] Spitfire fights in the sky. Those were marvelous machines. I can't say it was a good feeling, we were at war, and it was kind of scary at times.

'A Life's Souvenir'

The Americans did not come until 1942, I think. I met John in 1943. It's a funny story about how I met him. His unit was putting on a little show for the local people and I was invited. I didn't really get to know him at that time but his part in it was up on the stage with a top hat and cane. He sang 'Who Threw the Overalls in Mrs. Murphy's Chowder?' *[Laughs]* Then I met him through some friends. There was a service person's canteen there in the town of Cardigan. We started going out and then became engaged before he went back to Europe. He came over on marriage leave some months later, sometime in February. Of course, he could not get into the establishment; when I got up there, I was shocked to see him. He was here on marriage leave and I was not a bit prepared! My poor mother had a hard time gathering up stuff. She only had the C-rations, some food and clothing. But she managed to beg and borrow and maybe steal, I don't know. It was enough to have a wedding. Of course, his parents did not approve and neither did mine. They thought we should wait until the end of the war. But you never know what is going to happen in a war. They wrote and sent him packages. When John was leaving the States for Europe his father had told him, 'Don't be bringing home any of those limies!' And of course, he did, he called me his 'life's souvenir'.

My sister had a falling out with the local vicar because he was against our marriage and saying [bad] things about the American soldiers. My sister was in the church youth group and stood up for me, saying, 'That is my sister and she is married to an American. I wish you would not talk that way.' And she never went back to the youth center. There were reservations about it. Some had horror stories, other brides. I was lucky. Yes, we were warned about how there were mixed feelings about it.

John was sent back by an Army hospital because he had developed an allergy while he was in Belgium. They did not know what it was and shipped him to an Army hospital in Paris where he was stationed. It all turned out to be related to a stray dog that John had taken in, because he had asthma. He was assigned to a group that was called French Quislings, collaborators that had Nazi leanings. They put him to work with some of the French Quislings repairing the hospital equipment. That is where he got his X-ray burns. Of course, John did not speak French, they did not speak English, and they worked on an X-ray machine. There were some cross-signals, so he did not know the power was on as he was checking the machine. He leaned on it with his knee and his hand and got X-ray burns. He was in a hospital for over a year. It was pretty bad. They shipped him back to the United States for skin grafting. He was back here when the war ended; John was in a group that released some prisoners from a concentration camp. I don't recall which one. So he was finally shipped back to an Army hospital in the United States for treatment, which lasted a year. He came back in November of 1945. I came here to the States in April 1946.

*

I was on a Red Cross ship full of brides and babies of American soldiers, the *Willard H. Holbrook*, a lot of Red Cross nurses and mothers with babies and infants. It was a very rough crossing. We who were able to keep standing would crawl in and the smell of that nursery in the mornings was awful because so many babies were seasick. John met me in New York on crutches.

[Being a 'war bride'] was scary because of the reports we were getting that the American people were against us. They said we were taking up spaces that their soldiers coming home should have. They were told the soldiers were sleeping on park benches because of us. So it was not too great in New York. I said I wanted to get out of here, I don't like this place. We went back to Connecticut where he was from the next day.

VE Day

I was still in the Army when the end of the war was announced. Still stationed at the same place. I was in the South Wales Regiment. I had a Welsh Dragon as our insignia. I wore crossed swords, which indicated I was a Physical Education instructor. I had kept that patch for some time but can't find it now.

On VE Day, we had a great time. It was such a glorious moment meaning the war was over. There was dancing in the street and overall mayhem. I think Churchill announced it on the radio, I guess we were all called to gather around a radio so we could hear his speech. He was such a great man and really held the country together. It was wonderful just to hear his voice; he kept everyone's spirits up. Just to hear his voice was uplifting. We thought Field Marshal Montgomery was pretty great, too. We didn't know much about him really, but we thought he was a savior in many ways along with Winston. But I remember that several months later, there was still a lot of rationing. We went to a restaurant and one of the main meals was still baked beans or sardines on toast. *[Laughs]* Times were still hard, however, and the long ration cues remained; I stood in those lines too. You would hear about a store that got a shipment of cigarettes. They were little five-in-a-pack sizes. You stood in line for hours trying to get five cigarettes. And it is such a horrible habit! I'm glad I don't do it anymore.

[How do I feel about the German people today?] Oh gosh, that was then and this is now. I have no bad feelings about the Germans; it wasn't the German people, it was the Nazism that we were against, but it still disturbs me that we did not know [that the Holocaust] was going on. It was a horror.

Joyce Griffin passed away on March 20, 2017 at the age of 94.

One of four children, Joan Hoffman was born in Canada in 1923. At the age of six, her father had saved up enough money to send Joan, her mother, and her three siblings to Cambridge, England to visit relatives for six months, but just when the Hoffman family was preparing to head back to Canada, a cable was sent from their father which stated to stay in England, and that he was going to join them in there, managing a horse riding school where she would grow up and meet the American GIs who came to ride in their off duty hours. She eventually wound up marrying one of them and emigrated to the United States after the war.

Joan Hoffman

I was born in Canada in 1923. My mother and father went to Canada after the First World War, and we were there for about six years, and there were four of us born there. And then my father sent Mommy and we four kids home to England for six months to meet our relatives, because he was one of thirteen children and Mother was one of nine. And we were getting ready to come back to Canada, having visited everybody, when Mother got a cable from Dad saying, 'Stay there, I'm coming home!' And you know in those days, children never asked any questions of parents. And the only thing we could think of was, Dad never had a decent job in Canada. He worked in a flour mill and a mine. And I think he borrowed the money to send us there but stayed and worked there until he got the money and paid for it and then came back to England. So, we were in England from then on.

The Riding School

We were fortunate because when we first went over there, my father got a job managing a riding school. So, we had horses. Basically, our lives revolved around the horses. The stable yard was in the middle of Cambridge, which was a big university town. We went to school, but you had to walk to school, and it had to be a good mile or two from the house. We walked and we rode bicycles. We never had a car, but we had horses. And kids... I never knew it until after I was talking to some girls that I graduated with. We went to Perse High School for girls. And they used to be talking and saying, 'Let's go for a swim,' because the river Cam went all the way around Cambridge. And they had two or three places which were made into bathing steps so that you could go swimming there. And I used to feel, 'Oh I wish I could go with them.' But I knew I had to go home because my father needed me. We worked in the yard. I mean we had grooms there sometimes. We had the horses' livery there. But I mean, the horses had to be fed every day and the stables mucked out and groomed. So, we were always busy with the horses. But the other girls, I heard, were so jealous. They used to think, 'You can go riding anytime you like.' We used to have to go riding whether we wanted to or not, because you know, it was just one of the things. That was even after I left school and got a job, he still would sometimes call me early in the morning, because we had a field that was two miles from the house. We used to turn out a couple of the horses there if they had been working very hard, let them have a day or two in the field. They could just relax. But when you wanted them again, he'd sometimes call me at 4:30 or 5 in the morning and say, 'I want you to get up and go fetch the two horses.' So, I'd walk the two miles and get the horses and come back and have breakfast and give the horses to him. And I get changed and then go to school.

Leading the Horses

But I have to tell you, it was war time and just up the road from our field, there was a small factory that was making some small article that was necessary for the war. And every morning as I was coming home, I would see these... oh, many, many dozens and dozens of elderly men, older men riding their bicycles to go to the little factory further up. And I just saw them and used to say hello. But one time I was starting to lead the two horses, and I couldn't get on them, and so I was walking them home and one of the men riding his bicycle said, 'Would you like a leg up?' So, I said, 'Oh, thank you.' So, he got off his bicycle and put his bicycle down and put his lunchbox down and gave me a leg up. So, I didn't have to walk home. I saw them every day. They didn't know who I was, and I certainly didn't know who they were, but it was just nice. And you won't believe that fifteen years ago, the last time I went back to England to stay with my sister, I was told she had a group of ladies with her. And I was talking to one of the ladies and she said to me, 'Do you still live in Cambridge?'

I said, 'No. I married a Yank. And I've just come from the States to visit my sister.'

So, I said, 'Do you live in Cambridge?'

She said, 'No, we live on Madingley Road. But you would know that because that's a road that goes outside of Cambridge.'

I said, 'I know Madingley Road because we used to have a field up there. And my father used to send me up there to get horses when he needed them.'

She said, 'Would you believe that when we were living there years ago, we'd be in bed and it would be 5:30, maybe quarter to six, and we'd hear clip clop, clip clop, clip clop.' And she said, 'I couldn't understand what that was, so I'd get up and move the curtain and look outside.'

And she said, 'There'd be a young girl and a young boy riding horses and they would be singing. And they would look and if they saw me, they would wave at me.'

I said, 'Well, that was me and my brother. Because my brother said if we're awake, everybody should be awake. So, we sang loudly.'

But what are the chances of meeting a lady? I mean I've been here sixty-three years, so I've been gone from them for forty-five years to meet someone who actually knew or saw us.

I lived in Cambridge. And Cambridge is in East Anglia, which is a flat part of the country, and there were airfields around and a couple of them were taken by the GIs, taken over by the Americans when they came. There wasn't too much in the way of entertainment around. So, they went and bring the GIs in; well, any of the people, servicemen, would be brought into Cambridge in trucks if they had a forty-eight-hour pass. And the largest hotel there was taken over by the Red Cross. I was four when we went to England. I finished school when I was seventeen, and worked for a couple of years. And then got involved with one of those GIs. To tell you the truth, we as kids or even growing up, we never knew much about what was going on. Of course, everything was rationed, the normal people—I don't mean lords and ladies, those who had plenty of money. But those who had a car had to just leave them or get rid of them because the gas was rationed, and people couldn't afford it. We rode bicycles. When my youngest brother was born, they had seats that you sit behind them and babies that could sit up. Mother did all of the shopping with a basket in front of the bicycle, very different from the living you notice now over here too, you know. But it was good, it was good. And my sister went into the Navy, the WRENs, the women's Navy. My brother, just younger than me, was in the tank corps. And he was stationed in Italy, and he married an Italian girl and took her home. They said our family was like the League of Nations, but it was fun. It was very good.

My mother was a volunteer in the large hotel that was given to the Red Cross, and it was GIs that stayed there. And she was in charge of the breakfast on Sundays. And she worked with a friend of hers, who had a small restaurant.

Air Raids

My father, of course, had the riding school. But during the war, he joined the [Home Guard], they used to have places where people would go and sit, and anytime a plane came over, they would report it to headquarters. And he did that during the night. He would work during the night. When the sirens went off for a bomb attack coming, wherever the planes were coming from, there were several of these places. And the one that he worked with was like in the cellar of the Chamber of Commerce. It was a huge room. And they had a huge table with a map of the whole of England. They had to say, 'Well, there's a bomb coming over and it's going northwest and it's going...' so that they knew where they were, you know. We had a siren going off almost anytime, I would say almost every day. But there weren't many bombs dropped on Cambridge because we were surrounded by airfields. And of course, anti-aircraft groups around the airfields were taking care of them. And I only know of one person who was killed by a bomber, and it was a teacher who taught second grade. She and her mother lived one block from the school. And there was one night where we had air raids and there were a couple of bombs dropped, and one bomb dropped right on her house and the two of them were killed. I mean, there were one or two others but really no real numbers from Cambridge. Although, as I say, theoretically, when we had an air raid siren, we were meant to go downstairs. A lot of people had air raid shelters done in their yard. They'd dig a little and then put corrugated metal roofs. And they'd have like bunks in there. The government also supplied tables made out of metal that you put underneath your table. If you had a square table and if there was an air raid and you had children and you didn't have anywhere to go outside, you would get under there. Because that would be like steel protection. That's what we did. An air raid shelter, especially in London, of course, they had lots of them down there. But they were underground places. And in London everybody went to the train stations, and they put up bunks in there. And people would sleep in there because you were underground. London was a very busy place. But they say that during the war, I think the trains stopped running. Whole families used to go down there and sit there with the children in the bunk and stay overnight. We knew that they were building those things. There were big air raids in some parts of the towns. As I say, they dug them out. Anybody could go there. If you lived there, you'd go. But we didn't have anyone. Well, Father was working. He wasn't there, and Mother was busy. We just stayed in bed. We really didn't have many bombs dropping in Cambridge.

The GIs in England

There was plenty of room for the GIs to stay. There wasn't too much to do. There were only two movie houses, and one restaurant had a dance every Saturday. And then, of course, they could go on the River Cam and punt. No boats were allowed with motors on, just, you know, a canoe or something like that. So, they used to walk through town and our stable yard was in town. And they'd come to the stable yard. There were horses for hire and my father would greet them, 'Hello, can I help you?'

'We want to take a ride.' And my father had one question he asked. No matter who it was, if it was somebody he didn't know, he would say, 'Have you ever been on a horse before?' Because we had some horses that needed to have a rider on it. And there was one guy that came in, sometimes six or seven or eight, but some member of the family had to take them out because they didn't know how to get out of the town of Cambridge to get out into the countryside. So, we literally met up with hundreds of different GIs. It was a very interesting time in our lives, you know, but it was good.

War Bride

Well, there were two GIs that came to ride one day. My father greeted them and said to them his usual thing. And so, he said, 'Have you ever been on a horse before?' And one of the GIs said, 'Sure, I have.' He said, 'I came from Iowa. I've had horses.' So, my father said, 'Okay, fine. My daughter will take you out.' My sister took them out for a ride. And we used to ride.

There were several different places that had horses for hire, but most people used to rent them out for an hour and pay by the hour. You want a ride, it'll cost you so much an hour. But my father wouldn't do that because what we found out is if anybody paid seven and six to ride for an hour, they'd go as far as they could in that hour, and then so they wouldn't have to pay extra if it took them longer to get back, they'd turn around and race the horses back so that they got back within the hour, depending how much trotting and cantering they did. My sister took those out and the next week they came again, and she took them out again. And a third week they came, and she took them out. They had finished riding and said hello and goodbye and they'd gone back to the field.

My father came to me and said, 'Look, if those two GIs want to ride again, you make an appointment and you take them out. And for heaven's sake, teach that one to ride. He's ridden my horse three times. He still looks like a sack of potatoes tied in the middle, and I won't let him ride my horse again.' He said, 'It's a disgrace to my yard; you take them out and teach him to ride.' So, the next time they wanted to ride, I took them out. The streets in the older part of Cambridge were very narrow. You couldn't have horses. So, in town you rode in twos. When my sister took them out, she rode and had the one guy from Iowa ride with her, and the other guy just rode behind. Well, when I took them out, I had him riding beside me. I didn't know at the time, but he came from Jersey City. He had never seen a mounted horse except when the police patrolled the parks. Apparently, I was very strict with him, and I taught him to ride. They never came to ride again. [*Laughs*] But he started dating me, and I eventually married him. So, he taught me to drive his car when I'd been over here six years. And that was the hardest decision he ever had to make, to teach a woman to drive his most precious possession, his car, even though, apparently, I taught him to ride. [*Laughs*]

We met literally hundreds of [GIs]. They were very nice. One man came and he was a very nice guy. I took him out riding. And I was asking him where he was stationed. Anyhow, when I came in that night, I said, 'I had one of your GIs riding today. And I took him out, and we had a nice ride.' Two days later, he came to me and said, 'I was talking to one of the GIs when we were having dinner,' or something and he said, he told me, 'You know, two days ago, I went into Cambridge, and I went for a ride. And I had a wonderful time. It was a very nice girl that took me. And I'm going back there again.' So, my husband said, 'Was the girl a blonde or a brunette?' He said, 'Oh, the girl was a blonde.' My husband said, 'The blonde is my wife.'

He said, 'Oh! I didn't know that.' He never came back again. There was nothing wrong. There's nothing much you can do when you're both on horses, you know what I mean. We laughed at those things. We met many, many lovely guys. We had a good time.

London

In 1944, I was asked to go to London. The firm that I worked for was Pye Radios that was outside of Cambridge. And before the war they made radios for everything, cars. And they were just beginning to make the TVs, but they hadn't started selling them yet. But then they started making radios for tanks or submarines or airplanes. They were doing all war work. And I worked there for some time. And then they said they had an office in London and they said they really needed someone to go and work in the office because the girls that worked there had evacuated. During the war they evacuated many families from the big towns and sent them to the smaller cities and found houses, families who would take them. Well, we had a house with plenty of room. But when I was asked if I wanted to go, I said yes. So, I went up to London and got accommodations right in the place near where I was going to work. There was a youth hostel for young girls who were going to live in London for the first time. And you could only stay there for two years because they figured if you'd be in London, and had a job and worked for two years, you could find somewhere else to live. But I didn't know how long I was going to be there. So, I got a job there. My bedroom was on the third floor.

Every time there was an air raid warning, you had to go down to their cellar. And then when the all-clear went, you'd go back to bed. Well, sometimes you'd do that three times a night. Because as the waves of bombers came over, another siren would go off. But then another batch would come. I got tired. I said, 'This is ridiculous getting up two or three times a night and having to go back upstairs.' So, they had a small air raid shelter in their yard, and it had six bunks in there. I said to this girl, 'I'm going to sleep down there.' So, instead of going upstairs to our bedrooms, we slept there. We could hear the siren, and we could hear the bombs go. But that was the beginning of what they called the 'buzz bombs'; the first bombs at this time had motors on them. After the air raid siren would go, you'd often here this 'putt, putt, putt.' And you knew that it was a bomb coming over. But all of a sudden, it would stop, and then it fell.

I was only there for six months, because, well, I was going to get married. So, I went home and got married. I wanted to go back to the company I was in, and I told them, I said, 'I might have to leave without very much notice.'

They said, 'Oh well, we don't want you here then.' So, I had no job. My husband was in the Eighth Air Force. He wasn't a flyer, he was a secretary. So he got all of the letters and information that came in first. He came in one day and said, 'We just got a notice today that at the end of the war, the Eighth Air Force is going to be sent to Germany in the Army of Occupation.'

He said, 'If I'm in Germany in the Army of Occupation and I get leave, they won't give me leave to go from Germany to England to see you. They'll give me leave to go from Germany to the States where I'm from.'

So, he said, 'The best thing to do is to get you there now.'

So, we went up to the embassy. I had my paperwork and because I had a Canadian birth certificate, I would be returning to the continent of my birth. And they issued me a non-cultural visa. Now for the thousands of other girls that had to wait until the end of the war, I don't know. But they said, 'Go home and pack your clothes, pack whatever you want to take with you, and be ready to leave in twenty-four hours' notice.'

So, we went there to Cambridge, and I said to my mother, 'I've got to pack everything because I have to be ready to leave in twenty-four hours' notice.'

She said, 'All right then, pack.' So, two days later, I hadn't heard anything. And I said to my mother, 'Would you wash the clothes that I'm wearing, because I have to be ready to leave and I would like to take them with me.'

Well, we didn't have a washing machine or anything. So, Mother washed them by hand, you know. And two or three days later, I said, 'Would you wash these?'

After doing that for two weeks, she said to me, 'Look, I am not going to spend the rest of my life washing your clothes. If you get the notice to go, and you've got dirty clothes, either wear them dirty or pack them dirty or leave them here and I'll take care of them. They didn't send me any notice until six months later! So, it was just as well that she hadn't been washing all that time.

I just sort of went about my business. Because the company that I had worked for in London, 'If you're going to leave without giving us two weeks' notice, no, we don't want you.' So, I worked with my father. When the GIs came to ride, it had been mostly my sister who would take them out. When I was there, I worked with my father. My husband was very fortunate. He used to get a pass to come into Cambridge every night. So, after he'd finish his work in the office, he'd get on his bicycle and start riding the fourteen miles to Cambridge. And I would've been taking GIs or whoever else went riding. So, if I finished the night, I'd get on my bike and go and meet him. And then he'd ride and stay overnight and get up at four or five in the morning, and I'd give him breakfast. And then, I would ride my bicycle with him back, but I wasn't allowed on the base, because I was just a civilian. So, he'd say goodbye to me and he'd go on and he was there. And then I'd turn around and ride the fourteen miles back by myself. But that's what you did.

'She'll Never Leave Me'

We were called by the embassy in London and told on a Saturday. They sent a cable; because I was out riding with four or five

GIs, and my youngest brother knew where we went riding, he came on his bicycle, 'Joan, you got a cable! You gotta go! You gotta go!'

That was Saturday afternoon. The cable said: 'Report to the embassy in London at nine o'clock on Monday morning, being prepared to pay your passage and sail.' So, I packed up and everything, and we went up to London. My husband of course couldn't go. They sent me by train from London to Southampton, which is in the south of England, because that's where the boat was. We got on board, but my husband wasn't allowed to come to the boat with me. So, he went back to Cambridge to say to my mother and father, 'I've sent her on her way.'

Now they both liked him, but he said to me afterwards in a letter, 'It was a little chilly about your father.' Because somebody had once said to him, 'Cap, what are you going to do when your daughter leaves you?'

He said, 'What do you mean when my daughter leaves me?'

He said, 'Oh, I'm sorry. I heard she'd married a Yank.'

He said, 'She did marry a Yank.'

And he said, 'Oh, well I presumed that he would be going to the States.'

He said, 'She married a Yank, but she'll never leave me.' So, when the time actually came, see, it was a little bit of a shock to him.

Singing With the Wounded GIs

We got on board ship, and they pulled the boat from Southampton and on the southern part of England, the southern coast there's the Isle of Wight. And we pulled in and put down our anchor. And we sat on that boat for five days before we moved. And when I was complaining to somebody, they said they were assembling the convoy. It was still wartime, and we came in a convoy. And although our ship was a small ship, it was the *John Ericsson*, we were the largest ship in the convoy, but a convoy could only go the speed of the smaller ships. And occasionally we'd see the destroyers or whoever was guiding us or guarding us when we were coming over, but it took us twenty-three days to get here. And there were no seats on the boat, you know on the deck, very strict. I was in a cabin with five other girls. It was three bunks. [*Points three up high, right/left*]. I got very friendly with one girl. So as I say, we used to walk around the deck. There was nowhere to sit down, but we used to sit on the deck underneath our porthole. And I always take my knitting wherever I go. I would sit there, and I knitted myself a sweater while we were onboard. My girlfriend sitting beside me said, 'Wish I'd thought of bringing my knitting.' She said, 'You have anything I could do?'

I said, 'Yes, I've got more pins, and I've got plenty of yarn. I'm making myself a sweater.'

She made the sleeves for me. We sat there and talked. We got to know each other well. But again, when we had to ride, whether we wanted to or not, we used to sing, my family, my brothers, and I. So I said, 'Let's sing a song.' We'd sing, and we'd be sitting there and there were wounded GIs on board. There were ninety brides, and three of them had babies with them. But there were many, many GIs who were bedridden. We never, ever saw them. They were in the cabins below deck. There were quite a few and they were wounded. One man had lost one arm, but they were walking around and that. They had nowhere to sit down either. So they'd come around and stand there; they'd eventually sit on the ground and we ended up having about thirty or forty of them every day. We'd sit under our porthole, and they'd sit down. And we'd sing, and they'd sing with us, and we taught them a couple of English songs, they taught us a couple of American songs, not the kind you'd sing in church or anything. We had fun and it made it interesting, because they would talk to us, and we would talk to them. I must say that when we were on board, there was one GI that almost lost his arm. He didn't want them to amputate it. He said to me, 'Since I've been in the service and have been abroad, my wife gave birth to our first baby. Could you make something with your knitting?' So, I made them a pair of baby booties, so he could take it. The only thing I knew about him is that he came from Scarsdale. I don't know his name or anything else.

The New York Skyline

In spite of the fact it was twenty-three days, it was March. I got on board ship March the first, and March the twenty-third, we pulled into the New York harbor. And it was raining, and it was foggy, and it was cold. And all of the GIs said, 'You wait until you see the New York skyline. It's the most beautiful skyline in the whole world. Well, we really didn't care about the skyline. It was freezing. It was snowing. It was miserable. I said to the girls, 'I wonder if they had said to us girls, 'Now, if you want to, you can go right around and go back home.'

I said, 'I wonder how many would go.' The thing is, my husband had said, 'You'll probably be put off at Ellis Island.' His sister had written and had told him that she would like me to go and live with her, because I had nobody over here. I knew nobody.

When she had written to the authorities, she said that she would provide a home for me. She had to do that, and she had to give them an estimate of her income, so that they'd know that she could afford to keep me and not throw me out of the house. The Red Cross in New York met the boat and took all the brides to the Red Cross headquarters and interviewed each one of us separately. When it was my turn, they said, 'Where are you going?'

I said, 'Wood-Ridge, New Jersey.'

'Have you made any plans to get there or is somebody going to meet you? How are you expecting to get there?'

I said, 'Well, my husband told me to go to the bus department and get a bus to Journal Square and then Journal Square change and get a bus that would go to Wood-Ridge, which was about twelve miles from Journal Square.'

She said, 'Well, you know exactly where you're going.'

I said, 'I'm going to live with my sister-in-law and her family. And I have a telephone number. And if we call her and if they're home, they'll come and meet us.'

So, the Red Cross lady called the number and said who she was, and they said, 'Oh, yes. We'll be there in about a half an hour.' They let me say hello to her on the telephone. And I waited. Now, a lot of the girls had to go much further, if they were going to California or anywhere else, I mean, they had to go by bus or by train. But it was very easy for me. They came to meet me and took me home. They even brought my mother-in-law.

She lived in Jersey City. So, on their way, they stopped and picked her up. And they had a five-year-old girl, daughter with them. And they picked her up and took me to Wood-Ridge. I was there. It was very, very lovely. They were very, very kind. Of course, I was new, and they showed me around. I can remember the first day when I got there.

'Life in America Was Very Different'

She showed me the house and where the bathroom was and she said, 'Anytime, all you want, go to the bathroom, we have showers and everything.' Well, we didn't have showers in England. We had bathrooms but just with a bath, you know. I think it was the next day. I thought, I'd like to take a bath. But she had said to have a shower. And I thought, well that would be good. So, I walked into the bathroom. She had the most beautiful shower curtain. It was... I've never seen any since that was so pretty. When I got there, I thought, 'Oh, my goodness. I don't want to get this wet.' So, I put it outside the bath and took a shower. Well, I didn't know all of the water was going outside the room. I mopped it up very quickly. It was silly things like that I didn't know, that I never met up with before.

She was very good to me. I actually got a job. Their neighbor was the manager of the telephone company, and I had always wanted to be a telephone operator. And she called me and asked me if I'd like a job and I had nothing to do. I used to help my sister-in-law, and I used to walk her little girl to school every morning, but nothing else really. After the one thing I made such a mess of, I don't think she really wanted me to help them out much. When the chief operator called me, she spoke to me for quite a long time. And then she said, 'Would you like to become a telephone operator? Do you have any questions?'

I said, 'The only thing is, I wonder if they would understand me.' Because this was before the dial. Everything had to be done by voice.

So, she said, 'I'm enjoying this conversation very much.' So anyway, she said, 'Report.'

So, for the first two weeks, they had one supervisor with two students. And for that first two weeks, the first day they made us get acquainted with the board where they had all of these lights, and if any person picked up the telephone, a light would come on. So, you'd pick up this and plug in that light and say, 'Number, please.' And then she'd tell you a number and you pick up the wire. She was in the back one and I was on this one and put in the number. I enjoyed that very much. It was good.

When my husband came home six months later, his mother lived in Jersey City and that's where he lived with her when he came into the Army. So, of course we were going there. So, we moved to Jersey City.

You had to learn how to pronounce that so everybody could understand me because that's how everybody else was saying it. I transferred to the telephone company office in Journal Square. I used to work from five in the evening until eleven o'clock at night, or six to twelve, because you got the same wage and even got a night differential that paid you a little more money, because the young girls didn't want to work at night. They wanted to be able to go on dates, but I couldn't go out on any date. But anyhow, the first day that I went there was a Sunday. They put me between two older operators. They knew I was new to the job. But it worked out. [My life in America] was very, very different.

PART FIVE

THE DISPLACED

"There was an expectancy of a better life; from what we read and heard, we knew that if we were to come to a normal life again, it would be in the United States. It would take time, it would take hard work, but eventually we will be normal living people. That is why I am against war, with every fiber of my body. Because I know what it does to civilian people, primarily mothers with young children... Who is going to take care of them? Nobody cared."

—Child Refugee, World War II

CHAPTER SEVENTEEN

The Refugee

As the world went about its business in the late 1930s, the clouds of war gathered as the policy of appeasement began to bear its terrible fruit. German troops had swallowed all of Czechoslovakia by March 1939; Hitler continued to demand the area known as the Polish Corridor and the outlet to the Baltic Sea at the city of Danzig, which had been lost after World War I. Secretly, he directed his foreign minister to enter into clandestine negotiations with the Soviet Union. Strange fellows bedded down in a 10-year pact of non-aggression, and the secret protocol called for the division of Poland between the Germans and the Soviets, the fascists and the communists. On September 1, 1939, Hitler rolled the dice once more as Germany invaded Poland on false pretenses of Polish aggression. Halina Roman and her family were victims of this division.

Halina was just ten years old, one of six children in her family, five girls and one boy. Halina's grandmother lived with her family and helped take care of all of the children. She attended school in what was the equivalent of present-day grade schools, but by the time Halina was ten years old, in June of 1940 the Russian secret police (NKVD) raided her hometown of Kuligi in northeast Poland.

Halina's mother, grandmother, sisters, and brother were evacuated by the Russians to Siberia. After several months of labor in Siberia, Halina and her group of family members embarked on a ten-year odyssey through Uzbekistan, Persia, India, East Africa, finally eventually settling in the United States. However, these travels took their toll on the family, and she lost four of her sisters and her grandmother.

After the long journey full of hunger, fear, and uncertainty, Halina made it to the United States for new opportunities and freedom in February 1951. This interview was recorded by her grandson in 2007, one of my students in the oral history project, at her home in Erie, Pennsylvania, when she was seventy-eight years old.

Halina Roman

I was born on August 28, 1929, in Kuligi, Poland. Kuligi was sort of close to the Russian border. My family consisted of my parents, my grandmother, and my five siblings. I was the oldest. My father was a farmer and we had everything on the farm, all of the animals you could imagine; in Poland at that time the farmers had to be self-sustaining. My father had seasonal help to help him around the place. I remember it was a nice place, we had lots of space. We had gardens, pastures, a river close by, and a couple row boats that you could go fishing in. On top of that my father had a fishery pond where we could just play around. We had a beautiful childhood along with lots of vegetables and food, which was why the beginning was very healthy for us. Then in 1939 when I was just turning ten, the war broke out and everything changed.

Between 1939 and the German invasion of the USSR in 1941, Soviet authorities deported well over a million Poles to the Soviet Union. The exact number unknown; many thousands were murdered in the Katyn

Forest and elsewhere. According to the United State Holocaust Memorial Museum, those "branded as 'socially dangerous' and as 'anti-Soviet elements' were forcibly removed from their homes and deported in cattle cars to labor camps in Siberia and Kazakhstan. These civilians included civil servants, local government officials, judges, members of the police force, forest workers, settlers, small farmers, tradesmen, refugees from western Poland, children from summer camps and orphanages, family members of anyone previously arrested, and family members of anyone who escaped abroad or went missing; in most of the camps, all prisoners were expected to work regardless of age or physical condition. Children were in charge of transporting water, gathering firewood, and collecting food. The grueling work and harsh weather often made conditions in the camps unbearable. With little food or medical care, prisoners died every day in large numbers."[14]

Arrest

My father was called into the office in Kuligi on official business because he was the leader of the hamlet of Kuligi. My mother never knew what happened to him, despite the war, and she never did see him again. As much as my mother and I tried, we never found out what happened to my father. Later on, however, we found out that my father was lost in a concentration camp. As for us, my mother, grandmother, and all the rest of the children, I don't know if you would call it arrested, but the NKVD came at six in the morning and pounded on the doors and gave us two hours to pack. This happened in June of 1940. My mother, being as nervous and devastated as she was, packed what she thought was easy to take and could be of value to trade.

Siberia

We were taken to the nearest railroad station, put into cargo cars, and taken to Siberia. The whole trip by train took three weeks, not counting the stoppages. In Siberia we came to a place called Salekhard, which to this day I remember, and it is still on the map. I think today's maps have a lot of names changed. They gave us a house that was abandoned and that's where we lived. While there, my mother became friends with a lady working in an office. By this time it was September or October of 1941. Through my mother's friend, she found out that an agreement had been signed between the Russian and Polish governments. It said that all the Polish people taken to Siberia be relinquished, but they had to travel to South of Russia. My mother got permission to travel, but other than that it was unsupervised and up to my mother how she got to South of Russia, to Kazakhstan. She sometimes had to leave the train to get food for us, which was sometimes not all that easy. In that period of time, I remember suffering from hunger, cold, and needless to say, fear. Fear of strange places and strange people, not to talk about the discomforts. When I watched my mom, I just felt so sorry for her.

I remember my brother Al was only four years old, he was just a baby, and my mother was stuck with all the children. Like all mothers, she only worried about keeping us warm and fed. In route to South of Russia we lost our grandmother, she was close to ninety years old. She got very sick, and my mom admitted her to a hospital, but when my mother went back in a day to see my grandmother, no one could give my mother a clue as to where my grandmother was, or what happened to her. To this day we do not know what happened to her!

'I Do Not Think I Could Find Their Graves'

As we went further south, one by one, we lost all four of my sisters due to malnutrition. There were instances where my mother carried my sisters to the nearest medical facility, but they could not help her. My mother and I had to dig out all the graves, two feet deep. If I could find those sisters who were buried in the hills it would be a miracle. Today even if I had millions of dollars, I do not think I could find their graves. Respectability for the dead was unknown during the war.

We did get south then and by that time there was a Polish army formed under the command of General Anders.[30] The families of these future soldiers of the Polish Army were allowed to leave Russia. My mother accidentally met up with her uncle, who was in the army. We were lucky; of course, at this time there were only three of us: my mother, Al, and myself. We were then put on crowded trains, shoulder to shoulder. Everyone on the train shared because Stalin agreed to give portions of food to soldiers, but not the families. However, the soldiers shared their small portions of mostly canned food with the children. That is how we got out.

Between 1939 and 1941, 1,680,000 Polish people were deported and dispersed all over Russia. We got to the South of Russia, Uzbekistan, and Tashkent was the name of the place. There were a lot of people that got the news about the amnesty; these people were all open, including those candidates for the army. They had to organize all of this, there had to be time for decontamination. They

---

[30] *General Anders-* Władysław Anders (1892-1970) was a general in the Polish Army. After the Nazi-Soviet Pact, he was captured by the Soviets but was later turned out to form a Polish Army to fight against the Germans. He also commanded the Polish II Corps in the Allied Italian Campaign, including the nearly impossible capture of German lookout stronghold of Monte Cassino. After the war, he was part of Polish Government in Exile in London.

had to place the civilian people wherever they could. We lived in just a shack; there was a floor and a mat on the inside of it. Through the roof of the shack, we could see the moon and the stars, and heaven forbid if it rained, we would be wet. I have to say in all honesty, we experienced a lot of sympathy and kindness from a lot of people. The family that let us use their shack asked if we could help them pick their cotton during the day in exchange for food. The food consisted of flat bread, rice, and lots of peppers. I had a very sad experience with the peppers. One time I thought it was salad. I took a mouthful, and I did not know what to do with it.

After this, they took us to the port of Krasnovostsk, where we would travel across the Caspian Sea by an overcrowded old ship. I remember the lines all around the ship just to get to the bathroom. I remember a lot of people in sacks being thrown off the ship because they did not survive. The ship landed in the Port of Pahlevi in Persia, or present-day Iran. Here we had to undergo a disinfection and decontamination process. Then by army trucks, we were taken to Tehran, the capital of Iran.

We stayed in what they called Camp #2, which was made of concrete blocks. These were left over and built by the Germans around the ammunition factory that was there years before. They were surrounded by a brick wall with openings to which we could get to Tehran with permission. While there, I remember that one morning I woke up and could not walk. My mother did her own remedies; she took two hot bricks and put them at the bottom of my feet, and I slept with them on my feet.

The next morning I was able to walk again. We stayed there until August of 1942. By train we then went to another place by the name of Ahwaz where we stayed for eight months. It was a transit point where we had to stay at a hospital because my mother was very sick, and I had typhoid fever. That is why we could not travel any farther because they would not send anyone anywhere unless they were well. They did not want any diseases taken anywhere else.

Then finally we got well, registered again, and through the Persian Gulf and Gulf of Oman we got to Karachi. There we stayed so we could get tested for diseases. We stayed in the army tents, and during the night to go to the bathroom you had to travel up the hills with a lantern. There were desert animals that howled so we had to travel to the bathroom in groups at night.

Then we were put on a big ship under escort across the Indian Ocean to East Africa to Mombasa on November 21, 1942. To give you some statistics, 77,200 left Russia, 33,300 civilians and 15,000 orphans. Those were the lucky ones considering at the beginning 1,680,000 Polish were in Russia. Some went to India, some went to Mexico, and like us some landed in East British Africa. Some of the orphans and civilians went to New Zealand.

The International Organization decided where to put these people by whether there was a certain number of adults that could work, or just children. In East Africa there were twenty-two settlements of camps, not only in the east but in South Africa as well. In each settlement there were 3,500-4,000 people. UNRA, the United Nations Relief and Rehabilitation Administration, were the ones that placed us in the camps. We had Polish school systems in Africa headed by The Ministry of Religious Affairs and the Polish Exile in London. There were 57 schools: 27 elementary, 7 secondary, 13 trade schools and 10 art, music, and craft schools.

Interviewer: Going back to the camps that you were in, could you describe what the conditions were like? What you remember from the camps in Russia, Persia, and East Africa?

The first camp was in Siberia. Salekhard was a city, but it was very small, and we were on the outskirts of it. [31] They assigned us to a very old Russian home with a big wooden stove used to keep warm; we had to burn wood in it. When we got there, I remember the first night. My mother pulled out the sheets and put them on the beds that were just rags rather than mattresses. We woke up in the middle of the night because we were itching and scratching. That place had a lot of bed bugs. We saw them coming down lines on the walls and my mother got the candles out and we started burning them. It took us a week to completely kill off the bugs. There were a lot of fish, and Eskimos were the ones delivering the fish to us. I will never forget when the first Eskimo came to our house, I thought he was an animal; his whole outfit was nothing but fur. He reached into the top of his body and pulled out this fish and he sold it to my mother. My mother bought the fish, but I was petrified of him. My mother used to take me to the store, and she gave this lady some kind of small gift so she would tell us when there would be a delivery of sugar coming to the store. She would say, 'Everyone in line is entitled to a quarter of a kilogram of sugar; if you bring your children, then each one of them is entitled to a quarter of a kilogram of sugar.'

It surprised me to see along the wall of the store what I thought were old branches of wood, but they were Eskimos on sleds being pulled by animals. I realized that they were animals pulling the sled and Eskimos came to the store too. I remember so vividly visiting one of the igloos and the whole place was built with ice with skins of animals inside.

As for the food, I did eat the fish my mother would manage to fry. It was a light trading basis. If my mother had something that

---

[31] *Salekhard*- Russian town on the Arctic Circle, used by the governments of Imperial Russia and the Soviet Union as a prison labor camp; Leon Trosky had been a notable prisoner there.

appealed to someone living there, they would trade. It was a remote area and delivery was of absolute basics. However, if you have a piece of gold, you can get anything. I remember my mother had my grandmother's glasses, which had gold frames. We used the frames and my mother's wedding band for food because that's the only thing that you could trade. We had plenty of wood, it was right next to us. I have recently started to paint, and I have painted a mushroom, a red one. We had plenty of these mushrooms in the nearby woods, which helped us too. My mother cooked them up and I do not know whether these went with fish or not, but they filled an empty stomach. I was young and I did not think much about it, I was not as bad as my mother, who looked ahead.

My mother tried to write letters to Poland to let my father know, but they never got there. Later, we found out that when he got out of wherever he was, he temporarily came home but then the Germans came and sent him to a concentration camp. My aunt was with him, and they never received any of the letters and did not know what happened to us either. There are a lot more details, but generally that is about all I remember from that camp.

Was there any forced labor in that camp?

If you could, my mom would have to go to work every single day in order to get rations of bread: dark, heavy bread. I used to go and help her and of course children were ordered to dig ditches. We landed in Siberia in what they call summertime, which was not as severely cold. It was not warm, but it was not frozen either. Most of us were kids. I do not know what good we did digging ditches, but we threw dirt from one place to another. This camp was only for women and children so they could not get too much out of us.

That camp was out of Russia. It was a place where we waited for our next step in our travels. In Tehran, we were in those cement blocks and literally the insides of them were huge empty spaces. There were no rooms, and it was just like a warehouse. All we got were blankets. We would put the blankets down and there would be two people and next to us there would be a family with a blanket with two or three people. We used to get rations of food and basics. In the community kitchen, we would get soup and tea or coffee. I do not remember much, but I remember the soup was lousy. My mother had my father's suit and traded it to a Persian to get private access to a canteen where she could buy some bread or some wine. We had a sort of dysentery from eating in the community kitchen that we were not used to. Next to us there was a doctor who said, 'Mrs. Kalicki, if you want your children to get out of here, you better get them away from that communal kitchen and put them on tea, wine, and dry bread.'

So that is what my mother fed us for a couple days. We survived and got stronger. That is also the camp where I lost the ability to walk for a brief time, but I got better. My mother and I were not there very long, but then my mother started to get really weak.

Our next stop was Ahwaz and that is where we stayed for eight months. My mother was very sick and there was an English doctor there. He took specific interest in my mother's condition because he had some medicine from England to treat her. She might have known, but I never asked what it was except that she got quite a series of injections. She got better and then I got sick with typhoid fever. That is why we were there for so long.

After examinations again, we finally got to Karachi where the big ocean liner was organized. We were under escort because there was still the threat of bombardment of ships traveling through the Indian Ocean to Mombasa. That was the second camp.

East Africa

Then we got to East Africa. From Mombasa, a port, we traveled by railroad to Kampala, which is the capital of Uganda. From there by truck about ten miles away was a camp by the name of Koja. That was in 1943. It was by Lake Victoria. In that camp we had schools, we had English teachers, we had a cinema, basic medical facilities, and local markets for fresh food. In addition to that we were given very simple types of huts. They were round with banana leaf roofs and beds that were constructed with four pieces of wood with legs, rope, and a mattress. We got nets because there were a lot of mosquitoes there. We were given blouses and pants because in the evening you have to wear those to protect yourself from mosquitoes. I went to school there. We had rations of food given to us such as oil, molasses, but whatever we did get we would separate it. My mom worked in a sewing center to make a little money. We went to markets and got fruit and vegetables. We cooked in very simple outside hotplates. There was a jungle that was not too far away, and on the outskirts, we could pick wild growing bananas, oranges, and potatoes. There were loads of bananas, all sizes. The bananas that you grow here are one kind, yellow. We had varieties of bananas, and the ladies of the evening would sit at the table and play cards and have a whole bunch of bananas. Do you know what passion fruit is? It looks like big plums, but it has a hard outside and on the inside a jelly-like sweet-and-sour taste. I spotted one at a local grocery store and they wanted two dollars for one. I got one, took it home and cut it open, and ate it. I thought how delicious this is! Then my husband Vic says to me, 'You did not save anything for me?' and I said, 'There was only a teaspoon of it all together, buy yourself one!' In Africa, right across the path was a field of passion fruit and I said to myself, if I had that here I could be a millionaire. We had a lot of food available, so we did not have to buy or trade for food. We had school and we had Girl Scouts in the camp. The administration of the camp arranged once in a while for the missionaries to come and they showed us their collection of butterflies.

I myself liked Africa very much. I was there eight years. That is why it came in handy, because when I came to the United States at least I could speak English, book English and not American slang. It was in British Africa, but it was not under British control. It was under control of the United Nations. The British agreed to take these camps because they were British colonies at that time. We had churches and I was in school there. I finished high school and two years' equivalent of college. I also worked as a secretary for priests. I had a lot of friends there too. Maybe that is why I remember because I was young and had friends.

When I came to the United States and married my husband Vic, I would say to him that I did not know anybody, and he knew everyone. At this particular time we had been in Koja for five years. By this time it was also the end of the war, and most of the Polish soldiers [in exile] had by then gone to England. All of the families of these soldiers started moving to our camp, so in the end the people that did not have any intentions of moving camps were moved to a different camp. That is why they moved us to Tengeru, present day Tanzania.

Tanzania

Tengeru at one time was the biggest camp in East Africa; it had four thousand people in it. The days there were very hot. The camp was close to the volcanic lake Duluti and at the foot of Mount Meru, near Mount Kilimanjaro. On any clear day, you could see the snow on the peaks of Kilimanjaro. Meru was closer, but it was a volcanic mountain that was not active anymore. It was a beautiful camp, which was where I worked as a secretary for the three priests. We had a YMCA there where you could go to dance, listen to music, or look at the magazines, and that is where we started to have a little contact with the outside world. My mother then realized that we would have to go somewhere else eventually, and she did not want us to be sent someplace we did not want to go.

To the United States

My mother got in touch with her brother in the United States. My aunt had to send us an invitation and pay for us to come to the United States. My uncle had to sign a guarantee that we would not be a burden to the United States. First, we had to go to Nairobi to go to the American Embassy to go through all sorts of tests so that we would not bring any disease to America. It took a long time, but finally in February 1951 we came to the United States from Mombasa on a merchant boat, back through the Suez Canal, to the Mediterranean, Italy, through Bremen, Germany, and then put on a big ship called the *General S.S. Stargitz*. Then we landed in New York on February 17, 1951. From New York I traveled by train to Erie, Pennsylvania, on February 19. I have been here ever since.

Going back on your experiences throughout your whole trip, what would you say is your most vivid memory of the whole experience?

My most vivid memory is of Africa, my eight years there. Despite the simplicity of life we had there, we also had social life and we were all in the same predicament. We enjoyed and cherished the simplest things, going to church, Girl Scouts, going on picnics, and sometimes we would dare the surroundings because we would go into the edge of the jungle. One time we ran into a wild pig, and we were so petrified we did not know what to do. The poor pig was probably more afraid of us. *[Laughs]* At night we could even hear lions. I enjoyed being in Africa. After Russia and all this traveling through different places, Africa was a sanctuary. We did not have to worry that much, even though there was communist influence and some uprising in tribes in Africa. I liked Africa; my most vivid memory was Africa.

Throughout your whole experience in Europe, you were a child. What did you make of everything at such a young age?

I was only ten. I was thrown out like somebody grabs a little plant, and pulls it out of the dirt and throws it on the ground. I was maybe too young to realize the severity of it. I always thought that my mother would take care of everything. No matter what, she would solve the problem for me. After a while, I realized that it was serious, especially when she was sick. I thought to myself, what would happen if she was gone? Here we are in a strange country with no one to lean on and we knew no one, but she survived and we with her.

'What War Does to Women and Children'

When you reached the United States, was there a sense of relief?

There was an expectancy of a better life, definitely. From what we read and heard, we knew that if we were to come to a normal life again, it would be in the United States. It would take time, it would take hard work, but eventually we will be normal living people. With other people around we will not have fears, we will not have hunger, and we will not have war. That is why I am against war, with every fiber of my body. Because I know what it does to civilian people, primarily mothers with young children. It was devastating and they suffered the most because military men, that is their job. Women and children are not soldiers, they generally suffer hunger, fear, and especially when the government decides that they are going to move people and throw them in God knows where. They did it without any care for the living, which is what they did to us. When they took us away from home, nobody ever gave a thought of how these people are going to make a living. Who is going to take care of them? Nobody cared.

*

I have a little conclusion. I am very proud of you for showing an interest in the events that took place over half a century ago! It disturbed millions of lives, and also caused global turmoil and suffering. It is important to keep up the memory of this horrible last world war and its victims to prevent it from happening again. I lived it as a child who remembers strange places, lots of fear and hunger, and do not forget my parents' devastation in particular, as well as the nations in general. Thank you.

Halina Roman passed away on Independence Day, July 4, 2017, at the age of 87.

CHAPTER EIGHTEEN

The German Schoolgirl

The Great Depression was plunging not only the United States but the entire world into new depths. In 1932, just as in America, a brand-new government was voted into power in Germany; here, though, mainstream politicians lay down with a populist upstart party that pushed a platform of vague and sinister promises to redress grievances and solve Germany's economic and political woes.

Eva Koenig was born in 1926 in eastern Germany in the state of Silesia just twenty miles from the Polish border. Only 13 years old at the start of the war, she lived with her older sister and parents in a little town, where they owned and operated an inn. In January 1945, everyone east of the Oder River was evacuated, including her family. Fearing the Russian advance from the east, Eva and her sister, who was eight months pregnant at the time, began to make their way to western Germany where the family of Eva's brother-in-law lived. The two sisters then began a trek that would take four days and four nights. Although her mother was still living with them at the time, she headed toward Breslau in an attempt to find their father, who had recently become a prisoner of war of the Russians.

After the war, Eva remained in West Germany until she came to the United States; after arriving in the country, she went to

Vermont. This interview was conducted in 2006 for our oral history project when she was eighty years old.

Eva Koenig

I was born in eastern Germany on March 31, 1926, and moved to the United States in 1958. The war in Germany started in 1939, and I was 13 years old.

[Before the war], the economy was very bad, people were without work, we had a lot of unrest and people were hoping that someone would come and help us out of the misery.

I had heard [about the hyperinflation that happened around the early 1920s] from my parents. It must've been terrible, they would make a million dollars in one day in their business, and then the next day when they went to the bank, they got maybe a few dollars for it.

[The Great Depression] was all over the world, depression, hunger, unemployment. Before Adolf Hitler came to power, there were two [types of people]: people who wanted him, because he promised work and jobs for everyone, and others who saw that he might not be so good for us. I did not really feel it personally so much; I was young.

In the big cities, [politics] did divide people, yes, to where there were actually fights by both parties against each other. When the war started, just like in this country, people tried to get together and say that 'we have to stand behind the elected president.' But deep down many of the elder ones, especially my parents and grandparents, feared that it would not come to a good end.

Many tried to stand behind [Hitler] because he was in charge of the troops, he was in charge of everything, and they were still hoping he would do good, because in those six years as chancellor, he had done a lot of good, he did find good jobs for those people. He built factories, he had people working. It looked like it could be getting better and better [for the] economy, but other people were not so happy with him; because he was a dictator, they felt that the leadership wasn't that good for the country. If anybody spoke openly against the war, they probably were incarcerated. I was very young; some talked about it among themselves. You'd hear it in families when just the family was together with good friends. They would have discussions about it, and arguments, but not in public.

The summertime 1936 Berlin Olympic Games were used for propaganda purposes, the unveiling of the concept of a master race and the showcasing of German might and militarism. An international boycott effort failed; Hitler's leadership and Germany's prestige was confirmed in the eyes of many at home and abroad.

I don't know if the 1936 Olympics in Berlin were really an accomplishment for the country, but it proved that he did something in all those years that he was president/chancellor. For the three years [prior] he had the use of the street, there were no trucks or anything like that, but [with] offenders of any kind, they would disappear; we often didn't know what happened to them. And whoever was out, they would learn how to do good things. We were actually in groups, and the girls and boys were separated. We did handicrafts. [Hitler] had organized something similar to the Brownies here, [Girls Scouts and Boy Scouts], one for the boys and one for the girls. That was the same, we met once a week in the afternoon and did different things. We had a leader, which was in our case a girl, who was maybe five years older than we were. She taught us all kinds of things, handicrafts. We helped the farmers in the summertime, and we went to elderly people and helped them. That's what we did in our small town. In the big cities it might have been a little bit more on the political side. We sung together, went to concerts together. Like I said, it was not political in our town.

'Our War Started'

It was 1939 when our war started. That's when the soldiers marched through our town, toward the border, and that's when the sad, sad part started. [We lived close to the Polish border]; quite close, we were twenty-five kilometers, which is less than twenty miles, but [before the war], nobody bothered us because there were very tight borders.

In the beginning, it was not very much for me as a child, because I was still in school. But what the girls in our youth group did now, when we got together, was that we started to knit for the soldiers, because some of them were in Poland and later in Russia. So we knitted scarves and mittens for them, things like that. We'd send packages; send letters to those who didn't have any family. Otherwise, of course, we had food stamps and a lot of things were not very easy to come by, because the factories were all changed into places where we made equipment for the war. We had our own business, so both of my parents worked in the business and so did I after I got out of school. All available women, unless they had a lot of children, they had to go to factories.

I had no 'teen years'; there were no dances or get-togethers. There was a movie once in a while, but it was a very sheltered life, really. We sat together in the evening, maybe reading or doing handicrafts, but there was no television. That was just the life; whether that was just because of the war, I'm not sure. Maybe I could only see the difference afterwards more than at the time because that was just life for me as a child.

Was there a lot of support for the troops? Oh, yes, naturally, because they were everybody's brother, father, son, so naturally we supported them. I didn't know of anybody who [vocally opposed the war, or who did not offer troop support.] And again, they probably would not have stayed on the streets [very long], or wherever they said it. They would have disappeared, because that's what they did, under dictatorship.

For the elder generation, people who were really involved in politics, I guess they saw [the war] coming. I personally did not. My father was very opposed to the whole politics of those days, and I remember that my mother often had to warn him to be quiet, not to talk too loud, when he spoke against it all.

After the years passed by into the war, city bombardment started up from the English. That is when we were fortunate to be in the east, because they never came to the east [at that time]; I guess it was too far to fly. [Then] only the western part of Germany was bombarded, so we didn't hear or see any of those terrible things. Soon when some of the cities were very much bombarded and they didn't even have enough housing for those people who had lost everything, they were starting to send those people to the east part of Germany, and we had to take those westerners into our home, so that they would have a home. We had one woman with a child, a school child, I don't remember her age.

Student interviewer: Did you know anyone who was living in the west?

My sister got married in 1944 and her in-laws lived in the west. But it was also in a smaller town, so there was really nothing to bombard because it was just people living there. But later on they started, it wasn't too bad there. We had relatives in Berlin, the capital of Germany. They brought a lot of their valuables to us actually because they didn't know what would happen there, but they were able to go to some other relatives nearby who were on the outskirts of Berlin, so they did not come to the east.

Some teachers might have talked about [the war] to us, about politics even. I had heard most of it through my parents, though, and like I said, from the radio and newspaper. For the teachers there maybe also was a little bit of worry; in case they said too much, it would hurt them. They might be taken off the job if they were saying anything against the regime.

*

My sister's husband was in the war, from the beginning to the end, wounded twice. We didn't have a big family, but I had two cousins who were drafted in 1940 or '41. And my father had to go in 1945, just a few months before the war ended. They drafted all available men in town, and even young boys. They had to go defend the capital of our state, Silesia, which is called Breslau. It's now Polish; after the war this whole part became Polish. He was fifty years old at the time, a World War I veteran. He felt terrible about it, he was very much opposed. But of course, he had to go; like most soldiers do when they are called to fight for the country, they go. It was very hard for him. He was a prisoner of war of the Russians, but since he was old and not very well health-wise they did not take him to Russia, they kept him in Poland, near Silesia actually, in a camp for just about three or four months and then they sent him home. He was not treated too badly.

'A Very Hard Time'

Before the war ended, that was really the worst part for us. We had to leave our home and house and flee that whole area because the Russians were coming from that side, naturally, and that was the worst part. We packed one suitcase each and we hoped to be back in a couple of weeks, once the war was over. That never happened because the Russians occupied that part, and from then on, Germany was divided.

We found shelter in that small town where my brother-in-law's relatives lived, and we had to start a new life all together. So that was very hard, and at that time there was really no food at all because like I said we had to go to the west, and the west was bombed out. So that was a very hard time.

'The Russians Were Reaching the Border'

Through some people who had to do with the government in our town, [we learned that the Russians were reaching the border]. They heard it, and they knew that our town would have to be evacuated. So they forwarded it to us, and in the morning at seven o'clock, we had to all leave. Since one of our relatives and neighbors was part of that town hall meeting, he came that night when he returned from the meeting. He came at twelve o'clock and informed us. So we had until seven o'clock in the morning. My father had already been drafted before that a couple of months earlier, so I was just with my mother and my older sister. My older sister was eight months pregnant. My mother decided not to go with us; she wanted to go in the direction where she knew my father would be, just somehow hoping to be able to help him. So my sister and I were the ones who actually went on a trek, they called it. Just trucks or whatever they had, horses and wagons, they put us on them so that we could leave the town. In our town there were no more trains leaving. We had some buses, but there was nothing coming. Everybody knew the Russians were close to the border because we could hear their cannons, so we wanted to go at that time because everybody was afraid of the Russians.

Difficult Journey

It was very difficult traveling with my sister with her advanced state of pregnancy; she was healthy, but the problem was that we had to go to the city, which would have taken us under normal circumstances maybe eight to ten hours per train, changing a few times on the way. It took us four days and four nights. Because there were hardly any trains going, sometimes we had to wait somewhere for hours and hours until something came. Try as we were able, the Red Cross was still working so they helped us because of my sister. They had blankets there, and some oatmeal for us to eat. Otherwise, there were no restaurants or anything for us to go into. Of course my mother packed both of us a knapsack we had on our backs, so we had food and water.

'We Left Everything'

We had to leave behind everything; we had a large house in which we rented apartments upstairs. So we left everything, we just had one suitcase, whatever we could carry, and my mother locked up the house hoping we would come back, but we never did. So we had to leave everything.

My sister was still living with us because her husband was in Russia at the time, so we were going to her in-laws. No, they did not know, because we had no way of getting in touch with them. Now, they had heard on the radio in the meantime that all of eastern Germany was evacuated, so they expected us, they didn't know when, but they had expected us. Quite a few houses [had been destroyed], but their house was on the outskirts of town, so that near there, there was no bombardment, [although the town was being bombed when we were there]. Every house during the war had to have one part of the cellar made stable enough, and emergency food had to be in there where the people who lived there could stay wherever there was bombardment. First the sirens would go off, terrible, through the whole town, drive you crazy and everybody was running across the street or wherever they would have to go—everybody knew where they would have to go in a shelter. The people were running with a few things in their arms, with their children in their arms, just to get there. Sometimes, of course, the bombs would come before they had even reached the shelter, but it was tough.

We had to sit in the shelter until there was a siren going again, telling us that it was clear, which sometimes could have been up to ten hours. So that was pretty scary. [At times this happened] maybe twice a week, it was not too much; like I said, this was a small town with no military there, or factories. Sometimes they'd just swoop a bomb down on the way home from the big cities when they had something left over. We stayed in this town from February until May 1945, when the war ended.

*

My mother and father were very close; my mother knew that my father was not too well. So I guess it was just natural instinct, but of course they would never let her into that city, so they told her to leave. The whole city was closed, and nobody could come in or go out anymore. We tried to protect it from the Russians but were unable to. For a few weeks and months, they did try to defend it, and it was completely destroyed because of it. She found a train and a few days after we had arrived, she came too. People were very much afraid of the Russians because they had heard so many bad stories of them, raping women, stealing and murdering, so there was great fear.

When we came close to the end of the war, we all got together, our small family, and we said, 'If we ever have to leave here, we will meet in that particular town.' And he was released in September from the Russians, and came right there, to that town.

My sister's husband was wounded again at the very end of it, and then he was okay. He still wanted to go and help, but gratefully he didn't have to fight against the Russians then, but against the English, then later Americans. Of course it was much easier for him because he was also a prisoner of war [in the west]; I cannot say for sure now if it was English or American, but they didn't keep him very long, and then he was released.

I mean during the war I can't really say [how most Germans view the British]; I guess that most Germans found them as the enemy because they were bombarding our land. We all knew that our politicians had started the war, but it's just very difficult because you don't know whom to believe and what to believe.

But definitely, [the western allies] were much more humane to prisoners of war, or even in our case, when the English and the Americans together came in our town, they were very kind to us civilian people. They even gave us something to eat when they had something. I mean, there was no question about it, decent. Oh, we were not scared anymore, we felt that that was the end; it couldn't get any worse than it was.

'There was No One Else to Blame'

Were you relieved that the war was over?

Yes, oh definitely.

By that point had most of the pride of fighting subsided and were the people getting sick of fighting?

Oh, [most Germans] had gotten sick of the war a long time ago. Everybody knew it was impossible to do what our chancellor wanted us to do, to more or less conquer the whole world. Therefore, we wanted it to end earlier. Many of the officers close to him wanted to end it, and tried to assassinate him, but it was not successful, unfortunately. They put bombs next to him and all kinds of things and he for some reason was never hurt. Then of course he went on the radio and made a big speech that 'nobody can harm me,' and all that. For us, we all hoped that somebody would finally be successful, but nobody was, and we had to just struggle along.

It was a long war, from 1939 until 1945, so I would say 1941, 1942, most people [were thinking], 'let's stop it.' But they couldn't say it out loud, but everyone hoped it would end somehow.

Hitler was a good speaker, but that was just for the ones who liked him. [*Chuckles*] You can make a good speech and still not say what they [the civilians] wanted to hear, and he'd tell them he didn't want to hear what they said. So you'd listen too; as long as the war hadn't ended, he had nothing else to say to us that we wanted to hear. In the end, actually, we didn't hear much from him or about him. He was in Berlin, and of course the Russians were coming from one side, the English and Americans from the other side, and finally, of course, he took his own life.

Was Hitler blamed for the war after it was over?

From the very beginning he was blamed. There was no one else to blame. He had a good propaganda minister there.

Did people realize that it was propaganda, or did they go along with it?

Well as always, different people have different impressions and ideas. Some saw it as if he said so it has to be good, it has to be right, and this was great and wonderful, and they went along with it. Then there were others who thought it was impossible what he promised. There were always two people and I think it was probably [split] fifty-fifty.

Did you hear any news about what was happening, as far as the Jewish people?

Yes. That's a story all by itself, a terrible story. I guess we didn't hear too much during the war, because it was so terrible, and he knew it. He knew that people wouldn't like it. So except for the propaganda which said the Jews were all bad, that's what they tried to tell us, which we knew they were not because we had friends who were Jews, we went to school with Jewish people, had businesses with Jews. So we certainly did not have that impression, but that was what was told to us: they are all bad. The synagogues were burned down, that was the terrible part of the Hitler Regime.

How did you feel when [you were told] that the Jews were supposedly bad, yet you had known so many?

It was unbelievable for us, because like I said, they were very good people. But there was nothing we could do.

What happened to your family after the war?

It was a slow start. I lived with my mother in one room; when my father came, he joined us. Then, after a couple of months, I had found a job as a maid with a business family where I could work and also have a small home where I could sleep. That started to be my home. We stayed in the west because we could never go back to the east.

Rebuilding After the War

They started rebuilding pretty quickly afterwards. Rebuilding after the war was very difficult, of course; what they did, especially in the large cities, since most of our houses are built out of bricks, not wood, they cleaned the bricks from all of the houses that had fallen down and rebuilt with those old bricks until they got new supplies, which took quite a while. They built shelters, of course, that everybody could stay in. And again, everybody had the house full, sheltering neighbors or relatives from another town. It was a few tough years after the war. I must say this is what we learned after the war. Everybody worked wherever it was needed. I remember we, as young girls, in our free time were taken to a place not too far from us with trucks, and they would get, I don't know what it's called now, but it was material to burn because we didn't have enough coal, we didn't have enough wood. But they could go into the earth, the people who knew about it, and they cut it in bricks. We young girls, we had to take it out and put it up on the trucks and carry it from one place to another. So that would be driven down and brought into the city and given to people, so that whoever didn't have anything to burn because it was cold, would burn this. It was not coal but as hard as coal, and I don't even know if it exists here in this country, but it was a form of heating the houses.

It took, I would say, until 1948 for things to get back to 'normal.' We had a new chancellor and good politicians; of course, Adenauer was our first one. In 1948 they brought new money, a complete change in the money, so we lost everything we had in the bank, but we started with new money. For some reason, we were able at this time with new money to buy a few things, but before that there was hardly anything that we had in those three years from '45 to '48. Everything was really down and that's how long it took. In those three years we didn't go anywhere, we couldn't do anything, just trying to rebuild and working to get something for ourselves, whatever we could for ourselves to survive. Do any job which came along and help out wherever we could.

Of course the Americans helped the Germans after the war. What was it called now? One of the generals or presidents sent food over; we got a lot of help from the Americans.[32] They came with planes, especially to Berlin, which was encircled by Russians, and they sent planes to drop food. Actually, we as a family, they found contacts for us through the churches, and a family from Vermont started to send us packages, which was very nice. When I came to the United States, they were the first people I met. [*Long pause*] It was wonderful to get those packages with clothes for us and food. [*She cries.*] Every few months we received them, and soon, they started to write letters. They'd put a letter in English, and we found somebody in Germany who could translate it. Then my father would answer them in German. Those Vermont people had neighbors who spoke German and who translated for them. It became a close friendship.

Eva H. Koenig passed away on February 4, 2018, in Minden, Germany, having moved back to be with family after her husband died.

---

[32] *we got a lot of help from the Americans-* The European Recovery Act, nicknamed the Marshall Plan after its chief architect, Secretary of State George C. Marshall, which provided 12.5 billion dollars for post-war recovery.

CHAPTER NINETEEN

The Holocaust Survivor

Whenever I look at the photos sent to my uncle before the war, I experience the same surge of feelings—pain, sadness, and great pity. I hurt because we all look so young, yet nobody survived except myself. Our family was one of hundreds of thousands whose fate was the same. Thousands of little children with potential for greatness in many fields perished.

Before the war, Poland had the greatest concentration of Jews with active writers, painters, musicians, and teachers. We were a community with high moral values, vibrant with cultural activities: newspapers, theaters, activities, and a variety of political parties.

[Following the war], the Warsaw ghetto was a huge, leveled, empty place. The skeletons of burned buildings and people are bulldozed into the ground. No one would guess what was once here. The people who died knew well they were not dying for a cause; most did not have the luxury of defending themselves. They were destroyed just for being Jews in the wrong place and time. All, without exception, asked to be remembered. We, who accidentally survived, owe them to keep their memories alive. As the Bible says: When a person dies, it is as if a whole world died because we carry within us a whole world.[15]

—Lily Muller, Memoirs

Lily Muller visited our high school on a few occasions to witness the reunions we hosted with World War II liberators and Holocaust survivors, as detailed in my 2016 book, A Train Near Magdeburg. *Indeed, her husband Oscar had been liberated on that train. In December 2007, one of my students visited with her at her home, when she was eighty-five years of age.*

Lily Muller

I was born in Lodz, the second biggest city in Poland, December 2, 1922. It was an industrial city; I was there until I was sixteen years old. I had a normal, wonderful life with my parents and my two brothers. I was going to a private school, which I loved, because the teachers were very close to the pupils, and I was doing well in school; I enjoyed school. We knew a lot of what was going on because my parents had a bookstore, and having a bookstore they got a lot of information from other things, and I myself saw a book printed in Germany which showed a photograph of people in camps, so [some of] the Germans themselves did not like their world view. Actually Mr. Hitler decided to put them there, to probably make them a little more to his liking. So, we knew that Europe was heading to a war, and we Jews would be very vulnerable.

In the meantime, we had in our bookstore windows all possible books printed against Hitler. When the time was near for them to come to Lodz, we had to take all those books and bring them to the house, and still in warm weather, burn those books; my parents, having lived through the First World War, had a very bad time then, there was hunger, and they knew we were not safe. I knew what it was going to be—not exactly, of course, [because if we knew what was going to happen], maybe we would have gone to the United States, where we had family. But I remember this book episode, because in history we ourselves read about things which happened previously to people who were not going along with the regime. We certainly did not [go along] ...

The Arrival of the Germans

The first of September, 1939, the Germans came into my town. A lot of Deutsche Polen, who were [of German extraction] and who had lived in Poland for many years, they were still German-oriented, they lined the streets—the German soldiers were bleeding, very heavily. Our town now changed completely because you could not be in the street. [Some] Jews were called in and made to dance in front of the Germans, who had a lot of fun, and who photographed it [for sport].

The schools were then closed completely. My uncle, who was part of the city government, had to hide in my aunt's apartment. It was just an awful time. Our store was closed, and we lost it; we did not own it anymore. I did not know how to deal with it, especially because my father and my brother went to Warsaw, because they thought that Warsaw would be spared. But there was such shooting on the streets in Warsaw, and there was no food, so he came home, and we were relieved very much that he was home. This had been going on for a long time and we found out that this particular city would be incorporated into the Reich. The family decided to contact some people my father had business with in Warsaw and asked them if we could go there, if they could help us find some lodging. Pretty soon part of the family went there, but my father did not want to make my mother sleep in one room like they put a few families because everybody was coming to Warsaw.

Before World War II, Warsaw was the epicenter of Jewish life and culture in Poland; 350,000 Jews made up its prewar population. This vibrant Jewish community was the largest in both Poland and Europe, and was the second largest in the world, second only to New York City.[16]

She [my mother] was supposed to wait for another opportunity to come a little later. It was very difficult there too, although we were not so scared because in our town, they were already talking about making a ghetto and closing it, whereas in Warsaw it was a few years until that happened. But of course, I worked because I had no school. I decided to open like a little kindergarten for the children of older women who were working; I think it was a good thing to do. But slowly I started work and saved change; my father opened a little library there, which I took care of. He found ways also to make some money so we could have some food to eat. It was hard, the people lived in one room, there was no food. You could buy food on the black market. Little boys used to bring the food from out of Warsaw city and where the war was surrounding us; the little boys used to put out bricks and put the food there and somehow get money for it. But many of them died, because when the Germans saw that somebody was doing it, they killed them. They did not care about killing people, it was just they really treated people as things. Food, I do not even remember what food we ate; we did not have much.

The Warsaw Ghetto

The Warsaw Ghetto was famous for hunger and for terrible sickness. A lot of people were sick from typhus, and a lot of people were just simply dying from hunger, a lot of children especially, all over the street. The next day you would not see them anymore; in the morning a little wagon would pick up all those people and take them to the cemetery. The people who still had money could maybe eventually save themselves, but generally it was very bad. The

Germans had a way of killing the Jews. First, they started with little things, taking away all your coats, took away all your radios, you did not have anything that reminded you that you were a human being. I was lucky because when I was in the underground, I had to bring bulletins from the radio, and because of that I knew what was going on, but otherwise, people did not really know.

Lily was able to slip out and smuggle food and munitions in to the ghetto fighters, she also worked to clean guns and create Molotov cocktails.

The Ghetto Uprising

As 1943 dawned, the SS returned to the ghetto for another major deportation. They encountered the first armed resistance from the ghetto fighters and beat a hasty retreat, leaving behind wounded and weapons, and temporarily called off the operation. For the next three months, the ghetto fighters organized and prepared for the final struggle. On the eve of Passover, April 19, the Germans returned again, this time with the aim of liquidating the ghetto once and for all, in time for Hitler's birthday on the 20th. By then, there were between 300-350 active fighters; the young were now the real leaders of the ghetto, having decided not between life and death, but rather, how to die.[33]

The Warsaw Ghetto was destroyed in 1943 when the Germans decided to [liquidate the ghetto], but before this even happened I worked for the Jewish underground, because I was promised I was going to get the first papers from my friend. They were [identity] papers taken from dead people that were brought in from the Russian side that would verify [if this person was alive or dead]. So,

---

[33] *By then, there were between 300-350 fighters*- Bauer, Yehuda. 'Current Issues in Holocaust Education and Research: The Unprecedentedness of the Holocaust in an Age of Genocide.' Lecture notes, International School for Holocaust Studies at Yad Vashem, Jerusalem, Israel. July 21, 2016.

they took these papers from dead people and [had us assume those identities], and then you could then go out of Warsaw and be out of the ghetto, if you had what they called a good face, that means a little wide, light, and you were could speak well, people survived on those papers.

At one time when things were bad, I decided to speak to my parents; we were in this camp together. I tried it; the first time when I tried it, it did not work out, but the second time I left this place. I was scared because you know our faces were very sad and it was very hard to always remember you are [supposed to be] very happy.

Photo from the infamous German Stroop Report, 'The Jewish Quarter of Warsaw is No More!' Credit: NARA.

I knew when [the Germans] were planning to burn the ghetto; I went out just in time.

*

The 1944 Polish Warsaw Uprising lasted for 63 days was initiated by the underground Polish Home Army to coincide with the Soviet advance, but the Red Army treacherously halted on the outskirts of Warsaw and allowed the German Army to suppress it, the goal being to eliminate Polish resistance to Soviet rule after the war ended. When that uprising, the largest in World War II, was over, the Germans forced civilian survivors to move. Wither her Aryan papers, Lily was sent to Germany.

I was there at the time of the [1944] Polish Uprising where everybody had to leave Warsaw. But the Germans sent us to Germany; they needed people to work in their factories.

Berlin

Unfortunately, they sent me to Berlin, where I was for over a year. Berlin was bombed twice a day, once by the English and once by the Americans. We had to go to a shelter so we did not show any signs of lights to the planes; every night we suffered through this, it was very hard. Eventually our factory was bombed and there was no more work for us. So, we were really afraid this was very bad for us, because first of all we were already depleted and were not fed very well because it was a very bad camp, it was very dangerous. I remember we asked a German whose older son had already died, it was toward the end, and she spoke to the boss, who was manufacturing caskets for the military. So we went there, and luckily for us, he took us.

I was afraid also of the Polish [slave workers] also in this camp because, you know, people started to become friendly, and some of them did not like the Jews, so I was not happy there. We could go down to Berlin, and in the end, [due to Allied bombing, we could not recognize any streets.

We were very lucky; there was a room of thirty people where there were all types of people. We also knew a little German, which was a little helpful. Where we washed ourselves there was only cold water and there were actually icicles hanging off the ceiling, but you learn how to adjust to it; that was something we could live with. When we went to our factories, they had showers for the men, so we used to go there very quickly and shower, dress, and go out, so we had a shower once in a while. Listen, this was no Auschwitz, but these six years of this terrible hunger and fear, I think that it took its toll on us.

'No One Survived From My Family'

I had two brothers. My brother went back to my town because my mother had an opportunity to come to Warsaw; we smuggled ourselves to Warsaw. I still think maybe if we would be together, we could have done something in Warsaw, but they were awful.

No one survived from my family. We were five people and we had grandparents on both sides, no one survived. My two friends, maybe more, from my schools survived, but my family, no.

'I Wanted to Live'

Student interviewer: What kept you going during the Holocaust, to keep pushing through and wanting to survive?

The fact that I was young. I wanted to live, and besides that, I wanted somebody to survive to tell the truth about what happened, because if Hitler would have won, there would be no humanity, no civilization. I knew in my bones that people have to prove that there is still humanity.

[After the war ended], they sent us to Brussels and we were very lucky we were there because there were already international aid groups. They also registered us with the city so we could get coupons for food; there was an international committee that started to take names and ask where you wanted to go. It took me five years only to come to the United States, can you believe this? *[Laughs]*

Have you ever gone back to Poland?

Yes. I went twice. My father had a house there and I wanted to take a little time to see it. I wanted to go to my room of our apartment; my heart was beating, and I went up there, I rang the bell, and the woman asked me what I wanted. I said, 'This apartment looks exactly like the one when we left. Our piano, the furniture, the pictures on the wall, everything.' I said, 'May I have one little picture, and she said, 'No, it is not yours!' Those people thought that they were entitled to it; of course it is hard. My friend, who was a pianist, went down to his apartment. He went there after the war because he survived, and they did not want to give him the piano. So, some people took advantage. [But] the biggest loss was the family, you know. I was still young when I left, I was sixteen when I did not see my mother anymore. Then gradually I lost everyone. I was still young, I do not know how to say whether we were less independent from the parents, but the families were very tight in Europe, like maybe sometimes you see here, Italian families who are very close to each other. That was characteristic of the Europeans.

*

I met my husband in Belgium. He came there from a camp, I never would have met him otherwise *[laughs]* because he was with the Russians later on, because this part was all east, so it touches where Ukraine is now. In Europe, every country after a few years changed their borders because of the wars. There were wars very often; they did this like a game of chess, and that is how it really was.

I found this work in a consulate; it was hard for me because I had to speak German, and French, and Polish, because it was a Polish consulate. But I did not know French, I knew German and Polish; I really raced to get to know this language that I should be able to speak with French people, but the learning process was very hard. I learned the French fast, then I started to learn English, because I wanted to come here.

To the United States

[When I came to the United States], I was living in Long Beach, New York; we lived there for fourteen years. You could go into New York in about an hour. I was working, making dresses to order, I was doing alterations, because that was easy. I did not have to learn anything. But this is also a war tragedy; I did not have a chance to go to college, and I had to work right away for myself. I could not pay for college, so I never went to college. I remember before the war, they planned for me, because I knew what I wanted for myself. I wanted a career. I wanted to be educated, but I made peace with myself about this. But I used to take different small courses, a few each year, each semester. I think that what I learned from it, that you can do a lot for yourself by studying, by reading a lot, by just being interested.

'I Know What War Is'

All I can tell you is, I am hoping there will be peace because I know what war is. I do not see much hope for it. I am eighty-five, I do not have much more to live. I was hoping people would learn from all this disaster. I am lucky my son did not get into the Vietnam War. We went marching and we were trying, and he is well educated, and my daughter is well educated; those were my goals. I have such wonderful visitors, and I admire you, too, for doing this job. Maybe somebody will find out that war is really horrible. Maybe they will do something about it.

Lily Muller passed away on December 2, 2015, at the age of 93.

AFTERWORD

To Keep Them With Us

In revisiting these stories, I came to realize that they are no less important than my previous books' tales of combat and sacrifice; in fact, they offer us a hidden facet of the story of World War II that is often overlooked. And these narratives were not easy to dig up; the simple fact was, many of the participants, until the sunset of their lives, had never spoken about their personal histories. Who cared to listen? They were frankly hard for me to find in the archives, but then again, I have a confession of sorts to make—I suppose my own biases and interests for the combat veteran narratives in the collecting phase took precedence. Although I never discouraged any student in our oral history project from talking to a civilian who lived through World War II, I just didn't emphasize that necessity at the time. Going through and researching and fleshing out the narratives, I realize how important these stories really are, and I'm proud of the ones who gathered them, many of them now the parents of their own high school age children.

Many of my readers, most of them children of the World War II generation, have written to me, or commented on my social media posts, remarking on how little their parents told them about their experiences during the war; they are thankful for the opportunity to immerse themselves in these recollections that must ring familiar to those of their parents, unlocking perhaps a mystery or two behind an unopened door. It is my hope that this volume of the series has in a small way rounded out another part of that story, and that in reading or listening to these late-in-life remembrances, we help to keep them alive, learning anew about the sacrifices they made for their families, and the world.

We honor their legacy by remembering their stories. We keep them close. We say their names.

*

MATTHEW A. ROZELL

THE THINGS OUR FATHERS SAW

OVER THE HUMP

THE UNTOLD STORIES OF THE WORLD WAR II GENERATION

CHINA/BURMA/INDIA

VOLUME X

THE THINGS OUR FATHERS SAW

VOLUME X:
OVER THE HUMP
CHINA, BURMA, INDIA

THE UNTOLD STORIES OF THE
WORLD WAR II GENERATION

Matthew A. Rozell

WOODCHUCK HOLLOW PRESS
Hartford · New York

Copyright © 2024 by Matthew A. Rozell. V.11.25.24. All rights reserved. No part of this publication may be reproduced, distributed, or transmitted in any form or by any means without the prior written permission of the publisher. Grateful acknowledgement is made for the credited use of various short quotations also appearing in other previously published sources. Please see author notes.

Front Cover: Merrill's Marauders in Burma, 1944, likely U.S. Army Signal Corps, possibly photographer David Quaid. Public domain.

Back Cover: Merrill's Marauders take a rest break, somewhere in Burma. U.S. Army Special Operations, public domain.

Any additional photographs and descriptions sourced at Wikimedia Commons within terms of use, unless otherwise noted.

Publisher's Cataloging-in-Publication Data

Names: Rozell, Matthew A., 1961- author.
Title: Over the hump: China, Burma, India: the things our fathers saw : the untold stories of the World War II generation, volume X / Matthew A. Rozell.
Description: Hartford, NY : Matthew A. Rozell, 2024. | Series: The things our fathers saw, vol. 10. | Also available in audiobook format.
Identifiers: LCCN pending | ISBN 978-1-948155-52-6 (hardcover) | ISBN 978-1-948155-51-9 (paperback) | ISBN 978-1-948155-53-3 (large print paperback)
Subjects: LCSH: World War, 1939-1945--Personal narratives, American. | Civilians--United States--Biography. |
www.matthewrozellbooks.com
www.teachinghistorymatters.com
Information at matthewrozellbooks.com.

Created in the United States of America

~To the children of
The World War II Generation~

"They say the coward dies a thousand deaths, the valiant dies but once. But possibly the valiant dies a thousand deaths too, if he is cursed with imagination."

— GENERAL JOSEPH W. STILWELL

THE THINGS OUR FATHERS SAW X:

OVER THE HUMP:

CHINA, BURMA, INDIA

THE STORYTELLERS (IN ORDER OF APPEARANCE):

MORGAN VAUX
JANE HANKS
PATRICK SCARANO
NORMAN HANDELMAN
ROBERT O'BRIEN
LEONARD 'RANDY' REEVES
KENNETH W. THOMAS
SAMUEL V. WILSON
PHILIP PIAZZA
MORRIS FACTOR
HERBERT CLOFINE
ROY MATSUMOTO
ROBERT E. PASSANISI
WARNER KATZ
DAVID QUAID
KERMIT 'TONY' BUSHUR

THE THINGS OUR FATHERS SAW X:

OVER THE HUMP:

CHINA, BURMA, INDIA

TABLE OF CONTENTS

AUTHOR'S NOTE 285

INTRODUCTION 291

COMMUNISTS AND NATIONALISTS 296
WORLD WAR II BEGINS IN ASIA 298
'VINEGAR JOE' STILWELL 299
'WE GOT A HELL OF A BEATING' 307

THE AVG STATIONMASTER 319

'WE WRECKED A LOT OF PLANES' 320
NO REPLACEMENTS.. 320
CHENNAULT'S EARLY WARNING SYSTEM 323
THE BURMA SALWEEN GORGE MISSION 325
CONDITIONS... 326
OTHER MISSIONS 327
'I WENT AROUND THE WORLD' 327
THE MARINES.. 329
BOOZE FOR SPARE PARTS 332

THE SLIT TRENCH ENCOUNTER 332
HOME... 333

THE FLYING TIGERS NURSE 335

'I FELT LIKE ALICE IN WONDERLAND' 336
A 'FOREIGN DEVIL' 337
GETTING BACK TO CHINA 338
'THESE KIDS, THEY'RE GOING TO FIGHT?' 339
SPENDING TIME WITH CHENNAULT 341
WAR 342
THE WARNING SYSTEM 343
MARRIED WITH A BLACK EYE 343
'WHEN THEY CAME BACK, THEY WERE MEN' 344
'THAT'S WHEN I LOST HIM' 346
HOME.. 346
'WOMEN DIDN'T TALK ABOUT THOSE THINGS' 348

THE CARGO PILOT.................................... 353

THE LIFELINE OF CHINA 356
HAZARDOUS DUTY.. 358
MEDALS... 359
THE COMMUNIST CHINESE 361
THE GRAND PIANO 362
THE CHINESE PEOPLE 365
GOING HOME 367
THE HOSPITAL SHIP 369
THE RESERVES.. 371

KEEPING IN TOUCH 372
CIVILIAN LIFE 373

THE B-24 RADIOMAN 375

SHIPPING OUT 378
TO INDIA 379
MISSIONS 380
WEIGHTLESS 383
ANOXIA 385
DETACHED SERVICE 387
COMING HOME 389

THE B-29 RADARMAN 393

THE B-29S 395
RADAR 396
MISSIONS 396
SINGAPORE 398
BOMBING JAPAN 399
'WE LOST OUR PILOT' 400
A SECRET WEAPON 401
AFTER THE WAR 401

THE ACE 407

PILOT TRAINING 408
INDIA 409
FIRST KILL 409

'I Believe I'm Going To Get Killed Tomorrow' 410
Purple Heart 411
'Pete, Don't Shoot!' 412
87 Missions 414
The Chinese 414
War's End 415
Japan Occupation Duty 416

THE THUNDERBOLT PILOT 419

The Test 420
Called Up 422
Pilot Training 424
The Thunderbolt 425
To The CBI 426
Burma 428
Marauders' Support 429
The Native People 431
War's End 432
Home 433
'They Were Soldiers' 435

THE VIRGINIA FARMBOY 439

'I Lied Like A Rug' 440
Forced Marches At High Speed 441
Stilwell's Goals 443
Winning Support of the Indigenous Peoples 443
Inspired to Learn 444

THE HEAVY WEAPONS COMMANDER 449

'I'M NOT ASKING YOU' 450
'A MINIMUM OF 90% CASUALTIES' 452
LIVING CONDITIONS 457
THE IMPERIAL MARINES 459
FIGHT AT WALAWBUM 460
WOUNDED 463
HOME 467
'GENERAL STILWELL JUST LAUGHED' 468
GOING BACK 470
'YOU VOLUNTEERED FOR THIS MISSION' 471
'I'LL TAKE CARE OF IT' 472
REUNIONS 474

THE ENGINEER 477

DEPRESSION DAYS 478
'YOU'LL GO WHERE I TELL YOU TO GO' 480
INDIA 483
COMBAT TEAMS 486
THE RIVER CROSSING 489
'WE WERE THROUGH' 491
THE END OF THE WAR 492
'HE BELONGS TO ME' 493
SOUVENIRS 495
STILL ALIVE 497

THE 4-F VOLUNTEER 501

Unit 'GALAHAD' 503
'Everybody Was A Marauder' 507
The Natives 508
General Merrill 510
'We Had No Dancing Girls' 511
Going Home 512
Observations 515

THE RADIO WIZARD 519

'I Wanted To Do My Part' 521
The 'Song Of India' 523
Mules 526
Shooting 526
'They Would Go Wild' 528
Marching Past The Hospital 530
Food And Sickness On The Move 531
Home 533
Last Words 533

THE IMMIGRANT 537

'You Become A Fatalist' 539
Point Man 539
'We Didn't Get Decorated' 540
'Killed In Action' 540
The Chief 542
The Ledo Road 544
'A Very Tough Thing' 545

Home 546

THE COMBAT CAMERAMAN I 549

Depression Days 549
Becoming a Cameraman 550
'We Need The Five Dollars' 552
'The War Was On Top Of Us' 553
'I Won World War II' 557
Going Overseas 560

THE VOLUNTEER 565

'You Have To Stay Home And Farm' 567
'You're The Son Of A Gun That Went AWOL' 569
In The Brig 571
'My God, A Torpedo!" 572
Picking Up The Dead 573
'One Day The Salvation Came' 573
'My Squad Leader Was A Convicted Felon' 574
'Poorest Goddamn Excuse For A Mule Skinner' 575
The Letter 576
'We Can Disappear In The Jungle' 576
Combat 577
Wounded 580
'I Can Save That Leg' 581
The Nisei Interpreter 583
'The Men Who Altered My Life' 584
Reconnecting With Truck 586

'I Don't Know What A Hero Is' 587

THE COMBAT CAMERAMAN II 591

Getting To India 592
Getting To Stilwell's Headquarters 593
The Chinese 598
Newsreel Wong 600
Going AWOL 603
Traversing the Mountains 605
'I'm No Damned Volunteer' 607
'The Most Important Thing In This Outfit' 609
Hit By a C-47 Air Drop 612
'I Had Never Cried In My Life' 614
"You're The Guy I've Been Looking For' 615

AFTERWORD 621

ACKNOWLEDGEMENTS 631

NOTES 633

Author's Note

"All Americans, they were ready to go and ready to fight. My thing, [today], is that I would like to see them outlaw wars."

—98-year-old Russell Hamler, at a ceremony honoring him, 2022

The newspaper from New York landed on my doorstep. A long obituary graced A-9 of the Weekend *Wall Street Journal*, circulation 610,000 print and over three million digital subscribers. A slight smile, tempered with a resigned sadness, spread as I noted the headline. At least someone was paying attention.

'Last of the WWII 'Marauders' Unit Dies'

The time had finally arrived—the last Marauder had passed, signifying the end of an era, and just as I began this book that very month to remember them and the other men and women of this most forgotten arena of World War II.

"Russell Hamler was born June 24, 1924, and grew up in Mt. Lebanon, a suburb of Pittsburgh. His father, Robert Hamler, worked with teams of horses moving dirt at construction sites. Young Russell's habit of roaming the outskirts of Pittsburgh earned him the nickname of Huck, a nod to Huckleberry Finn."

"When he learned that the Army was seeking volunteers in 'a high state of physical ruggedness' for a dangerous mission in an unspecified location, he put up his hand. It was simple, he said later: 'You joined the Army to fight the war.'"

"Soon Hamler found himself among nearly 3,000 volunteers in an Army unit that became known as Merrill's Marauders, named after their leader, Brig. Gen. Frank Merrill. They fought behind Japanese lines in Burma, now known as Myanmar, in some of the most hellish conditions faced by troops during World War II."

"In February 1944, the Marauders were ordered to march into Burma, ready or not. 'It was an organization that was never given time to organize,' Charlton Ogburn Jr., a Signal Corps officer in the unit, wrote later in a memoir, The Marauders. Amid bickering among the British, Chinese and American allies over strategies, Louis Mountbatten, the top Allied commander in Southeast Asia, assigned oversight of the unit to the American Lt. Gen. Joseph 'Vinegar Joe' Stilwell."

"The hastily trained and often ragtag unit lugged packs along twisting trails over mountain passes, endured ravenous leeches and tropical diseases, chopped through bamboo thickets and won battles against highly experienced Japanese forces. The Marauders' most famous exploit was capturing the strategic Myitkyina airstrip in May 1944, an accomplishment described by Winston Churchill as 'a brilliant feat of arms.'"[17]

After the war, Russell returned home to work for Trans World Airlines in Pittsburgh, Pennsylvania. It was there, in 1968, that he met a touring Lord Louis Mountbatten at the airport, and they had the opportunity to meet and chat about the Marauders, twenty-three years after the war. Russell left us quietly at the end of December 2023 at the age of 99.

*

In the writing of this series, I have been approached by people, generally children of combatants, and sometimes in slightly indignant fashion, wanting to know 'why there is no CBI Theater' focus in my books, as if I considered these men and women who served in that arena somehow less worthy of recognition and study.

The ordinary unfortunate explanation was simply that comparatively few Americans served there, a complex and confusing pocket of activity that technically is not even classified a 'theater' of operations in the sense of, let's say, the European or Pacific Theaters. It did not have a unified combat command per se; there weren't any conventional U.S. infantry divisions slogging it out in China, Burma, or India—most of the ground fighting was done by British, Indian, and Chinese troops. Only about a percent and a half of Americans in uniform during World War II were engaged here, most in supporting roles; less than 3,000 U.S. ground troop volunteers made up legendary long-range fighting forces known as Merrill's Marauders and others, who were pushed to the brink of extinction after just five months of combat. And so, the sad fact is that the sampling of archived interviews with these veterans is comparatively small, though some interviewers working through the auspices of the Library of Congress were able to attend a Marauder reunion or two in Virginia about the time I was undertaking my oral history project with my students.

This is not to say that it has been entirely forgotten; as we have seen, with the recent passing of Merrill's Marauders Russell 'Huck' Hamler, China-Burma-India was momentarily thrust back into the spotlight. Of course, there are more authoritative tomes out there, but it was the ordinary individuals like Huck who carried out the plans of 'gods and generals' who will be the focus of this book, including the Marauders and the brave men and women carrying out harrowing mercenary and support duties and 'flying the Hump' to resupply our Chinese allies. I hope that I have done them a degree of justice.

Matthew Rozell
September 11, 2024
Washington County, NY

Merrill's Marauders take a rest break, somewhere in Burma. U.S. Army Special Operations, public domain.

Introduction

To understand the significance of the China-Burma-India area of operations during World War II, the reader has to understand that from the Allied perspective, keeping China in the war against Japanese aggression was of importance not as a priority mission but as it related to keeping Japanese forces tied down as the war in Europe was won first. Here we will venture back to the political, military, and geographic origins of the 'War in the Pacific,' beginning with the root causes of Sino-Japanese conflict. From the American perspective, it is a fascinating and complex history, the remnants of which are manifested to this day, especially as we seek to understand China's rise as a superpower in the post-World War II and 21st century landscape.

*

In 1853, when Millard Fillmore was in the White House, Commodore Matthew C. Perry steamed into Edo (now Tokyo) Bay with his seven 'Black Ships,' equipped with the latest in military firepower, and let loose with a 73-gun display of firepower and intimidation to signal that the United States was interested in opening Japanese ports to commerce and mooring stations with the West. No would not be an acceptable response, and in 1854 he returned. The Japanese acquiesced to opening six ports, with concessions of extraterritoriality, or rights for foreigners accused of a crime in Japan to be tried by their own nation's courts. After 250 years of national seclusion, Japanese leaders shrewdly decided to 'Learn from the Barbarian'—sending students abroad to acquire the latest in

Western fashion and customs, but especially in industrial and technological advances that had passed the East by as China and Japan had closed their doors to outside interference and 'corruption' to their millenniums-old cultures. Japan now saw it had to adopt these concessions to the West to survive, simply by looking at what had happened in China only a decade or so before.[34]

By the end of the eighteenth century, Imperial China, with its history of dynastic rule spanning nearly four thousand years, was having none of the similar Western demands to open its doors to barbarian outsiders. Frenzied European demand for fine silks, tea, porcelain, and other goods was met with their contempt for outside trade goods; gold and silver were the only acceptable commodities. The British East India Company found a workaround in the illegal importation of opium cultivated in their holdings in India and a ripe market as addiction took hold in some Chinese ports. The destruction of British opium by Chinese authorities in the 1830s spurred the lopsided Opium Wars and subsequent humiliating treaties in which Western military superiority forced huge indemnity payments, the rights to open ports to Western zones of interest, and extraterritorial concessions; the British also got the port of Hong Kong for the next 150 years. China descended into addiction, corruption, rebellion, and civil war that ended their dynastic system on the eve of World War I.

Japan, on the other hand, by adopting selective cultural borrowing, adapted and thrived in her stunning transformation from a feudal society to a modern industrial state. As her hunger for raw materials and 'necessary' territorial expansion grew, she looked at

---

[34] Townsend Harris (1804-1878) was appointed the first U.S. Consul General to Japan. In that capacity, he promoted U.S. interests and navigated the intrigues of Japanese court life at the end of the 'Shogun' era. I mention this because he was born a fifteen-minute walk from my high school in Hudson Falls (then Sandy Hill), New York.

her neighbor to the east—Korea, historically a tributary state of China and now one that the Chinese viewed as still a dependency of China.

By the 1880s, Japanese military leaders also came to view Korea as 'a dagger pointed at the heart of Japan'; the Russian empire also was poised just to the north by this time, coercing a lease from the Qing Chinese authorities at Port Arthur.

The First Sino-Japanese War (1894-1895) revealed the gains made by Japan over the previous twenty years' crash programs of industrialization and modernization and whetted the appetite of the Japanese for further expansion into China. Japan acquired parts of Northeast China and Taiwan at comparatively little cost with a burst of nationalistic pride and Western astonishment and mixed admiration.

Japan's 1894 victory over China. Source: Japan Punch, 1894 Public domain.

This, after all, was the golden age of imperial outreach and conquest, and the United States' interest in the Pacific region was also peaking. In 1898, the war with Spain over Cuba resulted in a sudden surge, with the annexed prizes being a host of little-known islands that would take on such tremendous name recognition as World War II in the Pacific unfolded, including the Philippine Islands, Guam, Wake Island, and Hawaii. Three-quarters of a million Filipinos died between 1898 and 1901 in the failed independence uprising that followed.[18]

Back in China, anti-foreign sentiment was coming to a head. China's loss in the First Sino-Japanese War increased the likelihood that China would be threatened with foreign partition as Britain, Italy, France, Germany, Russia, and Japan continued to advance their overseas trading and colonial interests. The United States, now with Asian interests and footholds, sought to introduce the Open Door Policy, by which all signatories would respect each other's rights to sharing markets in China. A secret anti-imperialist group, the Society of Righteous and Harmonious Fists, quasi-mystics who practiced martial arts ('Chinese boxing' to Europeans) and came to believe they were impervious to bullets, began to target Christian missionaries and their followers in North China. The movement spread to the capital, Beijing, where foreign legations were put under siege with the blessing of the elderly Qing dynasty empress dowager Cixi, who issued an imperial decree essentially declaring war on foreign influence. Eight nations, including the United States, responded with 30,000 troops to counter the rebellion and extracted more monetary concessions, revealing fully the weakness and corruptness of the old imperial regime.

Russian incursion into Manchuria in 1902 in violation of the Open Door Policy inflamed tensions, especially with Japan over conflicting spheres of influence in Korea and Manchuria, culminating in the 1904-1905 Russo-Japanese War. Japan's victory stunned and shocked the world, curbing Russia's eastern expansionist powers and encouraging Japanese militarist sentiments. Her swift surprise attack at the Russian eastern 'warm water' fleet at Port Arthur on February 9, 1904, in some ways foreshadowed her future assault on Pearl Harbor. The Russian Empire, dealing with its own nascent revolutionary uprisings and an as-yet-uncompleted Trans-Siberian Railway (troops and supplies from the west had to be unloaded and then sledged two weeks overland to be repacked and retracked to the front in the far east), ran out of time and men to stem the onslaught, contributing to the decisive Russian defeat in the Battle of Tsushima in the Sea of Japan, the first naval engagement to be fought with steel battleships and wireless technology.

"A Righteous War to Chastise the Russian Destroyer Force's Night Attack," likely the Battle of Port Arthur, Shinohara Kiyooki, 1904. Japanese block print propaganda. Public Domain.

The Treaty of Portsmouth [New Hampshire] awarded Japan her newfound spoils and netted U.S. President Teddy Roosevelt a Nobel Peace Prize, the first ever for an American recipient (even though he was not even in attendance at Portsmouth). It allowed for the Japanese colonization of Korea, culminating in the outright

Japanese annexation of Korea in 1910. The table of Japanese aggression and the reward of overseas success was being set.

China's revolutionary turmoil boiled over in the Revolution of 1911, ending the Qing dynasty and thousands of years of imperial dynastic rule. China was declared a republic in 1912 under Sun Yat-sen as the first president. The Nationalist Party Kuomintang was founded, and Dr. Sun turned over power to Yuan Shikai, who then died in 1916, after which a period of civil war between warlords once again plunged China into chaos. With the outbreak of World War I, Japan joined the Allies with the promise of acquiring German territories in Asia, landing in China's Shandong Province to attack the German settlements at Tsingtao and later their Pacific possessions in the Marianas, Carolines, and Marshall Islands.

Japan then presented the Republic of China with its Twenty-One Demands, designed to cement control over China with the intention of making it a Japanese protectorate; Japan's position was strong enough that it was awarded the Shandong Province at the Paris Peace Conference in 1919, despite U.S. misgivings at the end of the Open Door Policy and Chinese objections.

Communists and Nationalists

In 1917, the Romanov dynasty collapsed in Russia as the Bolsheviks under Lenin orchestrated the world's first Marxist revolution amidst catastrophic wartime defeats and the economic turmoil of World War I. The new 'workers' revolution' appealed to revolutionaries everywhere as a possible alternative path to power, the parliamentary path viewed by them as hopelessly corrupted by capitalist and imperialist class influences. The Communist International, or Comintern, was organized to foment the worldwide socialist revolution; only then would the true Marxist state of communism exist. In 1921, the Chinese Communist Party was founded, aligning itself with the Nationalist Party as the left wing of the Kuomintang under its emerging leadership of Mao Zedong and Zhou Enlai. Dr. Sun Yat-sen sent Chiang Kai-shek, the head of the right wing of the KMT, to Moscow to study in 1924, but Chiang returned disillusioned with the Soviet model of governing for China. When Dr. Sun died in 1925, Chiang emerged victorious in the power vacuum that ensued in the KMT. As the commander-in-chief of the National Revolutionary Army, the military arm of the KMT, in 1926 he led the Northern Campaign to put down warlord factions and solidify the Kuomintang's power and authority over China. Troubled by competing communist influences in the ranks, in 1927 Chiang turned on the CCP and began purges and massacres of communists that would end their cooperation and foment civil war until the eve of Japanese full-scale invasion ten years later; in the famous Long March of 1934-35, Mao's forces evaded Chiang's pursuit and encirclement in a 5,600-mile retreat; out of the 65,000 soldiers of the CCP's First Army, just 8,000 weary but battle-hardened troops survived, with the support of local peasantry along the way, resentful of the heavy-handed treatment by Nationalist forces and government policies. For years, the peasantry had been subjected to over forty different taxes, some levied years in advance, controlling every aspect of a miserable existence where half the population already had a life expectancy rate of just thirty years.[19] Nationalist forces responded by laying waste to entire villages and communities suspected of aiding the communists, yet the remaining communist forces emerged battle-hardened on the eve of the Second Sino-Japanese War (1937-1945) when the two armies united to confront the all-out Japanese offensives for the conquest of all China.

World War II Begins in Asia

As we have seen, the stage was set for China's World War II conflict with Japan decades before 1937. Manchuria, about the size of France and Germany combined, with its fertile land and rich coal and iron resources, was key to Japan's expansionist ambitions. Already in control of railroads in the region, in 1931 the Japanese manufactured a railroad sabotage incident in Mukden that gave the pretext for a full-scale invasion, which led to the creation of the puppet state of Manchukuo in 1932. Worldwide condemnation resulted in Japan withdrawing from the League of Nations in February 1933, which was followed in October by Nazi Germany and signaled the death knell of the concept of collective security, though it was probably doomed from the outset, as the United States never joined the League due to the Senate rejection of the Treaty of Versailles in 1919.

In July 1937, an incident at the Marco Polo Bridge outside of Beijing escalated the tensions that would begin the full-fledged war with Japan that some historians place as the true beginning of World War II (in Asia, at least). While the exact cause is unknown, it seems that the occupying Japanese forces demanded entry to search for a missing soldier; shots were exchanged and skirmishes escalated. The subsequent Battle of Shanghai lasted from August 13, 1937, to November 26, 1937, and resulted in massive destruction and the Japanese capture of the city. Chinese forces suffered over 200,000 casualties, more than twice as many as the invader, and the Japanese had no qualms about using gas attacks and instituting the commission of atrocities on a large scale, soon to be amplified in the 'Rape of Nanking' the following month, which fell on December 13. A note of horror was a beheading contest between two Japanese officers, competing to see who could behead 100 Chinese captives first; the number was upped to 150 prisoners for the subsequent round. Consensus estimates place the number of Chinese massacred at around 200,000.

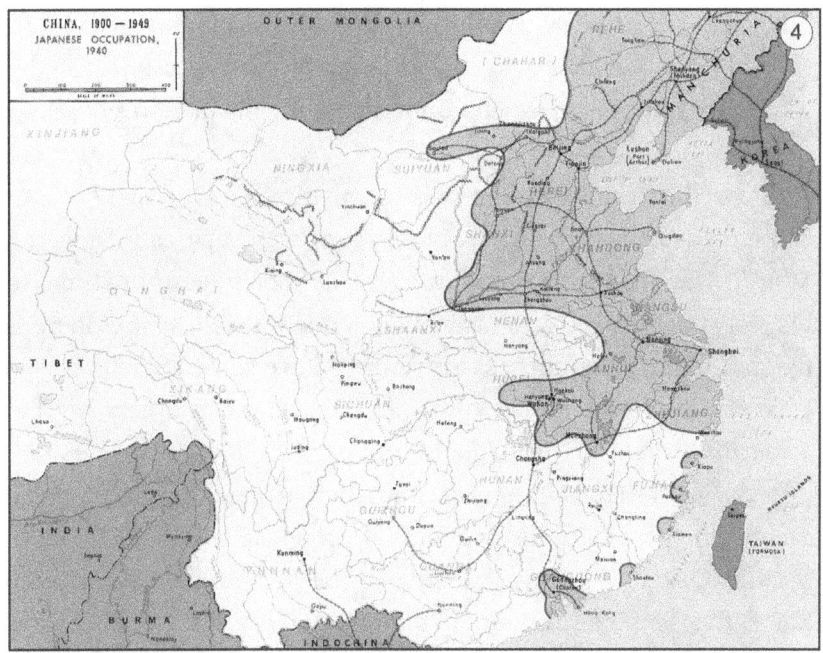

Japanese Occupation of eastern and northern China, 1940. US Army, public domain.

'Vinegar Joe' Stilwell

One American became the personification of the United States' efforts to keep China engaged in World War II and its efforts in the China-Burma-India arena.

Joseph Warren 'Vinegar Joe' Stilwell was born on March 19, 1883. With deep Yankee roots, he was raised in Yonkers, New York. Young Joseph pushed back against his strict religious upbringing; though a good student, he fell in with the wrong crowd in his post-graduate studies at Yonkers High and instead of the originally planned course of college study at Yale, his father used his influence to get him accepted into the U.S. Military Academy at West Point. With an aptitude for languages and athletics, he graduated in 1904 with his commission and a lifelong pride in keeping himself in top physical condition, especially running in cross country and track, which would pay off in many ways—most notably his retreat on foot through the mountains of Burma in 1942 at the age of sixty.

Stilwell chose the Philippines for his first posting in 1904, because as a product of the recently concluded Spanish-American War, it was an area that was still actively rebellious at the time. In his early twenties, he came away with some valuable lessons in midtropical highland country skirmishing before being posted in 1906 to West Point as an instructor in the Department of Tactics and as a coach. Restless and feeling a bit too close to home—Yonkers was just down the Hudson—his second tour of the Philippines commenced in 1911 with his new bride in tow. He was determined to see the 'Orient' with his wife before she departed for the United States for the birth of their first child, Joe Jr. (who would in later years serve as his father's chief of staff in China). They spent time in Japan before she left, and he continued on to see China on the eve of the Revolution of 1911, marveling at a culture nearly four thousand years old boasting 400 million souls, but also confiding disgust in his journal at the extreme ignorance and poverty he encountered in a country where 70 to 80 percent of the population remained illiterate.

Stilwell returned to the United States in January 1912 just before the old Chinese regime was toppled. He rounded out his twenties and entered his thirties on duty in California and back teaching at West Point. As the Great War in Europe unfolded, Congress authorized doubling the size of the regular army and in April 1917 entered the war. This period of exponential, unprecedented growth culminated in the Selective Service Act the following month, calling for the conscription of a million more men, an army that had to be trained before taking the field, a task for which Stilwell was selected at various postings until ordered to France as a newly minted captain to the Commanding General's AEF office for intelligence duty; his command of the language was sorely needed.

After the war, he sought a distant posting and jumped when the opportunity to serve in China came up. In the interwar years, he served three tours in China, picking up the language, studying the people, and making key connections, like that of his lifelong champion, George C. Marshall, whose own posting overlapped with Stilwell's for eight months. In his third posting to China, he was the military attaché of the U.S. Legation in northern China between 1935 and 1940, where he became acquainted with Chiang Kai-shek in late 1938. In between his tours of duty in China, he also held several staff officer positions in the United States.[20] He didn't care for pomp and ceremonies and overbearing discipline of subordinates, but he was a stickler for tactics and maneuvers, dishing out criticism without reserve to those he felt were not pulling their weight in the field. One disgruntled soldier drew a caricature of his head and face emanating spectrally from a vinegar bottle; upon discovering it, a tickled Stilwell had it copied and distributed to friends and posted on the board.[21]

After the fall of France to Germany in 1940, the Japanese government ordered the British to close the Hong Kong frontier and the Burma Road, the last backchannel of supply to China from the West. The British acquiesced, not willing to risk war with Japan while in a state of war with Germany and finding no assurance of joint action with the United States, still neutral, in the event of a refusal.[22]

In September 1940, Stilwell attained the rank of major general, having been assigned to command his first division, the 7th, that

July. He loved driving the draftees and whipping them into shape, a taskmaster who often accompanied them on hikes and maneuvers, acquiring the nickname Uncle Joe or Galloping Joe in his hiking boots, sweater, and crushed hat, blending in with the 15,000 soldiers and ordinary workers at the post in California. At the ceremony put on by his staff to address the assembled soldiers to acknowledge and celebrate his promotion, he kept it brief: 'The higher a monkey climbs the pole, the more you see of his behind.'

The same month, Japan joined the Axis alliance. Shortly thereafter, President Roosevelt and his service chiefs, including George C. Marshall (sworn in as Chief of Staff of the Army on September 1, 1939) agreed in theory to follow a Germany or 'Europe First' policy in the future planning for what now looked like an inevitable eventual entry of the United States in this world war, with the prevailing notion that Europe was the seat of world power politics, whereas China should continue on the defensive, with U.S. back-channel support, buying time for the time being—which would eventually define the China-Burma-India operations in the future.[23]

*

"Roosevelt's governing idea was that China should be one of the great powers after the war to fill the vacuum left by Japan. He was not unaware of shortcomings for he once acknowledged to his son that China 'was still in the eighteenth century.' Nevertheless that great and ancient country with its 500 million enduring people, however frustrated by endless misgovernment, was a geopolitical fact. Roosevelt wanted it on America's side in the future."

-Barbara Tuchman, *Stilwell and the American Experience in China*[24]

President Roosevelt had floated to the American public a naval quarantine of aggressor nations in an October radio address. In December, the USS *Panay*, in Nanking to evacuate Americans, came under attack by Japanese aircraft. American presence in China, including business and missionary interests, had been active for decades; the president settled at the time for an official apology and indemnity settlement, though diplomats were working the back channels to get the British on board with the idea of a quarantine of Japan. As 1937 turned into 1938, Prime Minister Neville Chamberlain turned down a proposal to discuss a joint conference on the subject, formulating his appeasement policy toward Italy and Germany; why provoke the Japanese? Without support from the Royal Navy, any idea of a quarantine was doomed, so it was scuttled.[25]

The United States finally instituted an oil and scrap metal embargo on Japan in the summer of 1941. Following the September 1940 invasion by Japan of French Indochina, ostensibly to cut off Chinese access to raw materials, American supplies of rubber, one of the few precious war materials the United States could not produce on its own, were greatly endangered. By then, the war in Europe was in full swing, with Warsaw and Paris having fallen to the Germans, and ten months later, France, Norway, and the Low Countries occupied. Chiang Kai-shek sought American support through the Lend-Lease Act and began getting financial and military aid. At the invitation of Chiang, Claire Chennault arrived with the 1st American Volunteer Group, the Flying Tigers, American fighter pilots in American aircraft affixed with the Chinese flag to do battle with the Japanese in the skies over China. Three squadrons would arrive to train in Burma after April 1941.

*

On December 7, 1941, General and Mrs. Stilwell were having an open house for junior officers at their home overlooking the Pacific at Fort Ord, California, when the news arrived over the radio that Pearl Harbor had been attacked. The Japanese, underestimated once again, had struck a stinging blow over three thousand miles across the Pacific. For the next several hours and days, Stilwell rushed to bolster his Southern California coastal command, chagrined at reports of logistical bottlenecks for men and materiel to defend the territory all the way to the Mexican border that he was responsible for. Thankfully, all the panicked rumors were false.

The Japanese continued their lightning blow across the Pacific. Guam and Wake Island fell on December 23. Hong Kong surrendered on Christmas after a century of British control. Manila fell on January 2, as did the Dutch East Indies shortly after. French Indochina, controlled by the Vichy French, opened its doors, cutting off the port of Hanoi as a resupply route for China. The invaders had cut the Malay Peninsula in half and began laying siege to Singapore. Thailand was also occupied, and the Japanese had begun to make inroads into Burma.

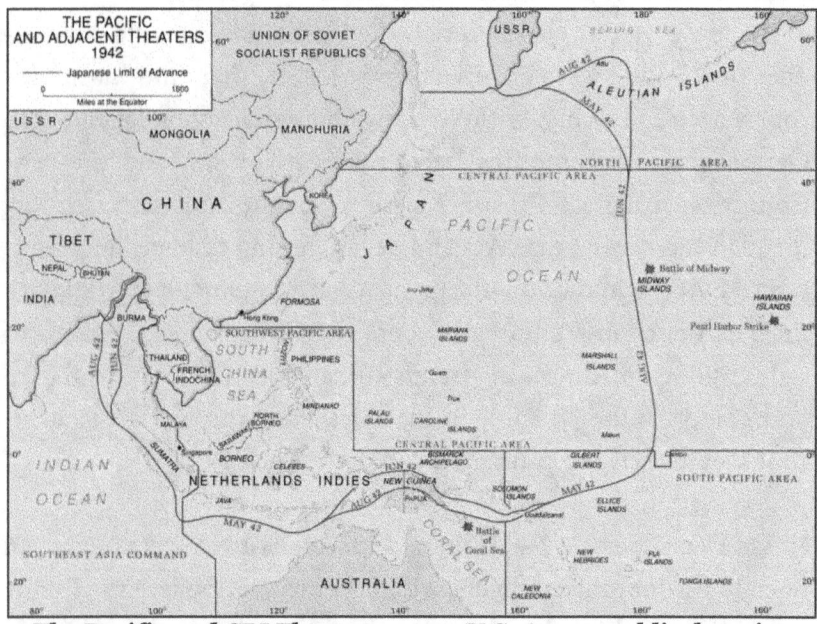

The Pacific and CBI Theaters, 1942. U.S. Army, public domain.

The conquest of British Malaysia and her rubber plantations was complete with the fall of Singapore in mid-February 1942. Britain, with its Asian colonial empire in tatters, was immediately concerned that the fall of Burma would remove the last obstacle to a Japanese assault on British India. While the United States had little interest in defending British colonial possessions, keeping China in the war to tie down over a million Japanese troops on the mainland was critical. The Burma Road resupply route to Kunming, China, from India had to be defended and improved. Lend-Lease supplies destined for road transport into the backdoor of China were piling up on the docks at the port city of Rangoon, Burma, in the south.

*

Universally recognized by now as a top commander, Stilwell was summoned to Washington for the joint British/American Arcadia Conference just before Christmas to help formulate the war direction, which would essentially boil down to 'Europe First.' Stilwell was initially selected to plan and command the Allied invasion of North Africa. He harbored some logistical doubts, however, and events pushed the invasion back; he also was not shy in his blistering opinions and criticism of British attitudes and how its officer staff carried themselves with swagger, and consistently referred to them as 'limeys' in his journal. Marshall called him in for mild reprimand, but also to pick his brain on a military point man to work with Chiang Kai-shek in China. When their top pick did not pan out, the chief-of-staff informed him, 'Joe, you have 24 hours to think up a better candidate, otherwise it's you.' Stilwell responded, 'I'll go where I'm sent.'[26]

In February 1942 Stilwell got his third star and as lieutenant general was assigned as commander of all U.S. forces in China, Burma, and India, deputy commander of the Burma-India Theater under the British, later to be led by Vice-Admiral Louis Mountbatten, and military adviser to Chiang Kai-shek and his Chinese forces. It was a complicated balancing act that would have been difficult for a tactful commander to pull off; dealing with egos and pomp was not

Stilwell's strong suit. While Japan was the common enemy, the British and Americans had different agendas. The British primarily wanted to protect their empire, especially in India, and would be wary of strengthening China too much, lest they experience a postwar resurgence to threaten Britain's interests; the two countries already had an uneven and complicated past. The Americans would hope to keep China from being knocked out of the war and wished to use Chinese coastal fortifications as a launchpad for the eventual invasion of Japan.

Stilwell would especially resist the effort to place his U.S. soldiers under British command. His main logistical military effort would be to use Chinese and American forces to keep and improve the Burma Road, though it was clear that Rangoon would soon fall. Planners were already envisioning building the Ledo Road to the north to connect with the Burma Road to Kunming, and flying supply planes over the Himalayas, a dauntingly skilled task that would be costly in men, planes, and fuel. A land route had to be maintained.

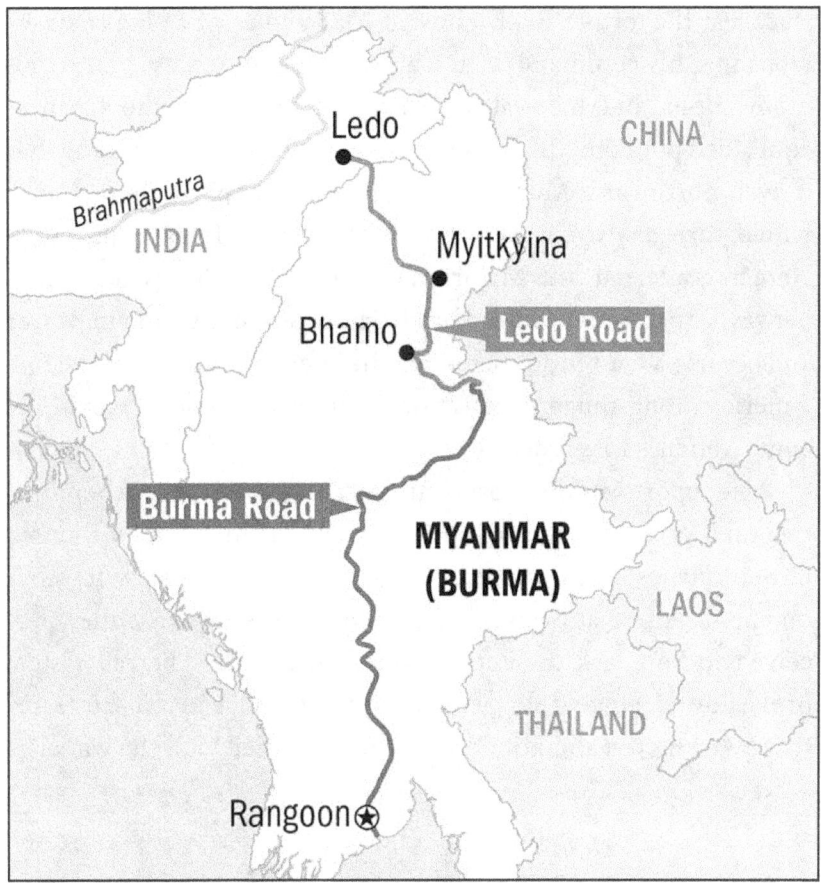

The Ledo Road would begin in India, connect with the Burma Road to Rangoon, (when re-opened from Japanese conquest), and pivot northwest from Burma to Kunming, China. U.S. Army, public domain.

'We Got a Hell of a Beating'

Stilwell arrived in China via Cairo and India in early March to present himself to Chiang and reacquaint himself with China and her troops, sorely in need of training and discipline. On March 8, Rangoon fell to the south; it was hoped to hold the line to contain Japan's advance up the Irrawaddy. It was not to be. Stilwell was in

Burma at the former British post at Maymyo east of Mandalay, establishing his command with Chinese generals amidst poor communications and medical facilities and disease as the Japanese continued pounding Burmese towns and cities from the air as they moved northward. Monsoon season was fast approaching, which would turn any eventual withdraw to defend India a quagmire. Here he conferred with Major Frank Merrill, another West Pointer he was acquainted with, who briefed him on the situation in Burma and became a trusted adviser whom he later selected to lead the first American long-range penetration force in Burma that would become Merrill's Marauders.

Air support was then lost in another surprise Japanese bombing raid on March 22 that caught RAF and AVG (American Volunteer Group) planes on the ground. Chinese troops were slow to move on the offensive at Stilwell's commands, upset at what they perceived to be a lack of support from the British. The rail system broke down; refugees clogged the roads. Stilwell was also frustrated that Washington and London were preoccupied with the war elsewhere.

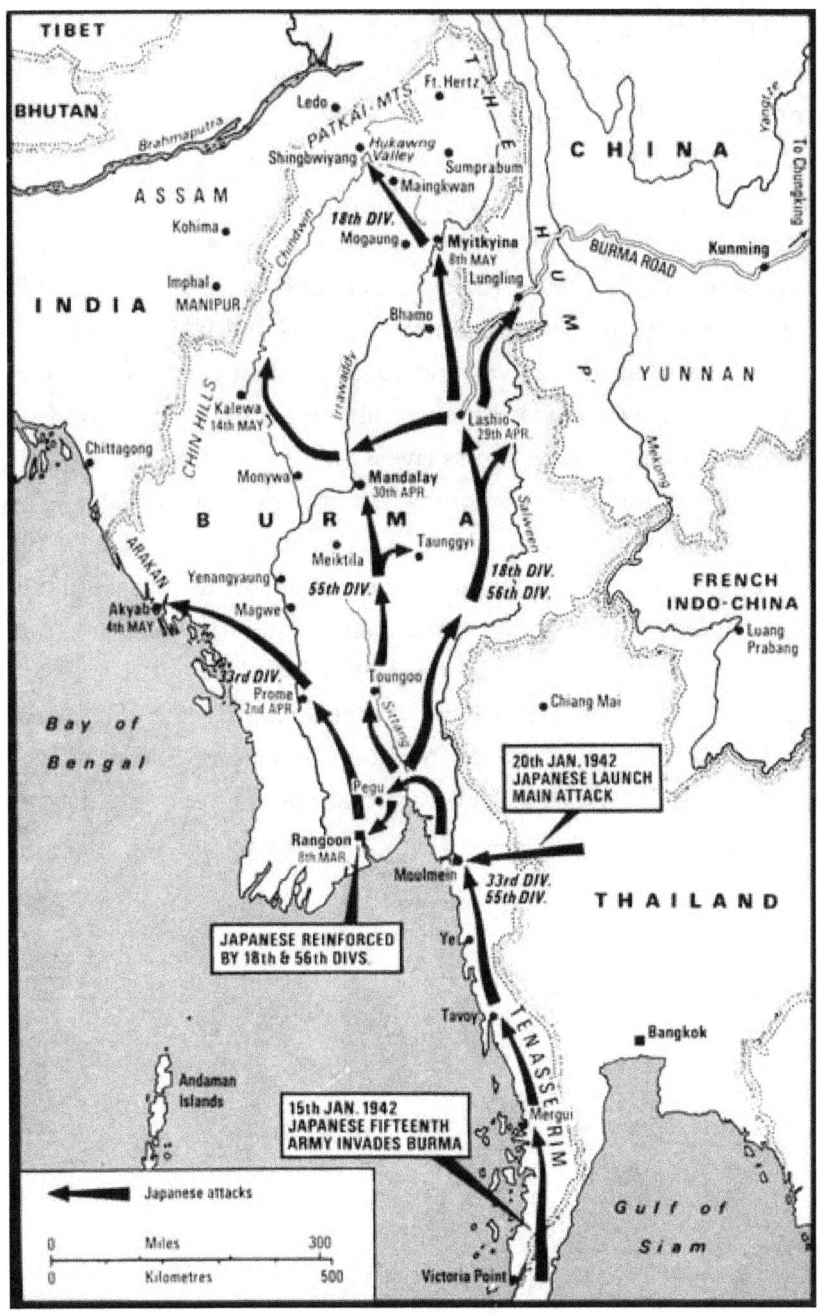

Japanese conquest of Burma, 1942. U.S. Army, public domain.

The decision was made to decamp to India with the Chinese troops before it was too late. Mandalay had fallen, the Japanese three-pronged attack now coming rapidly into wider focus. British leaders had left Burma, and Stilwell's staff was evacuated by air as Stilwell planned to move on to Myitkyina (pronounced 'Mitcheneau'), the main northern airbase, with a party of just over a hundred including Frank Merrill and other American officers, Burmese nurses, missionaries and Quakers, civilians and Chinese soldiers. Scouts reported the railway and roads heading there were hopelessly jammed. He decided they would take a rugged path on foot over the mountains and across rivers for 140 miles northwestward to Imphal in India. 'Keep moving. Don't stop for anything. By the time we get out of here, many of you will hate my guts, but I'll tell you one thing: you'll all get out.' Three-star generals command tens of thousands of men and materiel in an army corps. This one, carrying a rifle and no insignia, was leading a column of souls worn out by heat exhaustion, combat, sickness, and disease. The monsoon season began; men cursed as they slipped up and down the trails. Slowed by sickness and sunstroke, some were dragged along by others; Merrill, with a weak heart, was one of them.

*General Stilwell leads troops on foot out of Burma, 1942.
U.S. Army, public domain.*

On May 20, 1942, the day the Japanese completed their conquest of Burma, the party of 114 arrived in Imphal, India. He was bewildered at messages of commendation from Marshall on behalf of the president and secretary of war, and the press noted this exploit where he had not lost one person in the confused exodus from Burma that would kill 900,000 refugees.

Stilwell flew then to Delhi, where, pressed by hounding newsmen, he gave an impromptu news conference, chaffing at British characterizations of a 'heroic, voluntary withdrawal' and a 'glorious retreat.' He ended famously with, 'In the first place, no military commander in history ever made a voluntary withdrawal. And there's no such thing as a glorious retreat. All retreats are ignominious as hell. I claim we got a hell of a licking. We got run out of

Burma, and it's humiliating as hell. I think we ought to find out what caused it, go back, and retake Burma.'

The Americans would return.[27]

P-40 Flying Tiger in China. Public domain.

PART ONE

THE FLYING TIGERS

Many Americans have heard of the Flying Tigers, but not many understand that they were the best organized American mercenaries to fight in World War II, assembled and trained in a time of neutrality.[35] Their leader, Claire Chennault, with several tours of China under his belt, had resigned from the Army in April 1937, having been recommended for a medical discharge due to poor health brought on by two decades of open cockpit flying, though it was no secret that over the years he had had his disagreements with superiors, the last straw being passed over for a promotion. Retiring as captain, now a civilian, he was recruited to inspect and advise the Chinese Air Force. His recommendations to Chiang Kai-shek would lead to the formation of the First American Volunteer Group, recruited under the authority of President Roosevelt to support the Chinese in their war against Japan. The volunteer force was made up of American veterans of the Army Air Corps, Navy, and Marine Corps, and was nicknamed the Flying Tigers. Commanded by Chennault, bestowed with the rank of colonel by Chiang, he was essentially a civilian mercenary from the American military point of view during this period. He clashed repeatedly

---

[35] *American mercenaries*-another group that comes to mind would be the young American pilots flying for the RAF in 1941 prior to Pearl Harbor.

with Army brass, most notably General Stilwell, who disagreed that Chennault's original plan for raiding Japanese bases from the air would be sustainable as a successful use of scarce resources, and would be more likely to invite Japanese counterassaults that the Allies did not need.

The Flying Tigers began to arrive in China in April 1941; trained in Burma and given delays and growing pains, they saw their first combat less than two weeks after Pearl Harbor, flying in their P-40s with the distinctive shark nose art.

Officially members of the Republic of China Air Force, AVG pilots destroyed almost three hundred Japanese aircraft, while losing only fourteen pilots in combat; they were the first Americans to engage the Japanese in open combat after Pearl Harbor and brought a much-needed antidote to the cascading news cycle of calamities brought on by the lightning Japanese advances across Asia.[28]

The American Volunteer Group ceased to exist on July 4, 1942. Many pilots drifted back to their original branches of service, some went home, and five others folded into now-Brigadier General Chennault's new Army Air Corps 23rd Fighter Group in what would become the 14th Air Force in southern China, flying air support and conducting a war of attrition for General Stilwell's ground forces. Today, their exploits are fondly recalled by the Chinese people; in 2005, pilots were given a heroes' welcome upon their return.

Morgan Vaux in China. Library of Congress.

CHAPTER ONE

The AVG Stationmaster

Morgan H. Vaux was born July 21, 1918, in Watertown, South Dakota. He graduated from Kenosha High School, Wisconsin, in 1936, serving in the Civilian Conservation Corps during the Great Depression. He enlisted in the U.S. Army Air Corps in 1939, and in 1941, upon receiving a special discharge from the Army, he joined the American Volunteer Group (AVG), the Flying Tigers, and served in Burma and China until they were dissolved. He then enlisted in the U.S. Marine Corps in late 1942 and served in the Pacific theatre until 1945. For his service, he was awarded the Bronze Star, Presidential Unit Citation, and the WWII Victory Medal.

Morgan H. Vaux

I had basic training at Chanute Air Base and Scott Field Air Base in radio operating and mechanics, aircraft specialty. A hell of a training I got. After that, it was maintaining aircraft in the 39th Pursuit Squadron, and also working field operations with field radios. That's about it until I got the contract to go to China with the American Volunteer Group; that was when I used my training to be an early warning radio station as a stationmaster in China.

'We Wrecked A Lot of Planes'

The learning curve for many of the young pilots transitioning into the P-40 fighters was steep; three pilots were killed in accidents early on. On November 3, 1941, a day that went down in their history as 'Circus Day,' no fewer than eight P-40s were damaged by accidents and mishaps.[29]

In Burma, we were there from August 1941 until August 1942. We went there mainly for training, because Chennault and his people had leased Kyedaw Airdrome at a town called Toungoo, Burma, north of Rangoon, from the British Royal Air Force. At that airbase, the pilots were trained in all kinds of things—landings and takeoffs and maneuvers. They were from the Army Air Corps, the Navy, and the Marines. The Navy and Marines had never seen the planes we had; they were all new to them. In fact, one man was a flying boat pilot; he had to go from high-flying boat pilot to a fighter plane pilot. It took a lot of practice, landings and takeoffs, at Kyedaw Airdrome. We lost a lot, and wrecked a lot of planes, too; propellers bent and smashed when they landed the nose over the plane, hit too hard, and broke the landing gear because they were used to [landing on] carriers—most of them were carrier pilots. On the carrier landings you cut your speed and just kind of drop down on the ground, maybe a couple of feet. You can't do that with another type of fighter plane. You have to grease it, more or less, on the runway. So, anyway, we lost quite a few planes to start with.

No Replacements

There were no replacements. In fact, all during our tour over there we had no replacements to talk about in terms of propellers and tires, things wearing out and blowing out. The only replacements we were able to get were by air by the China National

Aviation Corporation. They were flying over the Hump from Kunming to India, and they would ferry in spare parts for us. But they had to come all the way across from the Ivory Coast in Africa, all the way across. I think they were shipped from there by air somehow. I don't know how they got to India.

Our fellas at one time were asked to go to the Gold Coast to pick up about, I think, four or five new model P-40 aircraft. We were flying the original old 'B' model, [before] we were flying Tomahawks. The new ones were Kittyhawks.[36] They had bomb racks on them, they had much better firepower. Anyway, we used those few planes to bomb the Japanese Red Dragon Division that was coming up the Burma Road.

---

[36] 'Built by Curtiss-Wright Corporation, the Curtiss P-40 Tomahawk was a single-seat, all-metal fighter and ground attack aircraft that first flew in 1938. 13,738 were built from 1939 to 1944. It is the third most-produced American fighter, after the P-51 and P-47. The P-40 design was a modification of the previous Curtiss P-36 Hawk. The design continuation helped reduce development time and enabled a rapid entry into production and operational service. The Tomahawk was used by most Allied forces during World War II. The P-40 remained in front line service until the end of the war. The U.S. Army Air Corps named the P-40 Warhawk. The British and Soviet air forces used the name Tomahawk for the 'B' and 'C' models and Kittyhawk for the 'D' models.' Source: HISTORY OF THE P-40 TOMAHAWK, Curtiss P-40B Tomahawk, www.americanheritagemuseum.org/aircrafts/curtiss-p-40b-tomahawk.

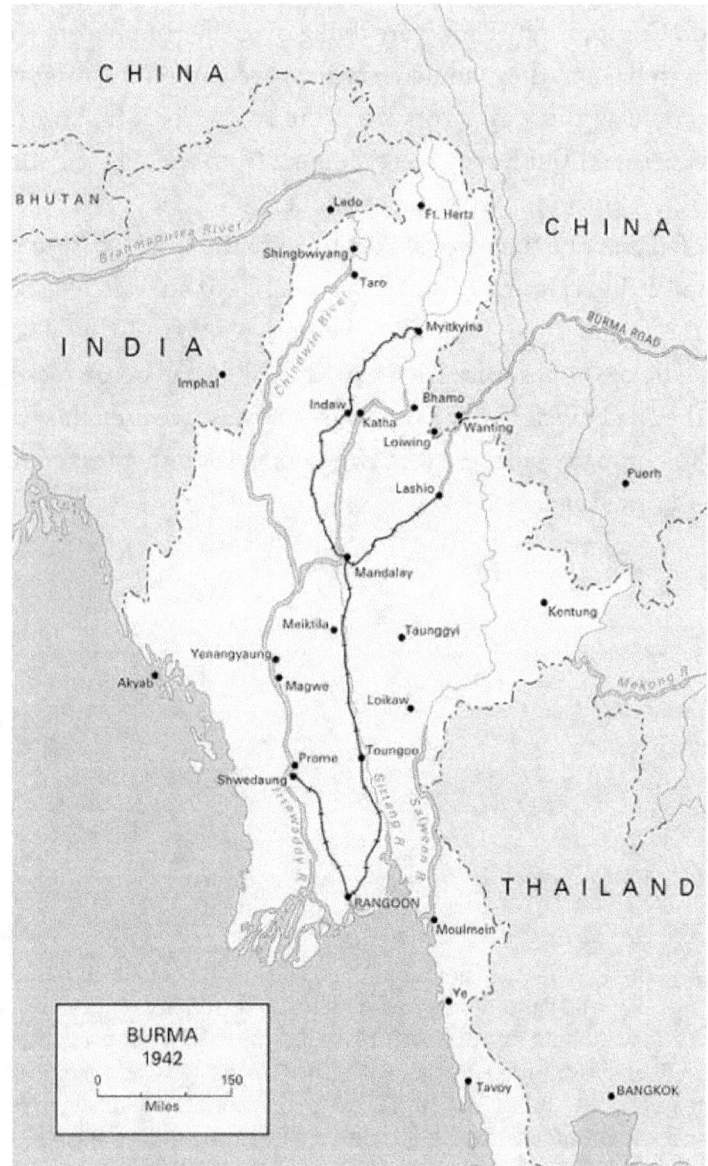

Burma, 1942. U.S. Army, public domain.

After they had bombed out Rangoon, everybody kind of got out of there if they could—they destroyed the docks, so we moved out of there up the Burma Road. On the way we had to detour. Over there we lost some men and planes because [we were used to the fact that] the British Royal Air Force had radar at Mingaladon Airdrome at Rangoon. That's where two of our squadrons were placed to help out the RAF, because they had only one squadron there; their American Brewster Buffalos weren't very good aircraft. Anyway, they took their radar with them when they moved out, so when we moved out, we had no early warning, we had no warning of raids. That's why [after that] we lost several men and planes there, due to there being no warnings. So we moved out of there as soon as we could. We had to move to Kunming then, up the Burma Road. Of course, pilots flew in there with P-40s.

Chennault's Early Warning System

'Starting from areas in Free China, in hundreds of small villages, in lonely outposts, in hills and caves, stretching from near Canton through all Free China to the capital in Chungking and to Lanchow, far northwest, are a maze of alarm stations equipped with radios and telephones that give instant warning of the approach of Japanese planes.'
-Life Magazine, August 10, 1942.[30]

Prior to that time we had another engagement with the Japanese from Hanoi French Indochina. They came up on December 20, 1941. Ten twin-engine bombers, they were headed for Kunming; they had bombed Kunming for years at their liberty, see, they had no protection at all there. So they came in and we got word of it. See, my radio station was down in an area toward Hanoi. Chennault had also set up a telephone reporting warning system. So he had Chinese Army Signal Corps guys down near Hanoi Airport. When those planes would take off, they would phone up my station. Then the telephone guys talked through my interpreter and told me what was going on, what was coming up this way. And I called in to report to headquarters at Kunming, and they got word of it in plenty of time. And planes of two of our squadrons hit those ten bombers. Needless to say, none of them ever got to Kunming; I think all but one was shot down. That was the first engagement of our Flying Tigers with the Japanese.

The first combat mission made a big splash in the news back home, hitting back against the Japanese, but Chennault debriefed his pilots with his chagrin at the overenthusiasm of some, believing that in the excitement of first combat, they had let down their discipline; instead of coordinated dives at the bombers, they had attacked them in a free-for-all that could have resulted in the AVG shooting each other down or colliding. Three bombers were confirmed downed, any survivors turned away.[31] Chennault concluded with, 'Next time, get them all!'

Then, of course, when the Royal Air Force asked for help down in Rangoon, that's when we got into the big fleets of Japanese coming in over from Thailand, where they had bases. They'd come over in huge formations, a hundred-some at a time. Of course, the British and we didn't have any more than, say, twelve, maybe fifteen planes, to go up at a time against those. That's where Chennault's tactics paid off [utilizing] hit-and-run. You hit them, dive off, and come back again; that way we saved our men and planes. Shot down quite a few of them, too, but it didn't stop them. They were able to bomb night and day. When they started doing that, we had to move out. I think in March of '42 we had to move out again until we had to move into Kunming. They made the big record down there right after Christmas time.

The Burma Salween Gorge Mission

The Burma Road was a supply line for the Chinese at that time because the east coast docks, all the east coast harbors, were controlled by the Japanese. The Japanese had the whole east coast [of Southeast Asia] pretty well tied-up. So the only way the Chinese could get supplies, maintain their country, was through the Burma Road. And I think our biggest effort we made was when we hit what they call the Salween Gorge of the Burma Road.

The Burma Road goes across this bridge at this gorge, to get to the other side of the mountain to go on toward Kunming from Rangoon. At this time, it was in around May I think of 1942, the Japanese were coming up that road with that Red Dragon Armored Division, a whole division. They were going to sweep up into Kunming and that would be the end of Kunming, as far as World War II, the Japanese were concerned, they would stop them right there because they would have no way of getting any supplies except by air and that could easily be controlled by the Japanese. They could shoot them all down. So we had three of those late-model P-40 aircraft with the bomb racks. We loaded 500-pound Chinese bombs on those racks. I think three of our former Navy dive-bomber pilots agreed to make a run on the Japanese lines coming up the Burma Road, and at the same time bomb and destroy that river bridge so they couldn't cross the Salween River, what they called 'The Gorge,' a big opening there. So they first destroyed the bridge. Then the army column was there, so they bombed against the wall of a mountain and had the mountain come crashing down on the line of troops down below, on the Japanese. Then they would bomb the road itself and then strafe all along there. They did that for several days. The Japanese never got up to Kunming; Kunming was able to continue the war effort. Let's see—that, I think, was the crowning effort of the AVG.

Conditions

I was at that little place, [a radio station near Kunming]. I was using an Army camp cot for a bed. My arm happened to fall down off the camp cot. Boy, one of those rats got me, bit me. It was the hepatitis, I got that somehow over there. A lot of that from poor food, poor sanitary conditions. At the radio station, when I moved over there, see, I stopped at Kunming Black Dragon Pool Factory. The Black Dragon Pool Factory got a Chinese transmitter, it was about a 60-watt transmitter they said, an old receiver that looked like it had been on at the docks somewhere in Indochina. Pretty bad shape. Anyway, it worked. And I picked up an old motor generator, put that on the truck. And basically they sent me some canned goods, quite a few canned goods, to last for a while. I was eating that down there at this pagoda where we set up the station. Then the cook decided he would go to the bazaar. We'd go over there and see what they had to buy to eat. Most of it was chickens hanging from wires. We had quite a bit of chicken. Then along with the canned goods, if I ran out of canned goods, I notified the head office up there in Kunming, the base, they'd try to get more to me. But I had to pay for that stuff. I was given 30 dollars a month extra to be living out there and live with regular meals. They were getting pretty good meals up in Kunming. So I had to pay for them. There was another [radio station] down closer to Burma. I forget the name of it. Another one up there closer to Chungking on the Burma Road. Three of them on the Burma Road. Then my first station was south of Kunming, down toward Indochina. That's where I worked until the end of the tour.

I think the Japanese were able to know about it, but the stations were too far away for them to do anything about it, I think. They didn't think we could do much anyway. They didn't bomb us, though they would strafe my station. They would come and strafe my station a couple of times, trying to hit planes on the airfield at Unanei. I was up here in a hill, then right down there was a field. They'd come strafing me and then hit whatever they could get down in the airfield. Usually didn't get anything, because we didn't have anybody there anyway.

Other Missions

After that, the Japanese never came up that far. After we destroyed their planes on December 20, coming up from Hanoi, they never came back that way either. From that time on, we moved east to an airfield called Kweilin. Formosa was operating under the Japanese, so they made raids on the Japanese airfields in Formosa. Then up farther they had advanced airfields we had made northeast of Kunming and used those airfields to attack Japanese airfields farther north. Before we left we were working in the area of the north-northeast China starting with the southwest part of China. The Burma Road went northwest up to Chungking, and that was somewhat due north. We did some operations toward the east, toward the ocean, toward the seaports in that direction, large cities.

'I Went Around The World'

[So that was a one-year tour of duty with the Flying Tigers]; I went around the world on that. I left my hometown of Kenosha, Wisconsin, by rail. I went by rail to Los Angeles, about one hundred of us met there, various air bases. We took a bus to San Francisco. We got the Dutch passenger freighter at San Francisco, the *Jagersfontein*, that took us to Hawaii. From Hawaii we picked up two cruisers and escorts because the Japanese had word we were coming to aid the British in Burma. So there was a cruiser *Salt Lake City* and a cruiser *Northampton*. We got escorted to the Dutch East Indies, as far as that went. From there a Dutch cruiser took over and went as far as the Dutch East Indies somewhere. We went to Singapore. So then coming home, we had no way to get out of China by ship or India by ship; [I'll explain why in a moment]. So the China National Aviation Corporation guys would pick up a few of us at a time, we'd manage to get as far as Karachi, India. In those days Karachi was Indian. From Karachi, India, our embassy, it or the consulate, was able to get us a trip over to Bombay. We were over there for a while. Then it took about a week before we could get a ship from Bombay, an ocean-going ship. We got a ship of the United States lines called *Mariposa.* That took us to South Africa, Cape Town, and we stayed there a short time. From there, that's where I got my hepatitis, it showed up there. Up until then it was dysentery. Went from there to New York, then from New York I took a train to Kenosha. I went all the way around the world on that trip. It was all by civilian boats really, wasn't any military transport at all.

You see, when our time was coming to an end up there in China—we had until July 4, 1942, that was the end of our contract—the Army Air Corps sent quite a few people to re-enlist us back in the service. They didn't care whether you came from the Marines or Navy, they wanted them in the Army Air Corps. I had dysentery pretty bad. I said, 'I don't think I can make it.'

'We will make you a first lieutenant if you come.'

I said, 'No, I have to get back.' Hell, I left the Army as a corporal. They wouldn't give us any time off. You couldn't go home on leave, we had to either stay or leave. The head of the recruiting team was a guy named Colonel Bissell. I will never forget that guy. He would not allow any planes to take us out of China. So, hell, I wasn't about to sign up with that dingbat guy. A lot of the fellas were unhappy with him, especially, and then they wanted to get home after a year fighting out there, living pretty tough. They wanted to get home so they had very few people that re-enlisted. It took us about, I'd say about a month, to get there, and I'd say it took a month on the sea to get home. But we spent about three weeks trying to get passage out of India just because of Bissell! I remember two or three of the fellas rented camels. They rode around the embassy building there at Bombay trying to influence the consulate, whoever was there, to get us a ship, transportation out of there. They rode around there about half a day until they got a detention of people there. It worked out pretty well, in a couple of days we had something, the *Mariposa*, and we were able to get home on that. Just about all the guys came home that way. But I spent the whole time coming up from South Africa, New York in the sick bay with hepatitis. Couldn't manage anything. Pretty sick guy. Then I got a sick leave. I got home 60 days. Colonel Bissell said the draft board would be waiting, he would have the draft board draft us as privates in the Army, that's another thing that turned the guys against him. He threatened us! When I got home, the draft board gave me 60 days' sick leave before I had to re-enlist. I didn't care about that. I was going to re-enlist anyway.

The Marines

[From there, I went into the Marines.] The Marines was a move from one darn island to another. Pack everything, get on a ship, and get off. Our main objective, when we were out in the Marines, was to destroy the shipping and the air facilities at a big island base at Rabaul—they had a big navy base there, they had an air base there.[37] We had the first Marine B-25s. Marines didn't have twin-engine bombers until we got ours. PBJ because it was a patrol bomber, they said. We did night bombing of Rabaul with radar. It was a confusing

---

[37] Rabaul was the principal Japanese forward operating base in the South Pacific at New Guinea, with tens of thousands of troops in reserve.

situation in the Marine Corps because I was trained with Signal Corps Army equipment. The Navy had different equipment. The radio, we had one set of radio, what they call a command set in the fighter plane for the fighter pilots to use. With the bombers you had a long-range set of transmitter, a receiver, besides a short range for the pilots. Then they had radar. I had never been to radar school. I didn't know anything about the radar. In fact, at that time the Signal Corps didn't have radar, the Navy had started it out at Chicago. So I was promoted to head of the communications of the squadron. I was to be in charge of every part of communication on the radios, so I had pretty much to delegate.

We bombed mostly by radar at night, bombing Rabaul. Rabaul was in the Bismark archipelago, near the Admiralty Islands. You would find it by going north probably from New Guinea, in that area. It was a big Navy base at Rabaul, they had a lot of anti-aircraft equipment. We even lost the planes at night, we did all the bombing at night, we lost planes and people due to the heavy anti-aircraft they had. We did some strafing of other islands that had some Japanese installations still there, small installations. I went on some raids, strafing raids with them, to see what it was like. Then I just did enough flying to get my flight pay. Usually I would get flight pay ever since I joined the Marines. But we did mostly that one island. I guess we were pretty effective because they weren't sending out fighter planes and raiding around very much after for a while there. We were pretty effective.

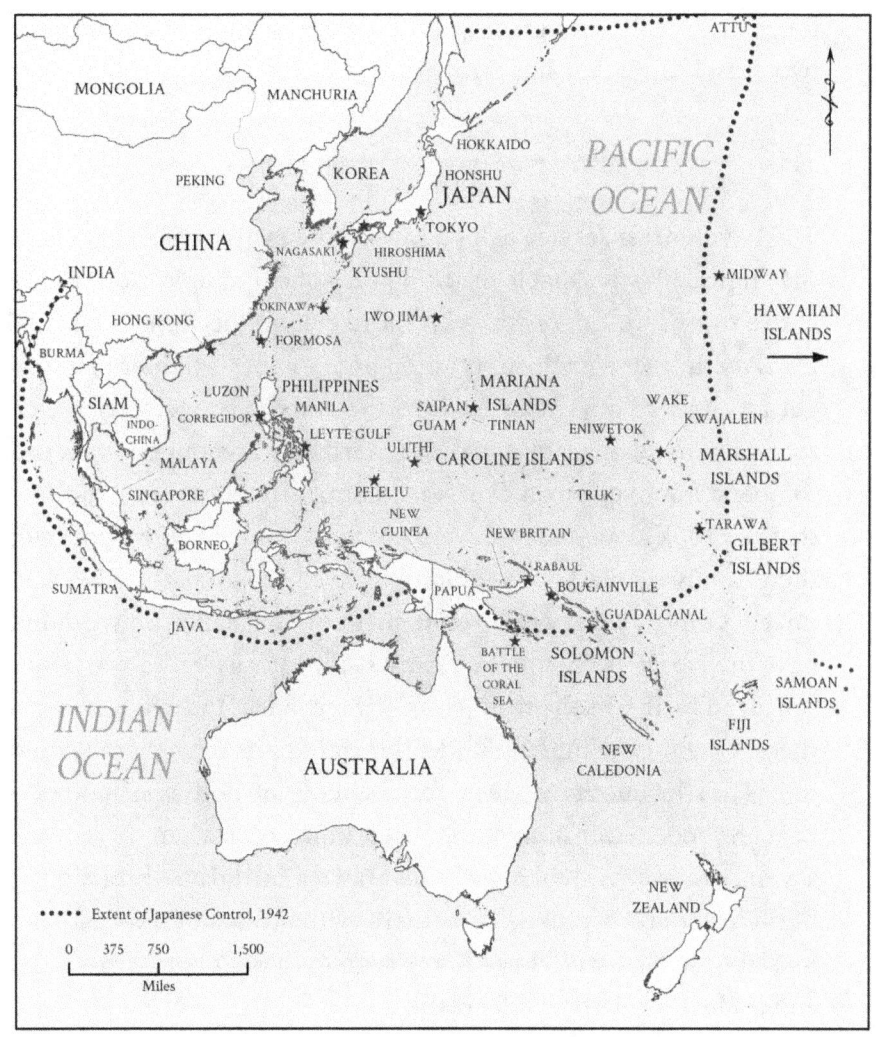

*Extent of Japanese Control in the Pacific, 1942,
Including Rabaul.
Drafted by Susan Winchell.*

We were out there in 1943. Then the war had moved up to the Philippines, up that way, so they moved my squadron north up to the Philippines. That's when they said, well, your time is up. I don't have to go to the Philippines. So I got a hop over to Admiralty Islands. I got on the troop ship, came home that way. Came home a long ways. Still other guys said their time was up. They had time overseas. I think they had Army time, Marine time.

Booze For Spare Parts

My volunteer service helped toward the experience. That's how they figured I was capable of taking care of communications of the entire squadron. There was a lot more communications [logistics] involved in that squadron, twin-engine bombers, fighter planes. I got a couple of guys who went to the warehouse, we pretty well took care of moving stuff out of the fourteen warehouses we needed to operate our squadron overseas, motor generators and stuff like that, we took along that we were going to need. Then we got over there, and we found out we didn't have any spare parts. They had mixed Army and Navy radio equipment on the planes. So we didn't have any spare parts for the Army stuff. Luckily there was a fire squadron, a P-38 squadron, over at Sterling Island when we got there. I went over there, found a bunch of parts over there I could use. They let me have them for a couple of bottles of booze. I brought booze over in my footlocker, in my tent where I was with several other guys; when we would have a birthday, I broke out a bottle of booze. I packed it in there with straw, Three Feathers; lousy booze. So I would use a bottle, go over there, the Army base, and trade it for parts for the planes.

The Slit Trench Encounter

Strange story happened when I was over there. It was on Sterling Island. We knew there was another squadron, the other side of the base, Army with P-38s. I never went over there but one time. One night we had a raid, not a raid, but Japanese search planes were running around one night. We had a blackout. I was in a slit trench there by the tent, some guy jumped in and just about jumped on me. I said, 'What the hell are you trying to do?'

Turned out to be, it's the strangest thing I ever had, thinking about it afterwards, because it was one of our guys in the Flying Tigers, a pilot, who had jumped on me in the slit trench over Sterling Island, in the Treasury group out there in the Southwest Pacific! Of all the guys you could think of, how could one guy from that one group over there in China, years ago, be jumping into my slit trench? He must have been visiting or something over in our squadron some of our guys; he was from that P-38 outfit. It turned out he was from Wisconsin. Years later I drove up to see where he was in northern Wisconsin. He was at a resort or something. I asked him about it. I said, 'Remember that time?'

He remembered it. But he didn't have much time to talk, he was busy, so we didn't talk much about it. I thought I would see him at the reunions, but the bugger never came to the reunion. All the years I am wondering if it really happened. That guy from our old Flying Tigers squadron would be in a P-38 squadron and jump in this Marine Corps slit trench years later. It was about a year after they left China. [*Laughs*]

Home

When I came back in 1945, I was 27. I enrolled on the GI Bill at 16 Lawrence College, Appleton, Wisconsin, and I graduated in 1949 with a B.S. degree. Then I went to the Civil Service Naval Electronics Supply Office at Great Lakes, until I got a transfer to the Air Force Material Command. I was stationed at Kingston Products in Kokomo as an inspector. While at Kokomo I was hired at Delco Radio, that's how come I came here, as a process and production engineer. So I was at Delco Electronics for 27 years.

Morgan H. Vaux passed away at 92 on August 3, 2010.

CHAPTER TWO

The Flying Tigers Nurse

Emma Jane Foster Petach Hanks, or Jane, as she was known, was one of only two women who joined the 120-strong American Volunteer Group, or Flying Tigers, in 1941, before Pearl Harbor and while the United States was still a neutral nation.[32] At 25 she was a registered nurse with them in Burma and China; known simply as 'Red' for her flaming red hair highlighted by her light complexion, she married a Flying Tigers pilot while there and lost him less than two weeks before they were due to leave for home. She returned to the United States a widow at age 27, but carrying the child who would become their daughter.

'About ten days before our contract was up, [Chennault] asked the fellas if they would stay over, because the army hadn't come in. He didn't have help [to train the Chinese pilots], and so some of the fellas stayed over. Pete was one of them... [pauses for a moment] ... and that's when I lost him. He got shot down bombing and strafing. I went home, and of course, my father wasn't... [trails off, then imitates father's voice, asking with incredulity] He said, 'You were a nurse, you were in the army, and you were in war, and you got pregnant?' And I never told him the truth, [which was that] I always felt [that with] Pete, we were never coming back together. And if I

was going to lose him, I wanted part of him, and that's why I deliberately had gotten pregnant. When I came back home, of course, my daughter was born.'

Jane Hanks

My maiden name is Emma Jane Foster. I was born February 14, 1916, [in Bellefonte, Pennsylvania]. As a kid, I used to say, since I was the youngest of six, I was my mother's heart because I was born on Valentine's Day. But as a kid, I was always adventuresome. And I remember they tell me when I was about a two-year-old, they found me in the outskirts of town, walking away, having a fine time because I was exploring everything. Since I was the youngest of six, I had to make my own way.

'I Felt Like Alice in Wonderland'

Ever since I remember, I was always interested in the culture in Asia. It fascinated me. I read all of Pearl Buck's books I could get my hands on, all that kind of material because Asia, especially China, intrigued me. And when I finally got to get my college education, I went to Penn State, and I found that they had an exchange student program at Lingnan University, Canton, China. Only men were going. And I thought, if men are going, no reason why women can't go. So with much—how will I put it? —'investigation,' anyway, I did get a chance. I was one of the first group of women that ever went that went to Lingnan University as an exchange student. It was the most wonderful experience of my life! I enjoyed every bit of it. I enjoyed the Chinese professors much better than the professors that I had in college because they were gentlemen. They were well educated, spoke very good English, and were very good to their students. It was such a wonderful experience for me that I always wanted to get back there somehow. But while we were there, we did a lot of traveling by bike, and I can remember going to formal occasions with my dress hanging over my arm, my formal dress. But we biked a lot through China. And during intermission from the sessions, the four of us went through the interior of China. And up there at that time, Beijing was called Peking. We went by bus and by train; there were just two girls and two boys. We stayed at the Chinese inns, and we never had any comment about that situation until we got to a missionary's house. And I was insulted that the missionaries would think anything was wrong with us!

When we got to Peking, I was fortunate enough to go to the Forbidden City. And I was there after the Dowager had left the city. There was a moat all around the city where the Chinese stayed. And I was lucky enough to go all the way through the Forbidden City. There was food still left on the beds, and the clothing was still on the beds.

I felt like Alice in Wonderland, because nobody was there but me. I went to all these little rooms and saw how they lived. I was just fascinated by the whole thing. When I came back to visit later, of course, they had taken all the furniture out of those little rooms and put them in a big room, so the Chinese really didn't believe that I had been there. But it was a fascinating experience. Chiang Kai-shek was there, and he had preserved a lot of this material, a lot of the culture, the Chinese culture. I went to the wall, the Great Wall, climbed the Great Wall, it was fascinating, and the culture was just terrific. And the Chinese were so respectful.

A 'Foreign Devil'

Of course, at that time, I was a flaming redhead, with blue eyes and light skin. So every place I went, I was surrounded by the Chinese. They called me a 'yángguǐzi,' foreign devil. The older, the more elite Chinese were embarrassed every time I told them about that. But I can see that I was taller than they were, except when I went to Beijing. And, of course, a different coloring, and they'd never seen anybody like me, so I always drew a crowd.

I took mainly political science and Chinese history while I was there. But as I said, we knew a lot of the officials because we were students and we were given special privileges, so we got around. I'll never forget the first time we were at a party for one of the officials. It was after our meal, and one of the officials burped and you could hear it all over the room. I was so embarrassed for him. I thought, 'it's a shame,' until I learned that that was a sign that they were congratulating the cook, that the food was so good. So, anyway, my experience there was just so great that I wanted to go back and help them.

Getting Back To China

I knew the best way to get back [to China] was in the medical field. But being a doctor took too long, so I went into nursing. I went to the Yale School of Nursing, got my master's degree. When I graduated, the only way I could get back to China was via the missionary field, and I wasn't exactly the missionary type, so I did visiting nursing in Minneapolis. Now, about that time, the American Volunteer Group was being organized. Chiang Kai-shek had asked Chennault to go to the States to get some help for him to fight the Japanese, and when Chennault went to Roosevelt, Roosevelt liked the idea, but the generals hated it. They said they already had their hands full in Europe, they didn't want another battle to fight, because we weren't at war with Japan. But since Roosevelt liked it, he helped set up a covert action group and the Chinese paid for us to do it. So he told us that we were there to protect the Burma Road.

Major Gentry was looking for his medical team, and when he came to Yale, he was looking for a nurse. Yale told him, 'Well, there's a girl, she's always wanted to go back. I don't know where she is, but I know she wants to go back.' So Major Gentry called my father. My father called me while I was in town doing work, and he said, 'You're going to get a call to go back to China. Go back and get it. Stay there until you get it.' He wanted to get me out of there; somebody with a master's degree shouldn't be wasting their time being in the slums! So Major Gentry called me, and within twenty-four hours, I was on my way back to China.

When I went to Shanghai, that was when I first met the AVG. I thought that they were just very young, very inexperienced, and I wasn't about to have anything to do with it. Those fellas were so immature! We were all waiting for a boat because in that time there weren't planes, and we were supposed to be the second boatload to go back to China. They took one look at two girls; said they had no room for the two girls! But we heckled and heckled, and finally we got our way, and they put us up on the top deck and they had set up cots. We used the children's facilities, and the captain did let us use his shower facilities for bathing, but it was fairly inconvenient. We also had a Victrola with really good classical music and jazz, and some of the fellas used to come up and we would dance on the top deck. I really had a good time on that boat, and that's where I met my future husband.

'These Kids, They're Going to Fight?'

My first experience with these AVGs, from the medical standpoint, we lined the fellas up to give them shots for Asia, and a couple of those big burly men took one look at that needle and landed on the deck! And I thought, 'They're going to fight?'

We landed in Hong Kong and Singapore, then we finally landed in Rangoon. We couldn't land in the other areas, really, because the Japanese controlled all the Chinese ports, and when we landed in Rangoon, they wouldn't let us disembark, because they had problems before, and the fellas were so frustrated, they threw overboard every portable thing they could find! And I thought again, 'These kids, they're going to fight?'

The next day we went by train up to Toungoo, which was north of Rangoon, and there was an old British base there and that's where we were going to stay. Now, since I had been in the Orient, I was expecting some primitive conditions, but I really didn't expect the conditions that we found in Burma. They were fat huts, really. The hospital had about ten beds and the nurses had quarters adjacent to the hospital, and other than having a sink, the facilities were all outside, so we had to go out to take care of them. And the beds were set in little cans of water, so that would keep the ants from getting up into our beds. And fortunately we did have mosquito netting over our beds, and it was very lucky really, because the rats would run around the ceilings and every so often they would fall on our mosquito netting, so we were glad that we had that mosquito netting! Another thing we had to be careful of was when you got into your shoes, you had to be very careful that there wasn't any living thing in your shoes!

In the first couple days we had a Burmese cook, and we had highly seasoned food—breakfast, dinner, and supper. That finally got a couple of the fellas, they weren't going to put up with that. They went home! Since we were under contract, we could go home. And the rest of us thought, 'Well, if they can't take it, they can go.' But then they got Chinese cooks, and they got screens at the windows, so we didn't have to fight the bugs to the food, and that food was much better.

Medically speaking, we weren't very busy, and one of the doctors was an ear, nose, and throat person and he was bored to death so he took out every pair of tonsils that he could find! I felt very comfortable because I used to help my father doing the same thing in the office, but it wasn't very long until they came down with malaria and dengue fever. And when they got dengue fever, they were really sick, so we were busy taking care of those fellas. But fortunately, we didn't lose any of them.

Spending Time With Chennault

After they got over that, we dealt with a lot of accidents, because they weren't used to those very fast planes. A lot of them had just come right off of aircraft carriers, and they hadn't experienced this real fast flying. So we worked in our days in Burma, we worked very hard during the day, and then we would get out and get down to Rangoon and party. So I had a good time in spite of it all, as I had a good time on the boat. Mister Chennault liked feminine company, so when he went to the very formal parties, he would take Josie, the other nurse, the other girl, because she was older, and when he went to the informal things, he would take me. I remember one time in particular, I was playing cribbage with a man, he was supposedly the best cribbage player in the east, and I was beating him. And Pete, whom I later married, was standing back of me; he was counting for me, because he could count much faster than I could. Well, Chennault [didn't take it well], and he said, 'Young man, that girl would do a lot better if you'd leave.' So Pete left, and I lost! And I've talked to Chennault's family since, and they said that's the way he acted with his family, he wanted to win. He was going to win! But when we'd go to parties with Chennault, sometimes when he was feeling very good, he would go to a step and try to reach the step below, and pretend like he was struggling, trying to reach this step. He [acted like] he couldn't do it, and so he'd bet his guests so much if he could make it, reach that lower step. And as soon as his guest took the bait, he reached the lower step! Another thing he used to do is, when he had guests for dinner, he loved these really hot pickles, and he'd take a big bite out of these hot pickles, and the guests would follow his lead, and they would [nearly choke]! They couldn't take that really odd stuff. [*Laughs*] In spite of working hard, we played hard, and we did have a good time in Burma.

War

Then the word came around that the Japanese had bombed Pearl Harbor. And then we knew that the United States was going to war, and now everybody wanted us. Right after, very close to that time, when we heard that we were at war with Japan, we heard that the Japanese were going to come over and bomb us. We had no air raid system, no nothing in Burma. And we dragged some of those fellas out and put them in ditches, because that was the only thing we had; they later said that they were all eaten up with ants. But fortunately, the Japanese didn't bomb us. They had heard about us, and they didn't think we were worth bothering with. And they have since said they were very sorry.

As soon as possible, the medical staff, or we nurses, were sent up into China, into Kunming. I wanted to go by the Burma Road, but they had me fly up to Kunming, and Kunming was our headquarters during the war. When we went up to Kunming, it was going to be our headquarters for the rest of the time, because we have this contract for a year. And Josie, the other girl, was Josie Stewart, from Dallas, Texas. I didn't know it at the time, but I was the only registered nurse.

The Warning System

Before the flyers got there, the Japanese came and bombed Kunming, and then we went out to the graveyards with the Chinese and stayed there until they finished bombing. The next day, our flyers came in, and the Japanese came back. They were going to bomb Kunming. But one of the most important things about General Chennault, he taught the Chinese to keep track of these Japanese planes, so they would follow the Japanese planes from their origin to where they were going. So we knew ahead of time where they were and how far away, so we could get them. And then the next time the Japanese came to bomb Kunming, Chennault's warning system worked very well. We met them outside of Kunming. They never got to Kunming and clobbered them there [before they could reach the city]. The Chinese were just so grateful that for once they weren't going to be bombed, and because of Chennault's warning system and the AVG being there, the Japanese never came back to Kunming, to bomb Kunming again. As long as we were there, they'd stay away.

Married With A Black Eye

The conditions for the living quarters in Kunming were much better than in Burma. It was a temporary building, but it was a building, and we were heated by charcoal. And we had about four beds in what was like a clinic, but when the boys were really ill, we would go down to the Chinese hospital. In the hospital, Josie and I would take one day on and one day off. They put up a cot and we'd sleep in the cot. I didn't tell you, we had three doctors. One was, as we said, eye, ear, nose, and throat. The other one was orthopedic, and the third one was a general medical person. We also had a dentist, and we had a chaplain, and we had these two girls. Chennault wanted us American girls to take care of his boys, and we were there to just take care of the AVG. We were busy with one day on and one day off, and of course, we didn't have all of the entertainment that we had before the war, but even then, I used to go on bike trips with Pete. Well, I was falling in love with him, and we wanted to get married. And it was generally understood that we [weren't supposed to] get married. And of course, at first, I didn't think I'd have anything to do with those fellas. But when we decided, we checked with Chennault, and he liked both of us, so he decided it was all right if we got married. As I said, I was falling in love with this guy, and he was doing a job trying to get me. So he would fly over our hospital and the fellas found out what he was doing, so he would fly over and wiggle his tail to make sure that I knew that he was doing it, and they got it, too, so that I could be sure that it was he that was out flying for me, letting me know. I said, 'I guess not very many women have had a courtship like that!' Bit by bit, he got me.

We were married in Kunming, in the French consulate. I only had a couple people there at our wedding. Padre Paul Frohman, who was our chaplain, was not there; he was out somewhere on the advanced post, so it was a minister in town that married us. And the night before our marriage, Chennault invited us to his apartment for dinner. I was Indian wrestling with Chennault, and if you know what Indian wrestling is, he gave me a big pull and I flew across the room, hit my eye on a corner of a table, and was married with a black eye! Then right after our honeymoon, we rode up briefly on Burma Road. After that, we stayed in my quarters, and he would run back and forth to the airfield.

'When They Came Back, They Were Men'

Later on, just about two months before our year was up, they shipped us to Kunming, Fletcher and Pete—John Petach was his real name—and the other nurse, Josie Stewart. I didn't know at the time, but I was the only really registered nurse with the crowd. But anyway, we went up to Kunming. We were there about two months before we were to leave—our time was up; our yearly contract was up. While we were there, one thing happened. It was the first time General Stilwell had asked our fellas to fly low over the Chinese airfield, and our fellas wouldn't do it, because if you fly low, that's then when a Japanese can punch in, and your survival rate would be practically nil. And they almost came to blows with Chennault.

One of the fellas says, 'We're not cowards, you know that.'

And Chennault said, 'I know. I realize that!' Well, they finally didn't have to do that.

Another experience that we had when we flew up to Kunming, General Bissell came to get us to enlist in the armed services.[38] Now, the fellas really worshiped Chennault. They would have done anything for Chennault, but they were tired. They had just about a year of just battling five-to-one, ten-to-one with the Japanese. I think talking about the experiences of the AVG in Rangoon, what they did is they would have one squadron at a time [at the main base]. One squadron was kept in Rangoon, and the rest of them were sent to advanced posts. Now, when those fellas went to Rangoon, they were fighting with two, four, six, ten, sometimes twenty Japanese airplanes after them! I remember that one of the fellas, his plane was shot down and he fortunately was able to get out of the plane and was going down by a parachute, and the Japanese were trying to get him, and he would shuffle around one side to the other [as the bullets went by], and finally he got tired and he just slumped down, and the Japanese thought they'd got him. And that boy is

---

[38] General Clayton Lawrence Bissell (1896-1972) was principal aviation officer for General Stilwell in China; in August 1942 he was named head of the 10th Air Force in India and Burma as the AVG contract with the Chinese government expired.

alive today. One of the things that was amazing, was startling to me actually, is when these fellas went to Rangoon, they were boys. When they came back, they were men. If I'd have seen that in the movies, I would have thought it was overdrawn. But they were fighting death the whole time; now they just wanted to go home and rest, and then they'd come back. But General Bissell was so nasty, and he told the fellas that, 'You will have a very difficult time to get home, and when you get home, you'll just be drafted.' But most of them went home.

'That's When I Lost Him'

About ten days before our contract was up, [Chennault] asked the fellas if they would stay over, because the army hadn't come in. He didn't have help [to train the Chinese pilots], and so some of the fellas stayed over. Pete was one of them... [*pauses for a moment*] ... and that's when I lost him. He got shot down bombing and strafing. So when I was on my way, when I was on my way home, our other commander, asked two of the fellas to escort me home, Bob Neal and Charlie Bond.[39]

Home

Well, then, when we got to Calcutta, since they weren't very fond of us, fortunately, one of those fellas, I think Charlie Bond, had gotten to Hap Arnold, and Hap Arnold gave me A-1 priority to go home.[40] So I flew home, we three flew home. I didn't have to go by

---

[39] Charles Bond is sometimes credited, along with another man, for the distinctive AVG shark face nose art.
[40] Hap Arnold- Henry Harley "Hap" Arnold (1886-1950). Major pioneer of strategic bombing theory in Europe, later head of the Twentieth Air Force command in the CBI and Pacific. He was named a five-star General of the

boat or anything. And when we landed in Miami, well, those boys were heroes, [they got a heroes' welcome]. They took those boys away and wined them and dined them. Now, I'd been very careful of them. Me, [to those in Miami], I was a camp follower, I was a prostitute. I was so embarrassed that I'd been well respected in every other country but my own, I cried for about two days, but I got over it. [*Chuckles*]

I went home, and of course, my father wasn't... [*trails off, then imitates father's voice, asking with incredulity*] He said, 'You were a nurse, you were in the army, and you were in war, and you got pregnant?' And I never told him the truth, [which was that] I always felt [that with] Pete, we were never coming back together. And if I was going to lose him, I wanted part of him, and that's why I deliberately had gotten pregnant. When I came back home, of course, my daughter was born.

I wanted to get a job in the States, but I was too well educated. They didn't want me. In those days, nurses didn't have any master's degree, but I finally did get a job. I was a health educator, and I stayed in Harrisburg, Pennsylvania. I was a health educator because I did have health information, and I was in that job for quite a couple years, and they did pay enough money that I could raise my daughter. That was another problem with some of the other opportunities I had. They didn't pay me enough so that I could raise my daughter. Then I became executive director of the Tuberculosis and Health Society, which was a voluntary organization. I was there a couple of years, and then I had the opportunity to be secretary of the Public Health Association in Harrisburg, the same place. And I really liked that job because we watched all the health legislation through the congress in the state. It was very interesting, and I liked

---

Army in 1943, placing him fourth in rank to only Marshall, MacArthur, and Eisenhower.

that. The Flying Tigers had a reunion every two years. And in those days, the China National Airway, which was the only other civilian war citizens group in World War II, they used to have reunions together with the Flying Tigers. And usually when I went to a reunion, I wanted to see my friends. I didn't pay much attention to the China National Airway, but one year, one of the fellas got my attention and.. we got together and we finally were married. I married Fletcher Hanks from Oxford, Maryland. He, of course, wanted me to come down to Oxford, Maryland, and, well, I moved, and it was a big change for me because I was used to going my own way, and I wasn't used to being adapted to somebody else. But we managed all right.

'Women Didn't Talk About Those Things'

I got involved in politics in Maryland, I enjoyed that. I was in a different environment because all the girls when they got together, talked about their children. And when I wanted to talk to the men about human events and other things, they looked at me as though there was something wrong with me. Women didn't talk about those things! But it's finally changing. But I got involved in politics and I enjoyed that for a while. I was president of the Maryland Federation of Republican Women for a couple years and I was a delegate to the convention for Ronald Reagan, whom I admired very much. The Flying Tigers have reunions every year because we're losing people so fast that we get together every year; every year I look forward to going to the Flying Tiger reunions because they're like going back to my family, since my family's all gone now and there aren't very many of us AVG left. One of the unique things about AVG was the same people who joined up were the same people who left after a year. Nobody came in between, [no replacements], so we had a closely knit group. And as I said, it's just like visiting somebody from your own family; we started out with about 350 and we're down to, I think the last count was 48. So we really look forward to that, do our reunions and see it.

[My husband and I], we both have a respect for China and admiration for the Chinese people. I should mention to you that we were never given veteran status. We were given veteran status only fifty years after we came back; we weren't recognized as a veteran until that time. We did get the Bronze Medal for our achievements in World War II.

Jane Hanks died Oct. 17, 2009, at the age of 93. Her and Pete's daughter, the only 'Flying Tiger Cub,' noted, 'To many who never knew Jane but recognized a tall, stooped, elderly lady doddering along with her American flag-bedecked walker, she was just another of Oxford, [Maryland's] elderly. What a shame they didn't know Jane, or 'Red,' the fiery Flying Tigers nurse, the dedicated public health nurse, the devoted mother, the nationally ranked cyclist, the consummate tennis player. A moment with Jane would have revealed there was no loss of acuity, no loss of wit, no loss of candor. Towards the end, Jane was frail, but her intellect never failed.'

The Curtiss C-46 Commando flying over the Hump. National Museum of the U.S. Air Force. Public domain.

PART TWO

THE HUMP

General Chennault's Flying Tigers withdrew their planes from Burma to China. In seven months of aerial combat, his volunteer force had destroyed nearly 300 Japanese aircraft. But for the next three years, the most vital use of aircraft would be getting supplies to China by flying them over the lower Himalayas in India. The Air Transport Command created to fly the treacherous 500-mile route between Assam and Kunming was nicknamed 'The Hump' by pilots flying over mountain ranges as high as 15,000 feet. They were subjected to extreme turbulence, unpredictable winds and weather conditions, and, after the fall of the airfield in Burma at Myitkyina, Japanese fighters. One peak in particular was called 'the aluminum-plated mountain' because so many cargo planes had crashed on it; over the course of that period of time, 650,000 tons were airlifted, at a cost of more than 600 planes lost and a thousand men killed.[33]

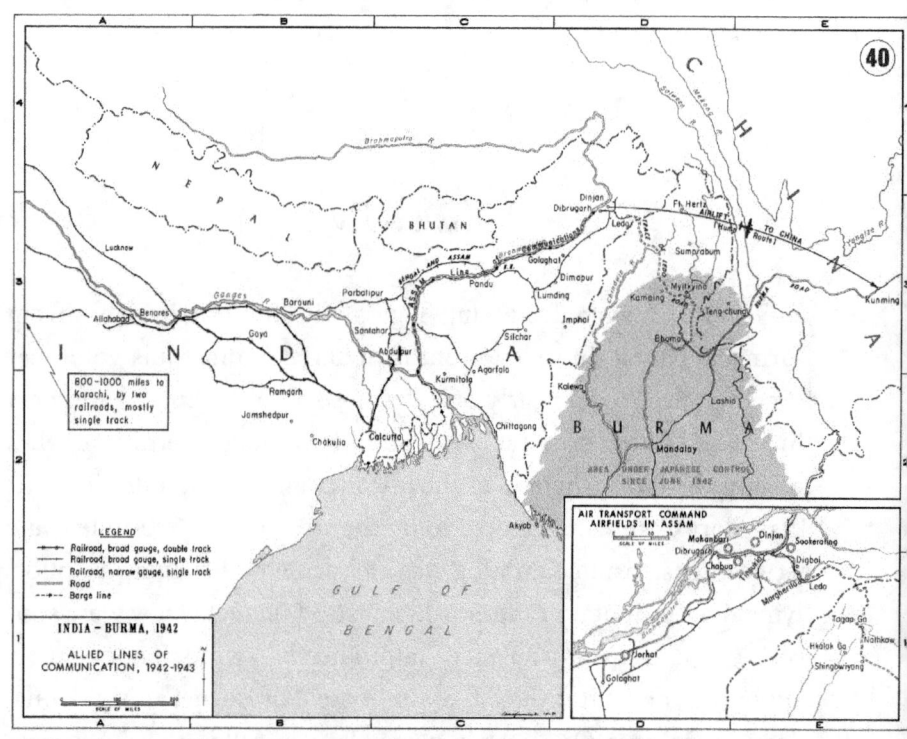

India-Burma-China lines of communication and air route over the Hump, 1942.
U.S. Army, public domain.

CHAPTER THREE

The Cargo Pilot

Patrick Scarano was born on April 14, 1915, in Cortland, New York, to Italian immigrants. He flew for Eastern Airlines in the early 1940s until he joined the U.S. Army Air Corps and wound up in the China-Burma-India Theater, flying multi-engine cargo planes over the Himalaya Mountains.

'Going back home, you are traveling westbound, into the face of the jet stream. So, it would take you longer. We'd head back to the Assam Valley, pick up a beacon, circle down to sea level as we broke out of the overcast, and land at the airport where we took off from. But here's the hazard—you'd get there early morning and there would be fog. So, you'd have to circle until the fog would lift or go to an alternate airport. If the fog did not lift and the alternate airport is too far away, you would run out of gas, then you would have to jump out of the airplane and lose the airplane. A lot of ships were lost that way.'

He sat for this interview in early 2001.

Patrick Scarano

Back in 1943, the war in Europe was getting worse and I was a pilot through the CPT, the Civilian Pilot Training program. I had won a scholarship after high school. From that, I started flying primary and then if I passed that, I'd do secondary and if I passed that, then cross country and then from there the instructor rating. I stayed there for a while and then the Navy man came through and was looking for recruits for the Navy. He said, 'Go to New York and take a physical at 50 Broadway.' I took the physical and they said I was a quarter of an inch short. I said, 'Oh my God, they want a 5'7"!' But then I heard that Eastern Airlines was hiring pilots, so I took a day off, went to LaGuardia Field to Eastern Airlines Headquarters, and they said they were hiring pilots for the military cargo division of the airline. Now, just about that time the government said they needed a lot of cargo pilots, so they hired me as a pilot with Eastern Airlines and sent me to school in Atlanta, Georgia. I went through their school, both the engine and aircraft instrument rating and all that.

Now, they were going to get C-46 Commando Airplanes from Curtis, from the government, and the airlines were waiting for the production. When they got that, they would put me on the Cargo Division of Eastern Airlines, flying C-46 cargo airplanes with cargo from the U.S. to Europe. In the meantime, while we were waiting for the airplanes to come in there, Eastern Airlines put me on a domestic run until the planes came.

I was on a domestic run for about four months, flying the regular routes from New York to Miami, Houston, and so forth. One day, Eddie Rickenbacker, the owner and president of Eastern Airlines, called us pilots into the operation room. There were about twenty of us pilots. He said, 'Fellas, I have good news, and I have bad news. First, I'll give you the bad news. The bad news is that we're not going to get C-46 airplanes anymore because all the production that comes through, the U.S. Army has taken. We have a surplus of pilots, and I am going to have to let you go. That's the bad news.' In fact, he said, 'That's the end of our cargo division of the airline. Now, the good news is that as long as we trained you on multi-engine aircraft, instrument rating, meteorology, and all that stuff there, the U.S. Army will guarantee that if you go to a ninety-day officer candidate school in Memphis, you will come out of there with a commission as a 2nd lieutenant and you will be in the service.'

So, I went to Memphis, Tennessee, and was one of what they called 'the ninety-day wonders.' After ninety days, I graduated, got commissioned as a 2nd lieutenant, and there I'm in the service. From there, they sent me on my first mission, which was the Air Transport Command, ATC. So, that's how I got into it. They said, 'Well now, Lieutenant, we're going to send you to Little Rock, Arkansas, to go through the instrument flight school.'

I said, 'Why do that?' I've just come out of Eastern Airlines, I've got a rating, instrument rating, FAA, and multi-engine rating.

This officer said, 'Well that's okay, but you've got to do things the Army way!' So, they sent me to Adams Field in Little Rock. I went through instrument school and, of course, it was a breeze. They said, 'Hey, we've got something really good here. We want to keep you here as an instructor on instrument flight.'

I said, 'What the hell, anything like that.' After I instructed a few classes, they made me the chief check pilot. Now, any of the students that went through the school would take a ride with me. It was up to me to either pass them or, if they were a little bit weak, to send them back for additional training. So, I was a check pilot and had been asking to be sent overseas because of the war effort. Finally, my orders came through. They sent me to Miami, Florida, for overseas duty. The first thing they did was to give me an overseas physical. They got about twenty officers in this one room in the medical division. They said, 'Strip.' So, we stripped. The doctor came in and said, 'Okay, fellas, anything wrong with you fellas, step forward. If not, put your clothes back on and go down to the airport for 1500 takeoff.' So, can you imagine that? That's an overseas physical. I thought they were going to give me an extensive electrocardiogram, blood tests and all that but if the body is warm, you're in! [*Laughs*] I was in Miami, but the orders said, 'We want you to pack winter underwear. Get your winter clothing, winter underwear, and that's part of your winter gear to go overseas.' So they sent me overseas. I am thinking, 'Oh my God, with heavy underwear, that means I'm going to go to either Greenland or a cold country.' Two days later, I ended up in the Assam Valley of India. Hot! It was hot, during the monsoon season. Ha, winter underwear! I think the reason they said to pack your winter underwear is if there were any spies telling the direction of our movement, they would say, 'The troop movement is going this way, sending them north or to a cold country.' They really created a diversion and sent them off the beaten path.

So now, I'm in Chabua, India. When I was with Eastern Airlines, they did have a couple of Curtis C-46 transports. We had a little time in it, but not too much, just a few hours to get acquainted with the airplane and check out as a pilot. So when they got their C-46 airplanes, all they had to do was assign us to the aircraft, load up, and go to the air with the load.

The Lifeline of China

I was in Mohanbari, India. At that time in 1943-1944, there was a blockade on the east coast with submarines and the shipping was bad there. Also, China had a blockade of submarines. So the vital supplies for China came by ship up to about Calcutta, India, and then from there to the Assam Valley. They had vital supplies, and they also had 100 octane gasoline. This is for the B-29 bases that flew out of bases in China.

Air Transport Command C-46 crosses the Himalayas.
U.S. Army, public domain.

My mission was to fly the C-46 transports from the Assam Valley; we would start at the Assam Valley at the beginning of the Ledo Road. Now, they would have vital supplies going down the Ledo Road, but they were also fighting the Japs and didn't have much time or material that went through. So they had to institute something better and that's when they called 'The Lifeline of China.'

We would start at the Assam Valley with a C-46 and about fifty or sixty 55-gallon drums of 100 octane gasoline. We would take off, usually a night flight, the operation beginning with us circling up to 15,000 feet so you could clear the Himalayas; the top of the mountains there were about 15,000 feet. Then we would spread out and then head east for Kunming, China. It would take approximately two hours; this was about a 400-mile trip, at 15,000 feet, mostly in the clouds. We'd get pretty close to Kunming, China, and turn on the beacon. We would home in on the beacon, spiral down, and land in Kunming, China. The trucks would be waiting there. They would pull up and unload the airplane. In the meantime, we'd go and have something to eat. They would refuel the airplane and get it ready for our trip back home.

Hazardous Duty

Going over to China, it was hazardous due to bad weather, but going back it was even worse. We had the jet stream that flew from west to east and sometimes it would be pretty strong, 50 to 60 mph, and in some cases, up to 100 mph. Going back home, you are traveling westbound, into the face of the jet stream. So, it would take you longer. We'd head back to the Assam Valley, pick up a beacon, circle down to sea level as we broke out of the overcast, and land at the airport where we took off from. But, here's the hazard—you'd get there early morning and there would be fog. So, you'd have to circle until the fog would lift or go to an alternate airport. If the fog did not lift and the alternate airport is too far away, you would run out of gas, then you would have to jump out of the airplane and lose the airplane. A lot of ships were lost that way.

A lot of airplanes were also lost in another respect. On the C-46 airplane, which was a very good plane, we would carry 55-gallon drums of gasoline. At sea level, the procedure was for one of the crew members to go in and see if there were any leaks. If we had a bad spot or a leaker, we would take it out. If not, a crew member would come out and say, 'Captain, everything is okay.' So then we'd take off, get up to 15,000 feet, where there is lower atmospheric pressure. So, with any flaw in that drum, it would leak gasoline.

Now, gasoline fumes flow downward in the cold air, so on the C-46, as you know, the gasoline fumes would flow downward into the belly [of the aircraft]. At sea level, it's warm, but when you get up to about 15,000 feet, it's cold. On the instrument panel of the C-46, there is a red button that you press for heat. However, if you have a lot of fumes that have flowed down into the belly and you got cold and pressed the red button, it could cause a spark. The spark would ignite the fumes in the belly and that was the end of that airplane.

I just got through mentioning the hazard of flying the C-46 over the Hump, the dangerous weather, the updrafts and the jet stream over the Himalaya Mountains. The War Department considered the Himalaya Mountains and the Lifeline to China a combat zone. As a combat zone, they had a criteria of 750 hours of total time in that area and you have rotation to go home.

Medals

They also mentioned that being in a combat zone, you were also awarded certain medals for the amount of time that you had flown over the mountains. So, the first medal I received and earned was this Air Medal, this medal right here. [*Shows medal*] This medal was given for 150 hours of pilot time over the Himalaya Mountains.

The next one was given when you accumulated over 300 hours and you would be awarded the Distinguished Flying Cross, which was a very good medal. When you kept accumulating hours, you'd have another medal. In other words, after 300 hours, I would earn a cluster to the Air Medal. After another 300 hours accumulated over the Hump, there would be another Distinguished Flying Cross. Instead of giving you the medal itself, they would give you a cluster for the medal they had already given you. So, what I have is the Air Medal with the cluster and the Distinguished Flying Cross with the cluster.

The war in China back in early 1945 was getting much worse. The government had to get troops from the northern part of China and bring them to the southern part of China to fight. They thought I would do much better being transferred to China on a C-47 airplane, which is basically the DC-3 Douglas. When I flew with Eastern Airlines, I accumulated a lot of hours and experience on the DC-3. So they thought it would be a good idea to send me to China to do some service with the C-46 airplane. So, my first mission was to go to North China to pick up troops and bring them back to Shantou in the southern part of China to fight the Japanese.

As I said before, the war was getting much worse. I took many trips up there, and at one time, we had to transfer a Chinese cavalry outfit from the northern part of China to the southern part of China. That was pretty tricky. They didn't have much time so they thought they would use the airplane. They took my favorite C-47 and made some stalls. In those stalls, they would put four horses. They would have a veterinarian go along on the trip. They would put the horses on the airplane, tranquilize them enough to be calm for a couple hours until we reached our destination, and then unload them, and everything would be okay. Everything was going along fine, and we did several trips with the horses. But then one night, we went for a cavalry outfit in North China, took the usual four horses, put them in the airplane, tranquilized them for the two hours, and when I got south to my destination after two hours the weather was very bad, and I could not land there. I had to either go to an alternate airport or wait out the storm. We went to an alternate airport, which took another hour and a half. In the meantime, the tranquilizer wore off for the horses and they didn't give them any more drugs, so the horses got up and became unruly. There was really nothing we could do; we couldn't land because the weather was too bad. One of the horses knocked its hoof through the side of my airplane, a hole about as big as a watermelon. It was a lucky thing that we had a C-47. The C-47, at the time, was not pressurized, so putting a hole through the cabin was just like opening a window and didn't have anything to do with the pressurization.

The Communist Chinese

We delivered troops and several cavalry outfits from north to south. There came another time when we had to deliver medical supplies to the Communist Chinese. The medical supplies that we had to deliver were to Yunnan, which was the capital of the Communist Chinese, about 70 miles north of The Great Wall. Occasionally, we delivered medical supplies to the Communist Chinese, but it was not on a regular basis. You had to get permission/authorization from the allies to fly the medical supplies to the Communist Chinese, which was another entity by itself. We did, after a while, deliver two or three loads there. The government in Yunnan did not have adequate airports. They had a small strip in a valley. It's a good thing we had the DC-3 because it could land and stop in a small space.

About this time, we had a surprise visit at our base in Chen Yi. Our base in Chen Yi had an airport that was about 90 miles north of Kunming and the elevation of the field was about 7,000 feet. We lived at 7,000 feet, and when we flew the airplane we would go from 7,000 feet to 15,000 feet. One day, we got a surprise visit from Generalissimo Chiang Kai-shek, the head of the Chinese government at that time. We were about forty pilots in the barracks, so we stayed at attention and then passed in review in front of the generalissimo. The generalissimo said, 'Men, I want to thank you for doing such a great job in maintaining the Lifeline of China. For that, I am going to award you pilots the Order of the Purple Cloud.' [Speaking of medals], that was a beautiful medal. I saw it but I never got it because, shortly thereafter, the [civil] war was getting worse in China and the Japanese forces were coming down from the north into the central part of China and into the capital. Chiang Kai-shek had to abandon his seat of government and go to Taiwan. You probably heard that he was in Taiwan. At that time, the raid came so quickly and not knowing about it, they had to leave in a hurry. The generalissimo left behind most of his important papers right there in his office. As it turned out, the order for my medal, the Order of the Purple Cloud, was in his office, with other orders. I never got the medal. Maybe someday, some Chinese ambassador might [bestow] me the medal. I hope I do get it.

The Grand Piano

One night, my roommate said, 'Patrick, I've got cargo going to China and what do you think is on the manifest? A grand piano assigned to Madame Chiang Kai-shek!' The generalissimo's wife was a concert pianist and very good. For some reason, our government wanted to cement relations with China, so they thought, what better way than to send this grand piano to Madame Chiang Kai-shek. So they put it in this cargo plane, instead of some gasoline and other supplies. My friend flew the regular course, and the more he flew toward China with his load, the madder he got and said, 'What in the hell am I doing for the war effort when I should be flying the gasoline for the B-29s, and I've got this darn piano assigned for Madame Chiang Kai-shek?' After a while, he bent down and shut off the gasoline on one engine and the engine quit. The standard procedure when you lose an engine is to jettison the cargo because you want to save the airplane and to hell with the cargo. So they went out back, opened the door, and kicked out the grand piano over the Burma jungles. [*Laughs*]

So when they got to Kunming, China, the truck pulls up to get the piano and the guy said, 'Where's the piano?'

The captain said, 'You know, I lost an engine over Burma and there was something wrong with the cross feed and I had to jettison the cargo. Then later on, I fooled around with the cross feed and checked the tanks and found there was a short on one of the valves. I opened another valve, the gasoline came in, and I started the engine and continued the trip here with both engines.' So, that was humorous. But maybe Madame Chiang Kai-shek got mad and told the generalissimo, 'Those pilots from Chen Yi who you told were going to get the Purple Cloud—forget them!' Maybe that's why I didn't get my Order of the Purple Cloud. [*Laughs*]

The Japanese were pretty smart people. They were smart pilots. [But] we had some basic radar, and we were flying mostly in bad weather anyway. [Remember, our usual pattern] when coming back to Chen Yi, where I was based, [was to] circle until we got the beacon, which was about five miles north of the airport. After we hit the beacon and knew we were at a certain altitude, we'd fly due south for about three minutes, descending until we broke out of the overcast and landing on the runway at Chen Yi. The Japanese, as I said, were pretty smart. They would see us someplace up the line and would follow right in back of our airplane so that when the beacon would pick up our aircraft, it would only see on the radar one blip. The Japanese fighter or bomber would be so close to our tail that the radar would only pick up the one blip. They would follow us down, and when we broke out of the overcast over the airport to land, the Japanese bomber would come right over us and bomb the field, without us ever even knowing they were coming in. That's what they did. That is the only encounter I ever had with the Japanese aircraft, them following me in and bombing the field over my head after I had landed. The only [enemy] ground fire that I encountered wasn't actually ground fire; they would come over and bomb the field. If we happened to be in the barracks, the standard order was to grab our gear and canteens and head for the trenches that were around the base. We would spend the night in the trenches until the bombing was over with and the next morning, we would get out of the trenches and go back to our barracks. That's the only encounter I had with ground fire or face to face with Japanese.

*

Very rarely we would see someone that came from the reserves before the war. There were a few but I didn't know exactly who they were, and they flew with the Flying Tigers. The Flying Tigers were very active in that area, and they started in the States with P-40s, and they gradually rotated to duty in China. We had quite a few of the Flying Tigers flying out of bases in China.

Most of the pilots I flew with were regular cadets that went to flying school that came there. Very few of the pilots were from another airline. There were a few but basically most of the young fellas were trained as cadets and got to fly there. The reason I got to be a first pilot as soon as I got there was because of my experience with the airline. I didn't have to ride as a copilot for three or four months to get used to the airplane and then go on to be the pilot of that airplane. I already had that experience so when I went there, I was immediately put into left seat as the captain of that airplane.

With the C-46 or C-47, we had a crew of three: the pilot (myself), copilot, and radio man. The radio man was also the navigator. He would navigate but have the communications with headquarters and transmit all these messages via radio and they could tell him, sometimes, about where we were. So, the standard crew was the three men. As I said before, I only flew the C-47 and C-46 and those were the crew members. There was no armament at all, not a bit. All we had was our trusty .45 caliber pistols that we carried all the time. Nothing for any guns or bombs, we had just plain airplanes. Later on, I got home and flew a hospital ship, which was a different story. That had the pilot (myself, the captain), copilot, flight nurse, and medical attendant. That was a four-man crew. We always had onboard, on every flight, our parachute. The equipment in the back of the parachute was some sort of survival gear. It had the machete, a couple of flares, three or four packages of soya biscuits to eat, and possibly, if we were over water, there would be some kind of lures to catch fish. That's about it other than mosquito repellent and the parachute itself.

[We never had to bail out], but there were a couple cases where we had run into ice. I was in a C-47 in the China area and had accumulated approximately 2 to 3 inches of ice on the wings. I told the crew, 'You better get your parachutes on. I'm going down as low as I can, and if we don't break out and we run out of gas, the red lights are on now, we're going to have to bail out.' At that particular time, my radio man called in and said, 'Hey, I've got great news! We're pretty close to Shantou, and this is the first time that the government has put in an instrument landing system. Here is the number, and if you will fly a course of 270 degrees for about ten minutes, you will run into the beacon at the end of the runway, and they will turn on the instrument landing system for you!' We did that, got to the beacon, called in, they gave us the signals, turned on the instrument landing system, and we landed. This was probably the first time an Army plane landed in China with the instrument landing system. This was in Shantou, which was one of the main B-29 bases to bomb Japan.

The Chinese People

The Chinese were good people. The reason I say they were good people is because I did duty in India. When I was in India and we had time off, we would go into a small town. We would watch the people just mope around; that was their way of life. Then, when I did duty in China, I'd land and go into a town like Kunming, I'd see the Chinese people and they were walking fast and seemed like they were busy. They were hard-working, studious people. They would respect us and when they saw us they would say, 'Yīqiè dōu hěn hǎo,' which means 'everything is okay.' [*Laughs*] Every time you go to a foreign country, there are always bad words that you pick up. There are also bad words in China. If they didn't like you and really wanted to give you hell, they would take their two fingers, point them to your eyes, and say, 'Nǐ chī sǐ lǎoshǔ.' That meant 'you eat dead mice.' [*Laughs*] On the whole, I respect the Chinese people. They were good workers.

Several times, we had to land in Myitkyina, Burma, and take on gas. That's the airport in Burma. I hate to say this, there was a colonel who was trying to make general. He did make it, of course. His name was Colonel Tunner. Instead of having our tanks full of gasoline, which would be about eight hours of flight, he would tell them to give us three hours of gasoline in the airplane. The other gasoline that was left over did not go into the tank; he would put it into the oil drums. At the end of the month, he would write down 'tonnage over the Hump.' If he put five or six extra drums of gasoline in my airplane from Assam to China, he could write that off as 'tonnage over the Hump.' We would have three hours of gas in the tank, fly from India to Myitkyina, take the drums off, and put more in for tonnage. Then he would put another two hours of flight worth of gasoline in my tanks. So, in other words, there would be about 800 gallons of gasoline in the airplane, and they would only fill me with 200 gallons.

One time, I said to the gasoline man, 'Fill up the tank.'

He said, 'We can't fill up the tanks, we can only give you about one quarter of your usual capacity.'

I got mad. The weather was bad, and I said, 'I will not fly this airplane unless you fill up the tanks.'

He said, 'I can't do that.'

I said, 'Go talk to your operations manager and tell them that I'm going to leave my airplane here, stick with my airplane, and I'm not going to take off until you fill my tanks.'

He came back after half an hour and said, 'We'll fill up your tanks.' So, they filled up my tanks, I took off, finished my routine flight to China, and there it was. Two months later, I saw in the service newspaper that Colonel Tunner was promoted to brigadier general for the excellent job that he had done flying supplies over the Hump. So there you are.

Going Home

I accumulated over 750 hours over the Hump and China flying and the routine was that you would be rotated home at 750 hours. This was in China. I came home from a flight one day and Colonel Keagan, who was our commanding officer, called me into his office. He said, 'Lieutenant Scarano, I want to thank you for the good job that you've been doing here but it's time to send you home. On my desk, I have two orders. I have one order promoting you to captain. The other order is rotating you home. They are both on my desk. Now, if I send them both in, they are not going to act on both of them. What they'll probably do is send you home as your present rank, first lieutenant. I would suggest, if I put in for your promotion first and then you wait two or three weeks, then I'll send in your orders for rotating you home. That way, you'll go home as a captain.'

I said, 'Oh, that's very good.'

He said, 'It's up to you.'

I said, 'Well, I'm anxious to go home. If I go home as a first lieutenant, there won't be much for me to do. But if I go home as a captain, I'll be able to swing a good position as a pilot on a bigger airplane. So, I'll take my chance. Send in the orders for my promotion first and then wait to send in my orders to go home.'

That's exactly what happened. He sent in for my promotion, that came in, and then, two weeks later, he sent in for my rotation home, and that came in. So, I went home as a captain. The bad thing about that, at that particular time, my orders said to leave Chan Yi, China, and fly by military aircraft to Karachi, India. From there, I would get a shuttle and go to Casablanca. [However,] when I got to Karachi, the minute I got into the airport and showed my orders, we heard about VE Day! The people in Europe capitulated. The problem was that they froze all orders to go home right then and there. They said for me to wait until further orders, and I didn't know what to do. There was a rumor that we were going to concentrate more on ending the war with Japan and that, instead of going home, they were going to divert us to another part of China.

I was downfallen. I was anxious to go home. While I was sitting there, a friend of mine that I knew back in the States at OCS came by and said, 'Pat! What are you doing here?' I told him that I was being rotated home, but my orders were frozen. What could I do?

He said, 'I'm flying a supply ship from Casablanca to Karachi. I'm going to unload that, get something to eat, refuel, and I'll be taking off again in about two hours back for Casablanca. But I cannot take any passengers. I have a C-46 airplane that's parked in the north ramp, number 766, but I cannot take passengers.'

I said, 'Oh, thank you, Jim. Good luck to you.'

So, after he left, I took my bag and snuck over to the north ramp, got into the airplane, got in the tail where the toilet was, and closed the door. An hour later, I heard the engines start up and then take off. About ten minutes later, I got out of the can in the back, went to the cockpit, and said, 'Hey, Jim!'

He said, 'Pat, I knew you'd take my hints.'

We landed the next day in Casablanca, the end of his trip and the end of my trip. I went up to the operations manager and asked, 'When is your next flight home?'

He said, 'How did you get here?'

I said, 'I came by military aircraft.'

He said, 'Let me see your orders.' The orders said to go home but that I was frozen in Karachi. He said, 'You know what you're going to do? You're going to take the next airplane going back to Karachi. You stay right here. You did something wrong, and you can't go home.' I sat there, downhearted, of course.

An hour later, the same officer came over to me and said, 'I hate to tell you this, but I've got some important papers to go to the States and they are to go by courier service. I can't send them with just anyone; I have to send them with an officer. You, as a captain, are eligible to take it. Would you like to take the courier to the States?'

I said, 'Do I ever!' Was I happy! They took this pouch and hand-cuffed the strap to my wrist with the important papers. I got on the airplane, and we had landed in Bangor, Maine. That was the end of overseas. Oh, I was so happy. I was the happiest man in the world. I came back to the States and went home on leave. I saw some of my family. I saw my daughter, who was born while I was in India; my three-month-old little girl, Charlene. She was a beautiful thing. I was so happy to be home. I was home for thirty days and then had to go on my next mission.

The Hospital Ship

They sent me to Romulus Air Force Base in Michigan to be a captain on a hospital ship. In Romulus, they gave me a copilot, nurse, and medical attendant. There were four people in our crew, and we had a C-47 airplane. We would take off from Romulus with a pocket full of money because we were going to be gone for a month. We would fly to either Metro Field on Long Island or Fort Dix in New Jersey. We'd take patients that came from the European Theater, usually about six litter cases and four or five ambulatory cases. We would fly them from the east coast, Metro Field or Fort Dix, westward and drop off these patients to a hospital nearest to their home. It could be St. Louis or Cleveland, and we'd pull up, land at the airport, drop off the patients, and work our way west from St. Louis to Kansas City to Denver. After dropping off our last patient, we would proceed to Hamilton Field in California. After a few days of maintenance on the airplane, refueling and something else, we would get ready for our mission going east. When we were in Hamilton Field, CA, we would take patients that were injured in the Pacific Theater and fly them east. We could drop off a couple patients in Ogden, Utah, and continue on to Wichita, Kansas, then Cleveland, and so on. When we finished dropping off all our patients, we returned to Romulus; after several days, we would do the same routine again.

While I was flying the hospital ship, one night in South Dakota, I was homing in on a beacon. Back in those days, they didn't control the airwaves. We had a radio beacon on this aircraft, and it would home in on a broadcast station. They would have music, etc. This one night I was tuned in on a station in South Dakota and heard that the Japanese capitulated and it was VJ Day. So, there was the end of World War II, flying at 12,000 feet over South Dakota, heading west. Shortly after that, I came back to Romulus, went home on leave, and was sent to Rome, New York, for separation from the service.

The Reserves

That was not the end. I stayed in the reserves. I retired in about 1972. I stayed in the reserves and was made a liaison officer for the Air Force Academy. I would go to a high school in uniform, talk to the seniors, men and women, tell them that we would like to have them in the service and after they finished high school and graduated, they could pick going to the Air Force Academy, Annapolis or West Point. They had to get to their Congressional representative and tell them they would like to be picked to go to one of the academies. The congressman would then have two or three students that he or she would send to these academies. I was a liaison officer and spent two weeks of active duty during the summer at the Air Force Academy. I would get to see the students I helped to get through there.

I stayed in the reserves for twenty years. We would meet once a month at an armory near our hometown, Cortland or Binghamton. We put in our fifty hours of studying or duty and that would be a satisfactory year toward my pension for retirement. It must have been about 1947 when the orders came through for making the Army Air Corps into the U.S. Air Force. They gave each one of the officers $200 to go out and buy a blue uniform. I took my uniform and went to Rome Air Force Base, went to the commissary or PX, and picked out a nice blue uniform and hat. From then on, I was U.S. Air Force. That was a memorable occasion.

[When the Korean War broke out], I was waiting to be called up. They never did call me but I had everything ready so if they said, 'Let's go,' I would have all of my household things in order and go just like that [*snaps fingers*]. So, I never went to Korea.

Another duty that I enjoyed very much was being a liaison officer for the Civil Air Patrol. One time, they sent me to Harris Hill as the commander for the encampment for the Civil Air Patrol

Cadets. They would send the cadets to Harris Hill, give them ground training, put them in a glider, and teach them to fly the glider alone so they could get their license as a glider pilot. I was in charge of fifty or sixty Civil Air Patrol cadets, both male and female. That would be my two-week tour duty at the encampment. Later on, I would go to the encampments and do whatever I could do to help the Civil Air Patrol. I got this Air Force Commendation Medal for the work that I did with the Civil Air Patrol.

Keeping In Touch

[I didn't really keep in touch with any flying buddies after the war]. Some nearby, I would, but they were from all over the country, including California. I did have a couple of buddies from Michigan that I kept in touch with. There was one officer from California that called me in the middle of the night. He said, 'Patrick Scarano?'

I said, 'Yes.'

He said, 'You flew over the Hump, right?'

I said, 'Yes.'

He said, 'I have your name here and about once a month I go down the list, pick out a name, call that person, and see how they are doing just for the hell of it!' I never went that far.

[My time in the war] was a good experience and the Lord was with me. The main thing back then, and I don't know if you could do it now, is if you are the commander of that aircraft, it is up to you as a commander to make sure you have a safe return of the airplane and your crew. In fact, to go back to that C-47 flight at 15,000 feet, when I flew the Hump I would tell my crew, 'Wear your sheepskin underwear and sheepskin flying suit, because when you fly with me, I do not turn the heater on. I fly blue and cold, but I return and so will you.' It is up to the captain of that aircraft to look after the crew and the aircraft, and return come hell or high water. There was a good many times when I was in China sleeping in an operation room at the airport and an officer would come up to me and say, 'You're Lieutenant Scarano?'

I'd reply, 'Yeah.'

He'd say, 'I'm going to take your airplane, we need it.'

I'd say, 'You're taking my airplane? How are we going to get home? Where are your orders? Look, you see what I've got over here? [*Points to his hip*] This is a 45-caliber pistol. You touch that airplane and you're going to get it! Get someone else's airplane!' He never touched my airplane. Like I said, take care of your airplane and bring it back home. When you're in Burma and they want to get you short on gas, you say, 'No way, put the gasoline in there or I don't fly the airplane.' As a captain of that aircraft, remember to do your duty.

Civilian Life

After the war, I went back to the airline and said, 'I'd like to come back because you promised me that when we got back from the service that we could come back here. How long will it take until you can check me out as a captain, because I've been in China and probably have 2,000 more hours in a C-47 and that's what they're flying; I'm a much better pilot now than when I left here.'

So they asked what my service number was, and I told them, '527.' I was a copilot with the airline then.

They said, 'Oh my God, you've got a very low number here. It might be two years before we can check you out as a captain.'

I said, 'Hey, I'm not going to fly as a copilot for two years waiting to be captain.'

As it turned out, about six months later, aviation expanded, and I could have been a captain. But I went home and got into the furnace and appliance business because there was a big demand for appliances and opened my store. I did that for a couple years and then I figured since I was still a young man and had a lot of flying left in me that I'd go back to flying. I made out a resume and sent it to some of the big manufacturers, stores, and firms in the Syracuse area. One man, J. Stanley Coyne, who ran the Coyne laundry system, called me and said, 'Patrick, I love your resume. Here is my airplane, you can come and fly with me to Maryland to see if you like it. You can fly three or four days a week and the two days that you don't fly, you can go out in the field and do some selling for me. You can sell garments to General Electric.' I went back to flying. I flew for this man out of Hancock Field for about twelve years. After that, I came back home and did charter work. That was about it.

I'm a member of the Hump Pilots Association and also joined the VFW when I got home. In fact, about two months ago, I was given a pin and emblem of fifty years for being a member of the VFW for fifty years. What else can I say, except that I was born in New York State, I'm going to die in New York State, I think [the governor] is a good man, it's an Empire State and I think I like it here. I want to thank the governor for giving me the opportunity to get my experiences documented for the people now and the people of the future.

Patrick Scarano retired in 1967 from the Air Force Reserves with the rank of lieutenant colonel. He passed away at the age of 97 in January 2013.

CHAPTER FOUR

The B-24 Radioman

Dr. Norman Handelman grew up in Brooklyn, New York, and became a radio operator and gunner on a B-24 Liberator bomber flying the Hump on several missions in the 10th U.S. Army Air Force, one of which included bombing the infamous bridge over the River Kwai. He sat for this interview at the age of 82 in 2005 in Manhattan, New York City.

Norman Handelman

I was born July 14, 1923, in Brooklyn, New York. I was in college at the time of the war. The college was very affected by the war, of course; a lot of people were being drafted from the classes. They started making edicts of all sorts. If you took enough courses of your major, then you could be forgiven the courses that were not major courses like arts, music, philosophy. Then as it came to 1943, I was drafted. It came down to that if you passed the midterm, you got credit for the term. I was drafted shortly after the midterm, which meant I got credit for the term, which also meant I got credit for the courses that I was forgiven. So, I had an abbreviated college degree; it was like a two-and-a-half-year college, I missed a lot of courses a lot of people take. So, I went into the service right from there.

[When I heard about Pearl Harbor], I was in my apartment and I was listening to a football game, the Giants or the Chicago Bears. That's where I was, and all of a sudden, there was a break in of some sort. Somebody announced that 'Pearl Harbor's been bombed.' Pearl Harbor, I had no idea where Pearl Harbor was. Anyhow, slowly the news started to trickle out. I think the game went on to the finish because nobody knew the enormity of it.

I ended up in the Air Corps. When I was drafted, I went down to Lexington Avenue Grand Central Station, the post office. There were several people there representing the Marines, the Navy, the Army, and the Army Air Corps. They all looked you over, looked your records over, and I was selected for the Air Force, the Air Corps.

[I went for basic training to] Miami, Florida. We were dressed—it was late spring—we were given winter clothing. We were put on a train, a coal burning train, I remember a lot of soot and all of that. I don't know how long it took us to get down to Florida, but we got down there. Nobody was going to tell us where we were going. It was top secret and all of that. There we were in winter clothing, going down to Miami Beach. Of course, we changed. So, Miami Beach was where I trained, staying at a small hotel off the beach. I have visited a couple of times just for reminiscence' sake. It was a beautiful beach; training was not hard. My image of what infantry training was like was that it was very arduous exposure to all kinds of things, but down there I just remember marching, learning right face, left face, about face, present arms, the right way to salute. There's a right way to salute!

After six weeks to eight weeks, we were on a train again out to St. Louis. At that point, they had done all kinds of orientation tests and the like. I wound up in radio school. We learned Morse code basically and we learned also how the Air Corps radio system worked. The planes were equipped with long antennas and there were what they called 'command units'; you have to change the frequency. It was a big, bulky tube kind of arrangement. So, we learned Morse code in varying steps. They gave us mock-ups occasionally. We wound up in a little compartment by ourselves. We were fed Morse code at varying speeds. I did well enough to get some kind of special days off when my parents came out to visit. I must say, for a sheltered boy living in Brooklyn where everything was gray and concrete and that sort of thing, it was a treat for me. St Louis was a treat because of all of the greenery. There I was in St. Louis with beautiful parks and wide streets. In Arlington, it was also lovely with very wide avenues, very big skies, palm trees, and a lot of exciting things to do.

From there I went down to gunnery school in Arlington, Texas. They gave us all kinds of instruction; we were taught to lead enemy planes. For planes coming in, you don't fire at him up there. You know he's coming in, so you lead him; depending on how far away, you lead him by what they call 'rads,' the circular vision of what the aiming thing is. So, we were learning to lead. We wound up with shotguns. We wound up with clay pigeons. We wound up riding on open trucks around a course where suddenly a clay pigeon would come out and you were supposed to get at them, you know, by leading it. I had a great time. It was like target practice for me. For me, it was kind of like an unreal experience. First of all, the [Army] Air Force was kind of sheltered. From basic training you're in the mud all the time, basically;n the Air Force, we weren't. Not quite coddled, but it was nice. So, we enjoyed ourselves. We were young kids playing at shooting and all those things. As I said, for me a sheltered boy from Brooklyn, the idea of shooting bullets and shooting [was fantastic!]

One of the things we had to learn at gunnery school was [stripping a 50-caliber machine gun]. Again, I told you I was a sheltered boy, as I said, I had never really done anything with my hands, I'd been studying all of the time basically. I learned, as everybody else did, to take a 50-caliber machine gun apart and put it together again blindfolded. You got to know the names of every last piece. I remember it got down to the smallest piece that had the longest name. I couldn't do it again, of course.

At gunnery school, we would go up in AT6s at the time. They're two-seaters. The pilot would take us up and there would be some [washouts]. Later I found out Women's Air Corps—WACs—would fly target planes pulling some targets for us to shoot at with this machine gun that you were given. I did poorly. So did most of us. That was the only exposure I had, the only experience I had firing a machine gun.

By that time, as far as we were concerned, the war was never going to end. It was something that you didn't think was ever, you lived in a war time, and that was it. For all you knew, you'd be an old man discharged from the service and the war would be continuing.

Shipping Out

So, I got orders to ship out. We went down to a collection point in Newport News. I went with a bunch of my friends from gunnery school and others that I had met in this collection point. One of them became a real good buddy of mine. We went on this big ship, the USS *Randall*. I remember that it was its maiden voyage; it was a troop ship, it carried thousands of troops. It was fast, it didn't need an escort. We went around to the Panama Canal, I remember watching us go through the canal, down to the South Pacific, all the way up through the New Zealand islands around to the west coast of Australia, where we docked in Perth thirty days later. Thirty days aboard ship!

To India

We stayed two nights in Perth. Some friends and I took suburban trains into Freemantle, things like that. Then we got on board ship again and fifteen more days. Again, we were not told where we were going. When you're going down [from the United States], and you're not going to Europe, and you're going someplace south, where could you go? Who knew we were going on into the CBI? It wasn't like until a couple of days out of Bombay that we knew because we went all the way around Madagascar to avoid submarines. At Bombay we were told we could let our people [at home] know. How could we let them know? We couldn't do anything, really. From there, again, we were waiting to find out what we were going to do because we were replacements. We got on board a train again and went across India by Indian third-class trains, where we'd sleep on slatted benches. You'd see exotic scenery. You'd see stuff that newsreels were made of.

We wound up in Calcutta. It was monsoon season at that point. So, we waited; I remember waiting with my group outside. Nice weather. All of a sudden, it just seemed like that, it poured. Beautiful blue sky, it just turned black in no time. It poured and then it stopped. The sun came out. We were soaked and then we were dry.

We stayed in tents for a few nights. Then we were transported up somewhere north of Calcutta. I've been trying to locate it on the maps. Kermatola, [on the east coast of India], stuff like that, not on the maps. This being the monsoon season, we hung around for a couple of weeks trying to get used to what was going on. I remember how I said it was like a game and all of that. When we got there, the bombing mission time was ending because you don't bomb during the monsoon season. You can't see your target. So, I remember a mission when we were in an orderly room or something like that there were guys coming back from a mission, coming in. The operations officer, a big, strapping Swedish guy, was crying and furious about the fact that his buddy had been shot down. I still remember—it registered with me, but nowhere did I feel like, 'Oh my God, this is terrible, I could die, it could happen to me!' That didn't register; I don't think for any of us it really registered. It was like it was your job. You're here. Something could happen down here on your way [to work], so you just do your job.

Missions

After a few weeks, we were assigned different planes because we were replacement radio operators. There's attrition of some sort. Sometimes people got sick, they got wounded or they died or opted out or whatever. So, we were assigned and then we went on gas hauling missions. We flew the Hump. We took gas. Every time I flew it was a different B-24. We flew on a lot of these hauling missions, which were dangerous, but being a kid and it being a job, it didn't feel dangerous.

[We were not under attack] on these missions. By the time we were there, the Japanese had finally been stopped; they had encroached into Burma, they were there close to the border of India. At the time, there were some Indian troops that really didn't like the British at all and were likely to throw in their hands with the Japanese. So, the Japanese were pretty close to getting into India, but there were all kinds of reasons why they were stopped. Supply lines got short; the jungles were terrible. By that time, they were starting to retreat a little bit.

I remember flying the Hump. The mountains there were very sizeable, I don't know, 15,000 feet or something like that. When you got over them, there'd be a sudden down drop midair. I remember I was never scared. I keep on saying that. I wasn't scared until, as a radio operator, I sat on the parachute. It was on the seat under me. I don't know exactly where I would have jumped out from. I sat on the chute until one day over this Hump, the engineer, a great friend, suddenly started to put his parachute on. I had never seen this before. I said, 'What's wrong?'

He said, 'Nothing.' I thought, he's putting the chute on. I thought if he's putting the chute on and he's the engineer, he must know something. From then on, I had my chute immediately available.

Later on, we went on bombing missions when the monsoon season ended. Then we came back, and yes, then we'd wear flak jackets. Sometimes flying high, we wore heat suits.

We took Atabrine, I believe, which was maybe a little bit later. Atabrine, we found out, turns you yellow. I started noticing my eyeballs were looking a little strange. It was the Atabrine. We were told to watch out for the waters, that sanitation levels were different. Someplace early in India, we were told to watch out for Indian alcohol, liquor. I was not a drinker. It didn't matter to me, but we were told to watch out because it can blind you. I remember seeing a guy coming back having drunk a lot and he was blind. It didn't last, but he was blind. He was terrified, of course. So, [we were warned of] that kind of disease or the idea of maybe consorting with prostitutes. A 'Pro Kit' included a condom to use and some kind of prophylactic ointment to put inside it and then something else to use after you finished the intercourse to inject into your penis to protect the penis from any intrusion of germs, and to wash, maybe some special soap. I think it was given to you on your leave.

For the Air Corps, the Air Force, between missions, there's nothing to do. We had it easy, I have to stress. I did not have a bad war. We didn't see any women except the Indian women, and we saw them at a distance. We had USO shows. One of them I remember was like the last USO show we got, because several of the guys got very disorderly and started making all kinds of obscene remarks about the girls—what he wanted to do with them, that sort of thing. The orders came down from the bigwigs, that's it, no more. We can't trust you guys.

I had this friend, as I said, who I see every couple of years or so. He's surviving nicely. He was my buddy in the war, in the India war; I know I have pictures showing me with a .45 automatic in a holster around my shoulder. We carried them around. There was a place for two automatic clips. Maybe we were given the clips when we left, when you go on a mission, even on a flight to haul gas, because there was always a danger of something happening to the plane. The jungles down below us were infested with Japanese. So, we were given kits to carry with us. One of the things we had, I regret not having taken it with me when I came home, we were given two small buttons. We had a flight suit, which had buttons on it, like copper metal buttons or something. We were given two of them to replace two of the buttons on the suit. When you do that, they're indistinguishable from the other buttons. One of them had a little bump on it, the other had two bumps. If you need it, you put them together and they were a compass. You put them down and they would magnetize, and they pointed north. So, that was one of the escape things we were given.

We also had carbines, small 30mm rifles. I don't remember where they were. They may have been in the planes.

The planes themselves, when we flew on bombing missions, we might have had some fighters had we flown into the Hump. We had these 50 caliber machine guns. By and large, until we flew the Hump, we flew at relatively low altitude. It was warm there, so we didn't have to wear too much. We could fly with the open waist window.

This war was never going to end.

Weightless

I was just remembering something, my lifetime experience with weightlessness. I hadn't flown for about a month overseas. My best buddy from all of the war from the beginning was shot down. We went on this mission. It was great fun watching the bombs dropping and all of that. He went on a mission a few days later and he didn't come back. I'm a little more upset now, thinking of it, than I was then. I was upset, though. I just felt like I couldn't fly. I just can't fly. I knew the policy there was you wouldn't be charged with any kind of major offense. They'd just ground you and get another replacement. So, it took me a long time.

Finally, I was going on a mission. We were awakened at 3:30 or 4:00 depending on how long the mission was, and we got very long missions from up in India all the way down into Burma. Sometimes they would go for twelve hours, fourteen hours. We bombed the bridge over the River Kwai. That's a long distance from India! That mission would be like sixteen hours.

Anyhow, I got grounded that month. I finally decided that I can't live this way. I want to fly. I want to fly, and I have a better chance of coming home at least for a furlough than if I just stay on the ground. This war was never going to end. So, I volunteered to fly on a training mission. The pilot was being trained for night flying, instrument flying. The training involved all kinds of maneuvers and the like, up and down.

With the B-24, way up front was the bombardier and, I think, the nose gunner. I'm not sure about that. Yes, the bombardier and the nose gunner way up front, downstairs. Then there was the cabin cockpit where the pilot and co-pilot were, then there's a narrow partition. On the right-hand side was where the radio operator sat with the radios. The major job of the radio operator on a flight was to listen to see if the flight has been cancelled or diverted. You have to know the code and the code name for the day. If a message comes, you put it down and you decode it. So, we sat with the headset on, on the right-hand side. On the left-hand side was the engineer. He's got his own desk as we did. Also, the plane that we flew there's various models. The plane we flew in you went up through a little trap door underneath the plane. You went up the trap door and then you were in a compartment. There was a gallon of fuel for a little engine. We called it the 'put-put' engine. It kind of warmed the major engines. It got them primed for starting. You got one more trap door, you open the trap door and come up and you've got a floor. That's where the radio operator sits, and the engineer sits. Then you walk straight through the walkway, the catwalk, through the bombs. There was a narrow catwalk about this wide. Then you got to the waist.

In this flight that we're talking about, the pilot was doing various maneuvers. At one point what he was doing was apparently checking out a stall instrument. He went up, then stalled it. This big B-24 started falling. I had no idea. We had no idea what he was doing. He was just being told by the instructor what to do.

All of a sudden, I felt like I was being pressed up against the ceiling of this plane. I thought we must be upside down. I started to try to right myself and I couldn't do that. Then I saw the trap door open and up comes floating this one gallon can of gasoline. I think something's wrong; I don't know it was weightlessness. Guys who were sitting in the waist—as I said, it was warm there—had the waist windows open and they were just hanging around. Before they knew it, they were starting to float toward the windows and float out and they were grabbing things. Of course, nobody got hurt. That was exciting. That was my experience with weightlessness.

To go on a mission, you're awakened. You go in, you have breakfast. You go into the room, and you'll be told what the mission of the day is. You'd be told, at one point, 'Watch out, here's a prisoner of war camp. See to it you don't bomb the prisoner of war camp, but you want to get the railroad station and tracks here.' Then, we would go out into another room to pick up our parachute. We also picked up a belt, it's like a life preserver belt like what we had onboard ship. Only the belt had, I forget what else it had in it, but it has a whole bunch of things to be used in case you're downed.

We had the blood chit[41] to help in one way but there was also a tin, and the tin had opium in it, it turns out. There was also American dollar bills, old bills. The old bills were so that if you were downed, you gave them to the people who were helping you, so that they couldn't be accused by the Japanese of having had these recently because they were so old. The opium was a special bribe to people to help us get out. I have a friend who was downed and was indeed taken out by the Chinese and it did help him all the way through. There were quite a few like that.

Anoxia

Let me brag about something else that happened. We were shown the dangers of anoxia in our training. We were taken into a decompression chamber where we were told that you want to wear a mask when you are above 12,000 feet because oxygen deprives your brain of the capacity to work well. It was hard to know so we're

---

[41] blood chit- military notice for civilians who may come across a 'friendly' armed-services member in distress, requesting assistance.

going to show you guys. Groups of us were taken into this chamber and they would slowly reduce the oxygen content. They reached 25,000 or sooner than that. Whatever it was, they showed at twelve, thirteen thousand your judgment is off.

I remember watching one guy. We are now pretty high. He was asked to write your name, rank, and serial number. In my case, it was Norman S. Handelman, 327…or whatever. I forgot what it was. Just keep on writing it. Just keep on writing it. I remember watching this guy writing and writing, then his hand started to tremble. He was uncoordinated. He dropped the pencil. He just stared blankly into space. He was out. Somebody gave him the pencil back, gave him some oxygen. We had this oxygen mask on. They're plugged into the oxygen circuit. He was told, because we were all wearing it by this time, he was told to unplug his. It was a male to female plug. Unplug it and do this exercise. So, he did. He was passing out. 'Plug your oxygen mask in. Plug the mask in. Plug the mask in!' He lost it. He just passed out. They plugged it back in for him. They gave him the pencil. He immediately started writing his name, rank, serial number as if nothing had happened.

I thought I was going to experiment with myself. I volunteered. What a jerk. Permanent brain damage. [*Laughs*] But I volunteered. I remember they told me this to unplug it, okay. I remember name, rank, and serial number. I felt so wonderful. I had never seen my handwriting this good. It felt so good, that's how it felt to me. They gave me this pencil. I started writing and all of a sudden I realized that I had passed out because there was a scrawl there and I hadn't known it. I figured that this is routine. I'm going to try something else. So, I volunteered again. I figured that I'll do the Gettysburg Address. So, 'four score and seven years ago our fathers brought on this continent. Four score….and dedicated to liberty'… and started repeating myself. They gave me the pencil again. At this point, I didn't know what I was doing. I just stopped and realized that I had passed out. But a routine matter, and you'd think you had been doing it all along.

For some reason, they needed more people in China so a bunch of us were sent into China to Luliang, which is near Kunming. We were established there, and we were to fly back and forth. We had flown over the Hump from Luliang before during the monsoon season. We were to be established there for how long we didn't know, of course. Where we would go back to India or pick up something in Luliang and fly to Sichuan or Guilin or other places where the Chinese were holding back or trying to hold back the Japanese and also supplying the 14th Air Force—Chennault's Flying Tigers. We supplied them with gasoline and stuff like that. We were in China for two or three months. I think two or three months. While there, I shared a tent with Bob.

Detached Service

When you come back from a mission, you'd be given a slug of whiskey and you'd work your way back to a room where they'd debrief you, tell what you saw, what happened, how much the flak was, where was it, the fighters, what the results of the bombing were, and so on. I came back from this mission. You're kind of tired. You got up early and it's intense. I got back and I'm starting to relax. Somebody comes from the orderly room saying the major wants to see you.

I said, 'What for?' I didn't know. I went to the office. They said, Pack up your clothing, you're going on a secret mission.' A secret mission! The hope of everybody there was that the mission would be to go back on a bond selling tour in the States! All I was told was that it's a secret mission.

I got back to the barracks. The barracks, by the way, we had it easy. We had bearers. We had men who cleaned the barracks. We slept on string beds with interwoven material on top of which were blankets and four posters so that there were mosquito nets to cover you. The cleanliness was taken care of. We had somebody we hired, all of us, probably eight to twelve of us in this room. So, I came back and everybody else was taking off their clothing. Here I am packing my bags. 'Where are you going, Handelman?'

I said, 'I'm going on a secret mission.' I figured that I've got something over them.

'What do you mean a secret mission?'

'That's all I've been told, it's a secret mission.'

'What do you think it is?'

'I don't know. Maybe it's a bond selling tour.' What could it be?

So I pack up. The next day, the truck takes me to the airport, to the airstrip. I get on the plane. God knows where I am going. Who knows? Maybe to Delhi. Maybe home. I get in. I get on the truck about twenty minutes later. Then we get on the plane. Twenty minutes later, the plane lands. That's a pretty short trip. I figured, that's not home. Maybe you've got to change planes there because it's a secret mission. For God's sake, its only twenty minutes.

We wait for the other plane. A truck comes and takes us to another airstrip where we were then—there were a whole bunch of us, several crews of us, we were replacements for combat cargo. We did then become part of combat cargo on detached service.

What we did then, we carried all kinds of cargo to the front-line troops in Burma. It was all kinds of stuff. We may have carried some ammo. I don't remember that.

That was out on detached service. Then, I came back. I logged many, many hours. We went by hour in terms of citations and the like. Well, it was a number of flights, but they were all varied. Some carried gas across the Hump. Some were bombing Burma or Thailand. Some were giving food and ammunition to front-line troops. In total, I had 60 flights flying in planes with high octane fuel, carrying fuel and carrying dangerous cargo into dangerous areas. So, I had 60 flights. That's the way it worked there. I came back and most of my friends had gone home by then because they had served their bombing missions, and I had been doing some lesser than bombing missions. I came back but I was scheduled for return home too. At the time, as I said, you got medals based on the number of hours you had put in. You got an air medal if you put in, I don't know, a hundred hours. You got an oak leaf cluster if you put in two hundred. You got a Distinguished Flying Cross if you put in three hundred combat hours. You got a third oak leaf cluster for another hundred, and another hundred would be another DFC.

I had just a few hours short of an oak leaf cluster. I did something that you're always told time and again, don't volunteer for anything. I figured I'd like to get that oak leaf cluster. So, I volunteered for a mission even though I knew I was going home I was told. Thank God, I'm here.

I was all set for the mission. It was supposed to be an easy mission, what they called a 'baksheesh,' a milk run. I get awakened. I get to the front line. Our plane is scrubbed. Something is malfunctioning. So, okay, I'll go. That's a mission from hell. The guys...some didn't come back. Some came limping back. It was not a good mission. It was Rangoon where all the Japanese had concentrated their flak and planes and that sort of thing. I got it, but I volunteered for a foolish thing. So that was my detached service.

Coming Home

Just to add insult to injury, when I came back, I didn't fly back. I came back by boat again. I got on a troop ship in Calcutta, went through the Suez Canal, the Mediterranean, the Strait of Gibraltar back at the same place I debarked from. Thirty days this time. I put in two and a half months at sea. Then, of course, I was one of the earliest people back. I came back because I got points for overseas time, combat time, medals, and all different points. I came back, and I was a changed boy by that point. I had experiences that I never dreamed of having.

I was onboard ship when Germany surrendered. There was a celebration, but at the same time the war was still on with the Japanese. I had been fighting the Japanese. It felt like it was okay, it was very nice that the war is over, that the Germans surrendered, but we're going back again. That was the prospect that we'd go back, and it would be worse because the Japanese would be concentrated. I was at home on leave when the atomic bomb dropped. I was delighted. So were all of my colleagues because that ended the war.

We were overseas when President Roosevelt died. He did. Oh my God, that's awful. That's terrible. Who's the vice president? Nobody knew who the vice president was. Nobody knew the name Truman. That was shocking, of course. What's going to happen next? I was discharged in New York City in October '45.

I made use of the GI Bill, very much so. We got the 52-20 club. Fifty-two weeks and twenty dollars a week unemployment. After a few weeks, I couldn't just hang around to collect the money. I had been trained basically as an accountant. I knew I didn't want to be an accountant. I just didn't. I had too many opening experiences in life at that point. An accountant sitting in an office scribbling numbers didn't appeal to me anymore. I was advised by a cousin, a knowledgeable cousin, who was a counselor to try it out. I tried for six months. Terrible. I just sat and wrote numbers, and I hated every minute of it. Finally, after six months of it, I quit. I started looking for what to do.

I went looking for schooling, looking for something to do, maybe journalism, maybe use my radio skills in an airline piloted plane but there was nothing there that I knew of. The journalism schools were closed by the time I looked to get in. So, I didn't know what to do. Somehow the idea of psychology, the idea of understanding people, had come to my mind some conversation I had through lunches. I went to visit the dean of the psychology department at NYU. He was very discouraging. There was no way to make a living. You can't make money or whatever. At the time, there really wasn't a way for a psychologist to make money basically. Not for many, but just around that time, a lot of veterans were coming home with a lot of mental disturbances. The Veterans Administration was swamped. They didn't have the facilities or the people to work with them. The number of psychiatrists was limited. I don't know how they got the idea, but they established training programs under the National Institute for Mental Health, the VA. They had a training program just at the time I was looking at getting into psychology. I took a test, and I apparently passed the test. I was accepted for a four-year training program in clinical psychology. At the same time, you were going to school, you'd work twenty hours a week. I had a lot of good training that way.

I joined AMVETS briefly. I didn't like the American Legion. I felt it was much too bound with tradition and didn't have the right political slant for me. Veterans of Foreign Wars. Jewish Veterans. They all seemed like organizations. So AMVETS came around at that point too. It had a very short life, but again, that attracted me, but I really wasn't focused on that. I was focused on getting my life together and becoming something.

I met my best buddy who had been with me in radio school and gunnery school; he was shot down in India, in Burma. Coming across on the ship, I met other people. I met this other fellow Bob La Canto, and we became quick friends. We had a lot of great conversations and shared a lot. We shared a tent in India. We became very close friends. However close you are, you're still at war. He went back to Ohio. I stayed in New York City. I contacted him briefly after the war, then I got involved in my own life, getting married, that sort of thing. Then about six or seven years ago—his name always stayed with me—I thought I'm going to look him up on the internet. I found several Bob La Cantos, five of them. I sent a postcard to each one saying I'm looking to get in touch with Bob La Canto. I got a call from this guy enthusiastic about hearing from me and so on. So, we became friends again. It turns out he became a professor of journalism in Illinois and other things too. I visited. We still share so many of the same interests, really, it's remarkable. We had very different backgrounds; we share much the same with one exception. He's crazy about flying. He has his own plane, which delights me, because when I go to visit him, I fly with him and it's fun. Here's this other old geezer flying a plane!

For me, I remember somebody once said you had a good war, and I did. I was fortunate. People there, I saw things I never would see. I escaped unscathed. I met friends with whom I still correspond and visit with.

CHAPTER FIVE

The B-29 Radarman

Robert D. O'Brien was born at home and raised and educated in the Bronx. He entered the Army Air Corps in 1943, and within two years he had survived thirty-six combat missions as a B-29 radar operator, gunner, bombardier/navigator in the China-Burma-India Theater and from Tinian Island in the Western Pacific. He was awarded the Distinguished Flying Cross, four Air Medals, the Asiatic Pacific Medal with silver star, and other awards. Unfortunately, right when he entered the service, his only brother, James O'Brien, was a victim of the war.

'Our plane was named before we got it. We got a war-weary one because we were new over there. It was called 'The Untouchable.' It was a good plane, and after several missions, they decided to change all four engines on it. Then we were assigned to take that plane and test run it, I guess good fortune for us. The officers were given a three-day pass. The rest of us took off to parts unknown. We didn't know that we had been assigned to that plane to test fly it. A young fellow that I had met just the day before who had graduated from grammar school with me, a fellow by the name of Morrisey, he took my place, and the plane went up, caught fire, the wing burned off, and the crew plus, I think, fifteen joy riders were all killed. Strangely enough, though it scared me afterward, it was almost

the anniversary of my brother's death. All I could think of, if I was on that plane and my folks got that message just one year after my brother, it would have been devastating.'

Robert D. O'Brien

I was born August 11, 1925, in New York City. I attended DeWitt Clinton High School in the Bronx. I really don't recall my reaction [to the news about Pearl Harbor], but what I do recall was going back to school after hearing of it. All of the windows were taped up. It was a scary proposition for me. It looked like the beginning of a war-torn area. There were all crosses, so the glass wouldn't shatter when the bombs hit us. During that time, I worked forty hours a week as an usher in Radio City Music Hall. I enlisted in the Army Air Corps after completing a testing program for pilot training in 1943. I wanted to be a pilot and after being called up, actually when I was called up I got my orders to report for February 2, 1944, and I left my orders on my parents' dresser, so they'd know when I'd be called up. I imagine they were very delighted to see my name wasn't on the list. They never turned it over to find my name beginning with the next list on the back page. I just couldn't understand why they weren't concerned about me going into the service. So, I got up early in the morning of February 2, prepared my breakfast. My father heard me stirring about, came in, and said, 'What's going on here?'

I said, 'I'm going into the army!' That roused the household. I guess, like all teenagers, I had that failure to communicate. First off, I went to Fort Dix for indoctrination. Then I went to Greensboro, North Carolina, and just about twenty days after reaching basic training, I got the word that my brother had been killed overseas. That was rather upsetting. He was in the Coast Guard. I thought it fitting that I should go home to be with my parents at that time, but I was told emphatically that no one left basic training for any reason. I went to the Red Cross to appeal to them, which was a waste of time. I went to the chaplain, which was a waste of time. I went to the base commander, and I don't know where I got the nerves, but I just let them know that I either go with a pass or I go without a pass. Lo and behold, I never saw the base commander, but a WAC assistant came out with a five-day pass for me and I went home. I had no money and appealed to the Red Cross and they weren't very helpful. My barracks mates, who I really didn't know at all, chipped in and collected money for me to go home. Years later, I realized that I never repaid them, and they never asked to be repaid.

The B-29s

I left basic training, and we went to flight training school in Florida. We never reached there. We found out that the flight training school had closed. The train reversed route and went off to Arlington, Texas, for gunnery school. After gunnery school, I went to Clovis, New Mexico, for flight training and to meet a crew. I was very fortunate the crew I joined had an experienced pilot. He was a pre-World War II pilot. He was a little older than the rest of us. It was a very intelligent group of people, so I was very fortunate they were so good. In Clovis, we had a lot of bad experiences. Many B-29 planes went down due to poor maintenance. A B-29, at that time, was still loaded with bugs. There were many crashes due to the [malfunctioning] engines of the plane, plus very, very poor maintenance. It got so bad that the commander of the post issued an order that there would be no permanent personnel on the base allowed to leave until the crashes stopped. Lo and behold, they stopped almost immediately—very poor maintenance.

When our training was finished, we were then assigned to go to a place called Kearney, Nebraska, to pick up a new plane to go overseas. We had no idea where overseas would be. Anyway, we got to Kearney, Nebraska. We saw the crews that were waiting there for their planes. They'd been there weeks after weeks, which didn't upset us too much. We figured we'd be safe for a while. Two days later, we were sent to Florida and put on a converted B-24, then took off for parts unknown.

Radar

When I was in Clovis—going back a step—I was trained as a gunner. They had already filled the slot for a tail gunner, right gunner, left gunner, top gunner, and I figured where's my position? They called me a 'roving gunner,' so I had to learn all positions as well as the bombardier's position.

In a quick order, they said to me you're a radar operator. I had never heard of radar. They sent me off to school, radar training. The radar sets were on a platform, and they showed us the switch one way to turn it on and one way to turn it off. Then they showed us how to read a map. So, that was my training. On the way overseas, I went to my navigator who I knew had been trained in radar.

I said, 'What is the radar all about? What does it do?' We were never told that.

He said, 'That's a military secret. I can't tell you.' [*Laughs*]

Missions

Anyway, we went overseas and wound up in India in a place called Piardoba. I was with the 58th Bomb Wing. We started our missions from there flying over the Himalayas into China to bring bombs and other supplies. So, it would be back and forth on several occasions. That was in November of '44. Then we started our serious bombing missions. A lot of missions, it took fourteen hours. You flew round trips. We were based in India. We were also based in China. We'd either bomb Singapore or Bangkok, those areas, from India. If we went to China, we had one bombing run into Japan and others to Nanking, Manchuria, and so on in that part of the world.

One disastrous one for many of us was to Omura in Japan where we were lost. One of the reasons we were lost, we didn't know about the jet stream at the time. We're blown so far off course. The navigator just couldn't understand how the winds could be that strong. He kept on compensating. He did find us. Actually, they were giving the order to bail out over the Himalayas some place, but he found our way home. One mission after another. Altogether, I had thirty-six.

Our plane was named before we got it. We got a war-weary one because we were new over there. It was called 'The Untouchable.' It was a good plane, and after several missions, they decided to change all four engines on it. Then we were assigned to take that plane and test run it, I guess good fortune for us. The officers were given a three-day pass. The rest of us took off to parts unknown. We didn't know that we had been assigned to that plane to test fly it. A young fellow that I had met just the day before who had graduated from grammar school with me, a fellow by the name of Morrisey, he took my place, and the plane went up, caught fire, the wing burned off, and the crew plus, I think, fifteen joy riders were all killed. Strangely enough, though it scared me afterward, it was almost the anniversary of my brother's death. All I could think of, if I was on that plane and my folks got that message just one year after my brother, it would have been devastating.

Singapore

We went and bombed Singapore and Bangkok on several occasions. By the end of February, we learned that we were going to be off to parts unknown. Our plane was no longer with us, so we had to go by ship. We went off and wound up in Tinian Island forty-seven days later. It was on Tinian Island that we completed most of our missions. We were finally assigned a new plane, which was unnamed and unpictured because some leading admiral or general's wife decided it was obscene to have the pictures on the planes and they didn't want any other names on them. So our final plane had no name. It just had a number.

We had one mission to Singapore I remember. We were very, very tired. The whole crew was very tired because we had been kept very busy with one mission after another when we were in India. But we went off on this one mission to Singapore. The pilot said to the copilot or vice versa, 'I've got to take a snooze. Put it on automatic pilot.' He reached over to put it on automatic pilot and, as he did it, he fell asleep.

We went in a very slow circle for I don't know how long. It was a question of should we abort this mission and go home and face ridicule. Everybody was sleeping on the plane except the navigator, and he was watching for a break in the overcast so he could take a fix on the stars.

Finally, there was a break, and he looked up and the stars were not where they were supposed to be. Immediately, he corrected our flight. We went on to Singapore and joined up with another crew bombing. We returned; we landed just about on fumes in the plane. That was seventeen hours and forty-five minutes of flying. The next mission, which was just a few days later, was three hours shorter. They didn't usually give us enough fuel to waste three hours of flying time. Due to our very bright engineer, he was able to save fuel.

I don't know if you knew about one of the raids into Singapore. One of our crews, I don't know which one it was, but they dropped a bomb right down the funnel of a ship, which was in the dry dock in Singapore. Rumor has it that the English government sued us for repair of that dry dock because we blew it to pieces. Then I went on another mission to Singapore a few days later with a crew that was without a radar operator. I was assigned to it. I was told it's going to be a 'milk run.' A 'milk run' is, don't worry about it, there's no danger whatsoever. So, we went on this recon mission that had no danger whatsoever. My duty was to take radar pictures over Singapore to see what was going on there. They issued me a 35mm camera to take pictures with. I had never in my life seen a 35mm camera. I had no idea how to operate it and they said press a button. That was my training on a 35mm. So, I went on the mission and took pictures galore. I have no idea if they ever came out or not. [But on this mission], we were attacked by a horde of Japanese fighters. They shot us up pretty badly, knocked out all communications on the plane, gave us a few scrapes, though nothing serious. We had to land at a place at the border of India and Burma. It was an English base. Our plane was repaired and fueled up. The next day, we flew back to our base in India, but no one had ever communicated the fact that we were alive. My crew were rather shocked to see me walk in.

Bombing Japan

I received the Distinguished Flying Cross. Actually, there should have been a couple, not to me especially, but to other members of the crew. We went to Japan. About the time we hit Iwo Jima on the way to Japan, we had a lot of engine trouble. Again, should we just land at Iwo Jima and abort the mission? Should we try to get back to our base on Tinian? It was decided to go on. We bombed Japan with one engine that was completely out. By the time we got back to our base, we were flying on two engines. By the time we landed, one was just about ready to quit. We landed actually with one engine. They thought that was a gutsy thing to do. I believe that's what it was for. But, as you know, they give out medals quite often based on the number of missions you complete.

On one mission, the doors just opened up and stayed open, which caused a lot of drag on the plane. The right gunner, the bombardier, and the engineer had to go into our bomb bay doors. There's two bomb bays—two doors in each bomb bay. These three people went into the bomb bay doors after we descended. We were just off the island of Japan and open to attack by planes. We were all alone because we were falling behind our squadron. We went down to a lower altitude. The three of them went into the bomb bay doors without parachutes, without oxygen. The tallest was the right gunner—Jim Sewell. They took turns sitting on his ankles as he lowered himself down into this open bomb bay door and hooked a cable to the bottom of the door, then he went around to the other side and hoisted it up and locked it in place. He had to do that four times, I believe, at a height of 17,000 feet. You get yourself killed at fifty feet! I read that other people doing the same thing got the Silver Star, other medals. He was never put in for anything at all, and he deserved it.

'We Lost Our Pilot'

We lost our pilot just about July of 1944. We were all assigned, again fortunately or unfortunately, we were assigned training missions. That July, we knew the war was winding down. New crews were coming over and needed a little bit of training. I was out goofing off swimming when my crewmate told me to get myself up to get on a plane for a training mission. I rushed up after a long delay. I was assigned to two different planes, one with my pilot and one with another crew, Captain Gay I believe it was. I had to train the newly arrived radar operators. They knew more than I did. They'd had a year's training in the States. They were all officers. When we landed, we found that my pilot's plane, which I was assigned to as well, had crashed and all aboard there had been killed. I think there were twenty-eight people on that plane, joy riders and so on. He was killed in July.

A Secret Weapon

In August, we had the atom bombs dropped. We didn't know what it was all about. When the bomb was delivered to our island, a rumor started. You may know the story about that ship the bomb was delivered on, the *Indianapolis*. When that ship came—we'd seen ships coming in before—that one delivered the atom bomb. We had no idea about it. The rumors started that a secret weapon was on the island. I don't know how the rumors started but most of us didn't pay any attention to it.

In August, the two bombs were dropped. I guess it was almost forty-five years later I was reading a book saying that our missions just prior to the dropping of the bombs were decoys. We had a mission to Japan. On our way back, the *Enola Gay* was going to Japan. The same with the *Bock's Car*. On our way back from Japan, the *Bock's Car* was delivering their bomb on Nagasaki. In September, they sent us home.

After The War

[You're asking me] how I think the war changed or affected my life? I actually only thought about that very, very recently. I think maybe I get cold. There had been many, many deaths around me, and for some reason, they don't affect me emotionally. The last one, my most emotional since the war, was my father. That got me; my mother's death didn't. I don't know why, except she had suffered, and I was glad to see her die. She was suffering. This wasn't lack of love or feeling. I just don't know. It just doesn't hit me emotionally.

After the war, I went to Manhattan College on the GI Bill, completed that. Went into industry, but my big desire always had been to study chiropractic. I was an accountant and financial analyst and even back then, I saw hanky-panky games with accounting. I didn't like it and unfortunately made my feelings known on a couple of occasions, saying things like, 'If it was that complicated, it has to be wrong.' Playing games is going to catch up with you. I got out of it. I got married, in 1957, I believe it was. She kills me because I can never remember. It was after college, anyway. I got married and was fed up with industry and decided to study chiropractic and talked about it at least. My wife said more or less do something or get off the pot. So, she signed me up for chiropractic college. I was still in industry. We had one child. She's going to kill me. I think it was 1954 when we got married. Let's put it this way, next year it's going to be fifty years. You can figure it out. We had one child. By the time I was finished with school, we had four and one on the way. That kind of killed my chiropractic career for quite a while because with that number of children you can't be that independent to just take off. It took many years later before I finally opened up my office, so I went into practice. Still practicing.

I joined the China-Burma-India veterans organization. Actually, the first one I joined was the VFW. I stayed in that a year. I joined that right after I came out of the service. I joined the China-Burma-India veterans because I kept on getting letters asking me to join a local 'basha.' I had no idea in the world what a 'basha' was. So, for ten dollars to join, I joined to find out exactly what a 'basha' was. A 'basha' was the [native type] barracks we lived in in India. My group called them 'barracks.' The old-timers called them 'bashas.' I joined that. I joined the American Legion. I joined the VFW again. I joined the 58th Bomb Wing Association, I joined the 20th Air Force Association. You name it, I belonged to it. I went to one reunion, the 50th anniversary of the B-29, which was in Seattle, which was unbelievable. They treated us like royalty there, an excellent reunion. I formed my own reunion. I found my crew after many, many years. I just made a concerted effort to try to find them. I found them all. I found that one was dead, and one was dying. We had a reunion. All but two of the remaining ones showed up at the reunion. That was in Chicago back twelve years ago, I guess it was. We made a pact that at least every two years we were going to have another reunion, [but we never had another one].

Robert D. O'Brien passed away August 2, 2010, at the age of 84.

PART THREE

FLYING COVER

"We were over Merrill's Marauders' heads from, God help us, their origin to their demise."

—Thunderbolt pilot, on covering missions for Merrill's Marauders in Burma

CHAPTER SIX

The Ace

Randolph Reeves was born in Texas on November 4, 1922. He joined the Army Aviation cadet program in April 1942 at the age of 19. Following flight training in California, Reeves graduated from the single-engine fighter school and then attended operational training in P-40s in Florida. In Karachi, India, Reeves received combat training and was then assigned to the 530th Fighter Squadron at Mohanbari in Assam, India. His combat missions were flown in P-51B Mustangs from five bases in India and Burma and eventually in Chengdu and Xi'an, China; he was credited with shooting down six Japanese aircraft. Following the war, Reeves served for three years on occupation duty in Japan; he built a career of service in the Strategic Air Command, retiring with the rank of lieutenant colonel with 25 years of active duty in 1966.

Leonard Randolph 'Randy' Reeves

I was born in Lisbon, Texas, on November 4, 1922. [I was raised on my grandfather's farm in DeSoto; my parents bought a house and moved the family to Lancaster in 1935. I graduated from

Lancaster High in 1940.] On December 7, 1941, I was seventeen and in Sunday school at the Baptist Church in Lancaster, and just as we were walking out of the church, somebody comes running up Henry Street. We lived on North Henry Street. They're saying that the Japanese had attacked Pearl Harbor. And, of course, I had no idea where Pearl Harbor was. I knew about the Japanese, but I had no idea where Pearl Harbor was. And so everybody's gathered around him. He said, there's probably going to be war. And that's when I heard about the attack on Pearl Harbor.

Pilot Training

I enlisted in the Army Air Corps Aviation Cadets in April of 1942, and I went to pre-flight at Santa Ana, California, to be a pilot. And then I went to primary flying school at Visalia, California, and basic flying school at Minner Field at Bakersfield, California, and advanced flying school at Luke Field at Phoenix, Arizona, where I graduated and was a second lieutenant and a pilot. And from there, we went down to Dale Mabry Field at Tallahassee, Florida, to get operational training in P-40s. But Dale Mabry Field was converting over training pilots from P-40s to P-47s. So we stayed there about a month, and all we did was dance with the co-eds at Florida State College for Women. [*Laughs*] They finally transferred us to Sarasota Army Air Base in Sarasota, Florida, and we got 85 hours of training in the P-40. We finished that up in December of 1943, went down to Florida to leave for overseas. We left the airport there at Southern Florida and flew down to Pelican Field, which is now Ramey Airport Space in Puerto Rico, and from there to Trinidad, and from there down to Natal and Belém in South America, and then across to the Ascension Islands and into the Gold Coast of Africa and from there down to Khartoum, from there up into Aden,

Arabia, they called it at the time, and from Aden we left and flew into Karachi, India.

India

We trained there at Karachi, India, with pilots that were coming back from combat. They flew with us, and we got 35 more hours training in the P-40, and after I finished that training in Karachi, India, I was assigned to the 311th Fighter Group, the 530th Fighter Squadron at Assam up in northern India;. Assam is the northern state of India. And from there I joined the 530th Fighter Squadron and we flew combat in India until General Stilwell and General Wingate started moving down through Burma, and then they cut strips out of the jungle, and we would move down to these strips and fly against the Japanese and do strafing and bombing for the troops on the ground.

First Kill

First, we went down to Akyab, which is [in Burma] close to Chittagong on the coast of India, attached to the British. General Wingate had parachuted into Burma; they parachuted behind enemy lines and fought their way out, so the only way they could get supplies was by airdrop, but the fighters of the British Air Force didn't have the range to escort the C-47s they called the Dakotas, the Spitfires and Hurricanes didn't have the range so they sent us down there to escort the Dakotas so they could resupply them. After, we would get the Dakotas back across what we call the bomb line, which is back into friendly territory. We went on a fighter sweep, and I was flying what they call tail end Charlie, and we had 24 planes up that day, and a Japanese got on my tail, and I was trying to holler that there was a Japanese on my tail, and the squadron operations officer who was leading it, Captain James England, was hollering, 'Randy, there's a Japanese on your tail,' and our transmissions were cutting each other out. So I finally just broke away and dove down and then I climbed back up and I saw a Japanese Zero and I was making a head on passing this Japanese Zero, and I could see his guns are blinking and I'm scooching down behind my instrument panel in my P-51, but just kept firing. And as he passed overhead and as I passed underneath, I pulled up in the chandelle and came around on his tail, and there was his plane going down. There was a parachute, the Japanese pilot had bailed out, but that was my first aerial victory on my way to becoming an ace. I had six aerial victories, four more probable, and had five that I destroyed on the ground.

*

In September of 1944, they decided to transfer our fighter group to China and remove a P-47 fighter group that was using too much gas, because everything had to be flown over the Hump to supply the troops. They moved them to Burma where gas came in by rail. They sent our squadron up to Xi'an China, the 530th Fighter Squadron, and we flew most of our missions out of Xi'an, China. I flew in all sectors of the China-Burma-India Theater. I spent a year in China flying against the Japanese.

'I Believe I'm Going To Get Killed Tomorrow'

I don't ever remember being scared at all. I guess we were so young and innocent that nothing scared us, and a lot of us had the idea that we went over to die for our country, so we didn't really think about dying—I know I didn't, but some of my friends did. After we moved up to China flying out of Xi'an, we went in on Christmas Eve of 1944 and destroyed 45 planes on the ground. And they ordered us back in, go back in on Christmas Day. Now I wasn't flying on Christmas Day, but a good friend of mine was flying in that day. And at night we were sitting around talking and Courtney Richard, said, 'Randy, I believe I'm going to get killed tomorrow.'

I said, 'Nobody knows when they're going to get killed.'

He said, 'Yes, I feel like I'm going to be killed.'

And I said, 'Well, let's go see JJ, and I'll fly for you.'

So we went to James J. England, who had become a squadron commander after we moved up to China. So we went to find Major England, and he and the operations officer were in Xi'an at a dinner that one of the warlords had given for the CO and the operations officer's squadron. So we couldn't find him to where we could change, and I could fly for Lieutenant Richard. And finally he said, 'Oh, heck, Randy, [you're right], you don't really know when you're going to be killed.'

I said, 'Well, I'll fly for you.'

He said, 'No, just forget it. So the next day they went out and attacked the same airfield, and destroyed 35 more planes on the ground, but there were some Japanese flying top cover, and they attacked them, and Courtney Richards was shot down in flames and killed. I guess a lot of people have a premonition of things. I never did have, but I guess if it's going to happen, you can have a premonition it's going to happen.

Purple Heart

I got the Purple Heart while we were flying out of Akyab to support the British. A Japanese got on my tail, and I couldn't shake him. And they shot 20-millimeter cannons where we shot 50 caliber machine guns. And one of the 20-millimeter shells hit the top of my armor plating and exploded and shattered all my instrument panel and what have you, and I got some shrapnel in my back and neck.

'Pete, Don't Shoot!'

[Despite that], I never was [nervous about flying]. In March we were sent to a forward base at Ankang in China, and it was just an airstrip with pierce planking, we called it, which was steel planking that they hooked together and made a runway. There were three squadrons on this base. Everything had to be refueled by a hand pump out of a 55-gallon drum. Major Fritz Coleman was the squadron commander at the time. Major England had rotated to the station, and he was taking eight or twelve planes down to the airfields around Nanking, China, and I was supposed to take eight planes and provide the air cover. The Japanese had twenty planes supposedly flying air cover over Nanking to protect the bases, and I was to take eight planes in to attack the twenty planes that were flying top cover. Well, four of our planes didn't get refueled, so four of us took off and two had to go back because they had [problems]. So Pete Beck and I were the only two left to go in and attack these twenty planes over Nanking. Pete and I went in at around 20,000 feet, and we saw the air cover up there, and the Japanese would send a slower plane out, and it acted like the pilot didn't know how to fly, and it sort of flubbed around in the air. And this plane got too far ahead of its cover, and I shot the plane down. Then we had really a dogfight with the other planes that were up there, and I shot down another plane that day, but I ran out of ammunition. So I called Pete Beck, who was my wingman. I said, 'Pete, I'm out of ammo. Let's go home.' I was watching Pete joining up, and it looked like he was pulling a pursuit curve on me, and I could see his guns firing, and I'm hollering, 'Pete, don't shoot! This is old Randy!'

About that time, something hit my plane, and it sort of blew it out of the sky, and I flipped over and went into a dive, but I managed to pull the dive out at about 5,000 feet and was flying back to Nanking by myself. And I looked around, and part of my wingtip was shot off, and the back part of my horizontal stabilizer was shot away. So as I got back to the base, I checked it at altitude to see if I could control it, because of all the parts that were shot away. I put my gear down and I could still have enough control of the elevator to pull my nose up; I put 20 degrees of flap down, but I didn't think about pulling full flaps to see if I could control it, so as I came in on the final approach and put down full flaps for landing, I didn't have any more back pressure, and I couldn't bring the nose up high enough to make a real smooth landing, and so I dumped my flaps really quick, and when I did, I just hit the ground real hard. I thought the struts were coming up through the wings the way I hit. And I taxied in and told Sergeant George Dobner, who was my crew chief, I says, 'Sergeant Dobner, do you want me to write up a hard landing?'

He said, 'No sir, I saw the landing. We'll take care of it.' I told everybody that Pete Beck was the one that shot me up, but unluckily, Pete didn't come home.

We went back to Chengdu, and about ten days later, here comes Pete. The Chinese had picked him up and brought him back to the base. 'Of course, I jumped them, but you shot me down.'

Pete says, 'No, Randy, there were three Tojos on your tail, I was shooting at the Tojos. That's what shot you down!'

He had run out of gas and had to bail out, and his idea of bailing out was getting his feet up in the seat and jumping toward the wing and the plane would move forward while he would miss the wing and bail out. But his foot slipped down the side of the seat, and when he leaped out, his ankle, his foot, was caught there, and while he was kicking trying to get loose, he fractured his ankle, but he finally got out, of course, and opened his parachute and landed. I said, 'Pete, it's a good thing you came back, because I'm going around telling people that you're the one that shot me up!'

87 Missions

I flew 87 missions over there in about twenty months of flying. In Burma, we flew quite frequently every month, but in China, we just didn't have the gasoline to fly. We were used a lot to protect the B-29s that were coming in out of India and flying up into Manchuria and to Japan Islands there. And so we had to reserve fuel so one of them had to land in the forward base, which one did, and I went over on patrol to fly until they could get the B-29 repaired and get it off, and get it back to Shantung and back to India. So we didn't fly as frequent as we did in India and Burma.

[When we were not flying], we played poker until four or five guys would corral all the money. And then we'd play bridge on a credit until the end of the month, and then when we got paid we'd pay our bridge debts off and then go back to playing poker. And we didn't have much to read and, of course, no officers club or anything like that. We lived in tents mainly and we just lay around our tents and talked or played some sort of cards there.

The Chinese

We had this one second lieutenant that was our interpreter from the Chinese Army, and the warlords would throw parties every now and then out of Xi'an there, and we'd go to parties like that. They had a lot of coolies working on the runway. Our group commander, Colonel Tex Chandler, was an ace. These Chinese thought there was an evil dragon following them. And if they could get by in front of one of those planes that were just landing, that prop from that plane would kill this evil dragon. A lot of them didn't make it, and Colonel Chandler had killed five of those people; coolies were working on the runway trying to get across in front of his plane to get rid of that evil dragon that was following him.

War's End

[When the war ended], I was onboard ship coming home. We got this ship out of Calcutta and there were eight of us, eight officers living in a state room, and from Calcutta we stopped in Ceylon, which is now Sri Lanka. And from there we went down to Fremantle, Australia, and we got to stay overnight. So some of us went into Perth, Australia, and visited. And the next day we went up to the Philippines. And while we were going up to the Philippines, the war was over. After we got out of the Philippines, they sent us up to Okinawa to pick up around 5,000 Marines that had been fighting when they took over Okinawa, and they were supposed to rotate to the States, so we picked them up and we went into Pearl Harbor and spent a night there. And from there, we were supposed to go into San Francisco to disembark. And the war being over, the longshoremen were on strike up at San Francisco, so they diverted us down to Los Angeles, and we pulled in to Los Angeles. And from there, I went to San Antonio, Texas, at Fort Sam Houston and got 45 days R&R to my home. And after that I reported back into Fort Sam, and signed up for an indefinite period in the service. I ended up spending 25 years in Army Air Corps and United States Air Force.

[My next assignment] was going to a fighter gun refresher course at Chandler, Arizona, but they were letting all the crew chiefs out. At Williams Field, they didn't have enough crew chiefs to man all the planes that would be found at gunnery mission, so they just closed the fighter gunnery school, and they sent me up to Wright Field, and that's where I met my wife and my downfall. I ended up getting married there after I met her. She worked at Officer Simon's section in Headquarters AMC and right after we got married, we went to Japan. We got married on the 7th of December 1946, and on the 22nd of December, I got orders to Japan. I went to

Japan in December of 1946, and my wife got over there in June of '47 and our first daughter was born in Japan. After Japan I went back to Wright Field. I was in the flight test division, and I was there for a year, then they sent me to a school at Lowry Field in Denver, Colorado, and I became a transportation officer, staff transportation officer. And so from there I went to Hill field, Utah, and then Los Angeles, California, and then from there to Biggs Air Force Base in El Paso, Texas. From there I went to Newfoundland for three years. My wife came to Newfoundland and my youngest son was born in Newfoundland and my oldest son was born when we were in my second tour at Wright Field. We spent three years in St. John's, Newfoundland, and then from there we went to Westover Air Force Base in Massachusetts for three years. And from there, we went to Seymour Johnson Air Force Base at Goldsboro, North Carolina. I was flying KC-135 jet tankers. And that's where my last daughter was born. I spent eight years at Seymour Johnson Air Force Base at Goldsboro, North Carolina, before I retired.

Japan Occupation Duty

When my wife got over there, we were assigned to a base outside of Japan, Showa Air Base, which was right close to Tatsukawa. We'd go into the city quite frequently to shop on the Ginza there. You could see all the embassies, just about all had been destroyed there with those firebombs. And most of Tokyo was destroyed, except for the Emperor's Palace. He was right in the middle of Tokyo there and had a big moat around the grounds and everything. I don't guess a bomb ever touched anything there, because I guess they were ordered not to bomb the Emperor's Palace. We had a house girl for free, and it cost us $6.50 every month for a house boy. So my wife sort of got spoiled with them, all these servants, and since we were just married, she thought that's the way the Air Force lived.

Randolph Reeves passed away on September 4, 2014, at the age of 91.

CHAPTER SEVEN

The Thunderbolt Pilot

In the China-Burma-India Theater, Kenneth Wilbur Thomas of Oklahoma flew strategic bombing and strafing runs in the 10th Air Force, 80th Fighter Group, 88th Fighter Squadron in support of the Office of Strategic Services. His missions included covering Merrill's Marauders on their long-range penetration missions in the Burmese jungle. He sat for this interview in 2006.

Kenneth Wilbur Thomas

[When Pearl Harbor was attacked], I was at my home in southern Iowa, still on the farm. At that time, I had a brother four years older than I who had enlisted in the Army. At the time, he thought he was enlisting for one year's training and then was going to come back in reserves, but it didn't work out that way. He was put in the MPs, and he was enjoying a truly great life. This would have been in late '30s or early '40s, because he was being assigned all over the country to watch the depots where they were transporting the soldiers to go and make sure the soldiers were conducting themselves in military manner, as long as they're in uniform. These were groups of seven or eight guys. They'd be stationed in an apartment, usually with a commanding car at their disposal, and getting more money than you could make anywhere else, because they were getting a per diem for their food.

He tried to persuade me to enlist and join him; of course, it was a great life. I thought, 'Hey, that's worth a try.' I went to Des Moines and sat down in front of a recruiting sergeant and told him I want to do enlisting in MPs. He looked at me like he thought that I was probably a little bit unpossessed, and said, 'You know, son, I've heard of military people being sentenced to serve the MPs, but I've never accepted that enlistment could be MPs. Why don't you think about it for a while?' [*Laughs*]

The Test

I knew at the time I very much wanted to be in the Air Corps. However, the Air Corps at that time required two years minimum of some college credit, which I didn't have, nor did I figure I could get it and in the end still get in the service. One September I was in Des Moines, Iowa, big sign on those sidewalks that said, 'College requirement no longer required.' I noticed it was right in front of the Air Corps, U.S. Army Air Corps enlisting station.

I went in and talked to him about it. He says, 'Yeah, you don't have to have college, just pass an equivalence test.' 'When are you giving it?' 'I'll be giving one at eight o'clock in the morning.'

'I'll be here!' I went out and took the test, of course, I reviewed it. There were several pages up. There were supposed to be 150 questions, and as I reviewed it I noticed there's about three blank pages. I thought, 'Well, that's funny.' I saw the room was crowded, and I thought, 'Well, I've got these three blanks, this guy probably got three other blanks. That way we don't copy each other.' I hustled through it, seemed like an awful easy test. Finished it up, looked around, and everybody else was still busy at their desks. I checked them one at a time all the way through. Everybody's still busy at their desk. Checked it again, took it up to the sergeant.

He said, 'Don't you want to check it?'

I said, 'I've checked it twice.'

'Fine, have a chair. I'll read them in a little bit. We'll know who passed.' At that time, the test was graded by an overlay sheet with a bunch of slots in it. Our answers were all marked with black and a slot. He just put an overlay sheet over it, and any slot that wasn't blackened got a red mark.

Then he'd count the red marks and total it up and find out what we made. He read the names of those who passed, and mine wasn't read. We had to get 85 out of 150 to pass the test. I said, 'Sergeant, would you please look...' I can remember the test number, we recorded not by names, but by test number. I said, 'Sergeant, will you look and see what number so and so had?' He looked. '78, not quite enough.'

I headed for my sister's house. She lived in an apartment in Des Moines, and I kept booting myself in the rear as I walked along.

'78 out of 150, what an idiot could I possibly be?'

Finally, the 150 number started eating at me, and I realized that I didn't have 150 questions, because the last sheet could begin with question 29 and after I got the blank sheet it might be question 41. I don't know, but I didn't have 150 questions. I hustled to the phone booth. They were a nickel at that time. I hustled to the phone booth, dropped the nickel in, and called the sergeant and said, 'Would you check the test number so and so?'

'Why should I do that?'

I said, 'I just got through taking it. I don't think it was all there. I had some blank pages at one moment.' He looked at it, came back. 'What the hell did you take this test for?'

I said, 'That's the one you gave me!'

Well, it had 'INC' right on the front of it.'

'What does that mean?'

'Incomplete, would you like to take it again?'

'When?'

'Nine o'clock in the morning.'

I'll be there!' First thing I did was to look at it, and all the sheets were full, all 150 questions. I went and passed through it. When they read the scores at that time there was only one boy who beat me. He was from Iowa State College, a second-year physics major and he had 138 out of 150. I had 135 out of 150 correct, with my high school education.

Called Up

I waited for my call. It was the following January, and I was called into a regular U.S. Army enlisted recruiting base, Jefferson Barracks, Missouri, in January. Bitterest winter I believe I had there; while we were there, they positioned us in these little old square huts, built out of green shiplap lumber with a square-pointed roof, and they had a little inverted funnel-shaped stove sitting in the middle of the tent. The pipe was a four-and-a-half-inch pipe that runs straight through the roof, a bit cold. Being a farm boy, I went out gathering wood, dead limbs and remnants of the construction, built a fire. That old stove got red hot in minutes. That worked pretty good, except the siding lumber was green, and the next morning when we woke up, there was a crack between each and every one of those green boards, and the snow would blow in, and was lying on our covers, not even melted, just white streaks. [*Laughs*] Well, we managed to survive it; we got extra blankets. We burned up the scrap lumber, but they got coal in there, and we survived that pretty well. We spent exactly 30 days in Jefferson Barracks learning how to soldier. 'That's how you march. This is your right foot you always start with it,' or whatever it was. They gave us another battery of tests there; never knew what it was for at the time, but that segregated us into groups. The first group spent one month in Jefferson Barracks, and then we got shipped out to a school. The purpose of the school was to try to replace this college [learning] that we didn't have. I got assigned to Creighton University in Omaha, Nebraska, beautiful Catholic school teachers, first time I'd ever seen a school uniform. It was a marvelous experience. At the end of the month, I had stuff all packed waiting to ship out, and lo and behold, I got the mumps.

They sent me to the Fork Brook Hospital. Mumps was treated with ice at the time. Of course, I developed the rarest case yet, swelling in every possible area at the maximum. This Texas nurse was always kidding me about my swollen organs, how horrible they were. That wasn't enough, because about the first week I was there, I saw her leading through a group of teenagers in civilian clothes. They were planning on going to nursing school, so she was showing them everything that she had in her hospital. Lo and behold, they moved into the mumps area, and I thought, 'Good Lord, she's always talking about my swollen organs. I wonder if she will talk about me?' Sure enough, here they came. 'Notice the swelling here, ladies, see how it's equal and how it looks, jaws and everything else.' Next move, 'Take off the ice pack.' She showed them what she claimed is the most classic case of mumps swelling she had ever observed. Of course, I was red enough to light a match to the cheek, and she recognized it. She thanked me profusely for being such a 'patient patient' so she could show this to the girls. I don't recall finding any other thing in the entire four plus years of service that was as embarrassing to me as that was. Guess it didn't shorten my life any. [*Laughs*]

Pilot Training

After we got through with Omaha, then they shipped us to San Antonio, which was all cadets at that time. That consisted of many months of pre-flight training, we called it, and a month of classification. We went through that, and then at the end of that preflight training, they divided us up into training schools. We all went to the same primary trainer, a little single-engine Fairchild PT-19, and my assignment was to Chickasha, Oklahoma, which I enjoyed very much. It was operated by civilians at the time. Next assignment was Coffeyville, Kansas, back in the army, tar paper shacks, forty men on one floor, and we took care of ourselves, marched the mess hall and everything else, beyond that was [like] basic training. We spent just about two months there, and then went to Victoria, Texas, for the advanced training and classification. They divided us into fighter pilots and bomber pilots. Much to my joy I qualified for fighter pilots and went to Victoria, Texas, for training in the AT-6. I'm training to be a fighter pilot, but I had one question left in my mind. I had heard of the Thunderbolt. I'd never seen one, but I wanted to fly it. That was the thought harboring in my mind: 'Maybe, just maybe, I'll get the Thunderbolt.' When we saw the assignment posted at the end of graduation, lo and behold, Richmond, Virginia, P-47s.' I got my last wish granted and we finished our training.

The number one thing [they would look at when classifying us in training] was how we handled the single-engine plane, and number two was our response [to emergencies]. They'd give us all these emergencies, like, you're out of fuel. They'd shut off our gas, make us find the field, go ahead. They'd make us go into the final approach to the landing before they'd switch the gas back on. Now, the responses we had to all of those things that the instructors could dream of, whatever it might be. And if we had at it and solved it with a great deal of vigor and glee, well, they kept us on the fighter list. Now, this is something I can't understand. The bomber, of course, is like driving a bus compared to a sports car. But the responsibility of a bomber pilot just boggles your mind. He's got ten men there he is responsible for, and one of them is a navigator, one of them a tail gunner. That's a lot of area to cover. And I am not sure what the criteria for the separation of it all was. Some of it was choice; some of the guys made that choice early on. The bombers were big and heavy, and they enjoyed driving big equipment, sort of like the guy that loves to drive a truck, so bombers were their choice. But I had opted for fighters and the thing that worried me at the time, I was at the exact height and weight limit for cut-off. Exactly. Six feet even and 180 pounds. And that kind of worried me, and I was mighty glad when I was given the decision.

The Thunderbolt

I'd seen a picture of the Thunderbolt, and I read that it was the most powerful and the most heavily armed fighter we had ever built. And I don't know. I worked with big horses; I wanted to have a big machine. Growing up on a farm with a big, two-horse team, a really big horse has always impressed me, so 2,000 horses was something I started vying for. Actually, it was a very easy plane to fly. Now, I didn't really get to understand the flying of the Thunderbolt until I got overseas. In training, we flew old, war-weary Thunderbolts on 90-octane fuel. Well, with the 90-octane fuel, we couldn't put that through [what the plane could really do]; I had to wait until I got overseas before I could really run that thing out and understand the joy I had in my hands. The only weakness I would say would be the fact that it required a pretty sturdy field to work from. Now, the British and the Americans in Britain flew them off grass fields. Their grass, I am sure, was quite different from the grass we had in Burma. I didn't see a single field in Burma that I'd want to put that seven tons down on. But they did that in England, and in France, and in Germany after the war was settled. I wouldn't say that there was a weakness, as much as it was a requirement. Its strength, of course, was the fact that it had eight 50-caliber guns, and we carried 420 rounds of ammunition for each gun. It would handle two 1,000-pound bombs or napalm tanks or whatever, and we could still carry a 50-gallon belly tank to extend the range. Its one weakness probably was the fact that it was a pretty good gas guzzler, but we learned how to cope with that, too. We had recommended settings for various altitudes, various requirements, but we discovered that if we boosted the manifold pressure beyond the recommendations and dialed the RPMs back to where we could hear the detonation from that specific setting, we could get by with about 85 gallons an hour instead of 120, so we stretched its range quite a bit just by learning what it could do. And that was, I would say, its only weakness, the fact that it required a great deal of fuel. As a weapons platform, I can't imagine anything nicer, because seven tons, you don't feel a lot of thermals in it. You can feel the jolt, but it doesn't move the plane. When you line that thing up on the sightline, that's where your bullets went, exactly where it went.

To The CBI

We had partial training in Richmond, and then moved on to Dover, Delaware, for gunnery and aerial bombing. Then we were shipped back to Richmond to await assignment. We were issued our orders to go to England, but we had a storm at sea that canceled our ship. We waited for the next ship. We still kept our cold weather uniform, so we again assumed Europe, England, somewhere. Just before we ship out, we get word that there's a German U-boat wolf pack off the Atlantic coast, so they delayed that shipment again. We're still sort of in limbo land there, getting tired of eating field rations in Richmond, Virginia. They loaded us on a train, and we headed south, still with our winter clothing. Where in the world would I be going, south with winter clothing?

We finally got to Miami Beach. They checked us in a hotel down there, and we turned in our winter uniforms and got some summer uniforms and started a round of tropical shots. We finally got that round completed, and they loaded us on a C-46 and we were jungle-hopping over northern South America. When we finally got to the town in Brazil, they parked C-46s and C-47s and gave us a B-24. We still didn't know where we're going. We'd take tropical shots and have summer clothing, and we were joined there by another U.S.O. tour, which included James Faulkenberg, Pat O'Brien, and three starlets whose names I don't even remember. Well, their first words, were, 'Oh, you guys are going to CBI too?' We didn't know, well, that's where we are going. Now we know! [*Laughs*]

That was an interesting trip too; the most interesting part of it for me came in the middle of the night. I was awakened by strong gasoline fumes. I looked out in the darkness, I could see our far-right propeller on the B-24 was feathered; the gasoline fumes were so strong that I couldn't sleep. I thought, 'We must be in trouble!' I looked down, all I could see was the fluorescence from those white caps and they rocked in the ocean for a mile, mile and a half below us. Next thing I noticed is another engine was shutting down. I looked and it was the other right-hand engine on that side of the plane! I hadn't flown four-engine planes, but I knew that if you had two on the one side that were bad, you had a problem of some sort. He's revving up these two left engines full forward and we're still doing pretty good. After a while, I see the engines finally restarting everything else. I was the only guy who observed that everybody else was sound asleep, snoring, and enjoying the trip. When we finally landed at Ascension Island, I cornered the pilot and I said,

'You're going to have to tell me, why do you shut down two engines on one side over the Atlantic Ocean?'

'Oh, we do it all the time. I was transferring fuel out of the bomb bay into those wing tanks, and that fuel line goes right behind that exhaust of those two engines. You've got to shut them down.' [*Laughs*] Well, that was educational to me.

Burma

We finally got across West Africa, out of the B-24 and back in twin-engine planes, and they got us across the African continent, across part of Asia, to India, one of the northernmost [British] colonies. We were assigned to the 33rd Fighter Group for orientation, they called it. I flew only three missions with them; within a month I was transferred across the mountain into a little strip of Shingbwiyang, Burma, which was in the most northern province of Burma, and joined the 80th Fighter Group. At that time, only the 88th Fighter Squadron was at that field. I got a thorough orientation and started the missions there.

When we got to Burma, the AVG had worked out of a field in Rangoon for a while, but by the time we went over there, by the time I got overseas, the AVG had been disbanded, and they were brought into the U.S. Army Air Corps, or they could leave the AVG if they wanted to. And we ended up with some of their mechanics on our flight line. They were good boys.

There were two typical missions we would fly. For a close support mission, most of the time, we just used the guns. We were over Merrill's Marauders' heads from, God help us, their origin to their demise. And what we would do, they would direct us in a direction, following the Burmese landscape. They could tell you to follow a river, but that was about all we had to follow. So they usually just gave us heading, and we'd fly, and we'd know that we could chart on the map what the distance was, so we judged it. And when the right number of minutes elapsed, we'd call in on the two-way radio, just like walkie talkies, 'Oh, yeah. We're close.'

'I can see you up there. You need about another minute.' And then we'd get down, they'd say, 'You're right overhead. Now circle. We'll describe the area.' And they would describe that area right down to the last detail of the land that they could see [where the target was]. They were looking through binoculars, and they could see the lines. And when they'd finally get it described, and we'd agree, 'Yeah, we think we got it,' they'd ask us for a short machine gun burst to make sure we were in the right spot. Well, often we were. And every now and then, we'd be asked to make a correction of a few yards one way or the other; if they asked us to make a correction, we'd give them another square at that correction. And then they would start bragging to us. 'Boy, get them. You're right exactly where they ought to be. Give them everything you got!' Then as we went through the motions, circling and passing—it was almost like a landing pattern—we'd make a pass, circle around, make another pass, circle around, make another pass. [*Rotates hands in the air*] Now, you wonder why we made so many passes? Well, those guns were bore-sighted for 1,000 feet, so if you're doing about 240 miles an hour, you've got an effective pass time of about three seconds, that's all. And in three seconds, you're probably going to square it up; out of all eight guns, you'd get probably less than 200 rounds total, so you'd make a lot of passes. Every so often they'd say, 'Well, that's pretty well wiped out there. Let's look at another one.' And then they describe another place. We'd move over there.

Marauders' Support

On the Marauders' early missions, the [Japanese-controlled] Myitkyina airstrip still had the problem of a Japanese gun emplacement off the far end of the runway. And so we'd take off, make short circles around, drop a bomb on it, come back and get another, take off. It was a totally crazy war. Some of those boys got in as many as six missions a day, but we eventually wiped them out of there and got them on the run. And then we, of course, after we occupied Myitkyina, we had to push them farther and farther. Burma was an area that was fought for very diligently. I had several missions in that area. And Merrill's Marauders, we actually patrolled over their heads as they were going down through the mountain, because the Japanese were famous for leaving back some expendables just to shoot people because they went by. They'd leave them there with nothing but a gun and a bag full of ammo. They could kill rats and eat locusts and whatever they could find to eat. But when these Marauders go by, shoot a few of them, you know. So we'd patrol over their heads, and if that happened, we'd zero them in and we'd take them out of the trees sometimes.

When we were carrying bombs, those would usually be loaded on only for specific purposes to go after a storage yard or a building that they thought was being used for storage or an actual weapons dump that they could see through the binoculars. All the bombs would be dropped one at a time for the very good reason that if one bomb does it, we got another [target] for the next one; see, all of our equipment—ammunition, gasoline, bombs and everything else—were flown over to us, and they always told us it took seven gallons of gasoline to deliver one gallon that we could burn, so seven-to-one was the ratio. A 500-pound bomb or a thousand-pound bomb took 7,000 pounds of fuel to deliver one bomb, so we used everything quite sparingly and for good reason.

The first place that we were based was located right in the middle of the rainforest. They'd whittled out a runway that was downhill. It didn't matter where the wind was; we took off downhill, we landed up here, and wind didn't matter because there were these huge trees on both sides of the runway. And at that place, it rained almost every day. The summer we were there, we had 200 inches of rainfall in that one summer, so everything was wet. Our uniforms, we'd have to try to hang them outside to air out so the mildew didn't set in. And with the rain going on, we couldn't always do that; everything around us was wet and soaked and sodden. We did, however, have latrine facilities and bath facilities. I don't remember anywhere where we didn't have that. We had dried eggs, dried potatoes, and dried powdered milk. But we were also blessed with a mess sergeant that understood all of those things, and he could make mashed potatoes. I couldn't have distinguished his from fresh out of the patch. He could take that powdered milk and the powdered eggs and make scrambled eggs, I couldn't wait to have them every morning. I was only one of the few idiots that they considered dumb enough to get up for breakfast. Growing up on a farm, breakfast was always the main meal, you know, 6:00 AM. If you didn't get that under your belt, you weren't fit for the day's work. So that was a habit I formed, and to this day, I still enjoy breakfast.

The Native People

[The local population, the indigenous peoples], they didn't really like the British at all then. The British had been there too long. And they were a little bit, I don't know what the word is, but they were treated like colonists. And it was their land, but the British occupied it, so they weren't colonists. And they seemed, when they worked in our tents and everything, they couldn't do enough for us, the Americans. They managed everything for us. They took care of shoe shines, making beds, sewing, making sure that the laundry was done and done right. We couldn't speak the language, but our house men would take care of it.

The other place where we were based was Myitkyina, [after the field was taken], in a prairie-like area. We had a lot of green pastures around there. Now, the farmers didn't use the pastures, but the wild water buffalo did; you could always see herds of those grazing around. Now, the air was nice and fresh, you could hang clothing out to dry, then you didn't have to hang them out just to air out. And that area was really quite nice, I enjoyed it. We had good facilities there. The area was so nice, the Red Cross girls even had a station around. We could get donuts and coffee down there, like that.

War's End

Within a few months, we moved forward to get closer to the battle lines to the strip the Japanese had built at Myitkyina. I flew the remaining combat missions from that strip. About May of '45, the British patted us on the back and said, 'Hey, you've been great, but we don't have to have you anymore.' I thought, 'Fine, we'll go home.' [*Shakes head*] Didn't. We went to an old B-29 base at Candi, India, which was about 90 miles west of Calcutta.

We got over there. There were a couple of bomb groups, the old 33rd Fighter Group is over there with their fighters. They've gone to P-38s, and we're being formed into something called the Far East Air Force. 'But the war is over. What's this for?'

'We still haven't beat Japan.'

We're bombing the heck out of them with B-29s, incendiaries killing them by the hundreds of thousands each and every night, but they weren't convinced that we were going to win. We were organizing that group for the sole purpose of supporting a land invasion of all five islands, one at a time. I had already heard what had happened in Okinawa. They had occupied that, and I knew that the Japanese mothers had thrown their kids over the cliff [at Saipan], and then followed them with the last leap. I thought, 'Good Lord, five Japanese islands. I wonder if the Japanese race will really survive, or will they all commit suicide?'

[The war ended]; we got all of our people who wanted to go home, and I had the points. I had 100 missions behind me, but I hadn't seen a single enemy plane in the air. In my mind, I hadn't really been [tested] yet. We were flying all these missions over the heads of the OSS, and they were cheering us like a winning football team. I landed our group at Djakarta and they told us, once we got on the ground, that the war was over, that we're going to pack up and go home. I get a screwdriver out. I want to recover that eight-day clock out of my personal airplane for a souvenir. I just parked it two hours before, but by the time I get out there, there's a tall soldier with a turban and a shroud. He must have stood six and a half feet tall. He was carrying an old British Enfield that was nearly as tall as he was, and as I get close to that airplane, 'Halt.' He pointed his bayonet about this close to my chest.

'You halt!' It turned out to be the only word he knew in English was halt. I tried to reason with him that I wanted to recover that eight-day clock, but the bayonet didn't move. I finally moved, and two days later, I watched the Corps of Engineers crush that plane with bulldozers at each end of the wings and to the tail until it was as small as they could get it and then sold for scrap.

Home

It took us about a month and a half to get on a boat and finally head for home. That was a tremendous experience because we boarded in Calcutta. They told us it'd take us 30 days to get across the Atlantic and home. For some reason, instead of coming across the Pacific, we went back around the Indian Ocean and refueled in Ceylon, then up through the Suez Canal and Mediterranean and back to New York, and then I reported back for my extra year that

I signed up for. Mind you, we docked in New York City. I went home to Iowa, spent 30 days there, then got on a train and went all the way to Santa Ana, California, for reassignment. The reassignment turned out to be St Louis, Missouri. I got to see a lot of the U.S., but I didn't get all the way around the world.

That last year in the military was probably my most memorable year. I ended up inheriting the last totally segregated black raw Air Corps recruits. They had been trained previously in Texas and Louisiana, but things were getting a little touchy at the time, and I'd read about some near riots. We had a bad colonel in St. Louis that was hoping to get one star before retiring. The colonel was trying to operate the segregated troops with all white non-coms. Those other white non-coms weren't accustomed to black troops. By that time, I understood the convenience and necessity of my black acting sergeants. I said to the colonel, 'Remove every white non-com from that area and let me appoint my own.' He didn't get his star, but he didn't lose his ego either. It worked out very well.

Interviewer: How do you think your experiences in World War II affected you later in life?

[Well, learning how to] just get along with people was one thing. Ninety-nine percent of us were shelled out of the same pod, and I think that the most remarkable achievement that any military group could attain was to establish a procedure that would pick up this very narrow strip of people, from here to there. That was the first thing. And then the second thing, of course, was getting accustomed to the fact that all of them were nice guys. Some of them hadn't been [raised] the same way we were, though, and things would come up missing. We had to learn to hide our stuff or lock it up or put it away. And then of course, [we learned to] the best of our ability to get results from people who you couldn't communicate with by language, the house boys and the various people we worked with. And probably the greatest thing was what coordination and cooperation can do. Soldiers on the ground, tired, not sufficiently armed, our planes in the air over-armed, doing the work together that had to be done. It was a marvelous training, [to see the coordination to achieve a common goal].

'They Were Soldiers'

I also learned I had absolutely no aversion to colored people in any way. I hadn't known any, and to this day, I don't have any, because some of those guys are the finest people you'll ever meet anywhere, and what I marveled at about that was that they could sense anything—just like a dog knows when you're afraid, he'll attack you and tear you to pieces, but if you're not afraid, he's your friend. Sensing that I had no enmity, they became the finest group of soldiers you'll ever see. I've got a picture, I guess it's at home, but I grew from that group of boys. I discovered we had enough musicians to make a band, so we formed a band. I had a second lieutenant there that was a musician. I had a band music major. And we put together a band and we held our own little Saturday afternoon marches. They loved that, anything, to march. And the colonel learned that we had a band, and we were marching, so he declared that every Saturday afternoon, we'd have a competition for every unit on the entire base ground field. And each winner of each Saturday would get a prize. So we went into that. And by golly, we took the prize off the first time. And when next Saturday came along, we took the prize off. Finally, we didn't always win, but we did win more than we lost. Finally, one Saturday there was a deal with Lord Louis Mountbatten, who was visiting the base for some reason. And we had this big old deal, my guys loved marching so much. When they'd hear the music play and we'd do the big eight-man turn, they practiced that. Eight men at the time, with an eight-man pivot, and to practice, they'd bump their head on each beat and take the short steps and bob their head, and it's kind of beautiful. Eight heads going up and down all at the same time! And so when we got in that last competition, I told the guys, I said, 'Hey, we're going to have to cut out on this because everybody else is here and everybody doesn't bob their heads.' But this day, I just got them in, lined up, and was ready waiting for the call to march off.

'Whose name is Thomas?' Well, I turned around and the colonel's pointing his finger at me! So I went double timing enough to see what he's doing. He said, 'Lieutenant, if you take the trophy home today, you'll be excused from any further competition.'

'Oh, yes, sir!' [*Gestures with a salute*]

'And just a minute, Lieutenant, do you suppose you could coax your men into doing their special pivot?' [*Laughs*] He wanted to see it! So I went back and told the troops, I said, 'If we win the trophy this time, we won't do this anymore. And not only that, but he wants to see our special turn.'

Oh, boy, did we mow them down! You get a lot of pride or something like that, and the fact that here are guys, some of them hadn't done anything, hadn't been responsible for anything until they got that uniform on. They conducted themselves with dignity in that uniform, and I recognized it by addressing them as soldiers. They were soldiers.

PART FOUR

THE MARAUDERS

"We are the forgotten people. Nobody ever recognizes the China-Burma-India Theater, but as far as I'm concerned, I think it was one of the most integral parts of the war effort because we were the back door running to Europe, and also it was important that we open up the road to get supplies from India on into China."

—*Officer, reminiscing on Merrill's Marauders*

In August 1943, the top-secret First Quebec Conference opened at the Hotel Frontenac in Quebec City, Canada, ostensibly to begin planning the invasion of Europe. The Southeast Asia Command, headed by Vice Admiral Mountbatten, had fielded an experimental long-range penetration force in Burma that spring to strike back at the Japanese and their astonishing inroads seemingly everywhere. This force would be comprised of British and Indian Gurkha elite soldiers skilled in jungle warfare and led by the veteran guerrilla campaigner in Africa and Palestine, Brig. General Orde Wingate. This force, nicknamed the Chindits (after the mythical stone lions protecting Burmese temples), was organized into columns that could act independently and move unseen and strike with deadly force seemingly out of nowhere, living off the land and traveling in the most inhospitable environments, but in a revolutionary twist, being primarily resupplied by radio and airdrops. They suffered huge casualties in Burma and had mixed results but were lauded for their ability to hit the Japanese repeatedly, which was played up in the press as a morale builder. Wingate was called to London to be presented to Churchill, brought to Quebec, and made a favorable impression on FDR, so much so that on September 1, George Marshall put out a call for three thousand volunteers for a top-secret dangerous mission. Codenamed GALAHAD, this force was to be modeled after the British long-range penetration force. But there had been an important American precedent—Major Robert Rogers and his hit-and-run Ranger companies of the French and Indian War days struck terror in the heart of the garrisons of the French empire in North America in the Champlain Valley region of the Adirondack Mountains, living outdoors in extreme conditions, in all seasons, moving under cover, striking quickly, taking prisoners for information, and blending back into the mountains like their native counterparts, the eyes and ears of the British Army in North America. Like their successors, the Rangers who landed in North Africa, Sicily, Italy, and Normandy, the newly formed 5307th Composite Unit (Provisional) would go on to become legends in their own right. Merrill's Marauders were born.

CHAPTER EIGHT

The Virginia Farmboy

Lieutenant General Samuel Vaughan Wilson was born on Sept. 23, 1923, in central Virginia, where his father ran a generations-old tobacco farm, and his mother was a schoolteacher.

He joined the Army in 1940 at the age of sixteen, and taught guerrilla and counter-guerrilla tactics at Fort Benning in Georgia. At the age of nineteen, he was on his way to Burma as 'Lt. Sammy,' becoming a chief reconnaissance officer for Merrill's Marauders. The lessons he learned and taught in the field behind enemy lines shaped his military career. This interview took place at Hamden-Sydney College in Farmville, Virginia, founded by his fourth great-grandfather in 1775 and where he served as president after a long and distinguished military career, which included awards and decorations such as the Distinguished Service Cross, Defense Distinguished Service Medal, Army Distinguished Service Medal with two Oak Leaf Clusters, National Intelligence Distinguished Service Medal, U.S. Special Operations Distinguished Service Medal, the CIA's Distinguished Intelligence Medal, Silver Star with Oak Leaf Cluster, Legion of Merit with Oak Leaf Cluster, Bronze Star for Valor with Oak Leaf Cluster, Army Commendation Medal with two Oak Leaf Clusters, Purple Heart, Vietnamese Gallantry Cross with Palm, and the Vietnamese National Administration Medal for Exemplary Service.[34]

Samuel V. Wilson

I was born twelve miles from here on a 150-acre corn-tobacco-wheat farm. I went to a small country high school and graduated in late May 1940. On the 9th of June 1940, I believe it was a Sunday, I was in the parlor in the farmhouse, which was our home, twiddling the dials in mid-afternoon, we would call it surfing the channels today. When I heard a man speaking, I noted that it was not an American accent. It sounded like an English accent that I had heard before. I was listening to WPTF from Raleigh, North Carolina, We Protect the Family, that particular station, which still exists. The speaker was Winston Churchill, and it was a rebroadcast of his speech on the floor of the House of Commons on the 4th of June, the day that the British Expeditionary Force and the French First Army were evacuated from Dunkirk. If you recall the speech, the words that have been lifted from it are, 'We will fight them on the beaches, in the fields, on the landing grounds, in the hills, in the streets. We will never surrender.' I looked around and said, 'Where's my hat?' That is what provided the impulse for my getting into military service.

'I Lied Like A Rug'

The next day was a Monday. It rained all day. I climbed up in the loft of the old stable to read, but I could not get away from those words that were echoing in my head leading up to, 'We will never surrender.' I knew enough about what was going on in the world to know that the Western world was in trouble, at least the free part of the Western world, including ourselves. Along about night, I could not stand it any longer without saying a word to anybody. I set off down to Fawn Lane on the right on Country Road, and ran through some thickly forested woods, several miles into the town of Farmville. Company G, 116th Infantry, was gathered there for its drill night that evening, the monthly drill night. I went in, raised my right hand, all 139 pounds soaking wet, lied like a rug, and told them I was eighteen; I was sixteen. That is how I got into uniform.

When they were asking me about the things that I studied, what skills I had and so on, I mentioned that I had studied music and that I played a couple of stringed instruments and bagged away on the piano, and that I also played the clarinet. They said, 'We've got ourselves a bugler.'

I said, 'No. You kiss a bugle or a trumpet, but you put the clarinet in your mouth, and you use your tongue to make the proper kind of noises.'

They said, 'Son, a horn is a horn. You are a bugler.' Took me three months to get rid of that bugle. I had to find my replacement in training.

Forced Marches At High Speed

My Christmas present, given to me along about Thanksgiving, was to exchange my M1A1 bugle for a 1903 Springfield, be promoted to PFC, and become lead scout in the rifle squad.

We were federalized and brought into federal service on the 3rd of February 1941. We trained for three weeks out of the Army and followed, and then we were trained up to Fort Meade, Maryland, by this time as an active Army unit. Our basic training and so on was accomplished there. I remember it well. Scouting, patrolling, long marches. Our battalion commander was from over in the Valley of Virginia. He was very much an aficionado of Stonewall Jackson. He wanted us to be able to move like grease lightning, so we went everywhere in a sort of jog or trot. We did move fast, and we moved great distances. He marched the dickens out of us. Every chance he got took us off. Forced marches at high speeds, which stood me in good stead later. We spent a lot of time on the range, firing all of the various infantry weapons. We learned, of course, everything about the school of the soldier. Extended all the drill formations, signals that would allow you to get quickly into the right kind of combat formation if you were in the field with fire upon, that kind of thing. These were things I took very much to heart. I was promoted to corporal, then to sergeant, then to staff sergeant. Wound up doing a lot of teaching myself as a non-com, which I loved.

At the age of eighteen, Sam Wilson was the youngest 2nd lieutenant in the U.S. Army.

I had graduated from OCS, and I had been kept back from my class for one year to teach light infantry tactics, raiding by infiltration, scouting and patrolling, and these kinds of subjects, there on the red hills of the Fort Benning Reservation, which meant that I had a year to contemplate, conceive, and teach the very things that I was going to be required to do in Burma. A very fortuitous combination, which meant that I was better prepared than I otherwise would be. I wound up in Merrill's Marauders as a first lieutenant, initially as a rifle company executive officer, and subsequently, after a few weeks, I became one of the intelligence and reconnaissance platoon leaders of the Marauders. I and another I&R platoon leader were used frequently, directly, by General Merrill on missions for the whole unit. We were behind the Japanese lines.

Stilwell's Goals

The Japanese were almost on the border of India; India was in a state of seething political unrest. The Japanese were toying with the idea of extending their reach into India, although they were already vastly overextended themselves. Stilwell, on the other hand, felt that the American objective in Southeast Asia and in China, Burma, and India was to keep the nationalist Chinese fully involved in the war and to ensure that the one million Japanese who were then occupying huge swaths of Chinese territory would be held there and would not be able to be transferred back to the home islands to assist in the defense of the home islands when the inevitable invasion by Allied forces, mainly American forces, occurred. So his immediate goal was to reopen the Burma Road.

We were trying to get supplies to Chiang Kai-shek and his Nationalist armies, but we were flying them over the Hump in C-47s and C-46s and providing only a trickle of what was needed there. We could only provide the tonnage over land that Chiang Kai-shek needed. Stilwell felt that the key to that part of the war was to get the Burma Road open and to be able to move supplies from India across Burma into Southeast China, to Kunming and that general area so that Chiang Kai-shek could continue to fight the Japanese sufficiently successfully that he tied them down where they were.

Winning Support of the Indigenous Peoples

We were behind Japanese lines. In most instances, when we moved to the Japanese, we were outnumbered. We had to rely on the combat multiplying factor of surprise, good intelligence, again, speed marches and mobility I referred to earlier, to be able successfully to stand up to the Japanese. We were fighting mainly the Japanese 18th Imperial Guards Division; the victors at Singapore who had come across to Rangoon and marched north had acquitted themselves extraordinarily well, driving Stilwell and two Chinese divisions out of Burma. This was in 1942. We had a tough enemy. We were in his backyard, and he didn't like it. What I'm leading up to is the assistance and support of the indigenous population was the sine qua non to our survival, let alone successful operations. That particular factor emerged as one of the most salient factors later in the war in Vietnam. Except in Vietnam, the situation had been reversed and the Marauders and the VC had been playing the same role. The fact that we had been teaching the same kinds of things that we would be facing in Burma was a great advantage. Then what we learned in Burma was a great advantage for me from then on.

Inspired to Learn

The story [of my becoming a foreign area officer and my subsequent military career] is a little complex, maybe a little long, but I'll try to tell it. As you know, there are lulls in combat. There are times when there's no firing when you're resting, recuperating, repairing equipment, cleaning your weapons, and so on. We had such periods in the areas of Japanese and North Burma. On those occasions, we would sometimes set up our wireless radios, SCR-284, for example, and experiment with the antenna around trees and bushes and so on, orienting them in different directions, to see what we could pick up from the outside world. It was amazing what we could pick up, especially when we were at altitude, when we were up in the mountains of Burma, the spurs that extend down from the mountain range. On one occasion, it was just before our third mission, we were kind of on our last legs, and by the time I was down, we'd lost a lot of people. We'd been watching the mountain pass, the kind of glade, the flat area. Set up our radio that night, and built fires because the monsoons were rolling in, and there were clouds between us and the valley, the Japanese were in the valley, but they couldn't see our fires through the clouds, but we knew it. We were wet and tired and hungry. It gave us a chance to warm up and dry out. We began to play that game with the radios, put our aerials up, and we began to pick up Radio Free Rangoon, which was a joke because it was under Japanese control. Radio Free Manila is another joke. BBC, some Chinese language stations. I knew only a few words in Chinese, but I could pick it up enough to know that they were speaking Chinese.

One station coming in rather indistinctly through the static was in a language I'd never heard before. One of my muleskinners was of Russian ancestry, and he said, 'Wait. That's Russian. Let's see what they're saying.' We fiddled a little bit, brought it in a little more clearly, and he began haltingly to interpret what was being said. They were talking about the Battle of Kursk, which took place in August 1943 and was a turning point in their war on the Soviet-German front. It was a propaganda broadcast. It was designed for home-front consumption, home-front morale, and so on. But as he talked, I realized more fully something I'd already felt, that that was where the war was really being fought. On a front that extended between 2,000 and 3,000 miles, involving from 100 to 150 divisions on either side, a war being fought on a scale and scope that we could hardly imagine, where we were, of human suffering and so on, involving a huge swath of the population. I sat there, and it dawned on me, we're pipsqueaks, we're sideshows, all the war we can handle right here because one man firing and being fired at is all the war anybody wants. But I listened to that, and it dawned on me, here we have a whole nation really fighting and sacrificing, dying by the thousands. Actually, they eventually lost 26 million, as you are aware. I stood up by the fire and I said to my guys, 'Fellas, when this is all over, I'll be a captain, I'm going to study Russia, and I'm going to get myself assigned to Moscow as an assistant military attaché. I'm going to find out what motivates people to fight, sacrifice, and persist in these horrible conditions for so long. One has to try to understand what are the dynamics at work, and I'm going to go find out.' And I did. It was my interest in the Russian performance during World War II, which was only possible because of the Russian people's willingness to sacrifice for the motherland. I wanted to comprehend that. I wanted to get my mental rope around that.

At the end of the war, Sam Wilson, as a Russia specialist, was assigned to the Office of Strategic Services in Southeast Asia and later worked as a CIA officer in West Berlin and a defense attaché at the U.S. Embassy in Moscow during the Cold War. In 1959, he became the director of the Army Special Forces School at Fort Bragg, pioneering a program of instruction for counterinsurgency operations that evolved into the 'hearts and minds' approach used with varying degrees of success in subsequent wars. As probably the most militarily distinguished surviving Marauder, he introduced the 1962 Hollywood film based on their exploits. He headed the Defense Intelligence Agency in the mid-1970s and is considered a father of the U.S. Army Special Forces; in 1977, he helped create Delta Force, the Army unit devoted to counterterrorism and hostage-rescue operations.[35] He passed away on June 10, 2017, at the age of 93.

Philip Piazza, WWII. Library of Congress.

CHAPTER NINE

The Heavy Weapons Commander

Philip Piazza was born in Connecticut in 1917. He passed up a basketball scholarship to enlist in the Army, a year before the attack on Pearl Harbor. He was posted to the Caribbean and then with Merrill's Marauders in the China-Burma-India Theater. Philip was wounded in the field; being evacuated under jungle combat conditions was no small feat. Like some other of the storytellers in this book, his family was mistakenly notified that he had been killed in action weeks before they learned he was alive.

'I was just telling someone recently about an instance that I saw on TV that this young ranger had just been wounded half an hour before and he's on a litter and he's talking on the telephone to his wife. I'm glad that they do what they do today. I think it's wonderful for the families because obviously when you're in combat and away from home, it's very stressful. I think it's as stressful for families at home as it is for the man up at the front line. In my particular case, my family didn't hear from me for over two and a half years, and initially, my mother received a telegram from the War Department stating that I was killed in action! Two weeks later, they sent a second telegram saying I wasn't killed, but I was missing in

action. *Two weeks after that, she got a third telegram stating that I wasn't missing in action, but I was seriously wounded, but they couldn't tell her what the nature of my [injury] was, so you can imagine it was rather stressful on my family, so I'm glad about what they are able to do with the communication that they have today.'*

Philip was awarded two Purple Hearts, a Bronze Star, and a presidential Unit Citation. Wounded and evacuated, he spent a year and a half in the hospital and then returned to active duty as an instructor at Camp Blanding, where he was tasked with finding the highest mountain in Florida to build a simulated Japanese village to teach the soldiers infiltration techniques. In 1995 he was inducted into the U.S. Army Ranger Hall of Fame; he was also the president of the Merrill's Marauders Association, which held its annual meetings since 1947.

He sat for this interview at their 59th annual reunion in Virginia in 2005 when he was 88 years old.

Philip Piazza

I was born in Stratford, Connecticut, in 1917. I'm the permanent president of Merrill's Marauders Association. Formerly with the Marauders, I was the commanding officer of the heavy weapons unit in the 2nd Battalion of the Blue Combat Team, Merrill's Marauders.

'I'm Not Asking You'

I went into the Army the year before Pearl Harbor because it was obvious that we were going to go to war, and in those days, the young people were pretty gung-ho about going into the Army because of the feeling after Pearl Harbor. As a matter of fact, I passed up a four-year basketball scholarship to Ohio State. I went in as a private. Within six months, I was promoted to first sergeant and then was sent to officer school at Fort Benning, Georgia. Immediately after that, once again, I volunteered to go fight in Africa. I was on a Dutch ship with three Dutch officers who were PT boat commanders. We were heading for Africa. We made a stop in Curaçao in the Dutch West Indies. While we were there, they got a radio message that they needed a junior officer in Trinidad. We had an air base in Trinidad, and we had an Army regiment in Trinidad at that time. They sent a Navy PBY plane to Curaçao to pick me up and flew me on into Trinidad. When I arrived in Trinidad, you had a certain rigmarole that you go through, what an officer does to report to the commanding officer and so forth. When I reported to the commanding officer, the colonel said to me, 'I'm going to assign you and three other officers, and you are going to build a camp.' It was the original Special Forces Mountain and Ranger Training Camp.

I said to him, 'Colonel, I'm a city boy from Bridgeport, Connecticut. I was never in a jungle in my life.' I remember the colonel laughed, and he looked me in the eye and said, 'Lieutenant, I'm not asking you.'

Well, the funny part of it is, nobody knew anything about jungle fighting or mountain fighting because we had just been involved in the war. What we did, we actually even built the buildings. We wrote the manual for the training and everything. The unit that I had been assigned to there was the 33rd Infantry Regiment, which eventually became the 2nd Battalion of Merrill's Marauders. They had been for many years guarding the Panama Canal. That was their duty. They were sent from Panama to Trinidad to occupy the island there and secure that area in the Caribbean because we had an airfield there, and at that time the route to the combat area in

Africa was from Florida to Puerto Rico to Trinidad and then to Africa, so it was very important to have American troops there.

A lot of people are not aware of the fact that at that time of the war, believe it or not, we had a French unit on the island of Martinique, right in the middle of all the Americans. That was before, remember when the French were siding with the Axis powers? My battalion's job at that time was to attack Martinique. My duty at that time was to take a squad, cross the Nariva Swamp, hit the island of Martinique, scale the cliffs there, and take out the harbor guns. Well, our intelligence informed us that the French soldiers that were guarding Martinique used to go into town to visit their girlfriends. We figured that what we would do then was hit the place at the time that they were not there. It's a good thing because those cliffs with the harbor guns controlling the harbor were rather steep. Fortunately, the morning that we were going to attack, they capitulated so we didn't have to attack Martinique. We had trained for three months on amphibious maneuvers, but fortunately didn't have to go.

'A Minimum of 90% Casualties'

A lot of people were not aware of the Marauders, nor were they interested in how we were organized. [The backstory is that] the British had just been kicked out of Burma; they had taken an awful beating. They had the British commandos, known as the Chindits, retreat out of Burma. At that time, General Stilwell had been training Chinese troops, and General Merrill, who at that time was a major, was one of his aides. They walked out over the Himalayas, back into India. When we went back in, we actually retraced their routes. Well, at the [August 1943] Quebec Conference in Canada, President Roosevelt met with Prime Minister Churchill, Lord Louis Mountbatten, General Stilwell, and General Merrill, and Churchill had requested from President Roosevelt to have a large contingent of American 'commandos,' they called them at that time, to go back in with the British commandos and try to recapture Burma; President Roosevelt was going to give Prime Minister Churchill a regimental-size unit, which was 3,000 men.

After the president had told Prime Minister Churchill that he would allow them a regimental-size unit, telegrams were then sent out to all theaters of operation at that time. It stipulated that, first of all, you had to be in perfect physical condition. We were all volunteers, and suddenly, it was the first time they had ever had an all-volunteer unit of that size. Generally, you have volunteer units for small missions, but as I said, the proviso was that you had to be in perfect physical condition. You couldn't even have a hangnail because we were told specifically that, first of all, they were anticipating a minimum of 90% casualties, which actually eventually transpired. We were also told that because we would be operating behind the enemy lines, there was no way for evacuation because we were just beginning to use helicopters at that time, but they weren't using them for evacuation as they did eventually in Korea, Vietnam, and in the current conflict. We were told that if you became ill or you were wounded, it was impossible to get you out.

We were originally assigned to the British Army as part of the British commando unit. We trained with them for four months in India prior to going into combat. We had no objection to fighting alongside of our allies, the British, but we always wanted to go in carrying our own colors. We finally prevailed upon them to be able to do that. That's how the Marauders were formed.

We trained pretty extensively in mountain warfare and jungle warfare because they had both of those in the climates of India. We took a long train trip across India to the border of India and Burma. We were regimental-size. We were broken up into six combat teams, two combat teams per battalion. The idea was that when we were fighting, we would, hopefully, when we ran into any action, we would join up and be able to fight the enemy that way. But unfortunately, as happened so frequently, each one of us had our own individual [team] firefights and quite often we couldn't join each other, except for the main battle at a place called Myitkyina.

What we did was, we carried silver money and trinkets for the natives, and we were told that in the event you became ill, or you became wounded, they would try to get friendly natives to take care of us. We were very fortunate in that we eventually didn't have to rely on natives. A group of young flying sergeants from the Air Force formed what they called a liaison squadron flying small Piper Cubs and were able to evacuate one man at a time in these little Piper Cubs. In that area, the vegetation is exceptionally thick when you're down in the lowlands. When you're up in the mountains, obviously it's thick too. It was awfully hard to find a place to land, but they would pick a spot on the bank of a river, or we would cut a small path in a rice paddy when we could find one so they could land. Incidentally, I have the greatest respect in the world for the Air Force. We would never have been able to complete our mission had we not had the backing of the Air Force for two reasons: our evacuation, which was very important, but also, they had to airdrop all of our supplies by parachute because there was no way that they could get supplies to us. Even today, in Burma, there was only one main artery, and at that time, we couldn't use any vehicles, so everything had to be dropped by parachute. Now, of the original 3,000 troops that comprised our regiment, we kept four to five hundred back in India, and they were the ones that did the paperwork and kept the records. They were the ones who arranged for our supplies to be dropped to us, which was very important because, once again, we wouldn't have been able to operate had we not had these people doing this superhuman job that they really did.

We had K-rations most of the time. Once in a while, we had C-rations, which I would have loved to have. But only a couple of times we got what they called a 10-in-one ration, a mountain ration that was fantastic. It had pineapple rice pudding, it had bacon, and eggs, all dehydrated, of course, but let me tell you, when we operated under the conditions we were operating under, anything was good. We only got that a couple of times, they couldn't get that to us. [As I said], everything had to be dropped by parachute because when you're deep in behind the enemy lines like that, obviously there's no way to get supplies in, so everything had to be dropped by parachute. What we would do is we would radio and tell them in three days, hopefully, we will be at these coordinates, this position. But quite often, first of all, when you're operating continuously in enemy territory that the enemy had held for a couple of years, they knew every inch of the trail and they were all over the place. When you're getting a supply drop, a plane doesn't come in one plane and drop it. You had numbers of planes and they're circling around up there and giving your position away. Quite frequently, we were attacked when they were dropping our supplies, and we would take off and run to get out of the area so we wouldn't be captured, and we would leave our supplies for the Japanese. That's a terrible feeling when you haven't had anything to eat for a few days and you have no supplies, you need medicine, you need weapons. Quite frequently, they were able to garner our supplies that way.

Those American planes are what we call DC-3s, the best plane that was ever built, believe me. How those pilots flew, the Air Force, what I said earlier, they flew what they called the Hump from India into China under the most miserable weather conditions there were. Those planes weren't geared to fly at extreme heights. We lost an awful lot of them that would crash into the side of the mountain. As a matter of fact, in the period that I was in one of the hospitals when they moved me from the one in Ledo to a place called Dinjan, which was the airstrip that the Air Force was flying over [to], they had me in a bag, then I had them put me in a bed by the window so I could look out. I was incapacitated, but I could watch the planes take off and they had these plywood auxiliary gas tanks because they needed extra gasoline. Many a time, I'd see these fellows struggling to get airspeed and they couldn't make it, and they'd run right into the side of the mountain and explode. They were fantastic and it's a shame that those pilots never got the credit, but pilots and other parts of the world had a rough time, like the 8th Air Force and many others, but these conditions were abominable, especially during the monsoon season.

Of course, the Air Force, once again, I can't say enough about them. A lot of people don't realize that we were always called the Forgotten Theater, and we still are today. The Air Force never got credit for what they did, and their flying conditions and flying the Hump with the air equipment that they had was the toughest anywhere in the world, and they did it. We lost an awful lot of them. The same way with us. We are the forgotten people. Nobody ever recognizes the China-Burma-India Theater, but as far as I'm concerned, I think it was one of the most integral parts of the war effort because we were the back door running to Europe, and also it was important that we open up the road to get supplies from India on into China.

Philip Piazza searches a dead Japanese soldier for maps and other intelligence. U.S. Army, public domain.

Living Conditions

Living conditions were abominable. Number one, obviously, we were operating deep behind the enemy lines, as we did for sometimes as much as 250 miles behind the lines, and we did that for seven months. Also, you have to remember that operating the way we did in that period, we never had any replacements. When you lost a man either through illness or wounds, there was no way to replace them because there was no way to get them in there, and it wasn't until we captured the airfield at a place called Myitkyina, which was the main hub for anything going on into China. It was the terminus of the railroad. It was the only all-weather airstrip and the only road leading into there. That was our main objective, actually, to capture the city of Myitkyina, and the airfield at Myitkyina.

By the time we [eventually] reached Myitkyina, of the 3,000 of us originally, we were down to less than 200 men. Of course, that includes injuries as well as disease. Well, that's another thing that I don't know if I had mentioned earlier, but it's bad enough when you're fighting the enemy. You are also fighting disease, and the incidence of disease in that part of the world is the worst it is anywhere. Now, we were inoculated against anything that they could inoculate us against. We were inoculated against typhus, but we ran into a mite-borne typhus where there was no inoculation. When a man got infected that way, it was so bad that at times we had to tie him to a tree because they'd go out of the mind, and they would be dead in twenty-four hours. Another thing, if you look at the historical records, and of course, we had mountainous terrain, and we had jungle, and the vegetation is the worst it is anywhere in the world. Of course, we weren't far from where they were fighting in Vietnam. It's similar territory. As a matter of fact, when the Department of Defense sent me back [on my trip over there], when we were flying from India over to China, we had a general who was with us that was piloting the plane. He sent the colonel back.

He said, 'Get Phil to come up and sit in the co-pilot seat.'

He said, 'Look down. Do you see that down there? This time you're flying over it. You're not walking over it.'

To be honest with you, when I looked down at the terrain, I wondered how we were able to do it. It's amazing what you can do when you have to, but you've got to remember one thing, too. We were the [first] class of the Army, the best-conditioned, best-trained troops that the Army had at that time. We were young, and we were all very physically fit, but it was still pretty hectic. By the time the campaign was winding down, we had all lost 40 to 50 pounds. You can imagine what I looked like. I lost 50 pounds, and by the time they got me back to the hospital, I went in at 142 pounds, and I lost 50 pounds. My mother was shocked the first time she saw me in the hospital.

The Imperial Marines

As far as conditions are concerned, things were rough in Vietnam, and those conditions were pretty similar to what we experienced, but it's bad enough that at that time we were fighting the enemy, who were actually Imperial Marines. When you think of a Japanese as rather a small individual, a lot of people don't realize that to be an Imperial Marine, you had to be a minimum of six feet to start with, and they were at the top of the Japanese Army, the unit that we fought against. If you read any of your history, they were the ones who captured Singapore when they defeated the British. They were also infamous for the rape of Nanking, when this unit—I was at the Smithsonian Institute the other day, and they had an article there in one of the books that I was reading—in Nanking, they had taken and murdered 300,000 civilians, and they just [lined them up] and beheaded them, and then about another 150,000, they lined them up and machine-gunned them to death, because they didn't have time to go [beheading people] down the line. That's why they call it the Rape of Nanking. It was one of the most horrendous things that was ever done, next to the Holocaust, when you talk about man's inhumanity to man; you can understand why that's why I still, to this day, have such a feeling for what they did there, and also my feeling about Pearl Harbor. It's awfully hard to be a Christian and say, 'You can turn the other cheek.' I will never forgive them for that, because at that time, I also lost an awful lot of my friends in the [Bataan] death march.

Fight at Walawbum

I commanded the heavy weapons; I was commanding officer heavy weapons, Blue Combat Team, 2nd Battalion. We were set up on the British [format] because when we were first with the British, we were set up on what they call a TONE, which is a table of organization. They used streamlined units. We streamlined the size of the companies and everything. We operated with two combat teams in each battalion, which meant six combat teams. Each combat team was designated a color: blue, green, white, khaki, orange. That's why on our insignia if you notice, the colors designate that. On our insignia, we show the Star of India and the Sun of China, and the lightning stroke is us going between the two countries.

That's our Marauder insignia, which the present 75th Ranger Regiment wears today.

It was funny, when we first went in to fight, we allowed our men to handle any weapon they wanted. We didn't go by the records that said, 'Each one had to carry a certain weapon.' None of my men wanted to carry automatic weapons because that meant you had to carry extra ammunition. We were carrying very heavy packs as it was; you had to carry everything on your back. I used the animals to carry our heavy weapons and our ammunition, the heavy ammunition. The men carried very heavy packs, similar to what the Rangers use today. When they jump out of a plane, they're carrying almost a hundred pounds of weight. So they didn't want to carry any extra weight if they could help it, and we never collected souvenirs, because if you collected anything else, you wanted extra food or extra ammunition.

We fought thirty-five [engagements] out there, and it's impossible in a short period of time to relate all the incidents, but I'll tell you, the very first major battle that we had was at a place called Walawbum. Our objective was to move in and put in a roadblock to keep so that when the Japanese attacked, you were supposed to be able to stop them. Well, my combat team and my battalion moved into this area, just short of the road, in the middle of a beautiful Burmese moonlit night, and a Burmese moonlit night is like bright daylight, the brightest daylight that you get here in this country. We were actually able to move in within a few hundred yards of this Japanese unit, believe it or not, without them detecting us. When we got our air drops of supplies, we used to have some of the equipment wrapped in burlap. I had horses and mules to carry my heavy weapons, and we took the burlap and wrapped the horses' and mules' feet in burlap. We wrapped all of our metallic equipment in burlap, so there would be no sound. Another thing was, you know how a mule brays? Well, obviously, in the midst of combat, if one of them brayed, or in a case like that, we were close to the enemy, if one had brayed, it would be pretty serious. The original group of mules that were sent to us were torpedoed on a ship off of India. They had been surgically debrayed; a lot of people don't know that can be done. They didn't have time to replace them with more of them that had been surgically debrayed. We had our mule skinners, the men who were responsible for taking care of their individual mules. Believe me, they looked after them like their own children. Whenever a mule started to bray, they would reach up and grab them by the nostrils to keep them from braying. You can imagine how hectic it was at that time.

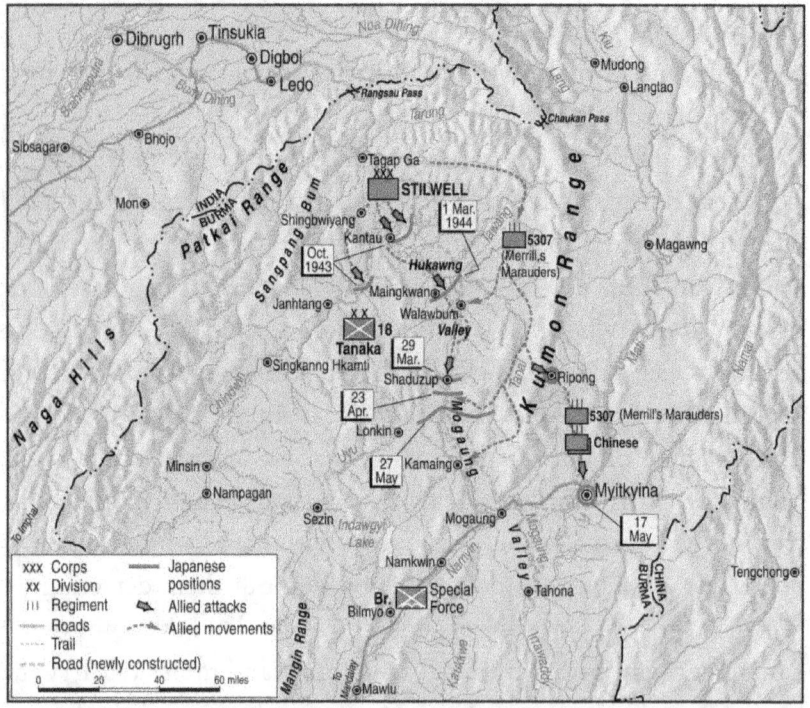

Merrill's Marauders in Burma. U.S. Army. Public domain.

We always talk to that man upstairs, and a soldier will always tell you he's always sitting on your shoulder looking after you. We were fortunate in that the Japanese in the middle of the night suddenly decided to vacate their foxholes and slit trenches and go into the city. When they did that, we immediately moved in and took over their positions; we didn't have to dig the foxholes and the slit trenches. When they returned, expecting to take over the positions, we hit them pretty hard. As a matter of fact, we killed 800 of them in that fight at Walawbum. If I remember correctly, I think we only lost a couple of men and a few wounded. But we were running out of ammunition, we were running out of food, and we were running out of medicine. We had to evacuate the position after we captured an area or an installation, and the two Chinese divisions would come in and secure it, and then we would move on to our next objective. We took off running.

We ran for five miles, carrying our wounded, feeding them blood plasma while we carried them on a litter. Once again, with that man upstairs looking after us, we ran down this trail that the Japanese had occupied, and because the whole trail was booby-trapped, one of our lieutenants took one of his horses, slapped him on the rump, and sent him running down the trail. As he ran down the trail, the horse set off the booby traps, so we had a clear path going down. The Japanese had all their guns set up and they were firing across the trail that we were running down, but they had their machine guns elevated, so they were shooting over our heads, otherwise they would have wiped us out. We ran five miles to a place called Wasaga, where we got an airdrop for supplies.

Wounded

I was wounded just before the Battle of Myitkyina. When I was wounded, we were in the midst of a terrific firefight. We knew that we were going to get hit at dawn, because all night long we heard the Japanese coming up on the only road that was there in Burma, and they were very noisy soldiers. They were good soldiers in some respects, but they were always very noisy. Well, we stress amongst our men discipline, and we stress quietness, because when you're operating behind enemy lines like that, especially, you have to be very quiet. But anyway, we could hear them getting off their trucks and banging the tailgates and jabbering away, so we knew that they were going to hit us at dawn. Then all day long from dawn until evening, they hit us with eighteen banzai attacks.

In a banzai attack, they come screaming at you. One thing about them, I have to hand it to them, their courage was exceptional. But it's like the Iraqis today, those stupid terrorists. It's an honor for them to die. As far as the Americans are concerned, we try our best not to let our men get wounded or die. We don't want to lose our men. When they attack you, it's an honor if they get killed. I had bodies piled up so high in front of my machine guns that I had to get out and kick the bodies away so we could fire our machine guns. That went on all day long.

When I was wounded first, I was outside the perimeter directing my mortar fire to my men. A machine gun got me in the head. As a matter of fact, I still have the two bullets in my head. Then later on, a 90-millimeter mortar [fragment] went through my ankle. At that time, the way we operated, we couldn't have any station hospital. All you had was medics. We were fighting all day long there; there was no way anybody could take care of me; all they could do was give me first aid.

When we pulled out of there, my men carried me on a stretcher for a while. Monsoon season was on. Conditions were abominable. It finally was getting so hard trying to carry me on a litter that I made my men put me up on a horse. I rode a horse for a while, back to Nhpum Ga (pronounced 'Niponga'), which was where my outfit was trapped on a mountain. It was seven days before I got to the hospital on the operating table. Yeah, a little different than it is today. Fortunately, today, you can evacuate the wounded so quickly with helicopters. But we didn't have those facilities. What they did at the time, one of the liaison pilots, the flying sergeants from the Air Force, put me in this little Piper Cub with my litter and flew me back a hundred miles till they had a DC-3 on an abandoned airstrip. That flew me the other 150 miles back to the hospital on the border of Burma at a place called Ledo, where the 20th General Hospital was the hospital that did such a fantastic job taking care of our sick and wounded. That was a unit from the University of Pennsylvania School of Medicine, commanded by, at that time, Colonel Ravdin, Isidor Ravdin, who eventually became a general. They were the ones that took care of us, and they did a marvelous job. I was at the hospital there six months because I was in such bad shape that they couldn't even move me. When they were finally able to move me, as a matter of fact, believe it or not, it was the day of the invasion of Europe.

I was in such a serious condition that I couldn't stand long flights or anything. On easy hops, they would put me into a hospital all the way across India to Africa. It was in Khartoum in Egypt, Africa, on the west coast of Accra. From Accra, we started across the ocean. Now, it was days and days that this took. When we left Africa, the route at that time was across to South America. As we took off from Africa, partway over the ocean, the engine on the plane kicked out, and we had to make a forced landing on Ascension Island. Now, you can imagine how barren that was. That was the island that originally they were going to banish Napoleon to, and they had decided it was too wild to put him there. What did they do? They put an American Air Force base there. Anyway, there was not a single tree on that island. Even though we had an Air Force base there, it was so rocky, there was a high cliff. When you land on the airplane, they have to run two jeeps down the strip to get the goonie birds off the strip to keep them from flying into the propellers of the plane whenever a plane came in. Also to get supplies to the men that were stationed there, they used to have to float it in barrels from the ships because there was no beach there to land on, that's how barren that place was. Anyway, they got another motor for the airplane, and then we flew from there to a hospital in Georgetown, British Guiana. Then it went up to Trinidad and Puerto Rico, and then to Miami. I was in an Air Force hospital in Miami until they could move me to what was then an amputation hospital in Atlantic City, New Jersey. In those days, when we went overseas, we spent years overseas. You didn't go away for weeks or months. You went away for years. What they tried to do when anybody was ill or seriously wounded was pick a hospital closest to your home that could take care of your particular ailment. In my case, the only thing closest was Atlantic City, about 200 miles from my home. But as a matter of fact, strangely enough, what was the hospital then was Haddon Hall Hotel. Today it's the International Casino, the big gambling casino. But once again, the feeling was so different in those days. The people in New Jersey treated us wonderfully. I spent a year there, when I was finally ambulatory, if you got on a bus, they wouldn't allow you to pay. Even a taxi driver wouldn't accept the money. If you went into a nightclub, somebody picked up the tab. People would buy your meals. It was a different feeling. It wasn't what unfortunately our servicemen experienced when they came back from Vietnam.

I was just telling someone recently about an instance that I saw on TV that this young ranger had just been wounded half an hour before and he's on a litter and he's talking on the telephone to his wife. I'm glad that they do what they do today. I think it's wonderful for the families because obviously when you're in combat and away from home, it's very stressful. I think it's as stressful for families at home as it is for the man up at the front line. In my particular case, my family didn't hear from me for over two and a half years, and initially, my mother received a telegram from the War Department stating that I was killed in action! Two weeks later, they sent a second telegram saying I wasn't killed, but I was missing in action. Two weeks after that, she got a third telegram stating that I wasn't missing in action, but I was seriously wounded, but they couldn't tell her what the nature of my [injury] was, so you can imagine it was rather stressful on my family, so I'm glad about what they are able to do with the communication that they have today.

Home

Home was Connecticut. Every stop that I made, because they could only move me for short periods, I would have to stay in the hospital until I was strong enough for them to move me because I was in a really serious condition. I was at the hospital in New Jersey for one year. I was anxious to get back to combat, but obviously, with my condition, they wouldn't allow that. I talked my way out of the hospital, went back to duty, and they assigned me to Camp Blanding, Florida. I was what they called G3, which is the operations or training officer. I was on the general staff there at Camp Blanding, Florida. I was there about six months, I'd say, before I got out.

After that, I went home. I was still in reserve, but I was in serious, still in bad condition from the head injury. Head wound, mostly. The leg was bothering me, but I managed. They managed to save my leg, even though I had been in an amputation hospital. But they managed to save that so that I eventually, even at my age, I played tennis up until just recently. But for many years after, I couldn't take advantage of the GI Bill because of the fact that I would spend maybe six months out of the year in the hospital. But I got my education in the service. I went into business in

Connecticut, but even then, for the first about ten years, as I said, I spent maybe six months out of the year in the hospital.

I was in Florida the day that the war ended. I had just built a replica of a Japanese airfield and a native village. I got orders to take my men out and blow it up. Then I was told to put myself under restriction in the bachelor officers' quarters and put my men under guard. In the barracks, they couldn't leave town because they were anticipating some really rough times with the men. It was a shame that we weren't even allowed into town. Well, I don't think I could describe to you the feeling that by then the war was over and we were going home. Of course, I stayed in a while to do some things for the general. I didn't get to participate in parades and everything that they had up north, but those of us who were in the war at that time were treated wonderfully after we came home, as you can see in the newsreels. It wasn't like what happened after Vietnam, which was a shame. We were treated terrifically. We cannot complain about that. There was a different feeling throughout the country. Well, you know what the women did when the men went away; the women went into the factories and even into the shipyards and everything. Unfortunately, if we were to go in a war, and we're not calling [the Iraq and Afghanistan operations] a war right now. But if we were to have to do the same thing today, I don't know if we could gear up as quickly as we did at that time, because we don't have the facilities right now.

'General Stilwell Just Laughed'

I hate to talk about the horrors of war, but when you look back, there are humorous things that happened at times. For instance, my battalion was trapped on a hill at a place called Nhpum Ga for two weeks until it broke out on Easter Sunday morning, strangely enough. But one of the men woke up one morning—in the Rangers, you operate in the buddy system. At night, there's always one man awake and one man asleep, hopefully. When he woke up in the morning, his buddy said, 'Boy, you look wonderful this morning. Who's your undertaker?' [*Laughs*] I always remember the one incident where I met the general, and I got the opportunity to talk to him later on a number of times. When we walked up into the Himalayan Mountains—initially, we walked 130 miles up into the Himalayas and over the Himalayas on into Burma. Well, at a place called Pangsau Pass, which was our jump-off point for combat, General Stilwell was standing there, and he happened to come through my area where my men were, and he stood there talking to me. He never wore insignia; he had a fetish [about it], he wouldn't wear his medals or all the fancy uniforms or anything. He always wore an old campaign hat. He always had a pipe in his mouth and a long coat. He was old, and some of the men didn't recognize him. But one of my men came up when I was talking to him. He took one look at him, and excuse my English, but he said, 'Jesus Christ, things must be pretty rough back in the States, when they send an old son of a bitch like you over here to fight!' [*Laughs*]

I wanted to dig a hole and just crawl in; here I am talking to the top general! Anyway, General Stilwell just laughed; as a matter of fact, he nudged me, he said, 'Don't let it bother you.' Well, I met him a number of times after that, like the time when I was in Florida and when he was a corps commander after that. He always reminded me of that. Just nine years ago when I was on that trip back to China that the Department of Defense sent me on, I was on one of the islands there, and I met his son, who was a forensic pathologist. Spent the night with him. His son told me, 'I was only a kid in those days. But I remember my dad telling me that incident.'

Going Back

In about 1996, I think it was, [I got to go back.] That was fabulous! What the Department of Defense did was they sent us and picked fourteen officers who had seen a lot of combat in that part of the world. I was the only infantry officer. The rest of them were Flying Tigers. At that time, they were just beginning to use a new C-17 plane that we have, a fantastic airplane. They wheeled in equipment and configured it the same as a first-class airline. They also sent three chefs from the Pentagon to take care of us. Every place that we went, not only there on the plane, they wined and dined us; every place that we went, either an admiral, an ambassador, or a general would throw a party for us every night! In China, the head of the Chinese Communist Party threw a party for us! It was a fabulous trip, 38,000 miles, three weeks.

We first went to Hawaii. The best part of it was that every place we went, we got three or four days to stay so that they would take us on tours of the area. As I say, every night, they wined and dined us, at either an officers' club or an ambassador's residence. I always remember the one in India. The ambassador's residence is really posh. I remember when we were having the reception, looking up the grand staircase and coming down this staircase was this Gurkha band with bagpipes! It was quite impressive. We went to Bombay, India, Calcutta, New Delhi. Then we flew over the Himalayan Mountains to China. We were at Kunming, which was the place where the Air Force in those days was supplied for their flights into China. We went from Kunming, where we had a big ceremony for the Flying Tigers, and then went on to Beijing. In Beijing, the head of the Communist Party gave us a party. Then we went from there to Okinawa, and from Okinawa back to Hawaii.

It was a fabulous trip. I wish my wife could have gone with me. As I said, they wined and dined us all the way, gave us all kinds of presents, and treated us royally. It was a wonderful trip, something I'll treasure. A funny part of it is, just prior to that, I had bought my wife a fancy new camera. Then I went out and I bought about 15 rolls of film to film the trip. Anyway, when I got back, I didn't use it properly, and all the film was ruined; I was on the verge of crying. But a week later, the Secretary of the Air Force sent me a big carton, and it had a big box full of blown-up pictures of the whole trip. Beautiful. We had his official photographer, a lady from Washington, D.C., so I had better pictures. [*Wistfully*] Yeah.

'You Volunteered For This Mission'

My final rank was captain. I had been promoted while we were in there, but obviously, when you're behind the entry lines, because my job called for a captaincy when I finally got it, my promotion was post-dated back to that. We have, of course, the theater ribbons, which all servicemen get, when they operate in [a particular theater]. We had the Presidential Unit Citation, and I was awarded the Bronze Star, and the China War Memorial Medal. I have two Purple Hearts, but actually, I was involved with three. I never put in for the third one. One thing that you'll find out, if anybody ever researches our records, and everybody is amazed at it, Merrill's Marauders has the least awards of any combat outfit that ever saw that much combat. The reason for that is that the officers put in a man for the award, you request it, and they were always rejected, in most cases, in my battalion, because the answer was, 'Look, you volunteered for this mission, so you were supposed to do the job.' After the war, I had many occasions. I was very friendly with General Merrill and my commanding officer, Colonel McGee, and they always regretted the fact that it happened, because people often say to me, 'How come an officer like yours did so much and got so few awards?' Well, it's like the Rangers today. They don't want to be publicized. You never see much about it in the paper. You hear a lot about the Marines right now, who are doing a good job, but you don't hear anything about Special Forces. They don't want the publicity. It really is sad, because I remember a few years ago when the president at that time took and awarded innumerable Medals of Honor to different youth. I don't believe you should—I'm not saying that they didn't deserve them, but I think they demean the medal when you give it out that indiscriminately. Our people should have gotten more awards than they did, but that wasn't why we were there. We weren't there to be awarded; we had a purpose, we had a reason for being there. We don't regret it. I don't. I often had people say to me, when they saw the records about volunteering for what they call a dangerous and hazardous mission, which the president had sent out to us, said, 'How could you be so stupid to volunteer for a mission that you're told that you're going to have a minimum of 90% casualties?' But once again, as I said earlier, it wasn't Vietnam, it wasn't Korea. There was a different feeling throughout the country completely.

'I'll Take Care of It'

[I encountered General Merrill several times.] As a matter of fact, General Merrill had a heart attack the same time I was wounded. So that's when we got to be very friendly. Even though he was very ill at the hospital, he used to insist on them bringing him over to my quarters so he could see me, and we got very friendly. Later years, I had a small business in Connecticut. I had a couple of retail stores, and I had a small wholesale business covering all of New England. I always made a point on my last evening before I went home to stop in Concord, New Hampshire, and visit with the general. Then after that, he attended every reunion, provided he was in the States, and he was very close to us. I think he was one of the most admired general officers there ever was. He was also, as a major general, one of the youngest field generals that we had at that time. He was in his early forties, and he was a powerful major general. Originally, when they went out of Burma when he was with Stilwell and the British when they retreated out of Burma, he was a major at that time. Eventually wound up as a major general, which is a two-star rank. When he retired from the Army and went back to live in New Hampshire, where his widow still lives, he was the highway commissioner in New Hampshire. They had a highway commissioners' convention in Florida. On his way back, he took ill in Fernandino Beach, Florida. The Governor of New Hampshire called me that night to tell me that he had passed away. So we arranged to have a ceremony up at where he went to school at West Point. We buried him at West Point. Stilwell was also buried there.

Merrill was very close to his men. Some fellows say he wasn't, but from my personal experience, I know he was. As a matter of fact, during the Korean War, I was here in Walter Reed for a brain operation, a craniotomy. General Merrill called the Surgeon General and said to him, 'This man's not only one of my former officers, but he's also a personal friend. I'd appreciate anything you can do for him.' The Surgeon General then got in touch with the commanding general at Walter Reed and said, 'You don't give him an aspirin tablet without letting me know about it.' Then he would call General Merrill and let him know what my condition was. Then General Merrill would call my wife, Emma, up in Connecticut and let her know how I was.

I got real wonderful treatment, same surgeon that operated on President Eisenhower the week before. As a matter of fact, right after my operation, that young colonel [doctor] had a heart attack because he had spent so much time in the operating room. Understand one thing, General Merrill didn't do that because I was an officer. He had always told me in our private conversations that 'if any of the men get in any problems, let me know. I'll take care of it. I don't want any publicity over it.' He didn't.

The same way with General Ravdin who commanded the 20th General Hospital and went back to the University of Pennsylvania. He always told me that if any of the Marauders had any physical problems and couldn't afford to have it taken care of, let him know. He went to bat for me a number of times where some of the men were rather indigent at the time. So it was a great relationship.

Reunions

I have been president of the Merrill's Marauders Association for fifty-eight years, since 1947, the first reunion. They can't get anybody stupid enough to take the job. [*Laughs*] [My wife will tell you the only time we missed a reunion was about four years ago, I resigned, I said, 'That's it.' What happened [at the one we missed]? They elected me back in and then talked me into taking the job again.

I think if anyone ever attends one of our reunions, [they will see that] there has never been a unit [with such camaraderie], and I have other service people tell me the same thing. We have met every year for fifty-eight years in different parts of the country. We have a special rapport. Maybe it's because of the unusual circumstances that we fought and lived under in those days, and incidentally, that applies to the present 75th Ranger Regiment, who are our successors. As a matter of fact, the 75th Ranger Regiment wears our insignia—one of the greatest honors I ever had, after the colors of the Merrill's Marauders were retired, was in 1969 at a ceremony down at Eglin Air Force Base in Florida. I had the honor of presenting our colors to activate the present 75th Ranger Regiment, which incidentally is the only Ranger unit in existence today. Those are the ones that are in—you don't hear much publicity about them, because they don't look for publicity, but they're the ones that are fighting constantly in Afghanistan and Iraq today, and we're very proud of this 75th Ranger Regiment. When you talk about rapport, I attend an awful lot of Ranger ceremonies, I go to every graduation; even though I live 250 miles from Fort Benning, I'm invited to all Special Forces ceremonies. There is a special rapport between Rangers and Special Forces people. It's hard to explain it to somebody else, but we really do have a special rapport, and strangely enough, the rapport between the old Rangers and the new Rangers is great. We meet pretty regularly at Fort Benning, and once a year we have what they call the Ranger Rendezvous for four days when we all meet, and we have all kinds of ceremonies. Generally, we have a change of command, and that's the time that we induct the incoming members of the Ranger Hall of Fame. As a matter of fact, I'm on both the Executive Committee and the Nominating Committee of the Ranger Hall of Fame.

Interviewer: How did your military experience influence your life or your thoughts about military or war, in general?

Well, if we're talking about war today or the conditions today over there, I'm not militaristic. I give an awful lot of talks. One thing I always say, 'Don't think us veterans are militaristic, that we love wars. That's not true. We don't want our children or our friends' children to have to go to war.' The same thing with what's happening over there. I'm sorry it's going on. Unfortunately, we're in a position right now where I don't see how we can back out of it like we had to do in Vietnam. To answer your question, I think the young Rangers today and the military people today are doing a wonderful job. Your young Rangers today I think are the best educated, the best disciplined, and the finest troops that we could ever have. We take our hats off to these young [people]. I don't mean just the people that are in combat, even service. I don't care if a person served in wartime or not, the fact that they're willing to wear the uniform. I admire them for it.

In closing, I can't think of anything else, offhand, but one thing I will say that in Tom Brokaw's book, he gives all kinds of accolades to us as the 'greatest generation.' I really think that the young people, today, are our future greatest generation, really. I think they should get their accolades, too. It's wonderful that they say what they do. The young people today, they're unbelievable! The problem is today the news media plays up the bad ones. They're a minority. Nobody says anything about the good ones who are doing the good things.

Philip B. Piazza passed away in May 2011 at the age of 94.

CHAPTER TEN

The Engineer

Morris Factor grew up in the west side of Chicago during the Great Depression. After Pearl Harbor, he decided to enlist, as he figured the draft was going to catch up to him, and he wanted to have a say in where he would up. The Army had other plans, and he would find himself in India, of all places, merged into the guerrilla force know as Merrill's Marauders. He sat for this interview shortly after his 91st birthday in 2012 in Chicago.

Morris Factor

I was born on October 7, 1920, in Chicago. I had two brothers. I had an older brother that died when he was 12 years old of pneumonia in the '20s. And my baby brother died, he was not quite two, also of pneumonia. You know, back in the '20s they didn't have penicillin then, and if you caught pneumonia you could say you're gone. They went to the hospital, and they died at Michael Reese Hospital, both of them, my older brother and my younger brother. I was the middle kid in between, the guy that was always in trouble. We ate every day, he paid rent, and when they got tired of an apartment, they used to move. One time they moved; they didn't tell me they were moving. I came home and they were gone. I came home from school, and they're gone out of the apartment, but I knew everybody on the block, and I said, 'What happened to my folks?'

'Oh, they moved to that building over there.'

Depression Days

My father, before the war, used to have newspaper stands on two corners, he owned both corners—I say he owned, but he had the stands across the street, and he sold newspapers to make a living. At that particular time, way before the war broke out, my father used to make if he sold 100 *Tribunes*, he made 60 cents. The paper was two cents a paper, on a Sunday he used to get two cents a paper. Of course, it was a dime a paper for the Sunday paper. And that's how my father made his living and supported the family. We ate every day. We paid rent and I went to school, and I used to help out after school or on a Saturday or a Sunday, while he used to go to sleep because he worked selling—he had to be there at 5:30 on a Sunday morning selling the newspapers. They used to drop off a whole load and he would sell them and whatever he didn't sell, he gave back, and he'd make 60 cents, or he'd sell a hundred newspapers, two dollars. Or he used to make more because he used to sell several hundred of them and I used to help out with it, and he had to go home and sleep.

Now after war broke out, my father got rid of the newsstands and he went to work in a defense plant, and he was making metal casings that they used to make for shells. He was the first guy there in the morning and the last guy to leave during the day. And the owners of the plant told my father—he was in his middle to late sixties when I came out—and they used to tell him, 'Harry,' you know they had him on a first-name basis, he never missed a day of work unless he was sick, and he was the first guy to come and the last guy to leave. He said, 'You got a job as long as you want.' And we used to holler at him. 'You're 65, I mean why don't you go on Social Security?' He didn't want to leave, you know. He was happy working. We finally forced him to leave, which was wrong. He lived 'til he was 93, I mean, but he was never as happy as when he was working. He could have worked a few more years, but the family forced him to quit.

In those years, they didn't have air conditioning, and unless you had a little fan, you used to leave the windows open, the doors open, sleep all night long that way, or we slept in the park, all the kids used to sleep in the park, boys and girls. I mean not together, I mean but we were teenagers, we'd sleep in a park at night, and nobody bothered us, and that's where we survived and lived in the Depression years.

I was always in trouble. Not criminal trouble, just trouble. I was going to Hebrew school and before I became Bar mitzvahed and I was what, about 12 years old. And the rabbi had a beard like this, [*gestures*], and I was always fascinated. I said, 'That beard must be false,' and I kept telling myself it must be false. I said, 'But how do I find out?' Finally with nobody even knowing, he walks by, and he stands there. I grabbed his beard, and I pulled. That's when I got thrown out of Hebrew school. My father came and got me back in. And I found out that it was a real beard. [*Laughs*] He didn't want me back at first, but my father was a member of the temple, so he did that. And my father was a religious man, and I was semi-religious. Most of my friends were not religious, unfortunately, even today. I go with some that are and some that are not. You know. So what can I say?

On our street we had Italians, we had Jews, everybody. And we were friends; we played ball together, softball. [Everyone got along.] If you go a block, two blocks away, then you had problems.

We had to walk three blocks to go to school. And when we crossed Taylor Street, we were in a different neighborhood, and the guys there used to come, and all of a sudden you were in a fight. Not with knives or baseball bats, I mean, or guns. With our fists, on an average of about I'd say maybe three times a week. I remember when we were playing in Sears lot, we were playing softball for the neighborhood championship, and the team we had to play was an Italian team from another neighborhood. So they came up to us and they said, 'If you guys win,' they said, 'we're going to pounce on you and beat the hell out of you,' you know, 'because we want to win and we don't want you to win.' It went in one ear and went out the other. We won. And believe it or not, there was a whole fight on the playground until they broke us up, you know. That was part of the life of growing up.

'You'll Go Where I Tell You to Go'

I went to Herzl Junior College for a year and a half before I went in the army. I enlisted in February of '42, right after Pearl Harbor. I went down to the draft board there and enlisted because they were going to take me anyway. So I figured to myself if you enlist, they told me that you can go into the branch of the service that you want. I found out then that they lied. I wanted to go in to become a photographer and go into something like the engineers or something like that. That's what I was more or less taking up in school. I was very good in math, you know. So when I went into the branch at Fort Sheridan to get inducted into the Army, when they called my name, I walked up. It must have been ten thousand kids in the place there, and they called them in alphabetical order, they called your name. So when they called my name and I come up, a sergeant was there, a corporal and a lieutenant were sitting in back, and I saluted, which I was supposed to do, I was told, I knew that. And they asked me my name and I told them. I said, 'Sir,' I called him sir, and he smiled at that. And I said, 'I understand when you enlist that you can ask for the branch of the service that you'd like to go to.'

He sat up straight like that. He said, 'What did you say, soldier?'

I says I only asked a question. I said, 'I understand.'

He said, 'You'll go where I tell you to go.' I wanted to tell him I'd like to tell you where to go, but I didn't.

He said, 'I'll choose what you want.'

I thought, okay, there's nothing I could do about it. So he sends me to the 954th Topographic Engineer outfit in Douglas, Arizona. Now their job was to make a map of the Mexican coastline. At that time in 1942, the coastline was very poorly charted in the beginning of '42. And my job was to do the math work for the surveyor on that. And they sent us in groups of four men, four men, four men and we're surveying the coastline. And they flew over by plane, photographed it from the air, and they correlated everything. And we were gone for about five, six weeks. When we came back, I asked for a furlough. I'd never—I'm in the army a couple months, I wanted to go home. And they said, 'You're in a cavalry, and you're going to a new outfit, and you've got to go up to Seattle, Washington, to Fort Lewis.' There were six of us that went there, we had a week to get to Seattle. We stopped off in Los Angeles for a few days, and we had a ball. And we come to Fort Lewis and the MPs at the gate, and we see all these beautiful barracks like Fort Sheridan. And we come up to the gate, and they asked to see our papers and we showed them. We said, 'Which building do we go to?'

He said, 'Do you see those tents out in the field about three-quarters of a mile away? That's where you go.'

I said, 'What are we doing in tents?'

He said, 'That's where you've got to report.' So we're walking over the grass carrying our duffel bags and everything, and we come there, and we see flags flying. It says First Ranger Battalion. I said to the other guy, I said, 'What's a ranger?'

He said, 'I don't know.' And that's when we found out that this was the First Ranger Battalion, and we got combat training from them for a few weeks, going out at night traveling by the stars, coming; we went into hilly country where they were training us. And finally we came back, and they'd bring us into Fort Sheridan, and we'd get assigned to the 930th Engineer Battalion, so now I'm in the 930th Engineers.

I went up to the guys and I said, 'Can I get a furlough to go home?'

They said, 'Sure.' They give me a furlough and I get on a train, and I come home. I get off in the station and I'm greeted by MPs. 'Let's see your orders.' I showed them my orders.

They said, 'You're one of the guys we're looking for.'

I said, 'How can you be looking for me? I just got here!'

He said, 'Well, your outfit's shipping overseas, you've got to go back tomorrow.'

I said, 'Oh!'

They said, 'We'll take you home, and we'll pick you up in the morning to bring you to the train.'

They wanted to know where I lived. I came home, I didn't go to sleep, I was with my folks and with some of my friends. In the morning they picked me up, put me on a train. I come back; they're all packed, and we get on a train, and we leave from Seattle, Washington, all the way to Newport News, Virginia. It took us a week to get there. Of course they stopped, but you couldn't get off. They had MPs at every door, and you stayed in the car that you were, no beds. You slept in seats.

They issued us winter clothing because we're in December, you know, and we were there two days or a day and a half and they says we're boarding the ship that's out there in the harbor at 2:30 in the morning. We were there and another outfit was there; there must have been maybe five, six hundred men on this ship, a Victory ship with bunks twelve feet high. Fortunately I was almost near the top so nobody could throw up on me.

They gave me a job clicking a counter to count how many people were coming for breakfast and lunch, that was my job when I was on the boat, because I didn't get seasick. I should have gone in the navy, but I was in the army. Now we were surrounded by destroyers, and they used to circle around us like we were nothing, looking for submarines. We were attacked by submarines, but not our boat. There were ships that had supplies like tanks and stuff on the deck that they were bringing overseas, that's the ones they went after. We were lucky, you know. It took us thirty-five days, and we landed in North Africa.

Rommel took off from Tobruk, and the war was over in Africa, and he flew to Germany. We were there and we knew that they were going to invade Europe. We thought that we were going to be in the group that invaded Europe, you know. And we're outside of the town, and all of a sudden, they said we're going back on a ship. I said, 'Oh, are we getting ready for the invasion?'

They said, 'No, you're going to the Mediterranean into the Indian Ocean, we're going to Bombay!'

We got strafed by German planes, but the U.S. planes were there, and they drove them away; nobody got hurt. We were down—we were told by the navy 'stay down below' because they had their gunners on top, and they didn't want us to get in the way, you know. I wanted to jump off, you know.

India

We landed in Bombay, and we were there for—that's when we were able to do a few things. We were there for a couple of weeks until they put us on a train and took us to Kharagpur, a town in India. And from Kharagpur, all of a sudden, we were no longer the 930th, we became [part of] the 5307th Composite Group. Our unit was the 5307th Composite Group, before we were named Merrill's Marauders. Before Merrill became the general, he was in Japan before the war, and he learned Japanese, and he became friendly with a lot of Japanese officers and generals before the war. And he knew a lot about the Japanese, he knew how to speak Japanese, and he was an engineer and very well trained, you know. That's why Stilwell took him. And the other colonels graduated West Point the same as he did. Hunter thought he was going to be the commanding general instead of Merrill, but he wasn't, he was just a colonel, and the three colonels were all West Pointers; they are not alive today.[42] They'd be about 115 years old if they were alive. None of the officers are alive. They are all West Pointers that graduated in the late '20s. They're gone.

Now I was under General 'Vinegar Joe' Stilwell. He wanted American troops to fight in Burma and he had Chinese troops, three divisions, but he didn't have [American commandos to spearhead any attack]. They had some Chindits which were part Chinese, they were like Indian Chinese, you know. And then they had the Kachins, which were Burmese. The Kachins hated the Japanese with a passion. They fought under Wingate. I don't know if you

---

[42] Charles Newton Hunter (1906-1978) was second in command, but is generally recognized as the de facto field leader of Merrill's Marauders, given Frank Merrill's medical emergencies and evacuation. He was the author of the 1963 book *Galahad*; author and field commander Charlton Ogburn noted in his own book on Merrill's Marauders that 'Colonel Charles N. Hunter had been with Galahad from the beginning as its ranking or second ranking officer, had commanded it during its times of greatest trial, and was more responsible than any other individual for its record of achievement.' Source: Ogburn, Charlton, *The Marauders*. New York: Harper & Brothers, 1956. p. 2. There is more on Hunter's story in Chapter 12.

ever heard of General Wingate. He was a British commando officer, and he trained—or he started to train the Chinese and trained some of the American forces. Wingate started the initial invasion of Burma.

'General Orde Wingate (center) with other officers at the airfield code-named 'Broadway' in Burma awaiting a night supply drop.' Colonel Frank Merrill far left. 1944. Wingate was killed in a plane crash shortly after this photo was taken. Imperial War Museum, public domain.

He sent commandos, Chindit commandos that he trained into Burma to hit the Japanese and then they pulled out. And then he wanted to train the Chinese and later the American forces in guerilla tactics up in Deogarh, India, until he got killed by accident, and we trained without him on that. But he was a commando general, I mean who trained us very well, but we trained without him on that. Now at that time they needed troops to form the American combat team. But where were you going to get American troops who are jungle fighters? So he asked, and the [British] generals there said,

'No American forces. Let the Chinese fight.' So [Stilwell] went over their heads to the States, and he got permission to gather up 3,000 men if he could, who were jungle experienced. They asked MacArthur at first. MacArthur then asked the troops that fought in Guadalcanal and the islands that they needed—these guys were out at the islands right at the moment—that he needed experienced jungle troops that are willing to volunteer for a dangerous mission; they wanted troops that had jungle experience, and they wound up with 650 experienced, tough New Yorkers to fight and those were the first group. But that's not enough. So he went to the States, and he got a group; some of them that were there were being trained in jungle warfare. So he got another group. He still didn't have enough. So he went to Australia, and he got a small group over there, and then finally the 930th came in to assist them to round out the 3,000 men that he needed.

With 3,000 men, we went up to India to Deogarh. It's a mountainous area. To get into Burma, you've got to climb up the mountains. Remember where the guys climbed up in the mountains 10,000 feet up? The Japanese figured that nobody could go over that there, especially an army because you can't go with motorized troops. So they figured that they were safe. They didn't know the army.

Combat Teams

We were trained in Deogarh with jungles similar to Burma, you know. They'd take us out in groups of five or ten, maybe ten, fifteen miles away from the camp. We looked at the stars and we took a reading, and we had to come back. They gave you a canteen of water and a cheese sandwich and you had to come back at a certain time. And we trained so that we would get harder and get in better physical shape. We were in pretty good shape, but we became even harder until they decided at that time—we didn't have any motorized vehicles, of course, you couldn't take motorized vehicles over the mountains. We had mules; they assigned 700 mules to 3,000 men and troops. Now what they did with the unit is, they broke it up into three units, a thousand, a thousand, and a thousand. Now they took the thousand units, we were still the 5307th Composite Group. They took and they broke each unit up into two groups, sixteen officers and about 460 men in number one, and the same in number two, and then another and a colonel in charge. Then another colonel. There was Colonel Olson, Colonel Beach, and Colonel McGee, the three colonels that were in charge of the three groups. Each group was broken up into a thousand men and then each thousand men was broken up into two groups. And they didn't give—they gave us numbers and colors. That's how we were identified.

White and red and white—or blue and green. I was in the number one group. I was in the white unit, under Colonel Olson. They broke it up so they could form like pincer movements. There were two groups here, two groups here, two groups there. We were not more than a mile and a half or two miles apart, as we were there. Anyway, we went in, we're in groups and over the mountains we came, high out there with the mules and everything. And some of the stuff, the mules had big, big packages on them. They couldn't climb. So we had to carry some of the stuff that the mules couldn't carry to bring over the mountains. And then we're walking almost 500 miles, we're walking for combat. And how many miles do you walk in a day? We're lucky if we walked ten to fifteen miles in a day because you're walking through jungles with cane and mud and everything down below. We had to combat two or three different kinds of mosquitoes, we had to combat leeches, we had to combat the different kinds of leeches. We'd scrape them off with our knives. You know, there's trees that were a couple hundred feet high. And there was the cane, and we had to chop that to get through.

Now, each group were fortunate that we had three or four Kachins as guides. Now they were born in the area, so they knew how to go on certain trails with us, and they went along with us. And I was really fortunate. One of the guys that was in our outfit was Japanese-American, so he was able to speak Japanese, and he would listen to the Japanese issuing orders, and he'd tell us. We were fighting different battles going along, and our first battle that we had to go down was down near Walawbum in Burma. Well, we were fighting battles as we went along.

Now, they broke up the 460 men, they took a unit, a platoon, and they became an intelligence reconnaissance unit. They picked up all the sharpshooters for this group, and these were hardened soldiers that they had in excellent shape. And they were reconnaissance. Then they picked certain ones that they made like medics in the group that—everybody had a job. And the rest of us were the soldiers that went along on that. I was a marksman, but I wasn't a sharpshooter, you know. I could hit the target, but a sharpshooter could hit the bull's eye all the time. I'd hit the target but not necessarily the bull's eye.

We'd travel a lot by night, because at daytime they can see you. The Japanese could be anywhere. You know, each unit of 460 men with our patrols going out and our colonel, we would be group one and color white or whatever, we would go a couple of miles and then we'd stop, we'd go a couple of miles and then we'd stop until we got to our objective. We had the Kachins that were with us, we knew where we were going, but you couldn't make it more than six or seven miles, eight miles in one day, you couldn't go any further. Maybe you could go ten miles, but that would be it. Don't forget, you had to go through cane and swamps and you just—you're not chopping it down because you couldn't chop it all down, it was impossible. I mean everybody had a job and they all traveled together. But the patrols went out without us and they—sometimes they got involved in a fight with another Japanese patrol. And they'd surround them, and they would get rid of them. There was quite a good deal of that.

But we went to all of these places, and we fought the Japanese. See, the Japanese had the 18th, the 55th, and the 56th division of Japanese. These were the three top hardened soldiers that conquered China under General Tanaka. Now he was under another general, but he was in charge of all of these troops, and we're going along, and our first big combat unit was at Walawbum. We had four major battles that we had going in.

The River Crossing

We were in the first big battle that we had, which is across the Irrawaddy River, and we're on the ground over there. And one of the fellows climbs a tree, and he takes a look across the river, and he almost had a heart attack. There must have been a thousand or more Japanese getting ready to cross the river at us. They thought that they would be easy to fight. You know, especially when we only got 400 men in that spot at that moment. The others were around but not close by. And he said, 'They're getting ready to cross the river.' And he was in a tree. He almost fell out of the tree. He said, 'Don't shoot until I tell you,' you know, so we're sitting there and we're waiting until they were across the river, and they were about 300 yards from us. They got a little closer and then he said, 'Fire.' Now all we had for weapons, no heavy equipment, because we couldn't carry it. We had .30 caliber machine guns, .45 caliber machine guns, Browning automatics. We had mortars; I had a carbine, and I had a .45 automatic and a trench knife, and we waited, and they came.

When they were all across the river, and they were coming toward us, and the last of them came, it must have been 100 feet away from us when they turned around and they took off and went back, and we're waiting there in the foxhole, and they came back again, and they took off. And now the Chinese were in back on the flanks with the Chinese army in case they tried to go a different way, the Chinese would surround them, and they would get the stragglers. We were in the middle with one.

There was a reporter from *Life Magazine* with the headquarters company under General Merrill. We also had Colonel Beach, Colonel Olson, and Colonel McGee. Each one had 1,000 men under him. What happened is after the first couple of battles, the guy from *Life* magazine sends reports back to the United States. You know, he's a reporter. So he called us Merrill's Marauders instead of the 5307th Composite, and that's how we got the name Merrill's Marauders from him. And we fought, as I say, altogether in Burma, we must have killed close to 3,000 Japanese. We destroyed the 55th and 56th and 18th Japanese divisions. It must have been 20, 30,000 men there, and we—they must have killed a third of them. We were almost finished as a fighting unit. We had dysentery, we had malaria, we had jungle fever, wounded different guys. And we didn't have semi-healthy guys, we had about 300 men left that were capable of fighting yet a little bit, and Stilwell wanted to take Myitkyina. Now the Burma Road was going through Myitkyina, and the airfield was in Myitkyina they wanted. That was considered a big city with 8,000 people. Now we didn't have healthy troops. So he tells General Merrill what he had, he says he didn't care as long as they can walk and carry a gun to go in and fight and take Myitkyina.

'We Were Through'

We fought the battle on the airfield and destroyed the Japanese in the airfield, and then from there, which they wanted, which the Allies, they needed the airfield, and you've got to remember, the engineers, the 930th that I was originally with, were building the road to Kunming, China. They had to go through that area there and join up with the original road over the mountains, you know, and nobody said you could build it. But General Pick had built, I forgot what dam it was in the United States, but he had been a civilian engineer, and he was in charge of the unit, had built a road, but they needed military protection. That's how the 930th Combat Engineers went along, and they protected them while they were building. But we were the chosen few. And anyway, after the airfield, we went in to take the town. And then after that, there was no more Merrill's Marauders, we were disbanded and they formed a new group called MARS, new recruits that came in, Mars Task Force.[43] Some of the Marauders joined up with them. A few did. They wanted to go to combat, and they went up. And I went in with a group, I was with a group of special forces that went into French Indochina and then we heard that the war was over. We didn't know that they dropped a bomb. You know, we found out afterwards, and our job was to go from there into Shanghai and help to collect weapons and make way for signing a surrender. And that's when from there, that's when I started to go home.

We had enough combat, and we had not only combat. What about the dysentery? What about the dengue fever? What about the jungle fly? What about the leeches? All of that we had. The guys, in order to unfortunately to move their bowels and stuff, they couldn't pull their pants down fast enough, so they'd cut a hole, a slit in their

---

[43] The Mars Task Force was the long-range penetration successor to the Marauders.

slacks, so all they had to do was bend down and open it up so that they could go to the bathroom. And they used to go to the bathroom, they'd dig a hole in their own foxhole and then they'd cover it up because they couldn't go out somewhere and move. I mean that's the story that we had. We ate K-rations when we got them. We didn't always get them; we had the Air Force; we had a group that took care of us. We'd call up by radio, and if we needed water or ammunition or food, within 24 hours the planes would come and drop it to us. This group was absolutely fabulous.

We were in I think about four major battles, and we couldn't—we were exhausted; I think out of all 3,000, 93 were killed, but we had about four hundred something that were with diseases and stuff and wounded and different things, and the rest were—everybody had a disease of some sort or another. I don't think there was anybody that didn't have one. But Stilwell said he didn't care, as long as you could walk and carry a gun, he wanted us to go in. We wound up with 300 of us, and we took Myitkyina, the airfield and the town, and that was our last battle, and then we were through.

The End of the War

I met Ho Chi Minh. At that time the war in Europe was over, and they were going to invade Japan, and in order to invade it, they had to invade French Indochina into China to the coast so we can invade Japan. He was with the officers in the group that were there. He seemed like a nice guy. [The unit was originally helping train him and his fighters to fight the Japanese], that's what they were doing. They were the rebels. The rebel [communist] forces that fought in French Indochina were not part of Chiang Kai-Shek's group. Chiang Kai-Shek was the regular Chinese army, and they didn't like each other. After the war, Chiang Kai-Shek's troops pulled way back, and they didn't bother the Chinese [communist] forces. In the beginning. I was out of China, you know about three or four months later, whatever, they started the invasion of China, and they wanted China, the rebels. [Later], they drove Chiang Kai-Shek and his troops into Taiwan [in 1949], and they took over China.

'He Belongs To Me'

They dropped an atomic bomb, and we got word to stop what we were doing. We said, 'What's an atomic bomb?' We didn't know. And we were going to be picked up by a C-47 and were flying into Shanghai, China, to make way for signing and surrender. When we landed in Shanghai, there must have been two or three hundred Japanese soldiers on each side, you know, standing there saluting us and with their rifles at attention, not shooting us. You know, the Japanese soldier, if you would tell him to kill himself, he'd kill himself. He did what his officers told him. And they told them when we came in that they're supposed to bring all of their weapons—you know what a Quonset hut is? They were to bring them there and bring in their swords and knives and guns to us. And that was one of our jobs, and to pick out suitable quarters for the American forces that were coming in for living quarters in Shanghai. And we're riding around, and that's when I'm looking and I see I've got 146 points, and they're sending guys home with 40 and 39 and 40 points, and I never was home. So when the Tenth Air Force came in, I was by myself when I went in and asked permission to see the adjutant general, and I came in and he asked me my name and rank and who I was with, and he says he heard of us.

He said, 'What can I do for you?'

I said, 'I want to go home.' And I told him I have 146 points, and they're sending guys home, and my outfit is going on to Japan.

I said, 'I don't want to.' I made a mistake, and I'll tell you, if I had to do it over again, I would have gone to Japan. I was a single fellow, and I had an opportunity to go to Japan and I didn't go. You know, and I could have lived high off the hog there. Anyway, I didn't go, and they typed the orders up.

When I came back, my colonel said, 'Where the hell you been?'

I told him; he grabbed me and brought me back and he said to the general, the general asked him, 'What can I do for you?'

He said, 'I want you to get rid of these orders and reassign this man to me. He belongs to me.'

The general said, 'He doesn't belong to you anymore, he's going home on the next ship.' And the colonel turned around, and he looked at me and he didn't even say good-bye. He turned around, walked out, and that's the last I saw of him. A week later I got on a ship and home I went.

[Once I got back], I was going to collect $20 a week for 52 weeks. You know, 52/20 club. I thought to myself, I'll be home, and I'll be unemployed and not do anything for a year. One week home and I was working.

My girlfriend's brother-in-law owned an auto supply business. And he traveled to Wisconsin and Illinois, and he said, 'I'll give you a job.' He said, 'I'll give you the whole state of Wisconsin.' And you're guaranteed when you start to work there, you're guaranteed to make a minimum of $7,000 a year. In 1945, that was a lot of money. 'Plus expenses and we'll give you—we have 35 accounts in Wisconsin, and we'll turn these over to you.' And he showed me. I would work out of a catalog like a dictionary. You would go into a place. The guy says I want a dozen here, a half a dozen here, and you'd write up an order. No problem, they showed you pictures. This is what you did. And I'm running here, I'm running there. I didn't know what the hell I was doing because I wasn't used to it. I was working for a few weeks, and I bumped into a guy in the middle portion of Wisconsin. I saw this guy before. And he walks up to me, and he said, 'My name is'—I forgot his name—he said, 'My name is so and so.'

He said, 'What's your name?' I tell him.

He said, 'What are you doing?'

I said, 'I'm selling automobile supplies.'

He said, 'Do you got the whole state?'

I said, 'Yeah.'

He said, 'Why are you jumping around like you do like a chicken that's out of a nest?'

I said, 'I don't know how to work it.'

He said, 'Break the state up in three sections: west, middle, and east. Pick the middle. Pick a hotel and have a standing appointment at that hotel. Then you go north, and you can go south for the week, but you work out of this hotel, and you have a standing room there regardless of it's snowing or what, it's your room.'

And I did that, I worked here, I worked here, and I worked there. And I was opening up new accounts. I made $35,000 in my first year and quit. I went into the drapery business. I didn't want to work on the road, you know, and be gone. I was gone in the army, and I wasn't home and I'm traveling five days a week, and it was a life I didn't want.

Souvenirs

When I came to the States, I had a carbine, I had a .45 automatic, and I had a trench knife. I wanted to turn it in in Shanghai. They told me that, 'You can't, we don't have any records that it was ever issued to you.'

I said, 'What do I do with it?'

He said, 'Turn it in in the States.' Okay, so I came to the States in the Port of Los Angeles, and I tried to turn it in, and they said, 'We don't have any records.'

I said, 'What do I do with it?'

He said, 'When you go to Fort Sheridan, they'll take it.'

Okay. I come to Fort Sheridan, and I want to turn it in, and they said, 'We don't even know if it was issued to you.'

I said, 'What do I do with them?'

He said, 'Do whatever you want.' So some guy from Chicago, I forgot his name, wanted to buy it. I sold him a carbine rifle, a .45 automatic and a trench knife for $35. I didn't want to come home with a weapon. About five months before I came home, I sent home a Gurkha knife that was presented to me by the Gurkhas, and a Samurai sword, and I came home. I said to my folks, 'What did you do with it?'

They said, 'We never even got it.' This was six months later.

I said, 'Well, I guess I can say good-bye to it.' Two months after I got home—you know, what they did is they piled everything up in big packages, and after the war they sent it all out—I got it. Well, I had gotten married since then, and I had it and the thing was in the basement, and I lived in a house and when I had a child, I said to my wife, 'I'm going to hang it on that wall.'

She said, 'You try to hang it on that wall,' she said, 'and I'll hang you on the wall with it!'

She said, 'No weapons are going up!'

I said, 'What do you want me to do with it?'

She said, 'Sell it.' So I sold it to a police officer in Schaumburg. And I sold the three units for $100; a Gurkha knife, a Samurai sword, and a .45 automatic and a trench knife. From what I understand, if I would have kept it a while longer, I could have sold it for several thousand dollars, but I didn't know any better. My wife told me to sell it, I sold it. I listened to my wife. She's dead now. She died; my girlfriend died. And now I'm by myself again with my friends.

Once in a while I still feel the dengue fever. I talked to my doctor and two other doctors, dengue fever is way worse than malaria. Malaria is minor compared to dengue fever and it stays with you. Once in a while I go to sleep, and I wake up in a cold sweat and I'm shaking like this. And in about an hour, it finally goes away, you know. Not that often but it comes. And I say to myself, well, I'm living with it, I'll live with it and there's nothing I can do, you know. We used to take Atabrine and everything else, and it was there. [Tough service]. And the monkeys used to throw coconuts at us. [*Laughs*]

Still Alive

How many men do you think are alive from the original group? I understand about a month and a half ago up at North Chicago, they had a reunion of some of Merrill's Marauders. I didn't know about it, I found out afterwards, but there weren't very many. There's only a few that came there. I would say to myself out of 3,000, they're lucky if there's maybe 50 of them that are alive, and they're up in my age. You've got to remember the war was over in '45. That's 67 years ago when the war was over. If they were 20 years old when the war was over, they'd be 87 or more. What does that tell you? How many guys are in their late eighties that survived? And I'm very fortunate I'm still here.

I haven't heard from anybody. At first, I thought there was nobody really in Chicago. I went on this honors [flight] trip. I went with a group from Chicago. Nobody on our plane was from the China-Burma-India Theater. Now there was another group from Texas and another group from the south. So roughly there must have been five, six hundred men there altogether. Nobody came from China; I was the only one. I asked all over. And they put up a memorial there, China-Burma-India, and we took a picture of myself in front of the China-Burma-India Theater that they had at the memorial there.

We were greeted—when we came back to Chicago, we were greeted by navy personnel on both sides, you know. And there must have been two, three thousand people in the airport waiting for us to come back home when we came home. It was nice to see. I can't tell you anymore. I remember what I remember.

Morris Factor passed away in 2017 at the age of 96.

Herbert Clofine, World War II. Library of Congress.

CHAPTER ELEVEN

The 4-F Volunteer

Herbert Clofine bucked a 4-F deferment to volunteer for World War II. He was a radioman in the Intelligence and Reconnaissance platoon, 2nd Battalion, Blue Combat Team of the 5307th Composite Unit (Provisional), better known as Merrill's Marauders. He gave this interview at the 59th annual reunion of the Merrill's Marauders Association in Arlington, Virginia, in August of 2005 when he was 85 years old.

Herbert Clofine

I was born in 1919. I was a member of the Merrill's Marauders, which was an infantry unit that served in Burma. Originally, I was a 4-F, unfit for military service, but it got to a point in September of 1942 when I felt that I could be of some value in the service, and I tried to get in but nobody would accept me. And I finally went to my draft board, and I said, 'Look, I'm a 4-F, and I've been to the Army, the Navy, the Air Force, the Marines, the Coast Guard, and none of them would accept me, so put me down as a voluntary draftee,' which they did. Six days later I was on a boat for Trinidad in the British West Indies, where I was assigned to the 33rd

Infantry, which was a regular Army unit before the war stationed in Panama and had then been transferred to Trinidad. I took my basic training there, and then eventually took radio training and became a radio operator. I had charge of an outpost on the coast at that time where we were watching for submarines, and eventually the call came out for volunteers for a dangerous and hazardous mission. And most of us at the unit volunteered, and we were flown back to the States and then eventually ended up in Pittsburg, California, where we boarded the *Lurline*, which is a transport ship, and sailed across the Pacific, taking 38 days, because we traveled unescorted during the war, and landed in Bombay. We trained in India and were formed into the 5307 Composite Unit, Provisional. Our basic mission was to take the only all-weather airstrip in Northern Burma, and the Japanese occupied that entire area. I was assigned to the I&R platoon in the blue combat team.

Our unit was divided into three battalions, the entire 5307th, which was nicknamed Merrill's Marauders by the press. The three battalions were each divided into two columns, red and white, blue and green, khaki and orange. I was a member of the blue combat team assigned to the intelligence and reconnaissance platoon as the radio man. I served with this unit until we took the airstrip at Myitkyina, and then was evacuated from the airstrip, which was the only way of getting out by plane, because we were a pack outfit. There was no motorized vehicles of any kind. I was put in, I believe it was the 110th General Hospital, where I underwent some surgery and then returned to the States. When I got back to the States, I applied for OCS and was eventually commissioned a second lieutenant. I spent six months at Fort Knox, Kentucky, as an instructor in the communications department and then eventually separated from the service.

Unit 'GALAHAD'

The unit, [code-named GALAHAD], had been put together at that time with various troops. We had one battalion composed of members that had been—come up from the Caribbean, and having been in Trinidad, we were part of that. When we got back to the States, we picked up additional troops, which formed another battalion. And then when we were crossing the Pacific, we made a couple of stops on a couple of the islands—I don't remember their names, some of the men will be able to tell you the names of the islands—and picked up seasoned troops who had fought in Guadalcanal and places of that type. When we got to India, we trained and eventually walked up the Ledo Road, and entered Burma. And each battalion naturally had their assignments, and being in the I&R platoon and the blue combat team, we were always out ahead of the rest of the unit, because it was our job naturally to see what was going on, and as the name says, intelligence and reconnaissance, find out what the situation was and report back, and I would report back naturally to headquarters. The first American soldier killed on the continent of Asia was a member of our platoon, Bob Landis. And we continued on and eventually worked our way down. Our entire unit fought five major battles and 32 minor engagements. Our battalion, 2nd Battalion, was at one point surrounded on the crest of a hill called Nhpum Ga, and for twelve days we could not get off until the breakthrough came, but we were eventually evacuated from that location to continue on. I was eventually pulled out immediately with a radio, and with my radio crew, to go back to the closest village to take an air drop the following day. All of our supplies were dropped by air, because we were a pack outfit with horses and mules. I stayed with that unit where I was assigned, which was called K-Force, and so we got to the airstrip at Myitkyina, which was our major objective. Once we had taken the airstrip, and we were in a position where planes could fly in replacements, the 5307th actually ceased to exist. And with the replacements coming in, I believe at that point it became called the 475th Infantry. We stayed on. As I said before, I was evacuated and went into the hospital for surgery and stayed in part of India there until we got our orders to come back.

*

[Some of the things that stick with me], one instance in particular, we were in a certain location and the Japs had occupied an area very close to it, and we were determined that there was some telephone lines that they had strung. So Sergeant Matsumoto and myself—he was one of our Japanese interpreters—were sent out that night, and Roy Matsumoto climbed up and tapped the telephone lines and got information as to troop movement, ammunition supply locations, and so forth, gave me the information, and I radioed it back to headquarters. That was a highlight.

Sergeant Roy Matsumoto was one of fourteen indispensable Nisei soldiers assigned to the Marauders. Born on a small farm in Los Angeles on May 1, 1913, he went to Hiroshima, Japan, at the age of eight to be raised by his grandparents, returning to the U.S. at age 17, finishing high school, and working for a Japanese grocery to support his family during the Depression. There, he learned many Japanese dialects as he delivered groceries to Japanese immigrant families in California, which would prove fortuitous when later fighting in the field.

When the United States began its mass arrest and incarceration of Americans of Japanese descent, Matsumoto and his family wound up in a concentration camp in Arkansas, yet like many young Nisei men, he enlisted in the U.S. Army from behind barbed wire. He was trained as a military linguist, and signed up for hazardous duty with the group.

SGT. Roy Matsumoto

That evening, I took everything out of my clothes. I put the helmet away and left the rifle behind, and I took the canteen, and the pistol belt off, and no weapon. The only thing is I had a bayonet, then a couple of rounds of hand grenades. If I was going to be captured, I was going to blow myself up. Anyway, when I took these gears off, then I told the boys, 'I'm going to come back here, so don't shoot just because you hear the noise. Recognize me first, then let me come in. Don't open up.' Then I crawled down the hill.

They're still talking, and the voice gets louder and louder, so I know I've come very close. I just sat there so I couldn't even sneeze or cough. I was that close, a few feet away.

Then they sat down, and they were talking to their buddies in the foxhole. Then they mentioned about next day at dawn, attacks. Then the other guy asked, he just got information from the commanding officer that they're going to attempt an all-out attack on the perimeter where they're pointing out the direction. I couldn't see it, but they're saying that way. That was the easiest access to come up because there was a gentle slope there, so I knew they would come, but they didn't want to make sure, so I stayed a little longer and found out it was daybreak.

LT. Edward McLogan

Roy came back, and we were all, of course, very quiet. Roy was talking up a storm, and I kept saying to him, 'Quiet.'

He said, 'Well, your area, your platoon is going to be hit tomorrow. The regiment that is surrounding us is going to make a last-ditch effort to breach our lines, and this is the platoon that they've picked to assault.'

With that information, we went back and talked to Colonel McGee, and McGee ordered us to withdraw farther back up the hill, maybe 100 to 200 feet. Further, he directed that we booby-trap our empty foxholes and dig new foxholes farther up the hill, consolidating our lines so we were all a little bit closer together in our perimeter.

The rest of the night passed quietly, but early in the morning, we first heard the enemy talking. Then we could hear them yelling. Finally, we could hear the Japanese screaming at the top of their lungs, 'Banzai!', even that trite 'Death to the Americans,' but in fact, that's what we were hearing, and they broke through into a clearing in front of us. There were two officers and maybe fifty men or so charging up the hill. They were only slightly halted or hesitated, I should say, at the empty foxholes, and at this time, Matsumoto yelled out to them, 'Charge!'

SGT. Roy Matsumoto

They had also reserves behind that were coming up, and then they mentioned about the retreating, so I gave them a counterman order, then I gave them a charge order, and I stood up so that they could hear me, and told them to charge. Then they heard me, so they started to charge up again. Then we come to our close, probably 15, 20, or 30 yards, and we opened up with all our, the platoon's, weapons.[44]

---

[44] In 1993, Roy Matsumoto was inducted into the U.S. Army Ranger Hall of Fame. He passed two weeks before his 101st birthday in April 2014.

Herbert Clofine

Other than that, it was just general operations all the time of—when the unit wasn't fighting, we were [on the move]. We were hiking through some very treacherous terrain. And I mean by the time we got to the airstrip at Myitkyina, those men that were still around—and we lost naturally I don't know how many men, you know, through gun battles and so forth—most of the men were pretty well beaten. When I came out of the jungles of Burma, I weighed 98 pounds.

'Everybody Was A Marauder'

Naturally, we were very close. And naturally, whatever we had done, everybody supported everybody else. And fortunately, that feeling of camaraderie has existed and that's why we are now in our 59th annual reunion, to which I have been to 56 of the 59 reunions, and we've become very close. We've had marriages within the organizations, sons and daughters from various Marauders got married and it's always been a family affair. And one of the interesting things about our reunions, whenever we have guest speakers, which we usually do, we've always made it very explicitly non-political. I mean nobody cares what party you belong to, what religion you are or anything else. Everybody was a Marauder.

Like I said before, out of the three battalions, and each battalion having two columns, there were six units actually operating, and each one of these units could operate by themselves, because they were formed in such a way that they were self-sufficient. So we actually never were active—we were never in combat combined as six units. Each one—and then when the time came and it was necessary, one column would support another. When the 2nd Battalion was surrounded on the crest of the hill at Nhpum Ga, it took the other two battalions to get us released, because we had no control. We couldn't get off that crest of the hill. The Japanese controlled the only waterhole there, and to the point where even water, everything we received as far as supplies had to be dropped by parachute. And up until the time we got to Myitkyina, the only evacuation for seriously wounded was by L4 Piper Cubs. That's the only way they could get out. There were times I can remember where we would carry men that were seriously injured on litters for miles, because we had to find a rice paddy that could, number one, be secured, and which was level enough for a Piper Cub to land on. My recollection is that there were at least a couple of Piper Cubs that crashed in the attempt to evacuate, but that's the only way men could be evacuated—there was no other way, because there were no roads.

The Natives

Northern Burma was primitive. I mean the people that lived there were very nice and everything, as far as, you know, but they were primitive. They lived in bashas that were thatched huts, and I know whenever the occasion did present itself that we were in a village, the natives were very kind to us. I can remember when we were evacuated off of Nhpum Ga and they sent me back to take the air drop with my radios. I stayed in the village that night, and the head man from the village came over to the basha that I was assigned, given, and I was able to get on my radio BBC, British Broadcasting, and it was something that these people never saw or heard. They were completely flabbergasted! So we saw another way of life that we would have never witnessed before, because everything was trails. I mean the terrain, there were places there where we'd walk through mountainous areas that had sheer drops of hundreds of feet. And horses and mules can go so far. As far as I'm concerned, a man will out-walk a horse or mule anytime. I mean they weaken.

And they had to carry any heavy equipment that we had, like our heavy machine guns, and in my case, my larger radio, the SCR-284 had to be packed.[45] If I had to go any great distance, I had the SCR-284 radio that I used to have to mount on a stand, and then have somebody with a generator to generate it, and put up an antenna 25 feet, which you couldn't do in most cases, because it would be a dead giveaway to the enemy, see?

Radio communications, SCR-284. U.S. Signal Corps manual, WWII.

---

[45] SCR-284-Paul Elisha, Joint Assault Signal Company radioman in the Pacific, noted: "Usually, we used what they called an SCR-284. It was about the size of a suitcase, on two folding legs. The lid would plop down and that'd be your workspace. The set was facing you in the rest of the suitcase. And then you have a cable going to a generator, which you turn; that was the worst job of the lot. We lost several people because the generator let out a squeal whenever you had to transmit and that gave away your position. You'd have one SCR-284, the large one with the generator. You'd have a couple of back-pack radios. Then with you, you'd have a few people for fire support if you ran into a hard time supporting your communications setup you had when you dug in."

510 | THE 4-F VOLUNTEER

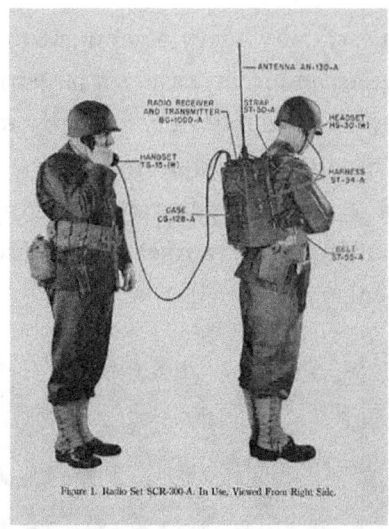

SCR-300 'walkie talkie' radio. Training manual, public domain.

I personally carried a radio on my back the whole time, which was an SCR-300. And the terrain was as much an enemy as the Japanese.

General Merrill

The reason we were called a provisional unit is because according to the TO, Table of Organization in the Infantry, a regiment was commanded by a full colonel. But they gave the command of our unit to a general, so in order to follow procedures in the service and everything, they called it a provisional unit, aside from which it was organized to accomplish one mission. And from what we were told afterward, Washington expected us to have eighty percent casualties. We lost several men, but unfortunately not only through gunfire, but disease. Malaria, typhus, dysentery, which was rampant there, and we survived practically the whole time on rations. So that was it. I mean you carried what you could eat. If you were lucky enough to be near a river, you could hand grenade the river and kill some fish and have a fish dinner maybe, but that was the extent of it.

It was very interesting that in later years we found out that in 1952, General Merrill, who incidentally had two heart attacks while we were in Burma and had to be evacuated, met with General Tanaka, who was the Japanese commanding officer of the 18th Division, which is the Imperial Division of the Japanese Army, who had taken Singapore, so it was their crack unit. And when General Merrill told General Tanaka how many men he had in the field, he was absolutely dumbstruck, because he had a full division of men. And a full division at that time was probably around 18,000 men, I imagine. And we actually had in the field just our 2,400 men; the balance of the men were in the rear echelon, because the rear echelon is where they had to pack everything that was dropped to us and maintain anything, from the statistical standpoint. But when General Merrill told General Tanaka that, he was absolutely amazed, and General Tanaka at that time told him that whenever they passed an area where an American soldier had been buried, his officers put flowers on the grave. So they had a lot of respect for us. Unfortunately we lost General Merrill in 1955. General Merrill was very, very, very well-liked by all the men.

'We Had No Dancing Girls'

I mean look, we had a mission to accomplish, and we—a lot of our boys were young. I know one fellow, he was sixteen years old—how did he get into the service? —who was with us. On the other hand, we some fellows that were older. I was about 24 at that time.

We were there. There was no alternative. There was no alternative. You didn't say, 'I'm going home,' you know, or something like that. 'I'm going to go down and catch a bus back to Calcutta,' or something like that. There was no such thing. You were there, period. [There was no time when you were off the line]; any chance you got, you just sat down or rested. Did the best you could. That's right. But there was nothing else, I mean nothing else, period. I mean whenever we stopped, naturally we had to have security out all the time, because you never knew when you were going to run into the enemy. [In the field], we received no mail that I know of. There might have been mail drops, I'm not sure, but there was no way for us to send out mail or anything like that. They used to send mail home to the families advising, you know, your son is 'killed' or something like that, unfortunately the other way. Someplace that we felt was secure enough, some of the guys would sit around and talk and shoot the bull, you know, like you would. But other than that, not much for entertainment. We had no dancing girls.

Going Home

Once we were evacuated from Burma and sent back to India, a lot of us ended up in hospitals. Like I said, I went into the hospital; I was evacuated from the airstrip on June the 6th of '44, and on June the 7th, I had some surgery done. It was actually why I was a 4-F to begin with. I had a weak wall in my abdomen. I had had a ruptured appendix as a teenager, and it left me with a weak wall in the abdomen. When you came to being evacuated from Burma from the airstrip, the medical officers were there— 'Why are you leaving?' You had to have a reason. So most of the cases it was FUO, fever of undetermined origin. In my case, I said I have an incisional hernia, so they evacuated me, and once we got out of the hospital and we were in a staging area in India, we knew that we would be going back. So evacuation was just a question of when, what your schedule was. You were tickled to death when you finally landed. I know we flew out of Karachi and made several stops in between. If I remember right, we stopped in Cairo, we stopped in Tripoli, and we stopped in Casablanca. And in Casablanca, we had to be put in a staging area to wait for assignment to fly back to the States. And it was usually a case of a day, or overnight, or whatever it was. And when we got to the staging area, a friend of mine and myself, we found out that about half a mile down the road was a roadhouse that served meals and everything else, so we crept underneath the fence and we got down to this roadhouse that night, and we had a great meal and a couple bottles of wine. My friend was a tech sergeant. I was a buck sergeant at the time. And by the time we got back to the post, we looked at the bulletin board and saw that we had missed our schedule to fly back! And they were having a lot of problems with troops that were taking off at that point and staying out, away, and they said if you miss your plane, you'd be broken in rank and lose two-thirds of a month's pay. Well, we didn't want this to happen. So this friend of mine and myself, we caught a bus down to the airstrip. And when I got there, I went up to the lieutenant in charge and I said, 'We're scheduled to fly out at such and such. Where's the plane?'

He said, 'Up there!'

I said, 'Uh-oh. What are we supposed to do? Look, we've been overseas for over two years. We fought in Burma and everything. What can you do for us?'

He happened to be a real nice guy. He said, 'I got a mail plane coming through 6:00 tomorrow morning. Go lie down on the bench over there, and when the plane comes in, I'll let you know, and I'll send you back on that.'

Sure enough, the mail plane came in, and Bill and I were put on that plane with nothing but mail bags, and he and I flew back to the States in that, so that made it interesting. We got back, and we were given leave at the time when we got back and told when to report back and everything, and then we were assigned to a post in

Louisiana, which they had just reopened, and they were converting troops from branches of the service other than infantry into infantry for the final push in Europe. And the first thing we did in there, we were lined up and we saw what was going on there, and I approached the captain. I said, 'What's happening here?'

He said, 'Well, we're training troops to go to Europe.'

I said, 'Sergeant Angelo and myself just came back from overseas. We fought in Burma!' I said, 'No way.'

He said, 'Well, that's what it is.'

I said, 'Well, I'll tell you what. We'll both go before an OCS board, Officer Candidate School. We both qualified.'

He said, 'Well, there's no board here. We just reopened the post.'

I said, 'Well, then, get me an appointment with the IG, the Inspector General.' Well, at the time they couldn't refuse you that privilege. So I went to the IG and told him our story. He says okay, and set up a board, and Bill and I were both assigned to go before the OCS board, which, of course, was a snap. And we both applied to go to Fort Benning, which was the Infantry OCS School. That's all we knew was infantry. And they sent him to Fort Benning. They sent me to Fort Knox, Kentucky, armored force. Well, all these motorized vehicles, I didn't even know how to drive an automobile, but I stayed on and graduated number one in the class and got my commission. And like I said, I stayed on for six months after I was commissioned and taught field operations in the communications department. That was already—that had to be '45, I believe. I was always in the retail business. I was a department store buyer before I went into the service, and I went back into the retail business. That's where it was, home, in Philadelphia.

Observations

A good part of my personal life has been my activity with the Merrill's Marauders Association. I have been active since the first reunion with the organization. This is our 59th, and I've been to 56 of them, and I've been the treasurer of the outfit now for the past 20-some years, whatever it is. I mean, your family gets to know that come this time of year, you're going to be in a reunion, period. And like I say, it's always been a family affair. There are people here now with their sons or daughters, grandchildren. We exist where a lot of other organizations, divisions that had thousands of men don't get the kind of turnout and camaraderie that we have. It's important to us.

[I guess my experience in the war influenced my thinking about war today]; of course, when I see what's happening today, it's so foreign. I look and I see the equipment these people have today. I mean they walk around with a radio that's [tiny]; I carried a radio on my back that was [huge], big, heavy thing, and it would only go so far. But today, they have [the newest] technology. They have these glasses that they wear that you can see at night. I mean, armor and vests. We had what we had on our backs. I think I went for months without a pair of socks even! And then, of course, the rains over there, we stayed wet for days at a time. You could only have what you could carry on your back. You can't carry a hell of a lot on your back, because you're carrying ammunition, and you're carrying your firearms, and in my case a radio, and it's altogether different, and I see what they have today. Unfortunately, the war today [in Iraq], I mean I don't consider—that, to me, is not even a war. Maybe it's an insurrection; I don't know what it is. I mean I see pictures in the paper that the press has, and it shows the people that are actually the enemy. Well, if the press can take pictures of these people, why can't you shoot them? That's my theory. Kill them.

That's what you're there for. You're not there to have a conversation. I don't know. I don't want to get into that, because I'm opposed to the whole thing. But equipment-wise and everything, compared to what we had... [But] I'll tell you, fortunately we had great medical personnel with us. That was very important, because they had to do everything in the field under adverse conditions. I mean they did amputations when they had to. They were great, and they've stayed active with the outfit, those that are still living. I think there's one left, he was supposed to be here, and he's out there in Johns Hopkins—his name is James Hopkins. He was the one who wrote that book we have, *Spearhead*.[46] Our medical personnel were great. And, of course, at these reunions, everybody's on a first-name basis. Nobody knows who was a captain, who was a major, who was a private. It doesn't make any difference. Everybody's the same.

*

I observed that in recent years, I think there's been more recognition of the Second World War than there was in the years before. I mean here lately, I see a lot written up about it, you know, the units and so forth. We've been documented in a lot of places; the History Channel did two documentaries on us. There's been several books written, a couple of books written by members of the organization itself. But other than that, I find that there seems to be a little—a little resurgence of interest in World War Two that didn't exist. They don't teach it in the schools. I walked into an elevator one day, and I wear these [Merrill's Marauders] shirts often, I have many of them I wear to the gym all the time. I got on an elevator one time, and somebody looked at it and said, 'Merrill's Marauders, what was that, a rock group?' Well, that's what it is. People have no appreciation, I don't think we appreciate what some of these guys

---

[46] *Spearhead*- Hopkins, Dr. James. *Spearhead: A Complete History of Merrill's Marauder Rangers.* Merrill's Marauders Assn. Inc. 736 pages.

in Iraq are going through today. Not knowing what's there, and they don't know what they're going to run into, because what they're doing there with these bombings and stuff, that, to me—that's not war. First of all, that whole Middle East thing, I mean that's ridiculous. Of course, it's become very political unfortunately. I feel sorry for a lot of them, especially the married men with families at home. I mean I look at the paper, and I'll read an account of somebody. He's got a wife and four children, but he knew that when he went in. Sure, he was going to get paid for the time he put in the reserves, but you don't do that unless you're prepared to accept the consequences. That's the way I look at it. You know, like I say, I only know certain things—being isolated like we were, especially in my platoon, which was all I&R, we were sometimes a day or two ahead of the rest of the unit, the rest of the outfit. The first man killed, Bob Landis, was in my platoon. And the first man to kill a Jap in our unit was Werner Katz, who fought on the islands before he came with us, and was a refugee out of Germany as a young man. Very interesting individual. We got a great group. That's about all I can tell you; I hope it's an experience I'm not only sharing with you, but for generations to come, because there will always be wars, honey, as far back as you can read.

Herbert Clofine passed away in 2009 at the age of 89.

CHAPTER TWELVE

The Radio Wizard

Robert Passanisi was born on July 24, 1924, in Brooklyn, where his father was a bricklayer. As the youngest of twelve children, he grew up with a fascination for radio, and as a teenager learned to repair radios from his older brother. In 1942, the 17-year-old altered his birth certificate so that he could join the Army, the only service branch recruiting high-school dropouts. Soon, like most of Merrill's Marauders, he found himself in Burma after volunteering for a hazardous mission, a radio operator and repairman with the 1st Battalion. He sat for this interview in 2005 at the Merrill's Marauders reunion in Arlington, Virginia, when he was 81 years old.

Robert E. Passanisi

I come from Brooklyn, New York. I enlisted at the Number One Jay Street, I think it was, and was inducted in Governor's Island. I had gone to see the movie *Bataan*, and I was so infuriated coming out of that movie. I was 17 years old and hadn't graduated high school yet, so the first place I went to was the Marine Corps. The Marine Corps didn't take anybody without a high school diploma at that time, although they did take 17-year-olds, see. I went to see the Navy, which also took 17-year-olds, but the Army was [the only service branch] that didn't require a high school diploma, [but was] only taking 18-year-olds and up, so I had to play a little game with my birth certificate to get into the Army. [*Laughs*] So I joined the Army and was given orders for basic training with my folder stating 'Signal Corps,' because I had been repairing neighborhood radios and was into radio from about when I was 13 years old. After the induction center at Camp Upton, Long Island, I was sent to Seagate, New Jersey, for basic training and then to Fort Monmouth, where I studied aircraft radio repair. After coming out of Fort Monmouth, we were sent to Fort Hamilton in Brooklyn, an embarkation center ready to ship overseas to Europe.

Somehow or another, the orders got mixed up, and on the day that I was to ship out, I was in the hospital, which I would have signed myself out of at the time. So now I'm kicking around at Fort Hamilton for a month or two where they were giving me leftover jobs. I wasn't the best-behaved soldier at Fort Hamilton. They gave a one-evening pass for about four hours, but since I lived in Brooklyn, that wasn't going to do, so I learned how to go over the fence by the parkway at Fort Hamilton.

After spending a few months at Fort Hamilton, I believe this was sometime in the spring of 1943, I was already in the Army for a year and was sent to A.P. Hill, Virginia. I was first sent to Fort Meade in Washington and found that the outfit was in training at A.P. Hill, Virginia. It didn't take long for me to see that this was not the organization I wanted to serve with. It seemed that everybody and his brother was an OCS washout, and the worst thing is to be with a group of men who think they're officers, but aren't.

'I Wanted To Do My Part'

I had already applied for paratroop training; I also had applied for commando training, and nothing occurred. I always had the feeling that I wanted to do my part. I had brothers in Europe, and I always felt that if I did my part, things would balance out, and they wouldn't have to do as much. So when the call came for volunteers for jungle warfare, preferably a radio mechanic, since they wanted radio men in the Signal Corps, I volunteered. Out of the 247 men in the company area, there was only one volunteer. If I needed justification for not wanting to serve overseas with that group, that was it.

Figuring that I had volunteered for various things before and the Army takes forever, I thought I would still have time. That was a Friday morning. That Friday afternoon, I was instructed that I was restricted to the company area, and on Monday morning, I was on the train to San Francisco! The following Monday, I was on the SS *Lurline*, the ship going overseas.

Now at this point, the request was for volunteers for a 'hazardous mission,' which had become a commonplace term at that time. The company was told there would be a three-month training and a three-month mission, and that would end it. It was indicated that it was going to be a dangerous mission, and that's why nobody else volunteered. Well, not only that, I heard, 'What are you, crazy? What are you doing that for?' from the background.

Anyway, I was on the *Lurline*, and we were out three days; while I was on the *Lurline*, the public address system had us practicing 'abandon ship' drills every day. On the third day, we didn't have any abandon ship drill. Lo and behold, on the fourth day, the first electrician of this merchant marine vessel approaches me and asks if I was Passanisi, and I indicated that I was. He just said, 'Come with me.' So, I went with him.

He takes me up to the bridge and introduces me to the ship's captain. I had just turned 19 now, and here I was on the bridge of a vessel like this, being introduced to the captain! If there was ever a time I was nervous, that was it. He takes me to the bridge, where they have a wall with the radio equipment and four racks of amplifying systems. In those days, they used tubes, which few people know about now. And I must have had some oversight from some heavenly instructions because I look at this entire system, and I'm awed by the size of it. I assumed that since nothing worked—none of the systems worked—the pre-amplifier unit, which was in the center, would be common to everything. So, I pulled the pre-amplifier unit out and discovered that there was a charred resistor. Resistors are those things that you find in your TV set. I knew enough about radio repair to know that the resistor didn't burn by itself. So, I checked further and found a leaky or shorted capacitor. Fortunately, the electrician showed me a cabinet that had every part number of every item that was in the unit. We took the two components, replaced them, put the thing back, and with the help of God, it worked.

Well, the rest of my trip on the *Lurline* was a very pleasant trip, because I didn't have to wait in the 12-hour chow line. The chow line was 12 hours long! You got on the chow line, you had two meals a day, and we had like 3,000 troops on the chow line, so it would take all day to serve them, and you'd be in time to get back on the chow line. So, you did your sweeping, your gambling, your washing while you were on the chow line. I didn't have to go through that anymore. I was able to eat after the officers left the mess. The steward was instructed to serve me whatever they had.

The 'Song Of India'

I met at this time another fellow by the name of Milton Gray, who was a radio announcer. The two of us, now that we had extra leniency, put on a music request show for the rest of the troops. We occupied the radio room and were able to broadcast onboard the ship. Our theme song was the 'Song of India.' We had found that out from the merchant marines about where the ship was headed, see, but nobody on board knew; nobody equated it; Milton Gray and I were the only ones who knew that the theme song meant something.

So, we got to Bombay, India, after about thirty days. Oh, we picked up most of the men from the 3rd Battalion. We had stopped in Australia at two of the ports. The total three ports that we stopped at were Perth, Brisbane, and I forget the other one, but we only stopped at two ports coming up, and I don't remember which one was which. We also picked up some men at one of the islands before going, which constituted most of our 3rd Battalion.

My first impression at the time we landed in Bombay, after looking over the side of the ship, was disbelief that the United States government, our government, would send us to this godforsaken place. The natives that came aboard ship, I was afraid to brush into them because everything looked so filthy and shocking. I never knew such a thing could exist, even though I was brought up in the streets of Brooklyn.

I carried a loaded Thompson submachine gun on the train, just in case. At that time, I was a Technician 5th Grade, which is a noncommissioned grade. I was in the communications platoon. The writer of the book *Marauders*, Colton Ogburn Jr., was my platoon leader. Another officer, Lieutenant Bright, was also assigned to the platoon, but he hadn't arrived yet. He was involved in the design and procuring of the first twelve units that we used for radio communication that were able to float. If you closed them up, they floated, and they were also more efficient than the radios that the Army had up until then. At that time, they used the radios on mobile troop carriers and whatnot, and you had to crank the radio energy by hand.

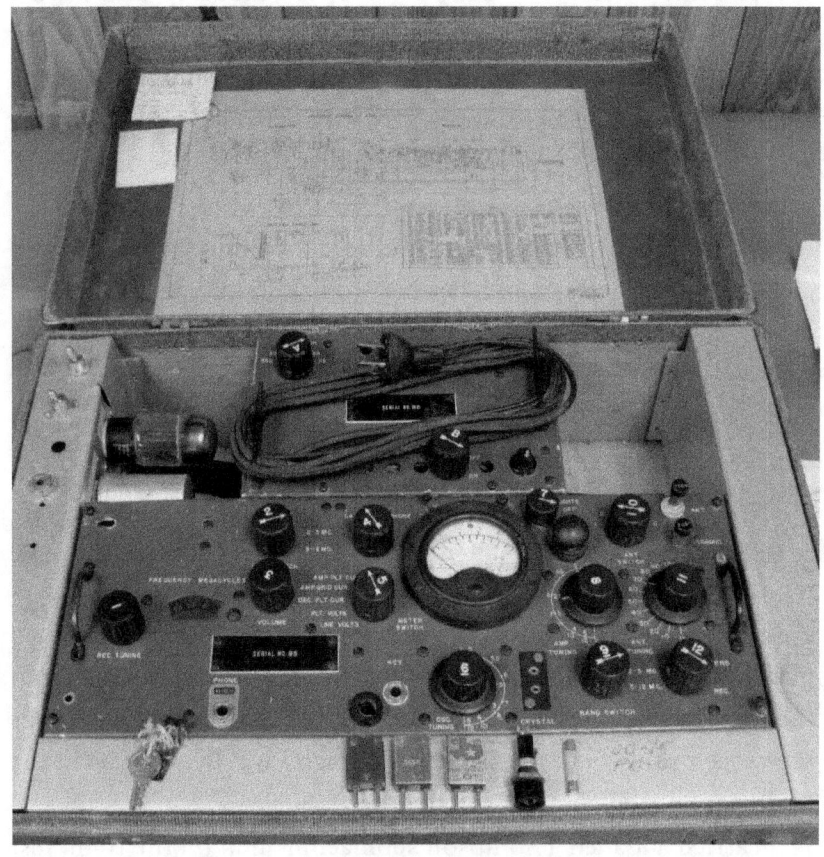

AN/PRC-1 Radio
"*Originally designed for use by Army Intelligence, some of these radios were used by the Office of Strategic Services. The radio is concealed in a suitcase.*" *U.S. Air Force photo, public domain.*

The radios were the AN/PRC-1 and AN/PRC-2. One was for the lower frequencies, and one was for the higher frequencies. At that time, a megahertz was considered a pretty high frequency. So we had radios from, let's say, one to two megahertz, and the higher frequency radios were from two to four megahertz. Nowadays, your cable is transmitted at gigahertz, which is a thousand times a megahertz. Radar is now up to the area of infrared light, around the 200-gigahertz area.

So anyway, the radios weren't difficult for me. We also had these portable radios, which were 18-tube transceivers that were good for about a 10-mile range in the jungle. You managed to get two or three miles with rather reliable coverage. We also had what they called the handy talkie, which was about double the size of a cigarette carton and shaped like that, which were absolutely worthless. We eventually threw them all away as they weren't good for ten feet in the jungle.

My job was to keep that equipment for the entire 1st Battalion going. The radio mechanic of the 2nd Battalion was a great guy, but he was predominantly an automobile mechanic. So, Sergeant Bellard, who was the radio man for the 3rd Battalion, and I, from the 1st Battalion, always helped out the 2nd Battalion, depending on who they were with. The SCR-300 was a tremendous asset that weighed about 65 pounds with a 30-pound battery. It didn't have any better ability than your wrist-type cell phone, but that was state-of-the-art then. The 18 tubes required energy to illuminate and heat up, so the batteries were very sizable. The hand-cranked generators for the other radios were the only way to power them at first.

To communicate with the liaison planes, they used a frequency in the 4 MHz region. The only thing we had that could cover that was a mobile-mounted-type radio, the SCR-284, which was very inefficient compared to the others and very hard to generate power for. For the liaison planes, the Piper Cubs that we used, I eventually got a hold of one that I was able to get onto for a moment. I hooked up one of the SCR-300s and jury-rigged an antenna on the plane to replace the whip antenna that the radio came with, and we used that to communicate. Now he could communicate with the walkie, the backpack, or the portable radios, and we didn't have to set up the hand-cranked generator. But for the airdrops, we still had to use the larger radio because it wasn't as easy to hook up a portable radio on the C-47.

Mules

Everything we had we carried on our backs or carried on our mules. But what was bad was when a guy from Brooklyn has to take care of this stinkin' mule. I have to say that after a while you became dependent upon the mule, and you appreciated the mule, and you took care of him, especially when you took a ten-minute break, and the mule sits down. But now your break is gone, because now you can't get the mule back up. You have to unpack the mule, get the mule up, and repack it. There's your ten minutes. So after a while you learn how to keep the mule from sitting down. Once they're down, they're not getting up until you unload them.

Shooting

Radio repairman was like a secondary item; during the daytime or while you're on the road in the field, you are an infantryman, the same as everybody else. My baptism of fire was at Walawbum. We were on a riverbank in Walawbum, and we dug in there. The Japs were trying to cross the river to get through it, but we had the ideal position. The 3rd Battalion, which was upriver from us, took the brunt of the attacks, but we had a couple of waves down where I guess they tested our area. Probably the reason we were so successful was that the Japanese were in the habit of charging these banzai attacks, where they would come in waves. A wave would run, firing at the enemy, then hit the ground, and the second wave would come to run over them, and they would then alternate. Whether there was a third wave or not, I don't recall. That's okay if you can overwhelm the enemy, but everybody had semi-automatic weapons, such as the Garand M1 rifle, which was an absolutely startling gun from my standpoint. You could fire rather rapidly; you could put 8 rounds in less than a second, and you could fire just as quickly as you could locate a target. I had grown up, in my earlier days, with a BB gun, and that's one of the reasons why I think that restricting youngsters from playing or having guns is not necessarily a great idea. I learned to shoot, to light wooden matchsticks at 15 or 20 feet. I don't know if you're familiar with them, but a wooden matchstick is about that long, and it has a head about an eighth of an inch in height. The little tip of it, the phosphorus tip, if you just strike it, would ignite the match. Nowadays, your safety matches have to be struck on the proper surface for them to light. Well, you could hit that little tip, just about an eighth of an inch in size, with a BB and light the match. That was the game. That means that when you start to fire a regular rifle, you have a more inherent feel of how you should aim and fire.

So with the M1, I must say that in basic training with the Springfield, I barely was able to make marksman. I've got a weak right eye, and the 1903 Springfield, which was the original rifle of World War I and still used in World War II, had a very small peep sight. When I tried to view through it, it would tend to blur out on me. The M1 had a slightly larger sight, and I could clearly see my target with my right eye and keep my left eye open on the target so I could see what was going on. This allowed me to call the shot, a very important aspect of shooting. Calling the shot means that you squeeze the trigger and don't know precisely the instant it will go off, but you keep your eye on the target, so you know where the bullet actually went. If you jerk the trigger, you have no idea. With the M1, I was able to achieve an almost perfect score, except for the standing position, where I couldn't hold the rifle steady enough to hit a bullseye every time. I felt that with the M1, anything I aimed at was going to hit. Therefore, I protected the front sight on that rifle because it was extremely important to know what I could aim at and hit.

'They Would Go Wild'

Our main training, I think, was with Lieutenant Ogburn. He was a great officer in training, and he got us running double time on everything we did. We went to the mess hall, we ran; we went everywhere running, which was good conditioning. In that manner, in the field or in the jungles, I would prefer him over most any other officers. He was a college graduate, a Harvard graduate, and I got the impression that he felt he was there serving his penance and that he shouldn't mar his reputation or his record, so he was entirely by the book, but one of the things that won the war, I think, is the free-thinking aspect of the American soldier, and this group was probably the most free-thinking you could get. You could throw a switch night and day. In the training at the agoge, they were the most undisciplined people you can get. I was still very idealistic and didn't stray at all, but about half of our unit was AWOL during the Christmas holidays of 1943. A couple of guys that were drunk in the company area managed to get some stuff called bullfighter rum, and it probably had 100 octane gasoline in it or something. They would go wild, and there was one incident where they were firing through the top of the tents, through all the tents, with machine gun tracers. The officer of the day, I think at the time, I don't remember who it was, but as I recall the incident, he wasn't able to control that, and it was too dangerous to try. So when General Merrill took over a few weeks later, he made the announcement that there would be no court-martials. By the first week of January, everybody who was AWOL, though maybe like 98%, 99%, returned. They were all ready to go, and General Merrill passed the word along that there would be no court-martials, so he became a superhero.

When I read the book *Galahad,* written by Colonel Hunter, who was a true strategist and a true combat officer—not really to put Merrill down, but Merrill was really Stilwell's representative—Hunter was a combat officer, no question. A lot of us owe our lives to Hunter's strategy. Anyway, in reading the book *Galahad,* Hunter naturally got extremely mistreated by Stilwell, and Merrill for that matter, so his book wasn't very complimentary. The reason why Merrill didn't have any court-martials was that Army regulations require that a general court-martial has to operate under the rules of the regimental command. We were a unit, not a regiment, and we had no regimental command. The only regimental headquarters was formed by Hunter, and the name 5307th Regiment was what he got as a designation, but I'm not even sure whether that was official. For about three days, we were the 5307th Regiment, and then when Merrill came in, because a general leading a regiment is kind of a put-down, they changed the name to unit.

So now you have a unit and it's provisional, which I always felt meant expenditures. So he couldn't legally court-martial anybody except at the company level for company punishment and such. So he took advantage of this great moment and whitewashed all court-martials, which worked because, I mean, everybody in combat, as I started to say, it was entirely different. You never had a concern about whether the guy who was supposed to be there was there. He was there. Everybody did their job. We didn't have anybody who slacked off or anything. We had one person, when we left Ledo, who was a misfit in our group. He had a mental problem, and we tried to get Sergeant Sylvie, who at the time was a tech sergeant in command, to get the medics to move this guy out and especially take his Tommy gun away from him. So while we were on the Ledo Road on this initial 100-mile trip, on the sixth day, I think, we went by the 20th General Hospital about that time, and he had put his Tommy gun into his mouth and pulled the trigger one night. I took it that he was extremely fearful of going into combat, and I could not understand why, if you're willing to die, why didn't you at least make yourself into a hero? I mean, if you're willing to die, that's the greatest thing you need is somebody who's willing to take every chance there is. So I could never understand that; I still remember that.

Marching Past The Hospital

Talking about the 20th General Hospital, the Japanese were within 25 miles of the 20th General Hospital, and the Chinese were losing ground all the time, and they were waiting for orders to pull out, and they couldn't understand why they got so frightened that their ward boys and such, the conscientious objectors, were going behind a hospital and starting to practice shooting a rifle. And then the one morning they wake up and they see infantry, American infantry, GIs—not British, not Chinese, there's nothing better than an American infantryman—and they see this endless column. It took us three days to pass the hospital. Well, we were ten feet apart per man, and between each squad there was like twenty, you know, we were spread out—the 1st Battalion went through, then the 2nd Battalion went through, and then the 3rd Battalion went through. So for three days they had this American infantry coming through, and it's like they were getting a new lease on life. The 45th Engineers or the quartermaster that were there, they got out the band, and they marched like ten miles with us, and then hurried back to pick up another group. They carried water and blister bags, blister bags maybe 200 pounds, and they would carry water, just whatever they could do. There wasn't enough that they could do for us. Of course, this was great because if you wound up in the 20th General Hospital, you got great attention, and that's what most of our boys did.

Food And Sickness On The Move

With the food, the worst situation was to eat K-rations and not even get a full complement of K-rations. You tended to get three days' worth of K-rations, but they didn't have to be a breakfast, dinner, and supper unit. You could have gotten five breakfast units or six supper units, and you can't imagine how it works. K-rations have a K-1 cracker and a K-2 cracker, so you would eat the two crackers when you start, and you find that you like the K-1s better or K-2s, and then you would be eating only the K-1 crackers, and then you reach the point, and you're trading K-2s for K-1s with somebody else, and you reach the point you can't eat another K-1 cracker, so you now are eating K-2 crackers, and that goes on for a couple of days. Now, the cracker is a hard cracker. It's about an inch and a quarter wide or an inch and a half wide, about three inches long, and about, the one cracker was like maybe a quarter inch thick and they would fit in the K-ration meal. The breakfast unit had supposedly pork and eggs, and it was the greasiest garbage you could ever possibly imagine. It wasn't really edible, but you could manage. The supper unit had the, I think it was corn, pork, loaf, which was worse than the breakfast unit. It was so bad but you're so hungry that I found that the burnt paper liner on the corn loaf was edible. The lunch unit had cheddar cheese, crepe cheddar cheese or something like that, but you can't eat all cheese, and you didn't get it all the time. You had a D-bar sometimes. That D-bar was an enriched chocolate bar about the size of a Chiclet package or Lifesaver package, and you also had Dextro-maltose tablets, which was supposed to be good for you, but they weren't that readily edible. The lemon also came in one of the units, I think it was the lunch unit, which was like very acidy. You couldn't make lemonade and use it. The breakfast unit had instant coffee, which went like fire, and the supper unit sometimes had bouillon powder. That went great, but then cigarettes, well, they must have been packed 50 years beforehand, because if you lit one of those cigarettes up, it would burn halfway down and flame out. So anyway, food was a terrible problem. We tried eating bamboo shoots because the mules ate them, but they weren't really digestible that well. If you managed to kill a couple of Japanese that were cooking, you got some rice, but the Japanese, if they were abandoning an item, they would urinate on the rice. That sometimes didn't make any difference, you know, but other than the staying alive from day to day, that was the most difficult item, and everybody had some form of diarrhea, some amoebic dysentery, but everybody had diarrhea, and bad. Everybody ran a fever. You had to run a fever of a hundred and three plus for three days to be considered sick. So when I got evacuated for running a fever, I was shocked because I didn't know I had that high a fever; I felt all right. I get to the 20th General Hospital, and I think I got a reprieve on life. I'm great. They wouldn't let you in a hospital. You stripped, dumped the clothes in a pile, they threw gasoline on and ignited it. [*Laughs*] Then you showered with GI soap.

So anyway, I'm talking to this nurse, thinking that somehow or another I feel like I got away with it, [being evacuated though I thought I felt okay]. And all of a sudden, I said to her, 'I feel faint,' and she took one look at me, shoved the thermometer in my mouth, took my pulse, and then went running and left the thermometer in my mouth! I took it out, and the last thing I remember was 105.2, and I put it back in. [*Laughs*] About two weeks later, I woke up; I don't know whether I was unconscious [the whole time]. They loaded us with Atabrine and quinine and sulphaguanidine, and fish-filled pills, and the requirement to drink, I don't know, was 320cc's of water, so you would wind up just throwing the pills in your mouth and doing it. But anyhow, your skin was all yellow, your eyes, you looked more Oriental. It took two to three months after I got home for my eyeballs to finally clear up, and when I got home, I was 125 pounds. This is after spending three days at Fort Dix and five days on the train and a couple of weeks in quarantine in Angel Island, I think it was, in the Pacific, and I was eating well there. So now I got home, and I weighed 125 pounds; [I was 185 before that].

Home

Now the first week I was home, the family was still on meat rationing. So I ate, I didn't realize it at the time, but I consumed my wife's and son's and my meat rations in the first week. So now I was eating eggs, like twelve eggs a day. I was eating raw eggs, hard-boiled eggs, sunny-side-up, scrambled, and that went on until, like the K-rations, you reach a point and then you couldn't look at another one. And I've never been able to give my wife a good enough explanation on how I came to volunteer to go overseas and leave a pregnant wife at home. [*Laughs*] I don't think there is any such thing as a good explanation... I had a baby boy who was born while I was overseas.

Last Words

Like every Marauder, it's only now starting to fade from memory, because probably everything is fading from memory now, but it was the most prominent time of our life. It's what has been embedded into your brain, and things that happened there keep coming about, like no other happening, no other incident or three-month time, or four-month time, has been recorded so thoroughly in your brain. And probably every single Marauder, when they came out of the service, weren't great guys to live with. I certainly look back and see some of the difficulties that people must have had with me. I couldn't stand certain noises, I was on edge a lot. Let's see, in 1950, we moved out to Long Island, and my first time that I wasn't working, and I was home during a weekday, Republic Aircraft jets were flying in, which was a common thing my wife was used to, but I wasn't. This is the first time I heard them, and that sounded to me like incoming artillery. I'm standing in the kitchen doorway, my son is there, my wife is there, and I'm looking to dive on the ground there, and this is five years later! When my wife realized what was happening, she calmly said, 'Those are the jets from Republic.' I wasn't as bad off as those that I've talked to on the internet, the family members that I talked to on the internet. Some of them took to drinking and never stopped. Some of them were divorced twice. Some of them left home. It was probably the percentage of Marauders that had domestic difficulties or difficulties adjusting to civilian life were probably much more than any other group. Today, they look upon it as combat neurosis or something like that, and, well, we didn't know about it then.

I'll [close with] my favorite statement. 'When America no longer is the home of the brave, it'll no longer be the home of the free.'

Like several Marauders in this book, Mr. Passanisi was an Army Ranger Hall of Fame inductee. He passed in 2022 at the age of 97, leaving less than a handful still alive.

Warner Katz, World War II. Library of Congress.

CHAPTER THIRTEEN

The Immigrant

Warner Katz came of age in Nazi Germany, a Jewish kid who felt the winds beginning to shift as Hitler came to power. He managed to follow an older brother to Italy as the doors were closing on German Jews by smuggling through Switzerland. When that too became uncomfortable, he arrived in New York in 1938 with the help of a friend of his uncle. His mother and her sisters perished in the Holocaust; his father died in Frankfurt. His brother later followed him to New York, where Warner basked in the freedom, struggling with a new language but holding down various jobs. He was drafted into the Army before he had citizenship and wound up fighting in Guadalcanal; from there he volunteered for hazardous duty and served as a staff sergeant and one of the lead scouts with the Marauders. He was credited with being the first American soldier to kill a Japanese soldier in the Burma campaign, and he was also likely the first one wounded, an occurrence which triggered an Army 'Killed in Action' telegram back home to his brother and family. He sat for this interview in 2005 at the Merrill's Marauders reunion in Arlington, Virginia, when he was 86 years old.

Warner Katz

Fifteen years old, and I'd been through the Swiss border and into Italy; I had a brother in Italy. I can speak Italian [besides German]— but they sent me, when I'm Italian and German, they send me to the Pacific. [*Chuckles*] I was drafted. [I had been drafted] in June 1941 [when I was twenty-one], before Pearl Harbor, [and I was in until] June or July 1945. I never had any leave until I came back to the United States. We never had leave.

I was in basic training at Camp Jackson, South Carolina, and I started December 7th. I was supposed to be in Maine, but I volunteered to go with 182nd on Panama Canal to Australia. We were the first troops to land in Australia.

We went through California training and the Marine Corps invaded Guadalcanal on August 7, 1942. The Army relieved some of the Marines in September and October. I went in on October 13 to Guadalcanal. When I came from Guadalcanal, we went to the Fiji Islands and one day they lined us up and they asked for volunteers for a dangerous and hazardous mission, and I volunteered. I wanted to get the war over with and I volunteered for the Marauders. It was called 5307 Unit. It wasn't then called the Marauders; later on, it was named Marauders.

I was only at my first citizen papers and the war started after December 7, but if you were drafted, you became a citizen. I never officially became a citizen until I went into Burma. Later on, I was in the hospital in India, from where General Stilwell would send us back to the front lines. I said, 'Before I go back there, I would like to be a citizen of the United States.' So a man from the State Department and four soldiers, one Mexican, one Scottish, and I think one Italian and me, we got our citizen papers in India. Finally, I became a citizen of the United States.

'You Become A Fatalist'

I went all the way to Myitkyina, all the way through all those five battles. I had already [had special training for this jungle warfare] on Guadalcanal. You know what I mean? First, I was a machine gunner and then I used to go every second day on patrol. So what becomes a veteran, and people get killed next to you, or you kill, and you get over that fear, you become a fatalist. You become a veteran, in my opinion. You know what I mean? You're always scared like hell, but you still keep alert. You know, you do your duty. You don't do anything [special], but you know and there's such a thing as heroes, but you do your duty. The hero was the guy that gets killed.

Point Man

I was the point man in the platoon led by Logan Weston. He was called the 'Fightin' Preacher.'[47] It was an I&R platoon, intelligence and reconnaissance. You're not mature enough yet to think, but you learn. You're not mature—you become mature in action. When you're in action, they say you become fatalistic. There was [something about] these Japanese that makes them go and use banzai [charges] and all that. They were a lot different than we were.

And I was one of the first scouts, you know, when we contacted the first Japs; that day I was the first scout going into the elephant grass. [I was] dreaming about [the fact that] I was already overseas over a year and a half, you know, [and I saw a man ahead] and I thought he was Chinese, so I went forward, but I stopped—I said to

---

[47] Col. Logan Weston (1914-2003)-Nicknamed the 'Fighting Preacher' or the 'Fighting Parson,' Weston's service awards through World War II, Korea, and Vietnam included two Distinguished Service Crosses, five Silver Stars, seven Bronze Stars, six Purple Hearts, and the Legion of Merit.

myself, 'My God, Japanese!' He started to fire at me, but I hit him before I [dropped] down; I found an indentation in the ground. A Japanese machine gun started to open up, but I was lucky enough to find the indentation. I had a big watch on, and that watch got hit, and the ricochet hit me in my nose, so I started to bleed. If it was a tenth of an inch more, I probably wouldn't be here today.

'We Didn't Get Decorated'

I had the distinguished distinction to be the first American who got wounded by a Japanese and the first American to kill a Japanese in Asia. That was the wound I got, then my first officer came in, he pulled me back. Logan Weston, who was later on a colonel—one of the most decorated men in the United States Army, but in Marauders, we didn't get decorated. We didn't fight for decoration; nobody in the Marauders got decorated because Stilwell didn't decorate, [outside of a Purple Heart for being wounded]. It was the first Purple Heart. At the same time, somebody else almost got killed.

When I was wounded there at the time, as I told you, it was a slight wound, but it was bleeding severely. They wanted to send me back, but we were already over 120 of about 200 miles inland, and the only way I could get back was with the natives and I was more worried about that than staying, because I got all the attention. You know what I mean, all behind Japanese lines. Our platoon, the I&R platoon, was always what I would say eight, ten—maybe even twenty, thirty miles ahead of the main group and combat teams—different combat teams.

'Killed In Action'

I was officially called 'killed in action.' I was wounded, I killed the first Jap, but I was [reported to be] killed.

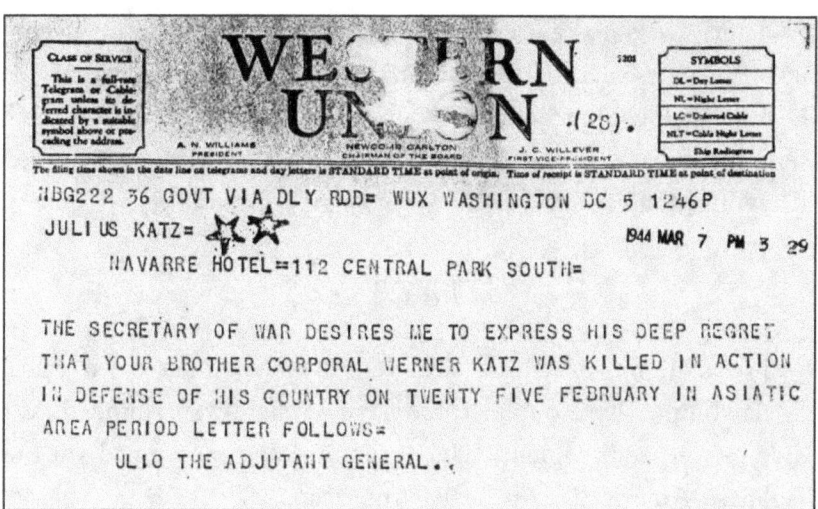

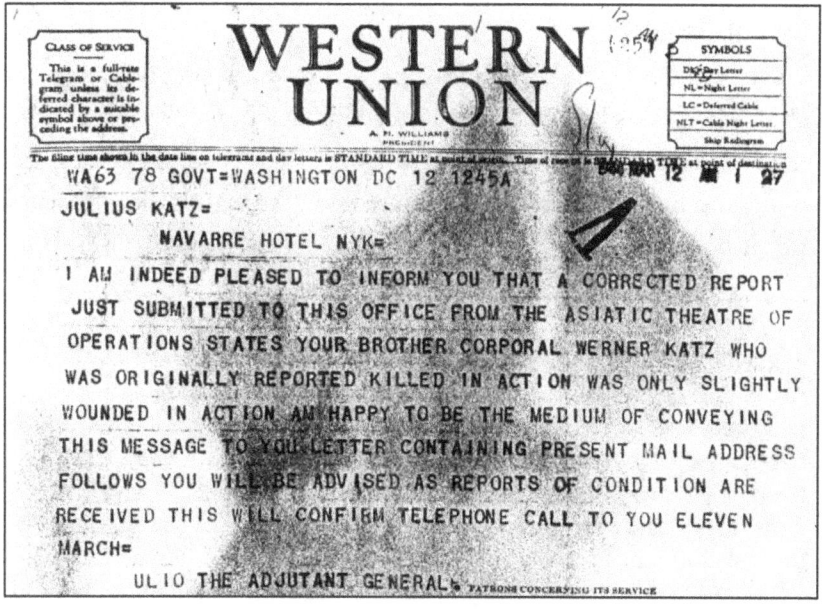

So my brother mourned me about two weeks; it took two or three weeks to straighten out. My brother didn't serve, he was nine years older, I think.

*

There were no replacements, and later on, as we went deeper into Burma, General Stilwell didn't have enough replacements, so he took the people who were wounded in the hospital and sick and sent them back to the front line. There was a little revolution [brewing] there; people didn't want to go back, you know?

The Chief

I was in more action. We went later on in a town called Walawbum, where our platoon was completely surrounded. We didn't even see the enemy. Under Logan Weston, we had with us Japanese-Americans, Mexicans-Americans. We had all types of people. We had American Indians—we had an Indian chief, [well, we called him 'Chief']. And if he wasn't there at the time, I wouldn't be alive today. I took a body of guys across a deep river, and the chief—Janis was his name—he looked in back of me from the original side, and in back of me was Japanese. It was a question of seconds, and he killed [several] Japanese and if he wasn't there, I would never be here today.[48]

---

[48] Gavin Mortimer, in his excellent book on the Marauders, elaborates on this incident:
"As we started to withdraw, Weston made a temporary litter and gave me and another fella the order to take this fellow [Lionel] Paquette across the river," recalled Werner Katz. Katz and the other man, John Clark, slid into the river with their cargo and struck out for the opposite bank. Katz glanced around and "saw a Japanese with a Nambu machine gun. I was praying, thinking 'this is it, I'm going to die.'" Katz, ever the fatalist, turned his face from the enemy and braced himself for the inevitable bullet. But on the eastern bank of the river, another soldier had seen the Japanese machine gunner. "He squatted down behind the gun, so I shot for his head," recalled Norman Janis, the Ogala Sioux known as "The Chief." The Japanese was dead before he had a chance to draw a bead on Katz. "Another one got in his place," continued Janis. "I hit him, got him out of the road. There was seven of them, dragging them away, and then another one. That last one, he kind of crawled back. I said, 'By gosh, I'm going to get you and keep you

I had malaria and even typhus. The doctor told me when I was in the hospital that it was probably typhus. People died next to me from typhus because we went in a certain area of Burma. I would say maybe half of us made it to Myitkyina. They were all disabled, wiped out. We were completely weak, but we made it. We had to make it. We had help from a local outfit called the Kachins, who were the natives of northern Burma. Thank God they were friends of ours because the Japanese mistreated them. [The Japanese had occupied Burma for some time, but the OSS had trained these people.] In the middle of Burma, I saw a guy in a Navy uniform in bell-bottom trousers. I didn't believe it when I went on patrol.

---

there.' So I shot him twice.'" Janis had a name for his M1 Garand: "Betsy." Betsy fired eight bullets across the river, and seven brave Japanese died as a consequence. Weston waded into the middle of the river and stood there exhorting his men to hurry, disdaining the enemy fire that threw up spurts of water on either side of him. Only when the last member of the I&R platoon was being pulled up the bank by their comrades did Weston follow "as calmly as he were out for a walk in the sun." The Japanese, furious that their prey had eluded them, charged across the river, but they were easy targets for Weingartner and his men. "They just kept coming across and we kept shooting at them," he remembered. Mortimer, Gavin, *Merrill's Marauders*. Page 71.

The Ledo Road

Marauders on the Ledo Road. U.S. ARMY SPECIAL OPERATIONS HISTORY OFFICE, Public domain.

Now, the Ledo Road was tremendous because our engineers built it; the English didn't think we could do it. The American engineers in fact were black troops, and they were wonderful. I remember when we walked and a hundred miles there was a black soldier, and they were the most wonderful people I ever saw, they were wonderful to us. I remember I stayed one night with them. I had to make an arrangement for a show; Melvyn Douglas was an actor. Later, I was down in South Carolina before the war started, and I remember I went to a football game for the first time. You know, I came from Europe in 1938, and there was a bunch of black soldiers sitting on one side and there was an overflow of people there, so they took the black soldiers off the stands, and they put white people in there. And at the time I didn't understand it; I thought it was terrible. You know what I mean?

Troops in Burma. U.S. Army, public domain.

'A Very Tough Thing'

I can tell you that Burma was physically a very tough thing. We had to walk, march, and walk. I'll tell you something. We went through terrain there over the mountains [seven hundred miles, seven thousand feet up]. I don't wish it on anybody. Even with the little breaks, I don't know how we ever made it. I'm very physically exhausted. I had poisoning of the stomach; I had to take 30 sulfa pellets a day. I was sick to my stomach a month. I had amoebic dysentery, and I had to take 30 or 40 sulfa tablets, I'd march a mile or so and lie down. I wanted to die, but they kept me moving, so we stayed in it. Yeah, if you ever would have seen our outfit going down into Myitkyina, you would have seen a bunch of dead people.

How I made it, I will never know, and I'm glad that the Japanese didn't attack us, like they attacked us later on, you know. They had gone through a lot of hell themselves.

We could really hit them, and then we run, and they didn't know exactly where we were. We had different combat teams in different places.

I know the last day when I left Myitkyina, I remember a Texan was singing 'When My Blue Moon Turns to Gold Again,' and I said—this was the nighttime, I said, they're gonna break through, and they broke through and that night two officers who had felt very secure [actually] slept in harm's way, because they got killed.

Home

All my education was minimal; really, I didn't have much education. High school, I learned in the Army. I learned a lot in life in the Army. I tell you, we had people who were in jail. We had people who went to Harvard. We had engineers. We had farmers. We had men from Oklahoma, from California, from South Carolina, from New York. We had people from all over life.

After the airfield was taken, I was brought out, they said I had a temperature of 105.5 degrees. In India I was in the hospital, I don't know if it was a month or two, and some of our people died there because they had typhus, you know. Later, I went back to the United States, somewhere in North Carolina [to an intelligence school]. It was very interesting, there were a lot of people there, a lot of language people, and I had to learn all about the German Army. I was born in Germany, you know. I got to know more about the German Army than the German officers, and I interrogated the Germans.

I was discharged at Fort Dix, New Jersey. I went into business, I got married five years later, I was married 54 years. She was a lovely girl.

This is an honor. [Thanks for listening to my story]; it was a pleasure, darling.

Staff Sergeant Warner Katz was inducted into the Army Ranger Hall of Fame in 2000. Mr. Katz passed away a little more than a year after this interview, on November 5, 2006, at the age of 87.

CHAPTER FOURTEEN

The Combat Cameraman I

David L. Quaid was born on March 27, 1920, in Glendale, New York. He was a cinematographer and director, the best-known picture that he worked on being the film *Arthur* (1981). As a young man, he had a single-minded pursuit in photography and motion pictures that would someday land him in Hollywood, after a detour to the jungles of Burma, a formative experience that stayed with him all of his life.

David Quaid

Depression Days

I was born on March 27, 1920, in Glendale, New York. I came from a typically Depression-struck family. My mother and father had five children; my father's boast of it was, 'I had five children and none of them went to jail.' But it was a typical, very difficult, Depression situation. My brother, who was absolutely brilliant, got the gold medal when he graduated from P.S. 121 in Queens. Brilliant guy, but he had to go to work. His sacrifice permitted my sister—who was also brilliant, actually, I come from a very interesting family—she was able to go through high school. Then I followed and I realized that this would be the limit of any education I could get, which would be high-school level. Now, strangely enough, in the years after the war, I've now taught in five major universities and no one has asked for my credentials, ever, okay? I mean, [I'm talking about] NYU, BU, School of Visual Arts, Rochester Institute of Technology, all these schools. I taught in all those schools on the basis of things I knew that they don't know. Anyway, because of obviously the sacrifices of the first three children, my two younger sisters went to college. That was sort of typical, I would say, of the [times].

Becoming a Cameraman

I was always interested in the motion picture business, and I was an Eagle Scout, so I got into the sort of senior program of Boy Scouts, and I met another young guy, Warren Rothenberger, who was also interested in motion pictures. The two of us basically educated ourselves in the public libraries on the books of Pudovkin, Eisenstein, and Paul Rother, and people of that nature. Then I decided to become a freelance newsreel motion picture cameraman and work with basically Paramount News as a stringer, not that they ever gave me any leads. I had to develop my own. I had a couple of good breaks. Crown Princess Martha of Norway was viewing some Norwegian dive bombers who were training in Canada at LaGuardia Airport. I managed to get some very fine footage of all these, of her, of Mayor LaGuardia, of Grover Whalen, who was the greeter for New York City, and what have you.

I also picked up some other stories. There was a riot down where they were building the East River Tunnel under the river at Battery Place, and the sandhogs were fighting the hard rock miners for jurisdiction.[49] I got some terrific footage on that, and also the first camouflage clipper that went to the embattled British, but the union newsreel guys would see me, and we'd get into fights, arguments, and what have you. Anyhow, I realized two things. One, I realized that these are the guys that I'm going to want to work with someday. I was doing a stupid thing; I was embarrassing them because since I ran around with a hand camera, they didn't get the kind of footage I was getting. Two, I realized I needed a regular job. What's interesting about this, Warren and I wrote to all the big shots of Hollywood. Now this is interesting. We'd get these letters back on embossed, heraldic letterheads from the executive secretary of Samuel Goldwyn. It would say, 'Mr. Goldwyn read your letter, and he's sorry, but there are no openings in the camera department at this time.' But finally, Mr. Cone of Columbia, who was considered the toughest producer in Hollywood, wrote back and said, 'Dave, if you'd find yourself in front of the gates of our studio, just present this letter. I'd like to meet you.' But at the same time, I was trying to get work in the industry around New York City. I got a job with an outfit called General Business Films and made industrial films. That's sort of interesting in a way, because Mr. Lawton, who owned it, he said, 'I'm very interested in your qualifications. But before we discuss further, I would like to give you a test.'

I said, 'Okay.'

He said, 'You know how to run a Cine Special,' which was a very sophisticated 16mm camera of its day.

He said, 'I'd like you to go out and shoot a typical autumn scene.'

I said, 'But Mr. Lawton, this is February!'

He said, 'Well, that's part of the test.' Then he said, 'I'd like you to shoot a scene of New York City at night.'

---

[49] sandhogs- underwater or underground excavation and construction laborers.

I said, 'But you know the film has an ASA of eight? I think you're asking a lot.'

He said, 'Well, that's the test. Take it or leave it.'

We went out to a place called Alley Pond Park where we used to camp with the Boy Scouts. There was this tree up on a bluff and it was blowing like crazy. We scratched around on the ground and found a beautiful red leaf, which I tied to the end of a branch, these bare branches. Now, this camera could run at 64 frames a second, which is a degree of slow motion. I had Warren grab palm loads of leaves and throw them in the air, and it'd come through the scene, this close-up scene of one leaf. In slow motion, it was absolutely, it was ethereal, I got to tell you. It was just fantastic, you know? Then we went to the top of the Empire State Building and now this camera would also run at four frames a second, I think it was, I could run that slow and pick up exposure. We got there just before dark; I really got a fantastic night scene of New York at night. Everybody looked at the shots and they were just pleased as hell. Then I got to know Elmer McGovern, who was the film editor. I said, 'What are you working on?'

He said, 'I'm working on a picture for the Better Light, Better Sight Institute.' He said, 'Yeah. We have one problem.'

I said, 'What's the problem?'

He said, 'Well, we're missing an autumn shot, we're missing a shot of New York City at night.' I got the job. It was a good learning experience.

'We Need The Five Dollars'

The war was developing all the time. Warren and I used to do backpacking when no one did it in those days. One Saturday, Palm Sunday, I remember that we were going to hike across Bear Mountain State Park. We hitchhiked and hiked up to the western entrance to the park. We started to follow this trail. Unfortunately, Warren had high-cut boots; for five dollars you could get an excellent pair of boots. Very nice. My Aunt Nora, my godmother, had given me five dollars and I was going to buy a pair of boots for them. But my father, who is a wonderful guy, said, 'Dave, we need the five dollars.' So I had a pair of old Oxfords, which had cardboard in them for where they were worn through, and I had a pair of rubbers. We started over this trail, and the hunters had shot off the trail markers and it started to snow. Before long it was a 19-inch blizzard. It was now getting dark. Anyhow, I was at that point breaking trail. It really snowed extremely hard. There was a light skim of ice on this small stream and snow on top of it. When I went over it, of course, I ended up to my waist in the water. Then it got bitter cold, and we realized we had better stop and do something about it. But all we had were these cotton blankets. By that time, my pants had frozen solid. We spent all night rubbing my legs. But what happened was they turned black, and it took a month and a half in bed with all kinds of techniques to restore the nerves and what have you. But that's the kind of, that's the things you did in those days. You couldn't afford to go do anything. You hitchhiked; you did things like that.

'The War Was On Top Of Us'

Suddenly the war was on top of us. Since I had 2500 vision, which is legally blind, I was rejected immediately. I was a very patriotic type of guy; that offended me terribly. But one day, in the newspaper it said that they got smart. I mean, why turn all these 1-A guys into cannon fodder when there are people that have minor problems? They were called 1-B. They had this program through General Hersey, who was the head of the draft, to start a 1-B qualification in draft boards. But you had to write a letter. I wrote my typical letter. I'm an Eagle Scout and all that sort of business, I know all this stuff, which I did. Then, like overnight, the draft board called me and suddenly I was in the Army. But some of my friends, who worked as film editors at the Senior Corps Photographic Center in Astoria at the old Paramount Studios, told Colonel Gaskell, who was in charge of training combat cameramen in what they used to call the IMO school. The IMO was a Bell and Howell hand camera, it shot 35-millimeter film, same as theatrical, and it weighed about 15 pounds; it was a very good camera for hand use. Through my friends, he heard about me and arranged an interview. This was early in the war, and he said, unfortunately, the Senior Corps has no priority comparable to combat arms. It's going to be very hard to get you, especially from a 1-B outfit. But as time went on, I progressed. I was in the first 1-B unit, which was the 1st Battalion's A Battery, 701st Anti-Aircraft. Because of all these skills I had as a Boy Scout, I was teaching all kinds of classes, so I ended up Chief of Range Section, which is sort of a computerized situation where you pick up an enemy plane and zero in on it. But I told Captain Potts, who was a very fine officer, I said, 'I'm going to do my best to get out of here.'

He said, 'Well, I'm probably not going to let you.' He said, 'In fact, you're going to apply for anti-aircraft OCS.'

I said, 'I don't want to apply for anti-aircraft OCS.'

Well, suddenly I was in front of all these colonels, and I was accepted, okay? I got orders to be transferred to Camp Davis. I had my barracks bag filled, and I had a command car waiting to take me to the train station. Captain Potts came out of his office to wish me well.

I said, 'Wait a minute, Captain Potts, I have a feeling what's going on here is illegal. How can you order anybody to become an officer? How can you do that?'

He said, 'Well, it does have its difficult interpretations.'

I said, 'Wait a minute, is it legal or isn't it?'

He said, 'Well, I would say probably sort of borderline.'

I said, 'Okay. Then I'm not going.'

I took my barracks bag, went back up to my bunk, and that was it. Then what happened was two films were made. Now, the war was going on in Africa at this time. The British were pushing from the Nile against Rommel's forces, and they had a Colonel McDonald who ran a photographic unit and they made a picture called *Desert Victory*, which was fantastic, black-and-white picture, beautifully done. We had, what was that idiot's name, a big producer, Darryl Zanuck, who was in charge of an American outfit that was shooting color, and the picture was called *At the Front*. Here are shots of Darryl Zanuck with a Tommy gun shooting at Junkers 88s up at 10,000 feet and all this sort of crap. It was a terrible picture, except for some shots of artillery hitting German tanks. What happened? Secretary of War Stimson and Roosevelt would look at movies together. They ran the British picture and then they ran the American picture and Roosevelt turned to Stimson and said, 'Wait a minute, aren't we the preeminent makers of motion pictures on earth?'

He said, 'How could the British make such a magnificent document? We made this awful thing.'

This is what the Signal Corps was waiting for. Stimson said, 'Well, we know there are men in the service, but we can't get them, we don't have the priority.' Well, at that point, the collators—collators were machines that they put cards in— [went to work]. Well, when I went in, you get an army specialist number and mine was 043, that's skilled motion picture camera. At that point, my card dropped down [by the collator] and unbeknownst to me, I was transferred to a signal photo company. I had an inkling there was something going on, and when I spoke to Captain Potts, he drew this red border letter out of his office desk, and this had me being transferred.

He said, 'We're not going to let you go, Sergeant.'

Now, a red border letter is what's called an immediate action letter. There's nothing you can do about it. When you get an immediate action letter, you have to perform it. By that time, the First Army, which I was in, had rejected the whole idea of my transfer.

Then, it went back to where it started. Then the red border letter came in again, and it chewed out the First Army. Suddenly, I was thrown into a command car and taken to a railroad station, and I was on my way to Camp Crowder, Missouri, where the 164th Signal Photo Company was. What's interesting about that now, you know, I had worked making industrial films and all that, but I never equated that to Hollywood technique. I was picked up at Camp Crowder station and the driver of the jeep was telling me this was a Hollywood outfit and all Hollywood people and all this other business. By the time I got there, I was sweating, I figured they were going to find me out, you know? I checked in and they gave me a bunk and the first sergeant told me to go to this certain barracks where they had set up as a projection room for training and they were running footage. They were like, 'You have to see this shot. It was magnificent.' I came there and it took me a while to get my eyes adjusted, and I looked at the screen and I'll never forget it until I die. Here was this paratrooper coming through the screen horizontally, with a parachute, fully inflated, coming through. I took one look at this, and I said, 'Quaid, you got it made.'

I said, 'He's obviously a still photographer and he took the motion picture camera and made it vertical.' This paratrooper dropping, he made vertical out of it, you know? It turned out that really what happened was that the motion picture industry wasn't going to lose their good people. I guess they helped organize some of these companies and I don't remember anybody who was a professional. Colonel Gaskell sent some good people in, and he devised courses for these guys, and they ended up doing a hell of a fine job.

'I Won World War II'

I was in Tennessee Maneuvers after training with this outfit and then I ended up in Tennessee Maneuvers, we all did, which was a huge enterprise.[50] You have no concept. There was this constant joke on the front lines, you know? 'You think this was tough, you should have been on Louisiana Maneuvers.'

'Well, you think this is tough, you should have been on Tennessee Maneuvers!'

Anyhow, they were short of lieutenants, and a photographic unit would consist of generally four or five men. There'd be a lieutenant, there'd be a motion picture cameraman, two still men, and a driver for whatever vehicle the unit had. Anyhow, two things happened. As I said, they were short of lieutenants, so they put me in charge of this unit. Now, the three men I had were Hatfield of the original clan, Cochran, and Beelen, and they were all very deep south guys or Kentucky or borderline states. Cochran, who was a staff sergeant, had recently been demoted to private and I never knew why, but these were three of the toughest men I've ever encountered. I take them out and for a week we'd do fine, because the maneuver went from midnight Monday until midnight Friday, and at that point, you camped next to the first creek there was and took a bath right out in the open.

On Sunday, I had finished chow, and I was sitting under a tree writing a letter home, and suddenly, I feel these shadows over me and there's Hatfield, Cochran, and Beelen, and they jump on me, and they pound the hell out of me and I pounded the hell out of them. But I realized they weren't really hurting me, I was hurting

---

[50] Tennessee Maneuvers- Large-scale Second Army training exercises involving more than 850,000 soldiers between 1942 and 1944; Middle Tennessee was selected because the terrain resembled that of France, Belgium, and Germany.

them, but yeah, they are bruising and what have you, nothing serious. They all got up and Hatfield said, 'Okay, Sergeant, you can run the outfit another week.' Okay? Next week these guys are fantastic, you couldn't wish for a better team.

Sunday comes, I'm under a tree writing a letter, but this time I'm looking, and I see the three of them come over this hill and I stood up, and this time they didn't pull any punches, they really belted the hell out of me, and I belted back, and by that time I was on the deck, and they were standing over me and Hatfield said, 'It's okay, Sergeant. We just want to know whether you'd fight.' You see, these boys were not going to go with anybody into combat that wouldn't fight. I never turned them in, never, you know? Actually, I should have, but I didn't. That, I earned a great deal of respect also, so we ended up a very fine team.

Last week, a relative, a cousin who I hadn't seen since before World War II, called up and dropped by, and her husband... See, I know nothing about him. See, I've been in motion picture business all my life. I was traveling all the time on projects. Anyhow, the husband of my cousin turned out to be with 4th Armored with General Patton. I said, 'Hey, 4th Armored. You were in Tennessee Maneuvers.'

'Yeah. We were there for three months.'

I said, 'I'll tell you a story.'

I decided to go out with 4th Armored with my unit. It's like 7:00 in the morning; a new phase of Maneuver started on Monday morning. By that time, temporarily, I got a lieutenant, and he was an ex-newsreel man from Florida.

I was lying on the ground while this briefing was going on. Now, they had a map of the military area, as big as that wall, and each of the colonels of Combat Command A, Combat Command B, each one would take notice what their outfit is going to achieve, and all that. And finally, one of them, Combat Command A, said, 'We're going to cross the Cumberland River at the bridge at such and such.' So, at that point, the general takes over and he starts his briefing, and I listen, and this General Wood, who was very well respected in Patton's Third Army, extremely well respected, and so was the 4th Armored. He points out where the Combat Command A is going to go across the river. Finally, he said, 'Any questions?'

I started to raise my hand, and Cliff Paul, my lieutenant, said, 'Shut up, Quaid!'

I said, 'Oh no, it's too important.'

And I raise my hand, and he looks at me, I mean, I'm the only one. He looks at me, and he's taken aback, like, 'What is he doing asking me questions in a major briefing?'

I said, 'Sir, if you'll check your map, at the point that Combat Command A is going to cross the Cumberland River—I'm a little distant. I realize, from the map, but that looks to me like it's a ferry symbol.'

'What?' And he goes and looks, and he goes, 'Yipe!' Now these three colonels come, and they all go, 'Yipe!' And he gets the radio man. He said, 'Call Combat Command A, put them in reserve.' Combat Command B was in reserve. 'We'll go for the bridge at Carthage,' and they changed the whole thing and stopped this whole thing.

Now, Combat Command A was moving out since midnight. So, I said to the guys, 'Hey, let's go down and take a look at that ferry.' So, we had a hard time getting there, because here's Combat Command A, all these Sherman tanks coming back the other way, [reversing direction]. We finally get down there, and the ferry consisted of this cable across the river and a barge that would take one automobile at a time. And what they did is, the guy that ran it, by angling the bow, the current of the river would slide this ferry across the cable, see? And all you could imagine is, what would have been happening to Combat Command A, [with their tanks trying to get] down to this muddy embankment, a disaster.

So, people say, 'What did you do in the Army?' I say, 'Well, I won World War II.' And I explain this whole story, because this is one of the prime tank outfits that we had. So anyhow, that night, we camped back with them, and I see this group of officers circling through this whole bivouac area. And finally, somebody points my unit out, and they come over, and it's General Wood. And he says, 'Sergeant, you have no idea what you have done for us.' See, don't forget they had umpires on all these units. And if this had happened, I guarantee you, they would break up the outfit, the whole officer corps would be gone. It would have been a disaster. And he went on, spent his whole time trying to find us to say thanks, but that's the kind of man, apparently, he was. He was extremely well-respected. But that outfit would have been junked, or at least the officers would have been. So that was Tennessee Maneuvers.

Going Overseas

Then, after that, they figured it's time to send us overseas, and we went to a port of embarkation: Hampton Roads, Virginia, Camp Patrick Henry. And there was nothing interesting there, except an outfit would have to take KP for this huge mess hall. But the whole outfit, it was so big, that every man would be involved. And so I was, at that time, a buck sergeant. And so, the mess officer of that installation said, 'Okay, here's how you lay out your men. You are going to run the officer's section here.'

He said, 'We're not going to issue any Kel-Bowl Paks today,' the little boxes of cereal that you could open up and pour milk into them. Do you remember?

'No one gets a Kel-Bowl Pak. Okay.'

So certain officers would say, 'Hey, I need something to put my cereal in.'

I said, 'Sorry, orders are we're not issuing them today.'

So, finally, this black colonel came on over, and he wanted a Kel-Bowl Pak. Well, I recognized him right away, he was Colonel Davis of the Tuskegee Airmen! And I said, 'I'm sorry, sir, but they're not being issued today.'[51]

And he looked at me as though I was another redneck of his life experience, and he just didn't believe me. And since I recognized him, it was rather excruciating to me also. So I understood his problem, and he refused to understand mine, that he was not going to get that damn thing, no way. I'm not going to get him a bowl, I'm not going to do anything against orders, period.

So, at that point, I see the mess officer, I said, 'Please come over here. You talk to the colonel,' and he told him that those were my orders, period. And that was the end of it. But I always felt bad about that. The guy probably had enough of this by this time.

*

So, then we went overseas, and finally, our time came to ship out, and we were on a British ship, *The Empress of Scotland*. I suddenly was put in charge of a group of twenty men, and we were supposed to work in a galley. There were at least 10,000 men on the ship, so it must have been an officer's mess; to feed 10,000 men is something else. So the mess officer had told me to tell the men that they're going to work all night, till morning, till dawn, and they would be excused from lifeboat drill. So, the cook who I was working with, a little bandy-legged Englishman, said, 'Now look, Sergeant, we got five jobs here. We got twenty men. I need four men cutting up herring. I need four men cleaning up around here from

---

[51] Benjamin O. Davis Jr. (1912-2002) was the commander of the Tuskegee Airmen and later was the first black United States Air Force general.

the last lane. And four men are going to help me with the bacon,' and all this sort of business. So, I tell the guys, 'That's what you're going to do.' Now, we left Hampton Roads in a violent storm, and I never get seasick, but I could see the guys trying to work [here on the food prep] and they had never been on a ship before. And so, the first guys I lose right off the bat are the guys cutting up the fish. I mean, that did it, I got to tell you. I would have figured they're out to con me, so I would not have permitted that. I really had to see the results, and I saw them [getting sick].

So then, the next group, the guys getting rid of the garbage, had whole big garbage pails, huge pails, and they would go into a small room, I'd say about eight foot wide, square. In the middle of it was this huge pipe with an iron cover on it, and what they were supposed to do was to take these pails of slop and pour them down this tube, and it'd exit out into the ocean. The only trouble is the ship was rolling. So, they took this mess of slop and poured it in, and the ship rolled, and this column of water came up this pipe. All the garbage, everything, hit the ceiling, all over these men. Four more gone. Four more wiped out. So then, finally, I lost the rest of the crew before I was done, and things like that happened. So, it was only the Englishman and myself to cook the bacon. Now, the way that was done, is we had these big black broiling pans, and the ovens were in ranks, serried ranks. It went from one side of the ship to the other, many of them. So we would take this bacon and throw it into the pan and put it into oven one, and go on, and as soon as we got to the end of the line, he would take one and I'd take the other and immediately go back and start pulling these out, and they'd be cooked pretty well. And so, finally, I'm dismissed, and I go back to my compartment, and all the guys are asleep and nobody else is in the compartment. They're up on lifeboat drill. So, at that point, all these officers come stamping down the stairs and, 'Sergeant,

Sergeant, what are these men doing in the bunks when they should be up on lifeboat drill?'

I said, 'Sirs, these men have been granted an excuse. The mess officer of the ship told us that they were free to sleep through lifeboat drill. They were on all night last night and they just got into their bunks.'

'Get them out. Get them up there.'

I'm like, 'Well, okay.' So I got them up and then [I started looking for] Captain Knight, the captain of the 164th Signal Photo Company. I found out where his cabin was, and I went up and I knocked on his door and he was very surprised to see me.

'What's your problem?'

I said, 'I don't have a problem, but you can have my stripes.'

'What do you mean by that, Sergeant?'

I told him, 'We were guaranteed that if we worked right through the night that we would be exempt, and you and the other officers rousted everybody out and there's no way I'm going to be in charge of men where what I tell them is not enforced by the officer corps.'

'All right, take it easy,' and he went up to the mess officer and the transport commander both, because this is pretty serious, lifeboat drill. And we got a reprieve and, of course, he demanded a great deal of credit for it, but son of a gun. So anyhow, that was our trip across. I mean, this is the stuff that nobody will ever tell you.

Mr. Quaid's story will continue.

Kermit Bushur, center, with soldiers from his first unit. Library of Congress.

CHAPTER FIFTEEN

The Volunteer

Kermit 'Tony' Bushur was born on March 22, 1924, in Neoga, Illinois. He worked for the U.S. Postal Service as a mild-mannered rural mail carrier later in life, but as a young man he had a penchant for mischief and fun, which landed him in the brig early in his military career. He kept being turned down as he tried to get drafted; he had to write a letter of voluntary induction in order to serve his country. Amazingly, he survived the sinking of a transport vessel in the Mediterranean by an advance radio-controlled German bomb, an attack which resulted in the greatest loss of U.S. life at sea due to enemy action during World War II, and the loss of his official orders and identity papers. As a man now without a 'formal identity,' he found himself in India picking up the famine dead before 'finding salvation' in volunteering for an unspecified dangerous mission assigned to the unit that would become the famed Merrill's Marauders, seemingly filling the role of 'everyman' before being evacuated with a leg wound so serious he was recommended for an amputation.

'My squad leader was a convicted felon. He had been convicted of killing a man in Tennessee; it was his wife's lover, and he killed a man with

his knife. He was sentenced to life in prison. I think there was more than Tom in our unit who were felons, but there came a time when they would let them go into combat if they wouldn't take any training, just take them right from the prison and go right into combat. Well, Tom took it. He said, 'That's better than sitting here in the jail!' And he was the best man I knew. I would follow him into the hubs of hell. He was really a wonderful fellow.'

He sat for this interview at a Merrill's Marauders reunion in 2005, when he was 81 years old.

Kermit 'Tony' Bushur

My mother was intrigued by the name Kermit from Teddy Roosevelt's son, who was Kermit. It was a heck of a name for me because I could not pronounce it. Whenever I'd go into town, the boys would ask me, what's your name? I'd say, Joe, John, Mike, anything but Kermit, because I couldn't even pronounce it. But eventually I grew to liking my own name. But in college then whenever you're playing football and you're going for a touchdown, you can't say, 'Go, Kermit, go!' So I used my middle name, which was Anthony, and Tony. I became Tony and I've stayed Tony most all of my life since then.

My brother and sister are both older than me, my brother John William was fourteen years older and my sister Helen Marie was sixteen years older. We were a poor family that did not know we were poor. My father provided us with a comfortable life, nothing fancy, just adequate, never going hungry or without clothing. He owned a 56-acre farm that started out at first being a fruit farm, then as the trees died off, it was converted to a grain farm. I do not remember the fruit farm. Sis used to tell me of Father's maverick ways of not conforming to the norm. Most fruit farms sold their products to cold storage houses that then shipped the fruit to the larger cities, such as Chicago and St. Louis. Father instead would load up the wagon and hawk his wares in neighboring communities. She remembered him coming home with a fistful of money. By the time of my birth, Father was in the grain farming mode. Again his maverick ways was seeking a greater return from the land, so he improvised to making it a pig farm. He would raise what grain he could on 56 acres, but that was inadequate for the pigs that he would prepare for the market. Therefore in the fall of the year we would scour the area to buy more grain to make pig feed. I walked many a mile driving a team of horses with a wagon of corn, walking to keep warm as this was usually a job for the fall and winter.

My education consisted of six years in a rural one-room school house, today it might be termed 'one size fits all.' The 7th and 8th grade was in a Catholic school, me being sent there for the purpose of confirmation into the Catholic religion.

Pearl Harbor happened the first year I was a freshman in college. I remember coming back to the frat house and everybody was glued to the radio, and they were being bombed at Pearl Harbor. It was a devastating blow, and I remember the look on many of the boys' faces. They couldn't believe it and some of them just wandered around in a cloud for a while and some even went down and they volunteered immediately to go into service.

'You Have To Stay Home And Farm'

I completed the year of schooling and then that summer, wanting something to do and trying to sort out what I was going to do, the government made available schooling, which was called NYA schools, and they were teaching machine shop, sheet metal work, and welding. I chose machine shop, and I took their training, and I then went to work in Chicago in a plant and that's where I was really then getting ready to go in the service.

I thought, well, I want to go in the service. I lived about 200 miles from Chicago, and on the way home one time, I went to the draft board to see why I wasn't being drafted—everybody my age was being drafted! Well, to my surprise, the factory had made my work very, very much needed, so they got me a deferment. Well, I went back up and I quit that job immediately, came back home, and I thought surely I would be called back up. Well, I was not.

Weeks went by and I was not being called up by the draft, so I went back to the draft board, and they said, 'Well, now you're the only son left on the farm. Your brother has been drafted and he's in service, so you have to stay home and farm.'

I said, 'I am not a farmer. You have drafted the farmer.' I said, 'I'm going to go in the service.'

They said, 'Well, I'm sorry. You're going to have to stay home and farm.' So I went home, and I left the farm to go to visit a sister in another area, and I thought, well, surely they'd see I'm not farming, they'll still call me. But they didn't.

I went to the draft board again and they said, 'Well, the only way you can get into service is by writing us a voluntary letter of induction,' which I did. I wrote them a voluntary letter of induction, and lo and behold, the next week I was on the train going to the draft board or to the examination area, which is in Chicago. Now in basic training, I went to Little Rock, Arkansas, and it was B-I-R-T-C, which is Branch Immaterial Replacement Training Center or Company or whatever it might be, but we were being prepared to enter almost any one of the branches of the service. It might have been quartermaster. It might have been engineers. It might have been many different things, but that's why they called it Branch Immaterial. So at the conclusion of the training we were put on the train and we ended up at Sharon, Pennsylvania, at the place, they call it Shenango.

'You're The Son of a Gun That Went AWOL'

I got word that my brother was getting married, and he asked me to be his best man. So I went to the company commander and asked to be on a leave to go home for the wedding.

He said, 'I'm sorry, we can't give you no leave because you're on orders. You're going to have to be going overseas.' So I just politely turned around and walked out, but I picked up a pad of passes, three-day passes on the way out and I went back to the barracks, and I started ironing clothes like mad.

I was charging a dollar a whack for a pair of trousers and a dollar for a shirt. And if they wanted the military crease in it, I'd charge another dollar. So when I had enough money, I went to Youngstown, and I bought me a round trip to go to Illinois and back. Now here's where those three-day passes came in. The passes would get me 300 miles. And that was the limit of the extent that you could travel on a three-day pass.

So every time I was at the extent of 300 miles, I'd write myself another pass. So, finally I got to Chicago. And from Chicago to home, you have to go through Rantoul, Illinois, which is an air base that they were teaching weather, I think, and some other Air Force-related things. But the train was just loaded with GIs and MPs. Well, I thought, oh, I don't want to get stopped this far from home. I'm really close now. So I spent about 50 miles in the bathroom while everybody was—when they got off at Rantoul, then I came out of the bathroom.

We had a very, very good wedding and I decided it was time to go back to camp because I was only home, I think about eight days. And I was in town at the bus depot. I had to take the bus to a train station. It was right across from that Western Union Station. And while we were sitting there, my brother and I, here came the

Western Union messenger. He came over to me and said, 'What are you doing, Kermit?'

I said, 'Well, I'm going back to camp.'

He said, 'Are you sure you're going back to camp?'

I said, 'Yeah, yeah.' So I showed him what I had and my round-trip ticket. I said, 'I'm just ready now to get on the train going back to Ohio and Pennsylvania.'

He said, 'Well, if you're going back, I won't show this to your parents.'

It was the telegram telling them that I was AWOL, and if they knew where I was, they were supposed to let the government know and they'd pick me up, you know. Well, he let me go and my brother took the telegram, and he tore it up. He said, 'Dad will never see this!'

So I get back to Pennsylvania into the camp where I'd come from, and it was empty; the area that I had been in was empty. There wasn't a person around. So I talked to one of the soldiers that was walking around on the street. He said, 'You got to go down to the dayroom down about a block.' So I went down there, and I saluted the lieutenant, and I said, 'Private Busher reporting from AWOL, sir!'

He looked up at me and he said, 'Oh, you're the son-of-a-gun that went AWOL before I got to see you. Well, your unit has shipped out!' So he said, 'I'll tell you what. I'll give you this quarter number and I'll set you up for a summary court martial tomorrow or the next day,' whatever it was, within three days.

So, at the summary court martial—in fact, it was early in the morning, and he hadn't even got out of bed yet when I had knocked on his BOQ, which is Bachelor Officers Quarters. And he just lay there in bed, and he turned the light on and picked up my papers and looked at them. He looked at me. He said, 'Well, you look like a pretty good kid. You weren't going to go—or desert, were you?'

I said, 'No, no, no, no! I bought a round-trip ticket, and I just came back to camp on my own!'

He said, 'Okay, that's good, in your favor. I'll tell you what I'm going to do. I'm just going to fine you fifteen dollars. You'll be on a shipment to go overseas; we'll send you on out just like you had been originally.' So that's how I got to Newport News. And at Newport News we got on the liberty ship, the *Betty Zane*, and we landed at Oran, Africa, after 21 days.

In The Brig

On the *Betty Zane* I befriended a fellow German; I'm of German descent. But his father had been in World War I as an officer for the German Army. And he came to the States after the war and brought his family to the States. His name is Ed Truckenbrote. Ed became a very close, a very good friend. He was a manipulator, and there was nothing that he wouldn't try to do. But we had a lot of fun onboard the ship. In fact, he and I made up a little skit, like he was a German submarine commander, and I was the crew. Oh, we sank a lot of convoys. And you know, it was funny that we had the crowd laughing and stuff like that, but somebody didn't like it. When we landed at Oran, they turned us in as maybe being spies. So we went to the brig.

Ed and I spent about a week and a half in the brig, and they ran security checks on our parents and everything like that, you know. And finally they decided—I remember some of the questions they asked me, which was ridiculous, but then it's just like they said, 'If you were on the battlefield and you had your sights set on a German soldier, would you pull the trigger?'

I said, 'Well, sure I would,' you know. These are the kind of questions that they would ask you and it would be irritating, but finally they let us go and he went one way, and I went another, and I did not see Ed on my stay in Oran. On Thanksgiving Day of 1943, I boarded a boat or a ship that was going to join a convoy in the Mediterranean. I had no idea where it was going, but we were just out a short time, and we were attacked by a group of German bombers and pursuit planes. They strafed us and things like that.

'My God, A Torpedo!'

We made it through that day. But the second day I was on the ship—I now know the name of the ship was the *Rohna*, but at the time I did not know the name of the ship. And I remember seeing this thing coming down from the bomber. It was very large. And my thoughts were, my God, a torpedo! It was so large. It wasn't a conventional bomb. So we were hit, and we were sunk in the Mediterranean there.[52] We lost 1,015 men, and I was picked up and found to be fit for duty. So they sent me on in the next convoy and I ended up in Calcutta—Bombay, then Calcutta. Now Calcutta or India at that time was in the midst of a famine.

---

[52] *we were sunk in the Mediterranean*-1,149 men were killed in the sinking of the HMS *Rohna* on 26 November 1943; 1,015 were U.S. personnel, with another 35 later succumbing to their injuries. The ship was sunk by a radio-guided, rocket-boosted glide bomb dropped from a Luftwaffe Heinkel He 177A heavy bomber. This sinking constituted the greatest loss of U.S. life at sea due to enemy action, even surpassing the tragedies of the USS *Arizona* and the USS *Indianapolis*. Details of the sinking were only released gradually over time; it was not until 1967 and the passage of the Freedom of Information Act that the U.S. Government revealed more details concerning the cause of the sinking, which makes Mr. Bushur's eyewitness account even more fascinating. Source: Naval History and Heritage Command, H-Gram 022: Loss of British Transport HMT Rohna, October 2018. www.history.navy.mil/about-us/leadership/director/directors-corner/h-grams/h-gram-022.html.

Picking Up The Dead

I better tell you also that when I left—when I left Pennsylvania, I did not have an officer, I had no company. I was by myself, and I was hand-carrying my orders—I hand-carried my orders. So when we went down, when the boat went down, I lost my orders! I had nothing. So I don't know what sent me off, but I ended up in Calcutta. And when I was in Calcutta, not having any company commander or anything like that, I was getting all the dirty details, and the dirtiest they had at that time was going into town and picking up the dead. See, the country was in a famine, and they were starving people, they were elderly people, but they came to Calcutta so they could bathe in the River Ganges. To their religion, they'd have to bathe in the River Ganges to be saved. Well, then they went into town. They'd unroll their little bamboo roll that they had, they'd lie down there and go to sleep and sometimes they didn't wake up. So every day there had to be a truck going through the entire city and picking up the dead. And then we would take them down to the river, put them on a big pile of wood, and burn them.

'One Day The Salvation Came'

That became very, very disheartening and very sad to see that happening. And I was catching that detail every day, every day! So that one day the salvation came. On a bulletin board they needed volunteers for a dangerous mission. They didn't promise anything except that you were going to be on a dangerous mission, but I think they did imply you might go home or something like that.

So there were three of us that volunteered. Lieutenant Dumpsha, Lieutenant Herne, and myself volunteered and we went into the hill country or the brush country where the Marauders were training. And I got the last two or three weeks of training before we went into Burma. So that's how I got into the combat.

Now in combat, I never did anything at all except be just a body count, you know. I did what I had to do. They told me to be a guard here and 'you're going to be in the right flank,' but I was in the Khaki Combat Team, Fourth Squad, the Fourth Platoon of I-Company of C-Battalion. Now, my battalion commander over there was Major Briggs. Some people called him colonel. I always called him colonel, but a lot of people, more people called him major rather than colonel.

'My Squad Leader Was A Convicted Felon'

My company commander was Major Lew, and my platoon commander was this lieutenant that I had volunteered with, Lieutenant Dumpsha, and I don't know why the Fourth Squad of the Fourth Platoon always gets called out for all the dirty work at the tail end, but here's an interesting thing. My squad leader was a convicted felon. His name was Tom Larson. He had been convicted of killing a man in Tennessee; it was his wife's lover. Tom was always quick to use a knife, he always kept a very sharp knife, and he killed a man with his knife. He was sentenced to life in prison.

And then that one time in the war—I think there was more than Tom in our unit who were felons, but there came a time when they would let them go into combat if they wouldn't take any training, just take them right from the prison and go right into combat. Well, Tom took it. He said, 'That's better than sitting here in the jail!' And he was the best man I knew. I would follow him into the hubs of hell. He was really a wonderful fellow.

My platoon leader was a fellow by the name of Rocky Curtain. Now Rocky was a very close friend of a Nisei interpreter by the name of Hank Gosho. The platoon guide was Whitney Dalmus. And that was the setup, more or less, of my unit.

'Poorest Goddamn Excuse For A Mule Skinner'

We, at that time, were not the Merrill's Marauders. We were just 5307 Provisional Composite Unit. Merrill's Marauders, everybody knows how that was just a media name, you might say. Some reporter used it, and it caught on and it became very famous. In combat, I don't know how to get to it, we had minor skirmishes [in the beginning], so I got the idea, you know, a guy could get killed out here. So I thought, well, I'm going to be a mule skinner, because I've seen these mule skinners bring the load up, deposit it, and then they go back to a safe area. So I thought, you know, 'That's for me. I want to be a mule skinner.' I got permission to go over and be a mule skinner. So the day I went over in that area, they gave me a mule and said, 'Now, this in your mule and this is your load. You're going to be responsible for this. So you are one of us now.'

So when morning came, I loaded that mule up, I got the pack all up on top of him. But the mule—and I think mules and horses do the same thing—they bloat themselves up a little bit with air. And like a horse now, if you put a saddle on them, you have to get that air out of them to get that cinch tight. I didn't realize that a mule would do that. So here I had this big load on top of the mule, and he was all bloated up and I didn't have no idea. So we take off. We go about seven steps, and he sucks in his air and that load just reversed from top to bottom. Here it had slid underneath his belly, you know. And he starts bucking and broke away from me! And everybody hollered, 'Loose mule, loose mule!' So here came the sergeant on his pony or horse. He goes down the trail after the mule and he gathers him in and brings him back to me and hands me the rein, and I'll never forget him looking down at me and he said,

'Poorest goddam excuse for a mule skinner I've ever seen!' At the end of the night, I was the BAR man—I said, 'Here, you can have your mule back. I'm going to get my BAR.' So I had one day as a mule skinner. It was just part of my life.

The Letter

In between fights, we would be dropped food and supplies, whatever we needed. And one day they dropped some mail along with the other things. So they were passing out the mail and said, 'Busher, who is that?' So I hollered and they sent it back to me. But it was an official letter, it had a little window in it. You know how they have the window? And it said, 'Private Kermit A. Busher.' So I thought, well, who in the heck could be sending me something, you know? So I opened that letter up and what had happened, when they refolded that letter, they folded it wrong so that the full address did not show up in the window. It was supposed to have gone to the commanding officer of Private Kermit A. Busher. Well, you know what that letter was? It was to hold my fifteen dollars. That letter is lost over in Burma somewhere. And I don't know if the government is going to come back on me now for my fifteen dollars. [*Laughs*] Well, that was just among some of the things that happened. You can look at it now and have a little chuckle out of it.

'We Can Disappear In The Jungle'

One thing I really thought that I would see was snakes. I did not see a snake! Now, I was amazed at the elephants. We would see an elephant herd ahead of us. And they would—you know how big an elephant is—and this is jungle that we could not go through ourselves unless we used a machete. That group of elephants can disappear into the jungle. It's streamlined, their trunk and everything like that, how they just slide everything over their back and everything like that and they're gone. But they're gone. You don't see them. And it was just—I was so—I was glad that I went into that area. First of all, when I was in Africa, I was afraid I'd be sent to Germany. And at the time they were having a lot of cold weather. The hedgerows, people were losing their fingers and toes and things like that, frostbite. And I thought, well, if I'm going to die, I want to be comfortable when I'm dying. So when I got into a warm climate, if you could be happy about it, I was comfortable with it, you know. What it also taught me, when we had Vietnam then, I could see—I could sympathize with the American troops that were in Vietnam because they were fighting guerillas. And we were guerillas; I could see what we could do. We could hit a base. We could shoot them up and we don't have to hold ground. We can disappear into the jungle. We'd be gone! That was the same situation in Vietnam. Those poor American boys, they had to stay there and hold the base. And the Viet Cong could attack at their discretion when they wanted to, fight as long as they want to and disappear. It was just reverse, what they were doing from what we had done. We were doing the same thing to the Japs that the Viet Cong was doing to the Americans. So I could fully sympathize with the American troops that were in Vietnam. That's one thing that my World War II experience did teach me on that.

Combat

We had one pretty heavy engagement called Walawbum. And I was not in the battle itself, I was on the right flank way out about three miles away from where the people were fighting in the community in the town itself; there was a right flank out there and a left flank and I was way up on the right flank. Well, it was quiet where I was. So I thought, well, after I had my foxhole dug and I had my

BAR all set up and being quiet, I thought, this is a good time—there was a river right in front of me—this is a good time to just get in that river. And it was my birthday. It was March 22, 1944, and I was born March 22, 1924. I'm 20 years old today and I was in the river bathing and paddling around when all of a sudden right across from me, vroom! The Japanese had artillery right across the bank from me! And I know that they had me under the gunsight, but they wouldn't shoot because they didn't want to disclose their position or anything like that. And what they had done, they had a well over there that they had lured their artillery piece down into and had it camouflaged, and then they could bring it back up when they needed to, and they could shoot. So they were using the artillery to shoot into the town or where the battle was going on! Well, of course, I broke all records getting back to my foxhole and sat there or lay there for quite some while, and then finally, I saw how they got rid of that artillery piece, how they used our Air Force.

Major Briggs, he was my commanding officer who was with us at the time, and I've talked to him since then, he said he happened to have the Air Force liaison man with him in that combat time. And he had them bring in two fighter pilots. And I saw this one way off high and to the side so that the gun just kept on shooting because they didn't think they were in any danger from that plane way off far away. But what he didn't know was that that fellow way off high was giving the coordinates to his buddy, who came in at tree-top level and dropped an egg right on him, and just blew him right out of there, you know. It was just cooperation between the two, how they got rid of that. And Major Briggs said, 'Boy, was I ever glad that I had the liaison man with me at that point!', you know.

Well, the battle was somewhat a success, but my company was not the company that did the battle. We were only added as a little added support. So now it was Blue and Green Company of the Second Battalion who were doing the battle. They pulled back and then we guarded their rear. They were going back, and they ended up—it took us two days to get to Nhpum Ga. And at Nhpum Ga—I don't know what you might know about the name or anything like that—Nhpum Ga was one of our major battles. And when the boys pulled through and they occupied the top of this hill or mountain or whatever you want to call it, that was Nhpum Ga.

The unit I was with then, we went through them and down into the valley and we were expecting them to come on down the next day, you know. But the Japanese were very angry because of the devastation that had been brought on them at Walawbum. So they were pursuing us; in the rear guard we had a few little battles with them, to keep them from following us too close. They were shooting artillery at us. And we had a terrible time trying to hit their artillery, like you try to knock them out also. And we found out later that they had mounted their artillery, they had mounted their mortars on an elephant, and they would shoot off of his back and then kick it in the butt and he would move on, you know, off to another side or something like that, so we couldn't pinpoint where they were. They kept avoiding being hit. They were very spirited in what they were doing on that, and we found this out later that that's what they had done. So at Nhpum Ga then, that became a major battle because the Japanese surrounded the boys [of the Second Battalion] at Nhpum Ga. And they were surrounded there for like ten days or something like that. And while we were down there in the valley, that's when the decision was made by General Merrill and another fella, Red Acker, that they needed artillery dropped to us.

General Merrill was on his way back for some reason and he said, 'I'll have that here tomorrow.' So they did drop the artillery, and he had two crew teams and there were two pieces dropped and they were able to get the boys off of the hill eventually. It took about two more days, but they broke the Japs up and they were able to get them off.

Wounded

I got wounded in that action at that point because before they got the artillery, we had to fight kind of a delayed action, and we had gone around to the back side of the hill and we started up toward the summit and gave the Japs the idea that it was a force that they had to reckon with; we were trying to draw fighters away from the encirclement and fight us. We lost a few fellows, and I got hit. And then it was two days later that the artillery was dropped in and they did get the boys off on Easter Sunday, April the ninth of that year. I got hit on the 4th of April and they sent me back then to 20th General Hospital.

There was no airfield there, but the airplane [I was evacuated by], it was an L-5, had landed on a sandbar, a short sandbar. And what they had done, they tied the tail down to something that would hold it and then they let the engine rev up as much as possible and they chopped the rope holding the tail and it had a catapult action, you know. But still, we didn't get to rise that quickly because I remember looking off to the side and there were monkeys looking around before we got above the trees.

I was wounded in the right thigh. It was a light machine gun. And I must have got about 15 or 20 bullets in this area. [*Gestures to right thigh*] They blew out my leg completely. I lost the bone, and it was just hanging there. When they carried me down the hill, I weighed about 180 pounds at that time. I was actually heavier there than I was at any other time. I don't know why I was gaining weight. And I was a BAR man. I needed all that weight, but when they got me down to the aid station, the doctor was Dr. Hopkins. And he's the fellow that wrote the book, *Spearhead*. And he has documented what my [injury was]—I think I'm entry No. 67 or something in his book. And he used that when he disclosed what he knew about everybody, and he made the remark in there that I was back in the hospital in 33 hours, which was unusual in World War II. Nowadays with a helicopter and everything like that, it's just a matter of almost minutes or hours, you know, that the wounded are taken care of. But I was back in the hospital in 33 hours. And another thing, as I said before, I was hand-carrying my records. I had no records. Phil Piazza and Bob Passanisi, they've all tried to find orders of me joining the Marauders, and they cannot find them. I am a nobody. If it hadn't been for me being wounded and Dr. Hopkins including me in the book, [no one would have even known], but that's my proof that I was a Marauder. So it's just one of those things that has happened in my life.

Kermit Bushur (L) and other Marauders recovering from their wounds, Gaya, India. Library of Congress.

'I Can Save That Leg'

I was wounded on the fourth. The boys got out on the ninth. Well, the hospital knew there was going to be a lot of wounded and sick people coming off the hill, so they had to make room at the

20th General. So they made up a planeload of wounded; most of them were walking wounded. I happened to be one of the better patients, but this is God blessing my life, really what happened, because when they sent me back to there, I was the first person that the doctor looked at because I was the worst wounded. And he was a Southern gentleman, and he was from Hot Springs, Arkansas. He was an older fellow and he just smoked a pipe, and he took my records. He looked at the hospital records, then he uncovered my leg, and he looked at it. Then he read the record again. He looked at my leg and the first words he said to me were, 'They're just crazier than hell.'

I said, 'What's this, Doc?'

He said, 'They have suggested I remove the leg.' He said, 'I can save that leg; if you want to spend some time with me, I can save that leg.'

I said, 'I'll be your brother. I'll be right here, I'll be closer than anybody you ever know!'

So he worked with me, and he did save my leg. He fixed my bone, he fixed my muscles and everything. And it's just today in the past three weeks that I've had to use a cane because I broke my hip now, and I've haven't got my strength back yet. But I've had no pain, nothing bothered my leg at all in all these years. And the Veterans Administration have checked my leg and everything like that and they said, 'You're just perfect. You're in good shape.' But it was this old, Southern doctor from Hot Springs, Arkansas, that saved my leg. They were intending to have it removed; of course, the first hospital was at the edge of the jungle, hot, damp, and the flesh wasn't healing good, so that was their recommendation. Probably if I would have stayed there, I might have lost a leg.

The Nisei Interpreter

We were in a pretty heavy engagement, and we had pulled back that night and we dug in. And Hank Gosho, [one of our Nisei soldiers], was not my friend, he was a friend of Rocky Curtain, who was my platoon sergeant.[53] But Hank came through, I remember him coming through the area. We were all in foxholes, and he found Rocky, and he said, 'I'm going to go out and see what I can find out here in front of us.'

Rocky said, 'You know you're not supposed to go out.'

'I know it. I'm going to go out.'

So Rocky said, 'Okay, you're going out, then I'm going out.' So the two of them did go out; they were in no-man's land, we had no idea what was out there. But he did find a [Japanese] phone line, which he tapped into [to get information, learning our unit was about to be encircled]. All of that night while we were digging our foxholes, we were fairly close to that road and we could hear the Japanese trucks—which were Ford trucks, by the way—we could hear them coming up and the tailgate would drop down and then these Japanese were jumping off and the troops—maybe there would be eight or ten in the truck, they were bringing in a bunch of them. So I knew we were going to be in for a big engagement.

Well, through the knowledge that Hank found out, then we knew they were on the move. They knew we were there, even though it was night. They were trying to trap us. So he told us and got us to go, get out of there, get out of this area. And what the Japanese had done, they had made kind of a horseshoe-like [perimeter surrounding us] with an opening at the one end. We walked out through that end. They knew we were on the move, but they

---

[53] Hank Gosho-Sgt. Henry H. Gosho, Nisei interpreter with Lieutenant Weston's platoon, one of 14 Japanese-Americans who had volunteered for the Marauders.

didn't know where we were going, so they turned loose their little dogs on us. Now see, these are dogs that they use for food, like the American GIs will carry their food. The Japanese, they pull a little dog as he's walking, so they don't have no weight, you know. All they carry is a bag of rice. They have hard-boiled rice, which is just a sling over their shoulder, along with that dog, you know, they could live for months. Well, when the dogs got over among our feet, they would yipe. In the jungle you shoot at sounds more than anything else. When they heard a yipe, they would shoot at us. So we killed a bunch of dogs that day. We had to wring their necks, you know, and we were able to leave that area.

So now that's where Hank got me out of what I thought was almost certain death. I had dug my foxhole, and being a BAR man, I had a supporting rifle. And after we got that foxhole dug, I know I remember turning around and his name was—why do I have to even try and think of his name now, [and I can't bring it up]—but I turned to him, I said, 'It's been nice knowing you. I'm glad that we had this acquaintance.' And I said, 'I hope we can continue our friendship tomorrow morning.' And we really thought this was it. Well, that was the prelude to the battle at Nhpum Ga.

'The Men Who Altered My Life'

I have a letter here from General Merrill where he sent me home. Now this is almost unbelievable that he sent me home. What I had done—I'm working in the replacement depot now, and there were fellas being sent home, and I had fallen through the cracks. I was still there, [but remember, I had no papers]. So I wrote him a griping GI letter, just bitching, you know, about things. He didn't promise me nothing, as you can see in that letter, he just said that he was sorry. He said, 'Your time will come,' and everything like that. But look at the date of that letter, the fifth of May. Now here's the date on this, the sixth of May, general orders from his headquarters were cut to send me by myself, so on the ninth of May I'm on the road home. He gave me also number three priority; it was a 66-hour trip that I made in 55 hours. Other fellas came home by boat, things like that, you know. I made the trip in 55 hours.

Now I'm back home. I have my thirty-day leave. I get this letter that General Merrill wrote; that was my first inkling of why I was being sent home; I had no idea why I was going home. But the letter opened up avenues for me. At Illinois, after my thirty days, I was sent to Miami for another leave of R & R. One day I was eating at the cafeteria, which the army had taken over, and lo and behold, in the front door came two boys that I had taken basic training with! One of them had the bunk next to me. His name was—it had to be a B because things were alphabetical. But they were my first knowledge of what happened to them after they left—see, I went AWOL from these boys, and it turned out that they had gone to England without me. Now, this is Miami. This is a boy right here that I'm talking about now, who wound up in England. Both these boys got hit on D-Day! They were on the beaches, and they lost 95 percent of their personnel, of which I would have been one of. See, there's again the Lady Luck. They were taken prisoner, and he spent all of his time in a German prison camp. [The other] was taken prisoner, and he was in an Italian prison. So all of World War II in Germany, these two boys that I had trained with had spent it in the prison camp! And they were the only ones that ever were able to tell me what had happened to my unit, so I was mighty glad. Now see if General Merrill hadn't sent me home when he did, I would have never gotten to meet these fellas.

General Merrill sending me home when he did, I also ended up in Camp Shelby, Mississippi. And I met a WAC. Before that, I hated WACs, because we'd heard so many stories about, you know at that time, well, it said all the prostitutes in Pittsburgh enlisted en masse.

So we just assumed that they were all prostitutes. But this one WAC changed my mind. We had a courtship, got married, and had a very good life. Now if it hadn't been for General Merrill sending me when he did, I would never have met my wife and then had the family that I did have. So there's the two men [who altered my life], Hank Gosho and General Merrill.

Reconnecting With Truck

After I got out of the jungle, I wrote to Truckenbrote's parents. I had his address, they lived in Chicago, but I did not tell them anything except what I had said, 'I have lost track of Truck.' When the ship was going down, there was a lot of chaos, a lot of people running around, fire, all kinds of explosions, stuff like that. And it was an old English ship that had wooden planks for a stairway, and they burned out in no time, so there were people down in the hole that were trying to get out. You couldn't throw a rope down, because it would burn right away. I saw who I thought was Truck down there, and I did grab a hold of the fellow and he slipped out of my grip, and he fell down, and then I had to jump overboard myself. So in my mind I thought that Truck went down with the ship, and that's what I was more or less asking his parents, what they knew about where Truck was or anything like that, not saying anything.

Their answer back to me gave me a little glimmer of hope. They said, 'We don't know what happened to him, he was badly burned, but he was in India.' He was not far from where I was! In fact, if you look at the Merrill's Marauders directory, you will find his name in there. Now see, I told you he was a finagler; I don't know how he got listed in our directory, but he is in the directory. So when I had made membership badges for all the Marauders, and I sent them to everybody that I could find an address for, and when I was going through the book, I see Truck's name in there, I thought, Truck was never a Marauder, so I was not going to send him a membership badge or card. Instead, I sent him a personal letter. I never heard an answer. So I said, 'Uh-oh, he knows that I know that he was not a Marauder.'

That was in 1995. So then I forgot about trying to get a hold of Truck again, until about four years later I wrote another letter again, and I get an answer this time. It happened that the first letter came at about the same time his wife had died, and he may have seen the letter, he may not have seen the letter, but he was not at New York. He was now living in the Catskills in Upstate New York. So when I found that out, I went to see Ed. He didn't deny to me that he wasn't a Marauder, but he said he was wounded by a stray bullet at Shaduzup. Now whether he was or not, I don't know, but it was so good to see Truck, you know, after all these years. And he is the only guy that could testify that I was on the *Rohna*. I had nothing! So he and I depend on each other; I'm in contact with him right now. And it was just really, really good to see him and then to find out everything that I did find out about him.

'I Don't Know What A Hero Is'

Interviewer: Any parting thoughts that you have or last words, if you will?

I try to save those for birthday cards. I try to think up something wise, something that they'll remember you by. But no, now I'm just about out of last words and things like that. It's been a pleasure and again, I'd say I was not a hero. What is a hero? What's your definition of a hero? I don't know what a hero is. I think a hero might be someone—he's a normal person who saw a need, and did it. I know I was not a hero, because I never had to go into a position where I had to make daily decisions like that, you know. You knew we needed ten men here; we needed a hundred men there. I was just part of that body count, and I was just following orders, something like that. [But] I remember one time lying on the hillside. We were pinned down and we couldn't move. And all of a sudden, I heard the darndest thing—I call it a roar. And I don't know why I called it a roar, but I turned around just momentarily and a guy by the name of Boshart rushed past me and I got to see his eyes, and I swear they were glazed. But whether his temperament had broken or what it was, he went up and he wiped out a machine gun right in front of us! What caused him to do that, see? He might have been a farm boy. He might have been a city boy. He might have been anybody, but all of sudden there for a moment he was acting on an impulse and he did something wonderful.

So what is a hero? I don't know.

Kermit Bushur passed away on July 11, 2009, at the age of 85.

David L. Quaid standing next to his motion picture camera, World War II. Library of Congress.

CHAPTER SIXTEEN

The Combat Cameraman II

David's boyhood interest in newsreel photography brought him to India in the Army, where he wound up on General Stilwell's staff and somehow got away with going AWOL to continue on the missions with Merrill's Marauders. In his assignment as a member of the 164th Signal Photo Company, he had to carry a heavy 35mm Bell & Howell motion picture film camera and still cameras along with his regular infantry gear, documenting their travails and exploits, suffering from the same tropical diseases and severe weight loss, and even survived being hit by a sack of mule feed during an air supply drop. He told an interviewer later that his survival was partly a matter of will. 'I've been shot at so much I just can't tell you. Sooner or later, a good combat cameraman will be a dead one. You just have to feel a little lucky.'

His military decorations included two Bronze Stars and the Legion of Merit.

David Quaid

Getting To India

We landed at Cape Town, South Africa, and we were given a 24-hour pass. And so, the guys I hung out with were an interesting bunch and we knew right away we want to get out of town, be all these GIs all over the place. So we went up into the hills and we found a pub run by an old lady, and she told us her son had been killed in North Africa, but he got mentioned in dispatches, which is very important, and it's like getting a decoration. So anyhow, Bill Safran and myself decided we should do something nice for this lady who was very nice to us, and we found a flower shop, bought some flowers for her, and then we went back into town. We were having a dance. And so, I'm paired off with a very beautiful young girl, and I said, 'What's your name?'

'Well,' she said, my name is such and such, 'but all my friends call me Chippy.' Well, I almost broke up because when I was a kid, a Chippy was a young woman of some doubt about her; anyhow, I almost died. And here's something, again, no one will tell you. You know what they did at these dances? The whole idea was to encourage white American guys to come back to South Africa and settle, to redress the balance.

And so, we get back on the boat and we head for Bombay. And halfway over, our ship goes up in flames, torpedoed. And then we took a train right across India to Calcutta, which I found very interesting, looking out at what was going on. We came to a place called Bilaspur, and as my train came in, another train came in. I opened the compartment door, the guy on this other side opened the compartment door, and there's Joe Rottenberg, my friend Warren's brother. It's amazing. I was on my way in, he was on his way out. And so, we get to Camp Kendrapara, which was a huge staging area for troops. And it was actually, in peacetime, it was some industrialist who had set that up as a retirement place for sacred cows, see, to get them off the streets, if you want the truth.

Getting To Stilwell's Headquarters

When we were still at Camp Crowder, they had sent three units of the 164th overseas. One of them went to China; none of us knew where they went. One went to Stilwell's headquarters, and one went with Merrill's Marauders. So, a guy from Stilwell's headquarters had been accepted for OCS and was on his way home and they needed a volunteer to go up and find General Stilwell's headquarters. Well, that's a pushover for me, old Eagle Scout, so I volunteered. And I must say, I don't think Hatfield, Cochrane, and Beeler ever forgave me for leaving them. They ended up in Karachi, 2,500 miles away from the front, but I couldn't accept that [kind of posting].

So they cut orders for me, and I took off. I got in a C-47, and two Red Cross girls loaded on when I did. And we were airborne for a while, and the pilot invited the two girls [into the nose] to see how you fly a plane. Then two pilots came out and said, 'Oh yeah, we left one of them in, and we put the plane on automatic pilot, and she thinks she's flying it.'

I said, 'You two, get your asses back in there! She could panic and grab something, and we're all going to buy the farm, come on!'

'Oops.' These Air Corps guys were, what, 20, 21 years of age?

I ended up landing at Chaba intact, but then, I had to find my own way down. As I remember, we used to get, when you're traveling, three bucks. It was a lot of money then. In fact, a great deal of money. And we get three bucks to handle our own food and things like that, when it couldn't be handled by some outfit that we would end up. So, at Ledo, they said, 'Don't go anyplace else but this Chinese restaurant. It's terrific.'

Well, it was terrific, but these guys were deserters from the Chinese Army from when Stilwell had to walk out. This was some of the 38th Division that decided to go into business at Ledo, but they were so damn good, nobody bothered them. You follow me? I mean, they should have been picked up instantly. Nobody bothered them.

So I put in for a flight into Burma on an L-5, [a small liaison transport aircraft]. Before that, I had to get jungle equipment and stuff like that. So, I go into the supply office and the supply sergeant says, 'Okay, give me your gas mask.'

I said, 'No, why should I give you my gas mask?'

He says, 'You're going to look like some horse's ass, the only GI in North Burma with a gas mask.' Well, it turns out they figured that Japs were not going to use gas. But they weren't as well read as I was, because I know the Japs did use gas on the Chinese. They flew over them, but anyhow, he won. He got my gas mask.

We fly into a place called Minh Quang in North Burma that had a small strip, and there's nobody there, just the pilot and myself in the L-5. And then another L-5 comes in, and we notice that the landing gear is [pitched on one side], it should be at 45 degrees, and one leg of it is, but the other is hanging this way, rocking back and forth. Well, that was because wherever he picked up this wounded Chinese man, the plane must have [clipped] a tree on the way up. Well, we started watching him as he came in, and the guy was terrific. What he did, after he made a turn, took a look at the strip, he came in like this [*motions with hands in a tilting motion*] and he angled the broken strut back at 45, and then it looked like he was going to crash. At the last minute, he [maneuvered] it over and the two wheels hit the ground. And, of course, it collapsed finally, and the plane spun around, and the pilot and I ran forward and helped him and the wounded man out. And nobody's hurt! It was a great performance. And then, finally, an ambulance came from the Seagraves Hospital Unit, which was beyond the trees, which I couldn't see, and picked him up.

I put my pack on and grabbed my rifle, and I know I have to go south on what was called the combat trace, which was just a jeep track; it's still over somewhere down there, no one seemed to know its exact location at the time. So I shot off.

Now, another L-5 circles the field and comes in. And at that point, a jeep comes from the south and goes to this L-5, and I see them unloading foot lockers and stuff like that into the jeep. And they get finished, they come by me and the jeep stops and Major Arnold turned up. His name was Major Arnold, one of Stilwell's staff, and he said, 'Hey, Sergeant, where are you going?'

I was all by myself. He said, 'Where are you going?'

I said, 'I'm supposed to go down to Stilwell's headquarters.' I said, 'I understand it's that way.'

He said, 'It is, but it's a long way.'

He said, 'Get in, we're going there.' And so, we get to Stilwell's headquarters, and they put me in a basha hut with his bodyguard, which was just about twenty feet from his tent. I think I'm going to have to get a glass of water. I was given the last bunk in front of the door where the rain blows in, naturally; I was the last man there. So, the driver and Major Arnold take this one footlocker and put it on what is now my bunk, and hook it up. And see, these guys had been up there for three months, had never gotten a PX ration of any kind, and Arnold was coming back from Calcutta, where he picked up a few things, like he picked up a whole bunch of corn cob pipes, some Prince Albert tobacco, oh God, what else? I mean, crazy stuff. Oh yeah, I remember a couple of Baby Ruths [candy bars], man. That's what they had. So, they parceled it out for the bodyguard, and there's two left, one for Major Arnold and one for

General Stilwell. So, he said, 'Gee, Sergeant, I'm awfully sorry. We didn't know you were coming.'

I said, 'Come on, I've been living [high on the hog]. You guys don't worry about it.'

So anyhow, he goes into Stilwell's tent, and he comes back, and he lays out the corn cob pipe, Prince Albert tobacco, two Baby Ruths on my bunk. I said, 'I thought he said that there's nothing for me.'

He said, 'The general would like you to have it.' It's a fact. He mentioned that there was a new man in, and he laid it all out. So then, later, and this is off the continuity of the story, but after going through the Marauders and all that sort of business, I ended up with typhus and malaria in 20th General Hospital. And you're not allowed to go back, but I had this wonderful pass, it had my picture on it, signed by Lieutenant General Joseph Stilwell, and it said, 'You are hereby directed to provide this man with any rations and assistance of any kind necessary to carry out his photographic mission.' Now I could have taken that pass and flown home, I mean that's how powerful that card was. I'd just have to show it and zingo, I'd be on my way to the States. So anyhow, even though I was ordered not to, I could never go back into Burma, I went down to the L-5 strip.

'Where do you want to go, Sergeant?'

I said, 'I want to go back to Stilwell's headquarters.'

So I get there, and I'm very weak—and I didn't get into how I bribed my way out of the hospital, that was interesting—but I decided to take a walk down the combat trace, I had a pistol with me, I had a 45. I was always a curious person, and I'm walking, looking down, and it's always muddy, and there was this huge paw print in the mud. As I looked at it in fascination, a single pearl of water came up in the middle of it, so then I thought, you know, 'this is fresh,' and I went up this tiny little game trail, so I knew it had to be a tiger.

I decided to track it, to see how close I could get, I wanted to see it, so I'm tracking it, and I'm getting closer and closer, I think. Then I noticed it veered to the right, and it actually had to break some stuff to do that, so then my Boy Scout manual came back to me—the tracker becomes the tracked, where they circle around behind!

So I went to the left, see, and I came to a chong, which is a river, and I immediately went into that, and went upstream toward where Stilwell's headquarters was. I figured that at least he couldn't track me in the water, but actually, they're not that worried about water themselves. I finally get on the other bank, and there's another trail following the river, so I'm going down this trail fast, and suddenly I stopped cold. I said to myself, 'What the hell's the matter with you?', and I started to look, and I saw a thin brown vine at eye level, coming down, and there it was, and against all this green, it was a little shocking, when you finally realize that in the crotch of the tree in front of you, there's a British hand grenade that this line is hooked to. Now, the British hand grenade was a wonderful weapon, because with the American grenade, where you pulled the pin, throw it, five seconds later, it exploded. Well, the British grenade had two screw-in fuses; one would give you a four-second delay, the other was instantaneous, so it made a marvelous booby trap, the instantaneous setting, and these had been all captured by the Japs at Rangoon.

So I just ducked under it, and I figured I'd leave that for the engineers to handle, and then I ran into what was a recent Jap encampment—I could tell it was a Nip encampment, and it was only, God, less than a mile from Stilwell's headquarters, and so I reported all that when I got back, and they sent some MPs in, and they shot the grenade out of the tree, and that was the end of that.

The Chinese

So I was with this Chinese outfit after I came back out of the hospital, after the campaign to Myitkyina. They had a weird sense of humor. By the way, I'm going to get editorial now, just really editorial. Now, the Marauders lived on K-rations and nothing but that for five months. The Chinese wouldn't eat it, so the Chinese were dropped corned beef, cucumbers, peanut oil, to cook all the vegetables we dropped to them, all this sort of business, but they couldn't seem to do that for us, I mean, that just seems dumb, and by the way, I went in 178 pounds, and I would come out in the 130s, and so did everybody else.

I was sitting on a big teakwood log that was lying on the ground, and the Chinese captain was sitting next to me. Now, we used to always joke with the Chinese and all that sort of business, we'd say, [foreign language] meaning American women are the greatest, and they would say, [foreign language] and would do these little monosyllabic things. Well, it was lunchtime, and I refused to use chopsticks, because I could always say that this bent spoon I had was much more efficient in eating than those damn chopsticks. This is part of the little competition, see, and so I was sitting next to this Chinese captain on a log, and he had his bowl of rice, and they just pour it in their mouth like this, and I was like a patrician eating my chow with my spoon, and I nudged this guy, and I said, 'fun tong,' well 'fun' is rice, 'tong' is dog, 'chowhound,' right?

He put down this bowl of rice, and he had a little bit of rice stuck here on his chin, and he picked up his carbine, and made a 180 degree turn for me, and went bang, now his men are falling down, because he's enraged, and finally, he ends up pointing it between my eyes, and there's a little bit of smoke coming out of the barrel, and my eyes are focused on the rice on his chin, but I was with the Chinese long enough, there's no way I'd lose face. I just looked at him, and maybe my eyes crossed, I don't know, but there it was, and then finally he put the carbine down, that was the end of it, but that's the kind of thing you run into.

Then, and then there was another time, though I was not present, but it was in my group, some of us had been issued what's called jungle hammocks then, which were excellent pieces of equipment, they were terrific, you hung them between two trees, and there was mosquito netting, zipped up, and then where your head is, there was a strap where you could put a .45, see, and the Chinese for some reason really treasured .45s.

One night, this Chinese soldier carefully unzipped the zipper and reached in, grabbed the .45, and the guy in there grabbed the Chinese and started to yell and the Americans got the Chinese. They notified his commanding officer, who came and ordered the soldier to dig his grave, and then he knelt in it and the Chinese officer took his pistol, killed him, but we all knew it was the Chinese officer that sent him to get the pistol, see. And that's what they did, and that's sort of typical.

These are vignettes. In the Battle of Myitkyina, I was with Bob Ray, who was a cameraman with the 101 Detachment OSS. The two of us were up with the 88th Chinese Regiment, as I remember it, and we were in the process of taking cover in a bomb crater. There were some Japs occupying a building up ahead, and the Chinese were wheeling a 37mm cannon. It had the wheel that came out of the arsenal on one side, and the other side was a wheel that came off a yak cart, one of the ancient wooden wheels. It was such a funny sight, but they were firing at the Japs, and the Japs were firing back, and also firing at Bob and myself. I hear something behind me, and I turn and look, and there's this little Chinese soldier, with a little pair of blue shorts made of parachute silk, and a white T-shirt made of parachute silk. And he's got a carrying stick, and on each side he had wooden boxes of British grenades he was bringing forward, and he came running forward, and I was yelling, 'Xiàng xià,' 'Down, down,' 'bad, it's bad, down!' and he came right to the edge of our bomb crater, and he looked down, and I grabbed for his leg to pull him in, and bango, he got it right dead center, he slid down and he looked at me, and he said, 'Méiguānxì,' that means, 'it doesn't matter,' and he died. That was the end of it, but you know, the Chinese, in those days, lived a day and a half away from salvation, all their lives, and they had a different point of view.

Newsreel Wong

So, now we get back to Merrill's Marauders—there's a lot of digression, but I'm either blessed or cursed with total recall, but I have it, take my word. So I would go out, for instance, with Newsreel Wong, you ever hear of him? Very famous, he was on the *Panay*, the gunboat that the Japs shot up, but he was a very famous cameraman, the reason he was called 'Newsreel' was so *News of the Day*, who he worked for, could reach him in China, because there's a million Wongs, see, so the Newsreel separated him from a million other Wongs. He is famous for making that shot of the little baby crying at the railroad station in Shanghai when the Japs bombed the railroad station, and this probably did more to hurt the Japanese than almost any action prior to that shot, I mean, everybody related to that baby.

Original caption: 'This terrified baby was one of the only human beings left alive in Shanghai's South Station after the brutal Japanese bombing in China.' H. S. Wong (1900–1981), Public Domain.

But Wong could travel anywhere, he could go to the Communists [or the Nationalists] in China, he was welcome anywhere, because I guess he probably did a rather disinterested job in a way, he didn't editorialize. So he shows up here, and he and I become friendly. And so I said, 'Let's get down to the front, let's see what's happening,' so I borrow a jeep from headquarters, and we get down, but we're stopped down the combat trace and there's all these tanks in line. This was Colonel Roswell Brown's Chinese American tank group. In those days they had the light tanks, and the Japs had climbed these trees, and they had picric acid, an explosive, about 10 inches square block, about 2 inches thick, with a hole drilled in it, that you had to put a fuse. But as these tanks came under these trees, these Japs jumped down on top of the tanks, lit the fuse, and tamped it with their bodies, and right into these five tanks, knocked them out. I see Newsreel chattering with this Chinese officer, and pretty soon I see Newsreel Wong lining up Chinese soldiers and directing them. So I said, 'The hell with that!'

There was a mopping-up platoon going into the mountain pass that separated the Hukawng Valley from another. The Japs were dug in there, and their line of defense there had been ruptured, so I went up with this platoon, and we were going to mop up there. Their defenses were dug under banyan trees. Now, banyan trees are at least fifteen feet in diameter, huge trees, and they dug in their machine guns underneath the roots of these trees, so even our artillery did nothing. Those are huge trees. When my back was turned while I was shooting film, a Nip threw a grenade at me, and he was killed immediately, so I went up, I got some very good footage. I sent it in with Newsreel Wong's footage, and when I tried to get it after the war, *News of the Day* owned it, see, I couldn't even get it, but in any event, it was amazing.

Anyhow, I finish up with my job, I get down, and Newsreel's done with his, and now we're driving back to headquarters, and I'm not saying anything.

And so we finally get to the basha hut, and he says, 'Dave,' in his Chinese, English accent, he said, 'You are upset with me, Dave.'

I said, 'Of course I am, what you did is phony.' I said, 'We don't direct action, we photograph action, we don't direct it!'

He said, 'Dave, a dead cameraman is good to no one,' and he said, 'The Japanese have $50,000 gold on my head!' When you think of 1942, that's a lot of money. And that's because of the baby shot, that wounded them terribly, worldwide, but I wouldn't let up, I told him it was not right. I did see a review from a British BBC researcher. I met her later, by the way, she gave me all her notes, and she said it was obvious that this is all directed action, because there's no movement. [Now, when she looked at my work, she said that] obviously the camera was on a tripod, the greatest compliment I've ever had, but I'd lean against trees and steady it.

Going AWOL

I am now Stilwell's motion picture cameraman, but I rarely had a chance to photograph him—he was a busy guy, mostly in his tent, actually. I went up north up the Hukawng River and photographed the aftermath of a tank battle, and I was getting short of film. I was near Meng Kwan, which was an airstrip, so I went back there, and at that point, they were evacuating Marauders, and we had a unit of four or five men in there, so I happened to look up as an L-5 came in, and there was Marvin Kirsten, one of the cameramen, so I went up to him, and I said, 'What's going on, Marvin?'

He told me that Anderson had died of cerebral malaria, and he had malaria and other digestive problems, and that Lieutenant Lubin was still in there, but when I got up there, Lubin was on a mule, and the mule bucked, and he broke his leg, and so there's nobody there. So I drove back to Stilwell's headquarters, and Clancy Topp, who was a captain, gave me an official document and I opened it.

S. Sgt. Signal Corps cameraman David L. Quaid peers out from the door of the ruined American Mission School at Myitkyina after the battle, August 1, 1944. Photographer T/4 Shearer. U.S. Signal Corps, Public domain.

It said, 'To Sergeant David L. Quaid, serial number 32355750, you are hereby directed to proceed without delay to Ledo, Assam, India, to become NCO in charge of the photographic unit documenting the construction of the Ledo Road. Sign by endorsement.'

So I told Clancy, 'Clancy, I'm leaving, I'm going in with the Marauders.' I said, 'There's nobody in there,' and I was a professional, you gotta understand, even though I was a young kid, I was a pro. 'It's an intolerable situation,' I said. 'I'm going in!'

'No, you're supposed to be here!'
'I'm going in.'
'What about this letter?'
I said, 'Send it back through channels.'

I was AWOL by my own signature, okay, I figured, you know, they'll catch up to me someday, and I'll go to Leavenworth, what the hell, but I'll be damned if I was gonna just not take care of what I thought was my problem, my responsibility. So I show my little badge to the guy that ran the L-5s, and then I started out.

Traversing the Mountains

I started to photograph the march over the mountains; I got some fantastic footage of General Merrill and General Stilwell, in the middle. He flew in right after me, and we're getting the last air drop of the camp, of the move down the mountains to Myitkyina. I got these fantastic shots of the two of them talking, and with a plane just going right over their heads, you know, all this beautiful stuff, but I kept following them, you know, with my camera, and when you look at the footage, you wonder what the hell they're doing, because they're walking this way, they're walking this way, they're walking that way, they're walking this way, and the whole thing is that they're discussing these final marching orders, secret. Here I am stuffing the camera in their noses, and they're trying to avoid me, and then finally they walk to his hut. And so I go trotting my way up to him and his big MP [grabs me] by the chest and says, 'Out.' But you understand, those two guys, you know, they were lieutenant general and major general. They could have done anything to me, but they knew I was doing my job. You know, it was amazing. I think kindly of them.[54] So then finally, when Stilwell left, I spoke to Merrill and I said, 'Hey, General, I'm going to come along with you. Any objections?'

---

[54] General Stilwell remains a controversial figure in Marauder veteran circles. General Merrill and Colonel Hunter promised the men much needed rest following the airfield fight; instead, Stilwell insisted that the exhausted men continue the fight for the city of Myitkyina in support of the Chinese in the weeks that followed, as long as they could walk and hold a rifle. Men were falling asleep under fire; one disgruntled soldier was overheard to have said, "I had him in my rifle sights. No one would have known it wasn't a Jap that got the son-of-a-bitch." In later conflicts with Chiang Kai-shek, he was relieved of command and returned to the United States, where he died in 1946 at the age of 63 after surgery for stomach cancer.
"I had him in my rifle sights"- Source: Tuchman, Barbara. *Stilwell and the American Experience in China, 1911-45.* New York: Macmillan, 1971. Page 539.

Brig. General Frank Merrill and Lt. General Joseph Stilwell. Burma, 1944. U.S. Signal Corps (Photographer David Quaid?) Public domain.

'Not a one; come on along.'

So after that, it was over the mountains, which was very difficult because the monsoons started that day, and we lost 18 miles off the trail. The Kachins said that the trail had not been used in ten years to begin with, and mules absolutely could never make it. Well, Merrill sent a platoon with Kachins and some of our men up, and we actually had to cut steps, to get the sure-footed mules up the cliff, but finally, eighteen of them fell and went over. When I heard the rifle fire, they were putting them out of their misery, but I thought, 'My God, already, and we've hit the enemy!' Actually, in the footage, if you ever see it, you can see where we would have to take the saddles off the mules. The saddles weighed 96 pounds. And then we'd have to put the saddles on men and have them climb up until you hit a place where the mules could handle it. It was pretty rugged, then I know they said, 'From now on, according to the maps, it's sort of all downhill.' It was worse than before, and it was terrible.

'I'm No Damned Volunteer'

So we finally hit a place called Ritpong. The Japanese had a full company there. The Chinese 88th Regiment was following us, and as the British term it, they were unbloodied, they'd never been in a fight, but it was determined that they would attack there. There were a lot of men doing it. They used to actually blow a bugle, and attack on a bugle. But anyhow, they did that. And before it was all over, myself and another photographer by the name of Warren Bucklin, who was with the *St. Louis Post-Dispatch* in peacetime, went up. Now, the Kachins used to, in the mountains, they would find a grove of large bamboo, eight or ten inches in diameter. And they would dig a trench around that. In the rainy season, all the rain would settle in and then suck up into the bamboo, and then when they had to travel through in dry season, they could cut into that and have water. So we saw a young soldier taking protection in one of these circles, and we jumped in with him and started to talk to him. His name was Page, P-A-G-E. He was telling me he came from Anniston, Alabama, and it was his birthday. I asked him why he volunteered for this.

'I'm no damn volunteer!'

I don't know how he got involved, but he was no damn volunteer. But at that point, the sergeant went by. An order had come to this platoon to move forward toward Ritpong, and the sergeant left to get more detailed orders. When he came back, I'll never forget Page saying, 'Sarge, did you talk him out of it? Sarge, did you talk him out of it?' Apparently, they didn't, because we started to move forward, and I lost track of Page. Suddenly, I heard this loud bang, like an M1, and this whimper-like cry.

I said, 'Well, we got one of them.'

We got some Chinese stretcher bearers in. They rolled this person on the stretcher, and who was it but young Page, on his birthday.

We had a guy of Swedish descent who was a medic and a conscientious objector. He volunteered for the Marauders, even though he carried no weapon. He said, 'Well, the volunteers are gonna need medical help.' And so he was a conscientious objector who did it through real conviction. He got Page out and we took a parachute and made a little aid station out of it. Captain Armstrong, one of our surgeons, was taking care of Page; I photographed Page, and Tony Colombo, Colonel Beach's runner, stayed with Page all night, kidding him along.

PFC Anthony Columbo

We had just gotten back from having about 20 or 30 wounded Chinese soldiers. They were all chewed up, and we got a call that Page had been hurt, and hurt badly. I went out with Dr. Armstrong, we set up a makeshift operation. I was no medic, but I just helped him. He was talking. He was coherent for the earlier part of the evening, and then he started to fade and fade away. He was afraid, and we knew he was going. He was going to die. I don't know. It's hard to explain. I was nineteen years old. He was eighteen. From what I understand, that was his birthday. I just sat there and held his hand. He lay there until I don't know what time in the morning, and then just expired.

David Quaid

Page died that night on his 18th birthday. [*Pauses*] Nice kid.

'The Most Important Thing In This Outfit'

Then, the whole idea, tactically, was for us to handle the Ritpong situation and let A Battalion slide through unnoticed and go down a trail to Myitkyina. We were a diversion. So we were sent again over the mountains to a place where we ran into this reinforced Jap battalion, and our first scout was killed, but we held there for two days, and I photographed real jungle combat. You could actually see the bullets flying through the trees and all that sort of business. But then, let's say there's a lull, so I wanted to see what had happened with our guys. One guy next to me was firing rifle grenades that killed a Japanese warrant officer and two privates. I wanted to find out what had happened, and I slid off this area down to a trail. It was a high bank that I came down, and then I found a place where

I could reload the camera. And now I started up the trail, right down the middle of it, and Bill Toomey, a machine gunner, was setting his heavy machine gun into the tripod. He saw me, and he said, 'Dave, Dave, what are you doing?'

I suddenly realized that I was walking right up the middle of the trail, which no one does. And at that point a Jap machine gun opened up, and the guy was very good. He walked it right down, and he expected me to fall; he walked the bullets right up the trail. Only I went to the right, where the trail fell off, and the Jap followed me, and I heard this 'sock,' like a meat cleaver hitting a side of beef. I rolled down, and I ended up behind about an eight-inch tree. And I'll never forget I heard this tinkle, tinkle, tinkle. And I sort of looked up without lifting my head; it was his machine gun bullets going right through the tree, and stuff was hitting my helmet. Father Barrett and Captain Armstrong had a theory that if you got to a man right away with plasma, and a friendly word, chances are he would not go into shock. So they would follow the skirmish line right up and do this. I heard Colonel Meade say, 'Damn it, you're my chaplain, and you're my medic. I order you to stop that. Lie back. We'll get the men to you!' They wouldn't do it. So suddenly, I saw Armstrong and Barrett come in. And I thought what I saw was that I photographed all of it, and Barrett was giving Toomey the last rites.

The Chinese stretcher bearers took him out. At the time, you see, you were not allowed to shoot, to photograph, American casualties during the war. I made up my mind—I was going to photograph Toomey. I mean, here's this guy, if it wasn't for him, I would have been dead, and the least I'd do is memorialize him. And so I photographed him being wrapped in his poncho and buried.

The guys were furious at me. They thought it was terrible. And Father Barrett gave a lecture, saying Dave was probably doing the most important thing in this outfit, showing people what war is really like, and so the guys laid off after that.

After the war, my young daughter was registered into a little parochial school in New York. And it was only six classes; they were building [the infrastructure] as they got money. So I came home one night from the studio, and there was this request for money, there's a few memorials left. And one of them were the bells that would be rung when the school was to change classes. So I said to my wife, I said, 'We're going to buy that bell for Toomey.' I said, 'He's buried in Buddhist country, but I think he may be a Catholic boy, and every time those bells ring, it will also call the attention of the Buddhist spirits where he's buried.'

So that's what we did. And his family has gotten in touch with me, and I actually sent them the footage. I told them, you got to understand you're going to see your brother get killed, better know what you're looking at.

*

After two days, we felt we had held up. We had allowed A Battalion to go for the airstrip. So then we started south, to get on the main trail south, and what I do remember vividly, of course, is it was a night march, and we were almost to Myitkyina, and I heard this sigh, and then something fell.

The next thing I knew, I tripped over a dead horse and fell. The horse had worked himself to death. Mules will not do that. A mule will stop and get its breath, but you can work a horse to that, and this one just died on its feet.

We come out on this Jap road, and what I remember is most of us are aghast when we look at the footage. We just walked down this road without flankers out or anything. A little strange, so, anyhow, they needed us at the airstrip. So Dave Richardson of *Yank Magazine* and myself went across with A.B. Weingarten's platoon to get to the airstrip. [Now, to get film out], I would send footage out with wounded men on a litter, I'd get plasma boxes from the medics, and I sent out two boxes of film. They went with the wounded until they hit Arang, which was a clandestine OSS airstrip. The plane took off again with a wounded man and my film and crashed into a tree; it was too short, but nobody was hurt, strangely enough. But they took my film and everything else they could on the plane and threw it into a drainage ditch. Dave Richardson of *Yank Magazine*, who was with the Marauders all the way from beginning to end, would have to leave after a portion of each campaign to go back and write up his stuff. So he flew into Arang to join up with us again. And he got out of the plane and saw two boxes of film. One is still up in the L-5 in a tree, but one box of film had my name on it. And he redirected it to the chief signal officer, New Delhi, India, before his pilot, who was flying back empty, could take off, he got it into the plane. Yeah, otherwise it wouldn't exist. [They made newsreel footage out of it]; oh yeah, it's very famous. It's really the only combat film that exists in the Marauders. There are plenty of very, very good stills.

Hit By a C-47 Air Drop

I'm the only human being that ever got hit from a free drop from a C-47 and survived. Yeah, I did. In fact, just in June, I've had this leg fixed from that. Unfortunately, I was opening a window at home, and I fell, and I'm afraid they were going to have to do it all over again. Terrible. I could go on and on and on forever. [But my war ended], and I can tell you that exactly. So, this was a Thanksgiving airdrop. And the president said, 'Wherever your sons or daughters are, on land or sea or in the air, they will have a turkey dinner.' And I was photographing this airdrop, to prove that the whole thing was a lie. [*Laughs*] And so I got hit with... now see, the trouble was that the first- and second-string troop carriers had been rotated home. They were great. We used to say they didn't drop to us, they stacked it, because if it went into the trees, it was gone. So these guys were special.

Now, they brought an outfit in from the ETO surplus unit, and they were dropping right on our trail, and they didn't have their radio on. One of our officers said, 'Get me two BAR men up here, and if this son of a doesn't turn on the radio, shoot him down!' And then they started the free drop of mule feed, well, that goes off in about thirty to forty 70-pound bags at a time. I heard them coming, and I was a good swimmer as a kid, and so I made a racing dive, but it caught me in the air. And if I had my feet planted, I would have been Jello. The force is so unbelievable. In fact, Captain Worley, a medic, came up to me. I mean, while this is still going on. Brave man. He says, 'Sergeant, how does it feel to jump off the Empire State Building?' And then there was a long pause. He said, 'And live?'

Then they started to drop the heavy stuff on parachutes, and there was one coming down directly on me, and I yelled to my buddy, I said, 'Bill, Bill, it's going to hit me!' And he stood up, and he said, 'Don't worry about it!' Oh, he tried to catch it; he would have been mud. But it just missed my feet, and so he didn't have to commit himself.

They put me on a plane. The morphine wouldn't work, they kept giving me syrette after syrette of morphine. Finally, I went out. I was at the 14th Evacuation Hospital.

I woke up, and there was an orderly with a flashlight.

'Hey, can you do something about that guy? He's moaning all the time. I can't sleep.'

The [orderly shrugged]. He says, 'Sergeant, you're the only one in here!'

So finally, they finally flew me back to 20th General Hospital. They hung me up in traction for five months; in fact, I have an eight-by-ten shot of Lady Mountbatten visiting me, and here I am with all these wires. I looked like a Wright biplane, you know? And so anyhow, then it came time to go home.

'I Had Never Cried In My Life'

This is what you really want. And they were packing me into a... [*pauses*] —I'll tell you something—I cried, and I never had cried in my life. When they were going to ship me home, I wanted to go back. I wanted to, I told myself and my friends that we weren't going to quit until we hit Shanghai. And I felt terrible. And so anyhow, a captain comes in and gives me wads of postal money orders, wads of them, because I never took any pay, I was always gone. And then he says, 'Raise your right hand, Sergeant.'

'Why?'

He said, 'Well, you got a field commission, but you've never been sworn in. So you've got to be sworn in.'

I said, 'Wait a minute.'

I said, 'Captain, can I do duty in the rank of a second lieutenant?'

He looked at me now—I was in a cast from here to the bottom with a stick across the legs, and he said, 'Sergeant, I don't see a chance.'

I said, 'Well, I'm not going to take any rank that I can't do duty in, period,' and I turned it down. So then they put me on an airplane, and they fly me to Casablanca. Now, by this time, I got kidney stones from lying on my back for five months and them pouring in calcium because bones don't knit in the tropics. They give me enough morphine to handle the kidneys, and now they're going to take me to this airplane. They put me in a forklift truck and stuffed me in the door. And there's these two big white-clad orderlies, and they grab me, and [they can't get me in the doorway].

'Okay. Turn him over.'

'Try it this way.'

'Try it that way.' Then, finally, they get me in by breaking the cast in many places. Now, we take off, and out came one of the officers, and the flight nurse. She goes down to the ambulatory guy, the first ambulatory guy. 'In the event of ditching, you put this over your neck, your thighs, by here, blah, blah, blah.' Yeah. Then she goes to the next guy, and the next guy, and the next guy, and then the last of the ambulatory guys. The two of them turn around and look at me, then they look at each other. She pats me on the forehead and says, 'Sergeant, don't be concerned. Regulations say, in case of ditching, the litter patients are offloaded first.' Oh God. [*Laughs*]

Then we landed in Florida, and they took me to Coral Gables Hotel Hospital, which was an Air Force hospital. They wheel me in on a gurney, and there's everybody crying.

I said, 'What the hell's going on here?' Somebody had passed. 'What's the matter with you people?'

'What's the matter with you? The president died!' That was when President Roosevelt died at Warm Springs.

"You're The Guy I've Been Looking For'

I had a long way to go. I'll give you one more. We set off to Rhodes General Hospital, which was for bones and stuff. I was a motion picture cameraman, so obviously I'm a projectionist. When I could get around, one of the things I had to do was wheel a projector around and show these combat films, including a lot of my own stuff, to these guys, because the war was still on and they're going to go to the Pacific. They didn't want them to lose their edge. But I would leave some of these wards afterwards with these guys [bouncing] off the ceiling, you know? So much for psychiatry. [*Laughs*]

So, I was supposed to help a captain on some photographic problem they had. He came in, and he was incoherent. He was trying to describe how one bomb could blow up a city, and he couldn't do it, because there wasn't much information at that point. I do remember when we heard that the war was finally over. We heard at night, and someone started to sing Christmas carols. That's what we sang all night.

Every Saturday, the board would come through. That's all these doctors, and they would go over your case, then they would board you in or out. Either you'd stay for treatment, or you would be boarded or discharged out to a veterans hospital. They kept saying, 'You're going to be sent to a veterans hospital.'

I said, 'Cut it out! You guys didn't give me the proper PT treatments,' which they didn't. I said, 'You guys get it fixed. I'm not leaving.' Well, I held them off. Then they finally say, 'This Saturday, you're out.' So, I was supposed to go down to the MP shack, like, you know, at the gate and everything where there'll be a bus to take me to the train to take me to some other place. Now, this one leg was at right angles, frozen like this. But I was on crutches, and I was good at crutches. So finally, the bus comes in, and some guys get on it. I get on it, and I'm up about two steps. A jeep comes around the corner. This black, curly-haired guy said, 'Sergeant! Sergeant! You get out. Get down there.'

I said, 'Who the hell are you?' and it was a major. 'What do you want?'

He said, 'This bus is for discharge. You're not ready for that.' I said, 'Who are you?' He said, 'I'm Major Perlman. I'm in charge of orthopedics. Get off there, come with me.'

He brought me into the MP shack, measured me. Laid me out on the desk, and he said, 'Now look, Sergeant, get in the jeep. You're going back. First of all, I want to know who boarded you out. Second, yeah, we can probably help you.'

He said, 'We can put you in what's called a turnbuckle cast that has a hinge here, and has a lead screw. You're going to have to take up two turns a day in that screw to break this loose.'

He said, 'It's going to hurt like hell for three months. But I guarantee you that you'll walk with a cane, or you'll walk without any. But you won't be on crutches.'

I said, 'Man, you're the guy I've been looking for!'

We did just that, and I ended up walking for six years on this leg. We needed more treatment, but yeah. Now, it's 1948. I always swore if I ever got into Cincinnati, where he was a big shot at George Hospital in Cincinnati, I said I had to go in and thank Major Perlman. So, it was a Saturday, and Truman was just about to be elected. So I went in and spoke to his receptionist, and she said, 'Just wait till we get rid of this load. I know the major is going to want to talk to you.' So he comes out, he recognized me right away. Well, we spent three months together. Then he bullied me because I wasn't exercising my thigh, and, you know, he said, 'Now look, how long are you going to be here?'

I said, 'I'm making a picture for Proctor & Gamble.' I said, 'I'll be here, you know, probably a couple more weeks at least. More than that maybe.'

He said, 'My wife's a great cook. I'm off on Wednesdays. How about you come to my house on Wednesday? My wife, I'm sure she's going to want to meet you.'

I said, 'Sure. Fine.'

So, Tuesday afternoon, somebody kicked a light, and I jumped off the camera crane and caught my heel in a camera cable. I went down on a deck, and I broke my arm. So, everybody wants to get me to the hospital and all the sort. I said, 'No way. No one touches me but Major Perlman.'

So, I went back to the Netherland Plaza Hotel. I had a copy of the *Weekend New York Times*, I got the magazine section. I wrapped it around the arm, and we have what we call camera tape, which is white tape. I wrap the whole thing in it. I went to sleep this way, up to my chest. Next morning, I grab a cab. Before that, I called them up. I said, 'Major, Dave Quaid.'

'My wife is very happy, we got everything set. It's going to be a wonderful evening.'

I said, 'Wait a minute. Hey, Major, we have to talk business.'

'What do you mean by that?'

I said, 'I broke my arm.'

'Please, meet me at George Hospital. I'll meet you over there.'

So I get to George Hospital. I identified myself, and the receptionist breaks up. 'Ha ha ha ha. So you're Mr. Quaid, who he has to fix up all the time. Ha ha ha ha.' You know? Finally, he got me repaired, and then it was time to go home. So he said, 'I don't want you to go home. I want to handle your recovery myself.' Then he said, 'But who's your doctor?'

I said, 'Dr. Rosenthal, in Richmond Hill.'

He said, 'Abner Rosenthal?'

I said, 'Yeah!'

He said, 'He was my roommate for four years in medical school!' See, it never stops. All right, that's enough.

John Easterbrook, retired U.S. Army colonel and grandson of General Joseph W. Stilwell, noted about Quaid's work and the estimated 23,000 pictures in total taken by the 250 men of the 164th Signal Photo Company: 'They made a significant contribution to the knowledge of Chinese history during the Allies-Japanese war. In some small way, these photographs also provided recognition of the American assistance to the Chinese people during those hard and difficult days.'[36]

David Quaid featured in a 1952 camera advertisement.

After the war, David Quaid went into commercial cinematography and direction, filming the very first television commercial (for Ipana toothpaste) and working in Hollywood feature films. He passed on August 19, 2010, at the age of 90.

Surrender ceremonies, 2,000 plane flyover, USS MISSOURI left foreground. National Archives. Public domain.

EPILOGUE

Afterword

"It is my earnest hope, and indeed the hope of all mankind, that from this solemn occasion a better world shall emerge out of the blood and carnage of the past—a world founded upon faith and understanding, a world dedicated to the dignity of man and the fulfillment of his most cherished wish for freedom, tolerance, and justice."

—REMARKS BY GENERAL DOUGLAS MACARTHUR, SURRENDER CEREMONY ENDING THE WAR WITH JAPAN AND WORLD WAR II, SEPTEMBER 2, 1945

"Can't we just let go of this war? My father spent four years in, [and] my uncles four years; they NEVER talked about it! Long dead soldiers, long ago war!"

-American commenter on one of the author's social media posts, highlighting the series, *The Things Our Fathers Saw*, September 2024

*

Was it really that long ago?

Seventy-nine years ago this month, Admiral 'Bull' Halsey's flagship USS *Missouri* was in Tokyo Bay awaiting the arrival of the Japanese delegation with General MacArthur and Admiral Nimitz aboard, positioned near the spot where Commodore Matthew C.

Perry had anchored his 'Black Ships' on his first visit to Japan in 1853. On display aboard the battleship that morning was the flag that flew on December 7, 1941, over Hickam Field at Pearl Harbor, and the 31-starred Old Glory standard of Perry's flagship from nearly a century before, now accompanied by hundreds of American warships. The Japanese delegation was escorted promptly aboard at 9:00 a.m., and at MacArthur's invitation, signed the terms of surrender. As if on cue, four hundred gleaming B-29 bombers roared slowly by in the skies overhead, escorted by fifteen hundred fighters.[37]

In the United States and Europe, it was six years to the day that the bloodiest conflict in human history had begun; after those six years of savage fighting, the devastation was unprecedented and incalculable. Between sixty and eighty-five million people—the exact figure will never be known—would be dead. Overseas, the victors would be forced to deal with rubble-choked cities and tens of millions of people on the move, their every step dogged with desperation, famine, and moral confusion. American servicemen, battle-hardened but weary, would be forced to deal with the collapse of civilization and brutally confronted with the evidence of industrial-scale genocide. Old empires were torn asunder, new ones were on the ascent. The Chinese Communists were victorious in China before the end of the decade; the British and other colonial powers began shedding their colonies in South Asia and elsewhere. In 1952, American occupation ended, lasting nearly twice as long as the war with America itself.

Now, the 'American Century' was well underway. American power and leadership of the free world was unparalleled and unprecedented. The Marshall Plan literally saved Europe. Enemies became allies. Former allies became adversaries. The Atomic Age began. And the United States of America rebuilt, reconstructed, and remodeled Japan. Of course, this 'American Century' was not free from hubris, error, and tragic mistakes, but all of this is part of the legacy that shapes us to this day.

*

In regards to the end of World War II, I can recall, in the early 1980s as a young history teacher in training, observing a veteran teacher describing the end of the war with Japan by making an analogy to his eighth graders:

'It's like two brothers who had a fight. The winner picks up the loser, dusts him off, and they go on as brothers and friends.'

Overlooked, perhaps, were the eight million Chinese civilians and millions of others in Asia slaughtered by Japanese troops in their imperial lust for conquest, the Allied prisoners of war brutalized and worked to death or executed in slave labor camps, the Allied seamen shot while foundering in the water at the explicit orders of the Japanese Imperial Navy, to say nothing of the deceitfulness of Pearl Harbor. I'm sure my twenty minutes observing the teacher in action left out what he hopefully covered in class; he must have known World War II veterans, just as I did. And these are things I suppose you learn later in life, as I did—but only because I wanted to know as much as I could learn. I was born sixteen years after the killing stopped, but ripples of that war have never ended.

If you are a reader of this series, you know how I got our veterans involved once I found my footing in my own classroom. My fascination with World War II began with the comic books of my 1970s pre-teen days, Sgt. Rock and Easy Company bursting off the pages in the bedroom I shared with my younger brothers at 2 Main Street. As a newly minted college grad a decade later, I was drawn to the spectacle of our veterans returning to the beaches of Normandy on the black-and-white TV in my apartment for the fortieth anniversary of D-Day. I was reading the only oral history compilation I was aware of, Studs Terkel's euphemistically titled 1984 release, *The Good War: An Oral History of World War II*, over and over. I studied that book, planting the seed for my own debut in the classroom. And in retrospect, I think I reached out to my students asking them if they knew anyone in World War II, yes, as a way to engage them in the lessons at hand, but also to satisfy my own selfish curiosity: just what 'resources'—really national treasures—did we have in our own backyard, surrounding our high school? I was going to find out. Man, was I going to find out!

Of course they 'never talked' about it! Why would they bring 'The War' up with their wives, their sons, their daughters? And frankly, most of the civilians they returned home to and surrounded themselves with at work, in the community, and even in their own families, weren't really all that interested in hearing about it. It was time to get on with life.

But then those guys headed back to the Normandy beachheads, now approaching retirement age, most in their early sixties, if that (about my age right now)...

Somebody was now listening! Somebody gave a damn! And maybe the old soldier could talk about that kid who was shot and lingered on for a while in the far-off jungles of Burma, the country boy far from home who was proud to be a soldier, the eighteen-year-old who wondered now if he was going to die. The combat photographer David Quaid spoke to his interviewers until he was too exhausted to go on. But somebody was interested, and he had things to say—things to get off his chest—before he would no longer be able to say them; like David, a lot of the guys I knew opened up like a pressurized firehose after all those years of silence. It was frankly cathartic, and maybe now they could 'let go of this war.'

Should we?

*

I didn't respond to the commenter in the thread, but another person added,

"I understand, but if there is no conversation, nothing gets shared—nothing gets learned! May your family all rest in peace!"

I know in my heart that opening up to others, even complete strangers, but especially to the young, finally brought our veterans peace.

*

A Final Thought

"I don't want to see [that] we are in a history book, and a page is turned, and we are forgotten."
-9/11 FDNY firefighter, 2024, in tears, called off at the last moment by a friend who took her place. Three hundred forty-three of her brothers and sisters died that day.

I finished this 10th volume on the 23rd anniversary of the 9/11 attacks; watching CBS's *60 Minutes* that Sunday before, I was struck profoundly by that firefighter's tears.

Which brings me to my final thoughts. Over the past nine years, I've strung together over a million words out of the mouths of our World War II veterans and Holocaust survivors. People will ask me now, are you going to continue to tell their stories of World War II? Are you going to do books involving oral histories of other American wars? The answer is, maybe; I just don't know. When I was actively collecting stories, the priority was on the oldest veterans still with us, and frankly many of the veterans of following wars and conflicts were just not ready yet; I know some of them felt in some degree intimidated by the World War II generation, and we know, of course, that many of our Vietnam veterans were mistreated when they returned home. What I think I really would like to do with the time I have left is help other teachers bring them into the classroom, connecting with our young people, keeping our history alive. School leaders need to recognize the importance of strengthening their community by encouraging the type of oral history projects that, in our case, have literally helped to heal the world; in fact, look for the four-part miniseries on my book *A Train Near Magdeburg* in 2025, in time for the eightieth anniversary of liberation and the end of World War II. I hope our work will inspire our teachers and school and community and political leaders to see the value of our veterans and this type of history education with our young people as a national resource for learning about our past.

I also plan on working on a much-needed sequel to *A Train Near Magdeburg,* having learned so much more, meeting and interviewing so many more soldiers, survivors, and second-generation survivors since that book's 2016 debut, not to mention all of the subsequent visits to the authentic sites of persecution and liberation, and connecting with the German schoolkids who are bravely keeping the history alive in their own backyard.

So, rest assured, I do have a few more books in me. I'll keep looking through my notebooks, getting ideas, keeping the history alive. With you and others reading, listening to, and embracing their stories, maybe our veterans and their friends won't be long dead. In the meantime, as always, thank you for your investment of time with us, and please keep sharing our *raison d'être*:

> *Dying for freedom isn't the worst that could happen.*
> *Being forgotten is.*

If you liked this book, you'll love hearing more from the World War II generation in my other books. I can let you know as soon as the new books are out, give you film updates, and offer you exclusive discounts on some material. Just sign up at the signup box at matthewrozellbooks.com.

Some of my readers may like to know that all of my books are **directly available from the author, with collector's sets which can be autographed** in paperback and hardcover. They are popular gifts for that 'hard-to-buy-for' guy or gal on your list. Visit my shop at matthewrozellbooks.com for details.

THE THINGS OUR FATHERS SAW® SERIES:

VOICES OF THE PACIFIC THEATER

WAR IN THE AIR: GREAT DEPRESSION TO COMBAT

WAR IN THE AIR: COMBAT, CAPTIVITY, REUNION

UP THE BLOODY BOOT-THE WAR IN ITALY

D-DAY AND BEYOND

THE BULGE AND BEYOND

ACROSS THE RHINE

ON TO TOKYO

HOMEFRONT/WOMEN AT WAR

CHINA, BURMA, INDIA

ALSO: A TRAIN NEAR MAGDEBURG

ABOUT THE AUTHOR

Photo Credit: Joan K. Lentini; May 2017.

Matthew Rozell is an award-winning history teacher, author, speaker, and blogger on the topic of the most cataclysmic events in the history of mankind—World War II and the Holocaust. Rozell has been featured as the 'ABC World News Person of the Week' and has had his work as a teacher filmed for the CBS Evening News, NBC Learn, the Israeli Broadcast Authority, the United States Holocaust Memorial Museum, and the New York State United Teachers. He writes on the power of teaching and the importance of the study of history at TeachingHistoryMatters.com, and you can 'Like' his Facebook author page at MatthewRozellBooks for updates.

Mr. Rozell is a sought-after speaker on World War II, the Holocaust, and history education, motivating and inspiring his audiences with the lessons of the past. Visit MatthewRozell.com for availability/details.

About this Book/ Acknowledgements

*

A note on historiographical style and convention: to enhance accuracy, consistency, and readability, I corrected punctuation and spelling and sometimes even place names, but only after extensive research. I did take the liberty of occasionally condensing the speaker's voice, eliminating side tangents or incidental information not relevant to the matter at hand. Sometimes two or more interviews with the same person were combined for readability and narrative flow. All of the words of the subjects, however, are essentially their own.

Additionally, I chose to utilize footnotes and endnotes where I deemed them appropriate, directing readers who wish to learn more to my sources, notes, and side commentary. I hope that they do not detract from the flow of the narrative.

First, I wish to acknowledge the hundreds of students who passed through my classes and who forged the bonds with the World War II generation. I promised you these books someday, and now that many of you are yourselves parents, you can tell your children this book is for them. Who says young people are indifferent to the past? Here is evidence to the contrary.

The Hudson Falls Central School District and my former colleagues have my deep appreciation for supporting this endeavor and recognizing its significance throughout the years.

Cara Quinlan's sharp proofing and suggestions helped to clean up the original manuscript.

Naturally this work would not have been possible had it not been for the willingness of the veterans to share their stories for posterity, with the New York State Military Museum's Veterans Oral History Project and the Library of Congress Veterans Oral History Project. Please see the 'Source Notes.'

I would be remiss if I did not recall the profound influence of my late mother and father, Mary and Tony Rozell, both cutting-edge educators and proud early supporters of my career. To my younger siblings Mary, Ned, Nora, and Drew, all accomplished writers and authors, thank you for your encouragement as well. Final and deepest appreciations go to my wife Laura and our children, Emma, Ned, and Mary. Thank you for indulging the old man as he attempted to bring to life the stories he collected as a young one.

NOTES

Source Notes: **Helen Quirini.** Interviewed by Michael Russert and Wayne Clarke, August 31, 2004. Latham, NY. Deposited at NYS Military Museum.

Source Notes: **Mabel Colyer, Frances Cooke, Ethel Severinghaus.** Interviewed by Michael Russert and Wayne Clarke, August 6, 2003. Deposited at NYS Military Museum.

Source Notes: **Ruth A. Bull.** Interviewed by Michael Russert and Wayne Clarke, May 19, 2003. Amsterdam, NY. Deposited at NYS Military Museum.

Source Notes: **Leonard Amborski.** Interviewed by Michael Russert and Wayne Clarke, May 6, 2008. Buffalo, NY. Deposited at NYS Military Museum.

Source Notes: **Jane W. Washburn.** Interviewed by Jennie Valyer, December 3, 2003, for the Hudson Falls HS World War II Living History Project. South Glens Falls, NY. Deposited at NYS Military Museum.

Source Notes: **Elaine Curren Sommo.** Interviewed by Jared Hunt, December 10, 2003, for the Hudson Falls HS World War II Living History Project. Hudson Falls, NY. Deposited at NYS Military Museum.

Source Notes: **Spencer Kulani.** Interviewed by Victor Ikeda, January 4, 2006, for the Hudson Falls HS World War II Living History Project. Hudson Falls, NY. Deposited at NYS Military Museum.

Source Notes: **Kathryn Goodman Frentzos.** Interviewed by Megan Seeley, January 11, 2010; Abigail George, December 6, 2010; and Alexandria Cartier, December 17, 2011. Hudson Falls, NY. Hudson Falls HS World War II Living History Project. Deposited at NYS Military Museum.

Source Notes: **Katherine G. Denegar.** Interviewed by Michael Russert and Wayne Clarke, October 3, 2003. Latham, NY. Deposited at NYS Military Museum.

Source Notes: **Lillian Lorraine Yonally.** Interviewed by Wayne Clarke, August 27, 2009, Colonie, NY. Deposited at NYS Military Museum.

Source Notes: **Rose Landsman Miller.** Interviewed by Wayne Clarke, November 5, 2009, Pine Plains, NY. Deposited at NYS Military Museum.

Source Notes: **Margaret Doris Alund Lear.** Interviewed by Michael Russert and Wayne Clarke, December 16, 2002. Saratoga Springs, NY. Deposited at NYS Military Museum.

Source Notes: **Helen Marcil Brennan.** Interviewed by Wayne Clarke, September 21, 2012. Troy, NY. Deposited at NYS Military Museum.

Source Notes: **Rose Landsman Miller.** Interviewed by Wayne Clarke, November 5, 2009, Pine Plains, NY. Deposited at NYS Military Museum.

Source Notes: **Kathleen Mary Davie.** Interviewed by Megan Shuler, January 5, 2006, for the Hudson Falls HS World War II Living History Project. Hudson Falls, NY. Deposited at NYS Military Museum.

Source Notes: **Joyce Griffin.** Interviewed by Sara Weiskotten, December 20, 2004, for the Hudson Falls HS World War II Living History Project. Hudson Falls, NY. Deposited at NYS Military Museum.

Source Notes: **Joan Hoffman.** Interviewed by Adam Armstrong, December 8, 2007, for the Hudson Falls HS World War II Living History Project. Hudson Falls, NY. Deposited at NYS Military Museum.

Source Notes: **Halina Roman.** Interviewed by Eric Roman, December 15, 2007, for the Hudson Falls HS World War II Living History Project. Erie, PA. Deposited at NYS Military Museum.

Source Notes: **Eva Koenig.** Interviewed by Lauren Ellmers, November 25, 2006, for the Hudson Falls HS World War II Living History Project. Hudson Falls, NY. Deposited at NYS Military Museum.

Source Notes: **Lily Muller.** Interviewed by Jackie Goodale, December 19, 2007, for the Hudson Falls HS World War II Living History Project. Hudson Falls, NY. Deposited at NYS Military Museum.

Source Notes: **Morgan Vaux.** Interviewed by Mark D. Doud. Undated. Deposited at the Veterans History Project, American Folklife Center, Library of Congress.

Source Notes: **Emma Jane Hanks.** Interviewed by Erica Sugar. Undated. Deposited at the Library of Congress Veterans History Project.

Source Notes: **Patrick Scarano.** Interviewed by Robert von Hasseln and Michael Aikey, January 23, 2001, Syracuse, NY. Deposited at NYS Military Museum.

Source Notes: **Norman Handelman.** Interviewed by Michael Russert and Wayne Clarke, January 11, 2005. New York, NY. Deposited at NYS Military Museum.

Source Notes: **Robert D. O'Brien.** Interviewed by Michael Russert and Wayne Clarke, July 30, 2002. Latham, NY. Deposited at NYS Military Museum.

Source Notes: **Leonard R. Reeves.** Interviewed by Sharon House. May 26, 2005. Deposited at the Veterans History Project, American Folklife Center, Library of Congress.

Source Notes: **Kenneth Wilbur Thomas.** Interviewed by Tony P. Lupo. Undated. Deposited at the Veterans History Project, American Folklife Center, Library of Congress.

Source Notes: **Samuel V Wilson.** Interviewed by Mark R. Franklin. May 15, 2014. Deposited at the Veterans History Project, American Folklife Center, Library of Congress.

Source Notes: **Philip B. Piazza.** Interviewed by Christy Chason. 2005. Deposited at the Veterans History Project, American Folklife Center, Library of Congress.

Source Notes: **Morris H. Factor.** Interviewed by Gunnar Gunnarsson. October 26, 2012. Deposited at the Veterans History Project, American Folklife Center, Library of Congress.

Source Notes: **Herbert Clofine.** Interviewed by Christy Chason. 2005. Deposited at the Veterans History Project, American Folklife Center, Library of Congress.

Source Notes: **Roy Matsumoto.** Deposited at the Veterans History Project, American Folklife Center, Library of Congress.

Source Notes: **Robert E. Passanisi.** Interviewed by Carrie Schneider. 2005. Deposited at the Veterans History Project, American Folklife Center, Library of Congress.

Source Notes: **Warner Katz.** Interviewed by Sheila Dyer. 2005. Deposited at the Veterans History Project, American Folklife Center, Library of Congress.

Source Notes: **David L. Quaid.** Interviewed by Aaron Swan. 2005. Deposited at the Veterans History Project, American Folklife Center, Library of Congress.

[1] Terkel, Studs. *"The Good War": An Oral History of World War II* (New York: Pantheon, 1984). Location 2239.
[2] *World War II and the American Home Front: A National Historic Landmarks Theme Study.* National Park Service, U.S. Department of the Interior. October, 2007. Location 4098.
[3] *World War II and the American Home Front: A National Historic Landmarks Theme Study.* National Park Service, U.S. Department of the Interior. October, 2007. Location 1985.
[4] *World War II and the American Home Front: A National Historic Landmarks Theme Study.* National Park Service, U.S. Department of the Interior. October, 2007. 10.
[5] *B-24 Liberator Assembly Line at Ford Willow Run Bomber Plant, 1944.* The Henry Ford, 2023. www.thehenryford.org/collections-and-research/digital-collections/artifact/369253/
[6] Rhodes, Richard. *The Making of the Atomic Bomb.* New York: Simon & Schuster, 1986.
[7] Recollection of Leona Gustafson. *World War II and the American Home Front: A National Historic Landmarks Theme Study.* National Park Service, U.S. Department of the Interior. October, 2007. Location 6604.
[8] Leonard, Chris. *World War II at 75: General Electric's key contributions. The Schenectady Daily Gazette,* July 27, 2020. dailygazette.com/2020/07/27/world-war-ii-at-75-general-electric-s-key-contributions
[9] Kannenberg, Lisa. *The Impact of the Cold War on Women's Activism: The UE Experience. Labor History,* 1993. www.ueunion.org/ue-news/2010/helen-quirini-1920-2010-fighter-for-equality-and-justice
[10] *their fellow women classmates would often pool their money and ship the body home-* Lillian Yonally obituary, *Albany Times Union,* Jan. 6, 2022.
[11] Source: *Women with Wings: The 75-Year-Legacy of the WASP.* National Air and Space Museum, Aug. 5, 2018.

https://airandspace.si.edu/stories/editorial/women-wings-75-year-legacy-wasp

[12] Source: *The Army Nurse Corps in World War II*. U.S. Army Center of Military History, p. 26.

[13] Source: *The Army Nurse Corps in World War II*. U.S. Army Center of Military History, p. 15.

[14] *Polish Refugees in Iran During World War II.* Holocaust Encyclopedia, United States Holocaust Memorial Museum. encyclopedia.ushmm.org/content/en/article/polish-refugees-in-iran-during-world-war-ii

[15] Muller, Lily. Unpublished Memoir.

[16] Holocaust Encyclopedia. United States Holocaust Memorial Museum. *Warsaw Ghetto.* www.ushmm.org/wlc/en/article.php?ModuleId=10005069

[17] Hagerty, James R. Russell Hamler, Last Surviving Member of a World War II 'Marauders' Unit, Dies at 99. *The Wall Street Journal*, January 26, 2024. Page A-9.

[18] *Three quarters of a million Filipinos died*- Bamford, Tyler. The Global Impact of the Spanish-American War. Aug. 14, 2023.https://usnhistory.navylive.dodlive.mil/Recent/Article-View/Article/3491710/the-global-impact-of-the-spanish-american-war/

[19] *half the population already had a life expectancy rate of just thirty years*-Tuchman, Barbara. *Stilwell and the American Experience in China, 1911-45.* New York: Macmillan, 1971. Page 181.

[20] *third posting to China/several staff officer positions*-Stilwell, Joseph Warren Sr. American War Memorials Overseas, Inc. https://www.uswarmemorials.org/html/people_details.php?PeopleID=1644.

[21] *drew a caricature/vinegar bottle*-Tuchman, Barbara. *Stilwell and the American Experience in China, 1911-45.* New York: Macmillan, 1971. Page 125.

[22] *Japanese government ordered the British to close the Hong Kong frontier and the Burma Road*- Tuchman, Barbara. *Stilwell and the American Experience in China, 1911-45.* New York: Macmillan, 1971. Page 257.

[23] *agreed in theory to follow a 'Europe First' policy*- Tuchman, Barbara. *Stilwell and the American Experience in China, 1911-45.* New York: Macmillan, 1971. Page 290.
[24] Tuchman, Barbara. *Stilwell and the American Experience in China, 1911-45.* New York: Macmillan, 1971. Page 261.
[25] Haight, Jr., John McVickar. *FDR's "Big Stick".* Proceedings of the U.S. Naval Institute, Vol. 106/7/929. July 1980. www.usni.org/magazines/proceedings/1980/july/fdrs-big-stick
[26] *you have 24 hours to think up a better candidate*- Tuchman, Barbara. *Stilwell and the American Experience in China, 1911-45.* New York: Macmillan, 1971. Page 295.
[27] *I claim we got a hell of a beating*-Tuchman, Barbara. *Stilwell and the American Experience in China, 1911-45.* New York: Macmillan, 1971. Page 362.
[28] Ford, Daniel. *Flying Tigers: Claire Chennault and His American Volunteers, 1941-1942.* Smithsonian Institution Press, 1991. pp. 30–34.
[29] *'Circus Day'*- Lendon, Brad. *These American Mercenaries were the Heroes of China,* CNN, July 24, 2020.
[30] Belden, Jack. *Chennault Fights to Hold the China Front.* August 10, 1942. Life. Time Inc. p. 70.
[31] *Chennault debriefed his pilots-* Eisel, Braxton. *The Flying Tigers: Chennault's American Volunteer Group in China.* Air Force Sixtieth Anniversary Commemorative Editon, Air Force History Museums Program. United States Department of Defense. Undated, likely 2007.
[32] Norton, Thomas. *Flying Tigers Nurse Jane Hanks Dies.* General Aviation News, November 16, 2009.
[33] *aluminum plated mountain/650,000 tons were airlifted- World War II: Time-Life Books History of the Second World War.* Morristown, New Jersey: Silver Burdett, 1978. Pages 64, 80.
[34] Brooks, Drew. Warrior, diplomat and academic: Lt. Gen. Samuel V. Wilson dies at age 93. *Fayetteville Observer,* June 12, 2017.

www.fayobserver.com/story/news/military/2017/06/12/warrior-diplomat-and-academic-lt-gen-samuel-v-wilson-dies-at-age-93/20606511007/

[35] Slotnik, Daniel. Samuel V. Wilson, Ex-Director of Defense Intelligence Agency, Dies at 93. *The New York Times*, June 26, 2017. www.nytimes.com/2017/06/26/us/samuel-v-wilson-dead-general-headed-defense-intelligence-agency.html

[36] Xu, Zhao. Cameras and carbines capture life during wartime. *China Daily*, August 14, 2018. www.chinadaily.com.cn/a/201508/14/WS5a2b40f7a310eefe3e99f257.html

[37] Dower, John W. *Embracing Defeat: Japan in the Wake of World War II*. New York, W. W. Norton & Company. 1999. P. 43.

www.ingramcontent.com/pod-product-compliance
Lightning Source LLC
Chambersburg PA
CBHW070040080526
44586CB00013B/864